Lutheranism

★ ★ ★ AND ★ ★ ★

AMERICAN
CULTURE

Conflicting Worlds

NEW DIMENSIONS OF
THE AMERICAN CIVIL WAR

T. Michael Parrish, Series Editor

Lutheranism

★★★ *AND* ★★★

AMERICAN CULTURE

★ ★ ★ ★ ★ ★ ★

THE MAKING
OF A
DISTINCTIVE FAITH
IN THE
CIVIL WAR ERA

★ ★ ★

TIMOTHY D. GRUNDMEIER

LOUISIANA STATE UNIVERSITY PRESS

Baton Rouge

Published by Louisiana State University Press
lsupress.org

Designer: Kaelin Chappell Broaddus
Typefaces: Garamond Premier Pro, text; TPTC Baldinsville, TPTC Chimborazo, TPTC
Foilhommerum Black, TPTC Squarzas Punch, TPTC Tredegar Italic, display

Cover photograph: Trinity Lutheran Church, West Franklin Street, Hagerstown,
Maryland, ca. 1870 (Library of Congress, Prints and Photographs Division)

Cataloging-in-Publication Data are available from the Library of Congress.

ISBN 978-0-8071-8520-9 (cloth: alk. paper) —
ISBN 978-0-8071-8594-0 (pdf) — ISBN 978-0-8071-8593-3 (epub)

For Emma, Ryan, Haddie, and Lydia,
a heritage from the LORD,
and Erika,
far more precious than jewels

CONTENTS

ACKNOWLEDGMENTS

This book has been more than thirteen years in the making and would not have been possible without the support and assistance of numerous people. I am thrilled to have the opportunity to express my gratitude to all those who have helped me with my research and writing.

Throughout my scholarly journey, I have been buoyed by the wisdom and generosity of mentors and colleagues. When applying to doctoral programs, I received encouragement and counsel from Kathleen Gorman, Lori Ann Lahlum, Matthew Loayza, Paul Koelpin, Mark Koschmann, Gaylin Schmeling, Tim Schmeling, and especially Chuck Piehl and Mel Piehl. At Baylor University, I had the privilege of studying under professors who modeled scholarly excellence: Beth Barr, Elesha Coffman, Barry Hankins, Philip Jenkins, Kimberly Kellison, Thomas Kidd, Michael Parrish, James SoRelle, Julie Sweet, and Andrea Turpin. While at Baylor, I was also blessed to enjoy intellectual camaraderie and develop abiding friendships with fellow doctoral students: Ryan Butler, Alyssa Craven, Paul Gutacker, Elise Henreckson, Joel Iliff, Sam Kelley, Liz Marvel, Matt Millsap, Tim Orr, Brendan Payne, Nick Pruitt, Paul Putz, Skylar Ray, Lynneth Renberg, David Roach, and Adina Kelley (now with the Lord). At Martin Luther College, where I serve as a professor of history, I am surrounded by wonderful colleagues. I would especially like to thank the other members of my academic division, Pete Baganz, Paul Koelpin, Kari Muente, Aaron Robinson, and Luke Thompson. Finally, as both a doctoral student and a junior professor, I have greatly appreciated the collegiality of fellow members of the Lutheran Historical Conference. In particular, I have received gracious mentorship from Mark Braun, Maria Erling, Kathryn Galchutt, and Mark Granquist. The people mentioned in this paragraph, of course, are only a partial list of the community of historians from whom I have learned so much.

In the research for this book, I have benefited immensely from the kind and knowledgeable assistance of librarians and archivists. I would like to thank the following individuals who helped me during various in-person visits: Mark Bliese, Daniel Harmelink, and Todd Zittlow at Concordia Historical Institute; Lyle Buettner at Concordia Seminary, St. Louis; Joel Thoreson at the Archives of the Evangelical Lutheran Church in America; Ron Couchman, Amy Lucadamo, Devin McKinney, and Carolyn Sautter at Gettysburg College; Peter Susag and Peter Watters at Luther Seminary; Sheila Joy, John Peterson, and James Ziebell at the Lutheran Archives Center at Philadelphia; Sandy Leach and Shannon Smith at Lutheran Theological Southern Seminary; Linda Miller at Roanoke College; Elli Cucksey, Donald Huber, Jennifer Morehart, and Ray Olson at Trinity Lutheran Seminary; Roberta Brent and Curtis Orio at United Lutheran Seminary in Gettysburg; Karl Krueger at United Lutheran Seminary in Philadelphia; Susan Willems at the Wisconsin Evangelical Lutheran Synod Archives; Suzanne Smailes at Wittenberg University; and Elizabeth Jacobs at the Zelienople Historical Society. Several other people were instrumental in the long-distance sharing of materials: Barbara Reuning at Concordia Theological Seminary, Fort Wayne; Elli Cucksey at Trinity Lutheran Seminary; Chris Fenner and Adam Winters at Southern Baptist Theological Seminary; Evan Boyd, Sheila Joy, Justin Saldarriaga, Cody Swisher, and Ron Townsend at United Lutheran Seminary; Emily Avery at the University of South Carolina; and, of course, the marvelous interlibrary loan staffs at Baylor University and Martin Luther College. This book is a testament to the tireless efforts of those involved in the crucial work of historical preservation.

Several individuals also played an important role in the writing of this book and bringing it to print. I am thankful for the careful reading of Michael Parrish, Elesha Coffman, Julie Holcomb, Tommy Kidd, and Andrea Turpin at Baylor University. Their adept suggestions helped to launch this book project. My friends Paul Gutacker and Nick Pruitt both took time away from their busy schedules to read the entire manuscript. Their excellent feedback came at a crucial stage in the writing process. In addition, I received valuable advice from April Holm of Ole Miss as I was preparing my book proposal. Throughout the publishing process, I have greatly appreciated the expertise and professionalism of Rand Dotson, Catherine Kadair, and freelance editor Todd Manza. I am also grateful to the two anonymous peer reviewers for their kind recommendation and sage suggestions.

Acknowledgments

A special word of thanks is due to Michael Parrish. We first met in January 2013, when I, somewhat fearfully, approached him with a rough draft of a prospectus on Lutheranism and the Civil War. "This isn't good," I recall him saying. "But it can be." Since that first meeting, he has never failed to offer timely comments, incisive critiques, and constructive suggestions. Most of all, he has provided unflagging encouragement to pursue this project and make Lutherans, in his words, "mysterious no more." I could not have written this book without him.

Throughout my research and writing, I have been blessed with a loving and supportive family. My parents, Brian and Ruth, stoked intellectual curiosity in their children and have encouraged me to pursue the calling of a historian and scholar. My in-laws, Ron and Barb, have supported my chosen vocation and have tactfully refrained from asking when my book is finally coming out. Both sets of parents have been enormously helpful when I was away from home on research trips by assisting with their grandchildren (though we did not have to beg them too much). My siblings and siblings-in-law—Jeff, Rob, Jill, Val, Michael, Troy, and Kelly—have offered encouragement and indulged my occasional soliloquys on the significance of nineteenth-century American Lutheranism, as has my cousin Jackie. For my nieces and nephews—Eloise, Nadia, Bridget, Carly, Arthur, Owen, Faith, Noah, and Maggie—I hope this book inspires them to continue to develop their love of reading.

The deepest gratitude I owe is to my wife and children. My only regret in writing this book (besides any errors it may contain) is that it has taken so many hours away from our time together. Throughout the ups and downs of this long process, Emma, Ryan, Haddie, and Lydia have been a constant source of joy. I love them with all my heart. And finally, I cannot express enough thanks to Erika, the love of my life and my best friend, for her unwavering support and unconditional love. Though she has listened attentively to my ruminations and offered thoughtful advice on big-picture ideas, she has assisted with no research and read no drafts. But she has helped me more than anyone else.

Lutheranism
★ ★ ★ *AND* ★ ★ ★
AMERICAN
CULTURE

★ ★ ★ ★ ★ ★ ★

Introduction

I
N THE LATE 1920s, two writers identified the central issue for understanding the history of Lutheranism in the nineteenth-century United States. The first was H. Richard Niebuhr, the renowned American church historian. In his *Social Sources of Denominationalism,* Niebuhr drew attention to what he called "an anomalous fact," namely "that the Lutheran churches of America should be so much more conservative in their doctrine than are the Lutheran churches of Germany from which they took their rise."[1] The second writer, Olaf Edvard Moe, a Norwegian Lutheran clergyman and professor, made the same point with even greater specificity. In an article on the three branches of the worldwide Lutheran church, Moe observed, "The peculiarity of American Lutheranism, compared with that of Germany and the Scandinavian lands, lies chiefly in its confessional firmness, its zeal for pure Lutheran doctrine."[2]

That Niebuhr and Moe noticed a divergence between European and American Lutheranism is unsurprising. Observers of religion in the United States from Alexis de Tocqueville to Dietrich Bonhoeffer, as well as many modern scholars, have examined the "Atlantic divide" that developed over the course of the nineteenth century. Every religious tradition transplanted from the Old World to the New was influenced by its interaction with the politics and culture of the United States.[3] In particular, the voluntary nature of American religious life shaped nineteenth-century immigrant churches. "Ethnic denominations," observed historian Timothy Smith in a landmark article, "were not transplants of traditional institutions but communities of commitment and, therefore, arenas of change."[4] Because of those factors, it is hardly remarkable that Lutherans also developed their own distinctive American identity.

What is surprising is the content of that identity.

* * *

From the antebellum era to the end of the Gilded Age, American Lutheranism underwent tremendous changes. In 1830, the various Lutheran church bodies in the United States totaled fewer than fifty thousand members, mostly descendants of German-speaking immigrants to the British colonies. Voices both inside and outside of Lutheranism believed that the best way to become American was by adapting their denomination to the nation's predominant form of Christianity: evangelical Protestantism. Over the course of the mid- and late nineteenth century, however, that situation was altered significantly. Large-scale immigration from Germany and Scandinavia dramatically increased the size of the Lutheran church. In seventy years, it grew at five times the rate of the U.S. population and numbered more than 1.6 million members by 1900.[5] But just as consequential was American Lutheranism's intellectual transformation. Rather than assimilating into the Anglo-Protestant mainstream, Lutherans in the United States created a version of the faith made up of both distinctively Lutheran and quintessentially American ideas. That creation was a synthesis of four components: theological confessionalism, ecclesiastical separatism, political and social conservatism, and American exceptionalism.

As both Niebuhr and Moe noted, the first and most noticeable characteristic of Lutheranism in the United States was its confessional commitment. A defining feature of most American Protestant theology in the nineteenth century was the insistence on the right and duty of Christians to interpret the Bible for themselves apart from the creeds of the past. Lutherans, though sharing many of the biblicist assumptions of other Protestants, differed in the weight they placed on their church's historic teachings.[6] Those teachings were found in the *Book of Concord* of 1580, which contained the three ecumenical creeds and seven Lutheran confessions—sometimes called "symbols," a traditional name for Christian statements of faith. By the end of the nineteenth century, the vast majority of American Lutherans agreed that modern believers were bound to pledge

2

themselves to those historic documents, particularly the Augsburg Confession of 1530, the oldest Lutheran confession of faith. For many other U.S. Protestants, however, such a requirement conflicted with their understanding of *sola scriptura* (scripture alone) and liberty of conscience.

Buttressing American Lutherans' insistence on confessional purity was a hesitation, and often outright refusal, to collaborate with other Christians. The majority of Protestants in the nineteenth-century United States regarded doctrinal differences as important, but they also believed that such disagreements posed little barrier to partnering in missions, education, and social reform, or to sharing one another's pulpits and altars.[7] But by the end of the century, most Lutherans rejected this vision of denominationalism. Instead, they argued that in order for members of different church bodies to work together, they must first be in complete, or nearly complete, theological agreement. In fact, some extended this principle to their coreligionists by refusing to work with Lutherans who differed with them on certain points of doctrine. While the most influential Protestants in the nineteenth-century United States viewed themselves as joint laborers in a "righteous empire,"[8] the majority of Lutherans either rejected or distanced themselves from this ecumenical outlook.

Along with doctrinal confessionalism and ecclesiastical separatism came a conservative view of politics and society. Though Lutherans were hardly united on every issue, in the final decades of the nineteenth century the majority criticized a host of ideas that they deemed either radical or revolutionary. In particular, most opposed the attempts led by Anglo-Protestant reformers to "Christianize" society through temperance advocacy or the various efforts collectively known as the "social gospel." Lutherans, of course, were not alone among American Christians, both Protestant and Catholic, in their political and social conservatism. But more than most other believers in the nineteenth-century United States, Lutherans disavowed the project of imposing their moral and religious views on American society.[9] Instead, most advocated not only a strict separation of church and state but also a sharp division between religion and politics.

Lutherans, however, were not complete quietists; instead, most trumpeted a particular form of American exceptionalism. Once again, they were not alone among Christians in viewing the United States and its free institutions as uniquely favored and blessed by God.[10] Yet whereas many Protestants viewed the nation's providential role through the lens of a presumed Anglo-Saxon supremacy,[11] most Lutherans grounded their understanding of American exceptionalism in the nation's religious liberty. This view took two forms. First, Lutherans argued that the freedom of the church from the state granted them the opportunity to establish their faith in its purest form. "Religious liberty in our great republic," wrote one clergyman, "has given our dear Lutheran church the opportunity to blossom and prosper as never before."[12] Second, Lutherans contended that religious freedom derived from the heritage of Martin Luther and, consequently, that they epitomized the nation's ideals. As one leader wrote, "Consistent Lutheranism and consistent Americanism are never and nowhere at variance."[13] Thus, by the end of the nineteenth century Lutherans occupied a paradoxical position: they viewed themselves as critical outsiders of mainstream U.S. Protestantism but also as the exemplars of what it meant to be truly American.

Each of those four individual components could find parallels and resemblances in other groups on both sides of the Atlantic, but taken together they formed a religious identity unique in nineteenth-century Christianity. For example, the theological conservatism embraced by Lutherans in the United States coincided with a confessional resurgence among their German and Scandinavian coreligionists. Yet European Lutherans, with rare exceptions, never adopted the same views toward interdenominational cooperation and church-state separation as their American counterparts.[14] Some other Protestant groups in the United States, such as the Presbyterians and Episcopalians, also placed a high value on their confessional identity.[15] Yet in no other American denomination could one find quite the same emphasis on the centrality of their church's historic confessions. Parallels can also be found between Lutherans and other "religious outsiders" and "minority faiths," such as the Dutch and German Reformed, Mennonites, and Roman Catholics.[16] Even so, American Lutherans differed substantially from these groups not only in their commitments to certain doctrines but also in their unique synthesis of ideas derived from their religious heritage and the nation's culture. By the end of the nineteenth century, then, Lutherans in the United States had established a faith that was both distinct from Lutheranism in Europe and singular among other forms of American Christianity.

The central thesis of this book is that Lutherans in the United States forged that distinctive combination of ideas—theological confessionalism, ecclesiastical separatism, political and social conservatism, and American exceptionalism—through their interactions with the debates of the Civil War era. In 1860, most

U.S. Lutherans belonged to the General Synod, a federation of church bodies that minimized theological particularity, promoted cooperation with other Protestants, and voiced political and social views in keeping with the Anglo-evangelical mainstream. Six years later, their denomination was fractured by sectional divisions and, even more significantly, by theological disputes shaped by conflicting views on religious nationalism, political preaching, slavery, and the meaning of the Union. Following these schisms, Lutherans turned inward. Most reacted to the early years of Reconstruction by adopting increasingly conservative positions in both politics and theology. Though their church became even more institutionally divided in the final decades of the nineteenth century, most Lutherans embraced a confessional conservatism that differed starkly from the version of their faith that had predominated in the antebellum era. The Civil War and Reconstruction were crucial to this transformation.

This argument counters two aspects of the standard narrative of Lutheranism in the nineteenth-century United States: that the larger cultural and political context was peripheral and inconsequential to American Lutheranism's theological development and that the rise of this confessional conservatism was driven by ideas brought over from Europe.[17] Both views are mistaken. First, while many of the doctrinal issues debated by Lutherans in the United States certainly had deep roots in their church's tradition, these disputes took place in an era of political crises, social upheaval, and war. As a result, Lutherans' intellectual transformation was shaped by their interactions with American culture, particularly the conflicts over the Union and slavery and the debates about reunion and reconciliation. Second, though the new arrivals from Germany and Scandinavia undoubtedly altered the church's size and ethnic composition, the principal leaders of Lutheranism's turn to confessionalism were either native-born Americans or immigrants whose outlooks were formed in the United States. Rather than an importation from Europe, the synthesis of ideas that came to prevail among Lutherans in the nineteenth-century United States was American-made.

★ ★ ★

Lutheranism and American Culture: The Making of a Distinctive Faith in the Civil War Era covers developments that took place over nearly a century. Because of this, those who possess even a passing familiarity with the complexity of this subject may worry that this book will overlook certain nuances or neglect certain events and people. Those worries are not unfounded. A study covering such a wide terrain, even of a single religious tradition, cannot come anywhere near comprehensiveness. In order to give the reader a better sense of what this study is—and perhaps more importantly, what it is not—it is worth providing a more complete definition of the three somewhat vague terms in its title.

I have chosen the term "Lutheranism" as opposed to "Lutherans" to indicate that this book is primarily concerned with the ideas propounded by church leaders—pastors, professors, and editors. Such a focus comes at the expense of the thoughts and experiences of laypeople. In particular, since the people in these positions of leadership were exclusively men, it obscures the role of women, who were not included in official debates about doctrine and church affairs. This is not to suggest that Lutheran women were uninterested in those matters or did not exert considerable influence in church life. They helped to shape local congregations, and by the end of the century, national organizations, particularly mission societies.[18] By and large, however, denominational meetings, church periodicals (save for the "family circle" section on the back page of some newspapers), and theological disputes were considered to be male spheres.

In fact, it seems that Lutheran women were more marginalized in the arenas of publishing and church leadership than their sisters in other Protestant denominations. In the early to mid-nineteenth century, there were no female writers in American Lutheranism comparable to the Congregationalist Harriet Beecher Stowe or the Episcopalian Sarah Josepha Hale, even on a much lesser scale.[19] Additionally, though some evangelical churches occasionally welcomed female preachers and exhorters, Lutherans, even those trying to emulate Anglo-evangelicalism, never adopted the practice.[20] Finally, in another divergence from other American Protestants, Lutheran church membership did not have nearly the same imbalanced female-to-male ratio as other denominations. Whereas the percentage of female members in Baptist, Methodist, and Presbyterian congregations was usually more than 60 percent, in Lutheran churches the figure was closer to 50 percent.[21] The extent to which Lutheranism's conservative transformation in the nineteenth century was the product of this gendered dynamic is a subject that merits further exploration.

Though I am aware of these limitations, my book focuses on "elite"—and consequently male—perspectives for two reasons. First, the dearth of scholarship on American Lutheranism forces prioritization. Before historians can more fully explore how Lutheran laypeople, including women, agreed with, dissented from, or altered the views of clerical leaders, we first must understand more clearly what those leaders thought. The second and more fundamental reason for this focus is that elite opinion mattered to "ordinary" nineteenth-century believers. As historian Mark Noll writes, "Many nonpublishing citizens read, pondered, and considered themselves part of the circles of debate created by . . . published theology."[22] For the most part, the American religious "marketplace" not only allowed people to choose their congregational and denominational affiliations but also compelled preachers and writers to address their message in such a way as to win prospective members.[23] Thus, even though the "Lutheran public" is mostly silent in the narrative, their presence has affected the selection of sources. In general, this study focuses on materials intended for their hearing and reading—sermons and addresses, books and tracts, and published denominational proceedings. Especially important are the church newspapers that enjoyed wide circulation and often defined the different Lutheran factions and schools of thought.[24]

Additionally, though this study is a history of religious ideas, it does not take the term "Lutheranism" precisely to mean "Lutheran theology." Certainly, disputes over doctrine play a central role in the narrative. Particularly important are debates about the historic creeds of the Lutheran church, especially the Augsburg Confession. Yet in no way is this book a comprehensive survey of American Lutheran doctrine in the nineteenth century. Instead, by "Lutheranism" I mean something akin to "Lutheran identity." Along with theological concerns, this definition includes an outlook on politics and culture and an understanding of one's place in nation and society. This book seeks to explain how a particular form of Lutheran identity became predominant in the nineteenth-century United States.

In order to do so, I analyze Lutheranism's intersection with "American culture," the second term in my title. Since the publication of George Marsden's *Fundamentalism and American Culture* (1980), many historians of Christianity in the United States have used this phrase or similar ones to distinguish their task from those of "denominational historians," who tend to examine religious doctrine and church organizations apart from the crosscurrents of their larger historical context. Though both theology and institutions are central to this study, my focus is on how Lutherans interacted with and were shaped by the surrounding "culture," which Marsden describes as a society's "collection of beliefs, values, assumptions, commitments, and ideals." *Lutheranism and American Culture* seeks to emulate Marsden's landmark work, as well as the many other studies that have followed in his footsteps, by examining how leaders of a particular religious tradition "responded to and were influenced by the social, intellectual, and religious crises of their time."[25]

The crises to which Lutherans were responding took place during the Civil War era, the final term in my title. Following the works of Orville Vernon Burton and Steven Hahn, I define this period in the broadest of senses. Both of these historians, though varying considerably in their interpretations of the era, have demonstrated how a comprehensive understanding of the conflicts over slavery, race, and nationalism must take a longer view than the typical periodization of 1848 to 1877.[26] A similar trend can be found among histories of Civil War–era religion. Over the past fifteen years, scholars such as Luke Harlow, April Holm, William Kurtz, Molly Oshatz, and Lucas Volkman have examined a wide chronological scope, showing the broad sweep of various religious developments from the antebellum era through the "long Reconstruction."[27] *Lutheranism and American Culture* resembles those works in viewing the Civil War as the pivotal point in a larger story. Though its narrative centers on the years immediately preceding, during, and directly following the war, this study covers developments from about 1830 to 1900.

Scholars of American Lutheranism have long recognized these years to encompass a critical period in the church's history, what historian Sydney Ahlstrom labeled its "Age of Definition."[28] Unsurprisingly, then, the corpus of Lutheran church history about this era is vast.[29] However, although denominational historians have produced numerous studies on individual synods (church bodies), ethnic groups, and prominent leaders, few have tried to tie the story of nineteenth-century American Lutheranism into a coherent narrative. Those who have attempted to do so have focused on explicating the convoluted details of the church's institutional development—what Noll has called the "thick alphabet soup of American Lutheran history."[30] Such a focus is understandable, as the myriad divisions in ethnicity, geography, and doctrine were central to nineteenth-century Lutherans' sense of identity. (In order to aid the reader in keeping track of the various theological schools, ecclesiastical federations, and church bodies, I have included a glossary and a statistical appendix.) However, this emphasis on U.S. Lutheranism's internal divisions has come at the expense of seeing its development as a whole and examining the larger contexts in which that development took place.

This book thus seeks to balance two goals: to tell the story of American Lutheranism without shortchanging its complexity and to situate that story in the broader debates, movements, and rhetoric of the nineteenth-century United States. This dual focus rests on two corresponding convictions. The first is that intra-Lutheran disputes and divisions that might seem obscure and inconsequential to twenty-first-century scholars were of great significance both to clerical leaders and to lay members in the nineteenth century. Historian Laurie Maffly-Kipp has made a similar observation: "Clearly, churches—including the antiquated intricacies of denominations—mattered to . . . [those] whose voices are now only a distant whisper."[31] The second conviction is that religious developments, including denominational "intricacies," never happen in a vacuum. As Marsden remarks in his classic study, "The actions . . . of the church are always intertwined with culturally conditioned factors . . . [and] shaped by historical circumstances."[32] Motivated by these convictions, I aim to show how the development of a distinctive identity among Lutherans in the United States was shaped by the larger culture of the long Civil War era.

★ ★ ★

In doing so, I also seek to demonstrate that Lutheranism should be viewed as a central component of nineteenth-century American religion and the Civil War era. Currently, this is not the case in either field of study. Since the 1972 publication of *A Religious History of the American People,* by Sydney Ahlstrom, himself a Lutheran, the space devoted to Lutheranism in U.S. religious history, both in comprehensive surveys and in books focused on the nineteenth century, has shrunk considerably.[33] In scholarship on the Civil War, even in the growing number of studies that focus on the role of religion during this conflict, Lutherans have rarely been present at all.[34] This conspicuous absence obscures the significant role of this faith in the nation's history. Jon Gjerde, the eminent historian of immigration and ethnicity, may have overstated the case when he wrote that "Lutheranism changed the United States just as the United States transformed American Lutheranism."[35] Yet his assertion is not too wide of the mark. The story of Lutheranism is indispensable to understanding religion in the long Civil War era for no fewer than three reasons.

Most basically, Lutherans matter because they were numerous. As the predominant faith of many parts of Germany and every Scandinavian nation, as a minority religion in other European nations and in North America, and as a missionary endeavor in parts of Africa, India, and the Americas, Lutheranism was the largest and most diverse branch of Protestantism in the nineteenth-century world. In the United States, the Lutheran church's more than 1.6 million communicant members made it the nation's fourth-largest denomination by 1900. (Only Roman Catholics, Baptists, and Methodists were more numerous.) Yet this sizable figure is misleadingly small. It excludes not only children but also adult "adherents," or those who attended Lutheran churches periodically and generally assented to their teachings but did not meet the requirements of church membership. Scholars of American religion have typically calculated that the inclusion of these groups increased the constituency of a nineteenth-century church by a factor of three or four. In sum, at the dawn of the twentieth century, Lutheranism was at least the nominal faith of as many as 6 million people, or nearly one out of every twelve Americans.[36]

Just as significant as their vast numbers was a second factor: their unique position in the American religious landscape. Throughout the nineteenth century, Lutheranism was, in the apt description of Gjerde, "neither part of the American Protestant center nor the Catholic 'other.'"[37] Though some of their fellow Protestants deemed them to be "half reformed" and even "in sympathy with Romanism,"[38] Lutherans' Reformation heritage ensured that they would never encounter the hostility endured by Roman Catholics, Mormons, or non-Christian religions. Similarly, while Lutherans' German and Scandinavian origins led some Anglo-Saxons to regard them as less than fully American, Lutherans rarely experienced the overt prejudice faced by Southern and Eastern Europeans, and certainly by African Americans and other racial minorities. Their "whiteness," a concept invariably bound up with religion in the United States, was rarely in question.[39] Lutherans' outsider status, then, rather than being thrust upon them by intolerance or nativism, was largely self-chosen. Yet their intentional separation from the Anglo-Protestant mainstream did not entail a rejection of American ideals. In fact, they exemplified how, in the words of historian R. Laurence Moore, "outsiderhood is a characteristic way of inventing one's Americanness."[40] Instead of seeing their faith as in tension with their national identity, Lutherans believed that their distinctive beliefs made them the best Americans.

Finally, the development of American Lutheranism speaks to scholarship on the political thought of white Americans in the lower North and Middle Border during the Civil War era. Over the past decade, several historians have explored the "moderate majority" in the loyal states outside of the Northeast.[41] Many men and women in these regions supported the federal war effort but viewed the conflict's principal purpose as preserving the nation and its constitutional order rather than freeing the enslaved and bringing about racial equality. Apart from a few exceptions, Lutherans exemplified this conservatism. During the Civil War, virtually all spokesmen for the church, including those who expressed opposition to slavery, insisted that maintenance of the Union was the war's primary aim. In the postbellum era, these same leaders repudiated various forms of what they perceived to be political and social "radicalism," thereby contributing to the retreat from the egalitarian goals of Reconstruction. In the ensuing decades, Lutherans' particular form of conservatism helped to shape the political culture of the areas of the Mid-Atlantic and Midwest where they were most prominent—in states like Pennsylvania, Ohio, Missouri, and Wisconsin.

While the subjects of this study influenced American religion, culture, and politics in a variety of ways, they are ultimately important for their own sake. The development of Lutheranism in the long Civil War era shaped the lives and beliefs of millions of men and women in the nineteenth-century United States, and the story told in this book continues to shape the lives and beliefs of the nearly 6 million people in the twenty-first century who are both Lutheran and American.

★ ★ ★

Lutheranism and American Culture follows a roughly chronological outline. Chapter 1 sketches the place of Lutheranism in the religious culture of the antebellum United States. After tracing the church's colonial origins and its development during the early republic, this chapter describes the three schools of thought that emerged within American Lutheranism by the beginning of the 1850s. New Lutherans, the most numerous and influential group, sought to incorporate their denomination into the nation's "evangelical empire" by modifying its historic doctrines and cooperating with other Protestants. Opposing them were the Old Lutherans of the Missouri Synod, by far the smallest of the three parties, who fiercely resisted assimilation into the Protestant mainstream and insisted that every doctrine in the Lutheran confessions was a nonnegotiable prerequisite for interchurch cooperation. The faction in the middle, Moderate Lutheranism, was cautious about theological innovation and hesitant to form alliances with Anglo-evangelicals but also put off by the "exclusiveness" of the Old Lutherans. Because of this, the majority of Moderate Lutherans chose to align with the New Lutherans.

The 1850s produced not only crises in the American nation but also conflicts in the Lutheran church. Chapter 2 examines the issues that emerged during this decade and would shape intra-Lutheran disputes in future years. The first was immigration, particularly the extent to which native-born Lutherans should attempt to "Americanize" their newly arrived coreligionists from Germany and Scandinavia. The second was a set of interrelated theological questions: To what extent must Lutherans pledge themselves to their church's historic confessions, and what should be the basis of church unity? The debates surrounding these issues prompted the founding of a fourth school in American Lutheranism, a confessional movement that aspired to reform New Lutheranism from within. The final area of controversy concerned the morality of slavery and the involvement of the church in politics. By 1860, most Lutherans had reached a compromise on their points of disagreement, with nearly two-thirds belonging to the General Synod, a national federation designed to hold together their denomination's various factions. As the nation began to break apart along sectional lines, American Lutheranism, with the exception of the Old Lutherans, stood more united than ever before.

That unity began to fracture with the onset of the Civil War. Chapter 3 discusses Lutheran debates over nationalism, patriotism, political preaching, and slavery during the first years of the conflict. Lutherans in the South, on the whole, quickly committed themselves to Confederate nationalism. Their northern counterparts were initially divided, with some promoting peace and neutrality and others embracing the war effort. However, by the spring of 1862, most had come to voice their support for the Union. Yet despite their mostly unified espousal of their nation's civil religion, Lutherans in the loyal states differed in their understanding of the relationship between religion and politics and in their opinions about the central issue of slavery. Their disagreements on these issues would sow the seeds for future divisions. The chapter concludes with a description of the first major reversal of American Lutheranism's growing unity, when various southern churches, which made up about 10 percent of the General Synod, withdrew to form their own federation in 1863.

Yet an even greater schism was looming, not a sectional division but a theological one over confessional allegiance and church unity, the very problems that supposedly had been resolved in the 1850s. Chapter 4 argues that different interpretations of the Civil War were instrumental in shaping and fueling these intra-Lutheran disputes. By 1863, northern Lutherans in the General Synod realigned into two competing parties: the New School and the Old School. These two factions interwove quarrels over theology with arguments about the war's origins and meaning. The staunchly pro-Union and more vocally antislavery Old School argued that any concession to error, whether in the nation or in the church, was wrong, and as a consequence they recanted their previous tolerance of doctrinal differences. New School Lutherans, for their part, contended that the war was precisely about the inability of differing parties to find common ground and sought to preserve the theological compromise reached in the 1850s. Their debates culminated in 1866 when the largest church body of the Old School, the Pennsylvania Synod, broke away from the General Synod and began inviting others, including the Old Lutherans they had formerly spurned, to form a rival federation.

Chapter 5 describes how different factions attempted to reconstruct American Lutheranism following these upheavals. As they had been during the Civil War, Lutherans were profoundly shaped by the issues and debates of the first years of Reconstruction. The vast majority reacted to the politics of the era by adopting an increasingly conservative posture toward civil affairs, and with the exception of those in the South, prioritizing the goals of reunion and reconciliation. With these commitments, northern Lutheran leaders worked to set aside political, geographic, and ethnic differences and to seek a "more perfect Lutheran union." The result, however, was further fragmentation. In 1867, leaders of the Old School founded the General Council, which sought to unite all "genuine Lutherans" in the United States, but several synods, mostly made up of Midwestern immigrants, either withdrew from the organization or refused to participate. The pursuit of sectional reconciliation also failed, as southern Lutherans rejected the overtures coming from their fellow Lutherans in the North. Capitalizing on this disunity was the Missouri Synod. Though these Old Lutherans had been a small minority in the antebellum era, their understanding of "true Lutheranism" proved to be compelling to those searching for certainty and order in an era of upheaval. In 1872, this church body spearheaded the founding of another, even larger union: the Synodical Conference.

Though the events of the Civil War and its aftermath had paved the way for the rise of this confessional conservatism, the developments of the Gilded Age cemented its triumph. Chapter 6 begins by summarizing the effects of postbellum immigration. New arrivals from Germany and Scandinavia altered the Lutheran church's demographic makeup; however, these immigrants largely adopted the version of the faith espoused by the Synodical Conference, the General Council, and the General Synod. Though differing in particulars, these three federations came to share a similar outlook. In the area of theology and interchurch relations, the majority of Lutherans, including those remaining in the General Synod, bolstered their commitment to their church's confessions, distanced themselves from other Protestants, and rejected theological modernism. Lutheran leaders also adopted an increasingly conservative posture on political and social issues, simultaneously arguing against various forms of radicalism and insisting on a strict separation not only between church and state but also between religion and politics. Finally, despite their status as religious outsiders, most American Lutherans, no matter their synodical affiliation, believed that their church epitomized the values of the nation they called home.

As they entered the twentieth century, then, Lutherans in the United States had created their own distinctive faith, defined by the synthesis of theological confessionalism, ecclesiastical separatism, political and social conservatism, and American exceptionalism. The book's epilogue traces, in broad strokes, the path of this religious identity from 1900 to the present. Though the American Lutheranism that exists today differs significantly from that of the long Civil War era, the debates and decisions of the past are still relevant to the modern church. If the story of *Lutheranism and American Culture* demonstrates anything, it is this: All religious traditions are shaped by their historical context and surrounding culture, including—and perhaps especially—those that fail to recognize it.

ONE

Three American
Lutheranisms,
1830–1850

I N March 1854, the Swiss American theologian Philip Schaff (1819–1893)
gave a series of lectures in Berlin on the "political, social, and religious
character" of America. The resulting book was published in New York the
following year and is still widely considered to be among the most perceptive
analyses of the nineteenth-century United States.[1] Yet American historians often
overlook the fact that nearly half of the book's first edition, published in German
rather than English, was devoted to explaining the situation of "the German
churches in America," that is, those denominations in the United States whose
origins stemmed from the Protestant Reformation in Germany. Despite belonging to the Reformed Church, Schaff devoted the longest chapter in this section
to examining Lutheranism, the most numerous of these German churches. As a
sympathetic outsider, he believed that "the Lutheran church has an important
calling in the New World." But he also pinpointed the central issue facing Lutheranism in the United States. The American Lutheran church "cannot fulfill
its calling," he wrote, unless it "faithfully preserves its gifts and powers and at the
same time engages in wise and cordial accommodation to the conditions of a
new land and people."[2]

Schaff identified three "main schools" in the Lutheran church of the United
States: the New Lutherans, the Old Lutherans, and the Moderate Lutherans.
"The New Lutheran party," Schaff began, "is an amalgamation of Lutheranism
with American-Puritan and Methodist elements. It consists mostly of native-born

Americans of German descent and hence prides itself on being emphatically the American Lutheran church." The Old Lutherans, he continued, "are still strangers and misfits in the New World." He described how they stood in opposition to the innovations of the New Lutherans but were also "extremely exclusive and narrow-minded." Finally, Schaff turned to the "Moderate Lutheran school," the group with which he had the most affinity. He saw this party's "true mission" as "to mediate not only between the churchly Old Lutheranism and the puritanical New Lutheranism but also between the European-German and American interests."[3]

Schaff's taxonomy was largely accurate and has been widely cited by historians of American Lutheranism.[4] He correctly identified the main schools of American Lutheran thought and he astutely observed the primary challenge facing Lutherans in the early nineteenth-century United States: how to be both fully Lutheran and fully American. Yet he erred in assuming that the chief difference among these three competing factions was their differing level of accommodation to American ideas. Each school—New, Old, and Moderate—had been shaped by the nation's religion, politics, and culture.

LUTHERANISM IN THE NEW NATION

The tripartite division described by Schaff in 1854 differed greatly from the situation of American Lutheranism just twenty-five years before. As of 1830, Lutherans were a mostly homogenous group of religious outsiders. Most could trace their heritage back to the migrations of German speakers to the British colonies in the mid-eighteenth century. About 80 percent of those colonial immigrants had arrived through the port of Philadelphia, and Pennsylvania would remain the cultural and intellectual center of American Lutheranism well into the nineteenth century.[5] Before the Revolution, some of these immigrants and their descendants had migrated southward into Maryland, the Shenandoah Valley, and the Carolina Piedmont, all of which encompassed what scholars have called "Greater Pennsylvania."[6] After independence, Pennsylvania Germans spread west into the Northwest Territory, settling in what would become the states of Ohio, Indiana, and Illinois. Settlements of German Lutherans could also be found in parts of New York, as well near the port cities of Charleston, South Carolina, and Savannah, Georgia. By 1790, German Americans, among whom the primary religious identification was Lutheran, numbered just under 10 percent of the white population of the United States, making them the largest non-British European ethnic group in the newly formed republic.

Though scattered congregations had existed in the North American colonies since the mid-seventeenth century, Lutherans did not establish an organized presence until the arrival of Heinrich Melchior Muhlenberg (1711–1787), often dubbed the "patriarch of American Lutheranism," in 1742.[7] Six years later, under Muhlenberg's leadership, German immigrants established the Ministerium of Pennsylvania and Adjacent States, the first Lutheran church body in America. Muhlenberg's theological and cultural outlooks—or at least the ways in which these outlooks were interpreted by his supporters and successors—shaped the American Lutheran church well beyond his death.

Most accurately described as an "orthodox pietist," Muhlenberg crafted his Lutheran identity from the "complex interaction of orthodoxy, Pietism and Enlightenment" in eighteenth-century Germany.[8] The most pronounced of these influences on Muhlenberg and other leaders of the Pennsylvania Ministerium was the pietism associated with the University of Halle, where many early colonial Lutheran pastors were trained. Though stressing an activist faith and devotional experience, Halle pietists eschewed the enthusiastic excesses of radical German pietists such as the Moravians and also emphasized the importance of the sacraments and liturgical worship. This explains the somewhat conflicted attitudes of Lutherans toward the revivalist evangelicalism that swept through the North American colonies during the First Great Awakening. Most welcomed the heartfelt piety of the revivalists while at the same time balking at their more extreme outbursts and antisacramental theology.[9] Thus, despite some affinities with Anglo-evangelicalism, colonial Lutherans were just as likely to partner with more churchly Protestants, such as Anglicans.

In the sphere of politics and culture, Lutherans were less hesitant to accommodate themselves to Anglo-American norms. Even before the American War of Independence, German colonists had adjusted to British notions of liberty, largely thanks to the mediation of "cultural brokers," the most prominent of whom were Lutheran pastors, including Muhlenberg.[10] During the Revolution, many embraced the patriot cause, others tacitly accepted it, and a few remained loyalists. After the ratification of the U.S. Constitution, German Lutherans were mostly at home in the new democratic republic. Two of Muhlenberg's sons served Pennsylvania in the United States House of Representatives, with Frederick becoming the nation's first Speaker of the House. According to historian Hermann Wellenreuther, most German Americans, including Lutherans, were, "if they must be categorized, a cross-breed between Jeffersonian egalitarianism and Andrew Jackson's common man, with the sincere piety of John Adams thrown in."[11]

Justus H. C. Helmuth (1745–1825), Muhlenberg's successor as pastor of St. Michael's and Zion Lutheran Church in Philadelphia, exemplified this embrace of American liberty. After the Revolution, he celebrated freedom from British tyranny as divinely ordained. In 1793, he praised God for "the spirit of civil freedom [that] has now and again spread much happiness." Yet in the same publication, Helmuth also expressed wariness that this liberty might erode Lutheran distinctiveness and allow any person to read "his whims and fantasies into [the Bible]."[12] In short, both during and immediately after the American founding, most Lutherans remained committed to the orthodox pietism inherited from the Old World, even as they were assimilating the cultural and political ideas of the new nation.

In view of this, the most important development in the first fifty years of Lutheranism in the early American republic was the church's almost complete separation from Europe. Already in the 1760s the migratory flow from the various German states and principalities had begun to ebb. After the Revolutionary War and until the 1830s, immigration from Germany, along with immigration to the United States in general, slowed to a trickle.[13] Additionally, Lutherans in America lost all but the loosest of ties to Halle and other institutions that had supplied pastors, publications, and other forms of support. An 1831 essay put the matter simply: "The Lutheran Church in the United States has no connexion with the Lutheran church in Germany." Though some Lutherans maintained a "fraternal correspondence with the distinguished brethren in Germany," the majority of Lutheran clergy and laity were born and raised in the United States, and their ideas and experiences were shaped by the political, cultural, and religious milieu of the young nation.[14]

That milieu was characterized by the ideology of republicanism, an emphasis on "common sense" reasoning, and the rapid growth of evangelical Protestantism. As Mark Noll has argued, out of these elements came a distinctive theological outlook that "defined the boundaries for a vast quantity of American thought, while also providing an ethical framework, a moral compass, and a vocabulary of suasion for much of the nation's public life."[15] A related effect was what historian Nathan Hatch has called "the democratization of American Christianity," wherein "popular religious movements," particularly the Methodists and Baptists, "did more to Christianize American society than anything before or since."[16] Though various scholars have offered nuances and challenges to the interpretations of Hatch and Noll, the overwhelming picture of religious life in the early republic was that of an intellectual and cultural environment shaped by Anglo-Protestant revivalism and American conceptions of liberty.[17]

Lutherans did not escape the assumptions of this emerging religious and political culture, even as they tried to maintain their separate identity. They fully embraced the rhetoric of "American chosenness" and the idea that the nation's free institutions safeguarded true religion. Additionally, in a trope that would be repeated frequently throughout the nineteenth century, they argued that Martin Luther was the progenitor of American civil and religious liberty.[18] At the same time, most Lutherans still clung proudly to their German heritage. The most dramatic example of this was the lawsuit and trial in 1816 surrounding the attempted introduction of the English language at Helmuth's St. Michael's and Zion congregations in Philadelphia.[19] This zealous guarding against the encroachment of English ways into religious life, however, was not incompatible with American national identity. As historian Steven Nolt has shown, Pennsylvania Germans, including Lutherans, "resist[ed] the claims of the larger society in the name of common American principles."[20]

One way in which Lutherans pursued this German-cum-American identity was through close relations with the German Reformed Church. The two communions partnered in educational ventures, publication projects, mission work, and even in some cases congregations. With this ecclesiastical collaboration came a de-emphasis of confessional particularity, as when the Pennsylvania Ministerium dropped from its constitution all references to the historic confessions of the Lutheran church. Some historians of U.S. Lutheranism have attributed these developments to the era's "spirit of rationalism."[21] Yet apart from a few outlying figures such as Frederick Quitman (1760–1832) of New York, the German Enlightenment had little influence on American Lutherans.[22] Others have found parallels to the Prussian Union of Frederick Wilhelm III, which united the Lutheran and Reformed churches into one Evangelical church in 1817.[23] However, there is little evidence that Lutherans in the early American republic, who were largely isolated from Europe, patterned their church affairs after the edicts of a

Prussian monarch. Ultimately, the ad hoc cooperation of the German American churches was a pragmatic means to retain cultural solidarity.[24]

Rather than its ethnically based ecumenism, the most conspicuous aspect of Lutheran theological development in the young United States was its lack of sustained intellectual inquiry. By the early 1820s, the church supported only two institutions of higher education: Franklin College in Pennsylvania, a joint Reformed–Lutheran school founded in 1787, and Hartwick Seminary in New York, a Lutheran institution begun in 1797. Both schools struggled with financial stability and attracting students.[25] In the realm of publications, the only widely circulated periodical, *Das Evangelisches Magazin,* another shared venture with the Reformed, lasted briefly, from 1811 to 1817. And while various German printers published scattered sermons, treatises, and books, the only press dedicated to producing Lutheran theological writings was that of the Henkel family in New Market, Virginia. Though the Henkels' influence would grow over the course of the antebellum era, their publishing ventures had little impact beyond Virginia, the Carolina Piedmont, and Eastern Tennessee during the first decades of the nineteenth century.[26] In both higher education and publishing, then, American Lutheran intellectual life lagged behind the more established Congregationalists, Episcopalians, and Presbyterians as well as the upstart Methodists and Baptists.

Lutherans in the young republic not only made little progress in the areas of education and publishing but also lacked a central denominational organization. During the fifty years following independence, the American Lutheran church divided into several autonomous synods. In some ways, this fragmentation was the product of the new nation's "democratic ferment," described by historian Gordon Wood, which allowed numerous sects divided by theological particulars to thrive.[27] Rather than doctrinal disagreements, however, it was primarily fears of centralization and losing local control that kept Lutherans separated. In 1820, a group of church leaders met to form the General Synod of the Lutheran Church in the United States. Yet the federation nearly became defunct after its first meeting, largely due to those who feared that an unwieldy national organization would infringe on their "liberties."[28] The General Synod survived, but barely. Ten years after its founding, less than 30 percent of American Lutherans belonged to this national federation.

Along with its ethnic insularity, paucity of literary and educational institutions, and ecclesiastical disorganization, Lutheranism in the early republic was marked by its slow numerical growth. By 1830, Methodist and Baptist churches had swelled to five hundred thousand and four hundred thousand members, respectively. However, Lutheran church membership, which had exceeded Methodists and nearly equaled the Baptists in the colonial era, stood at less than fifty thousand.[29] Yet despite these challenges, the theological fragmentation described by Schaff had not yet come to pass. Instead, most Lutherans shared a heritage rooted in the mid-eighteenth-century colonial migrations, the orthodox pietism of Halle, and the experience of the American Revolution. They were, in Nolt's phrase, "foreigners in their own land." Disconnected from the Anglo-evangelical establishment yet enthusiastic about their nation's freedoms, Lutherans were simultaneously at home and outsiders in the young nation.

NEW LUTHERANISM

Samuel Simon Schmucker (1799–1873) was a proud Lutheran but troubled by his church's lack of intellectual rigor and cultural clout. The son of a German American minister in Pennsylvania, Schmucker's desire to move beyond his parochial upbringing was already evident when he chose to attend Princeton Seminary for his theological education. Yet instead of seeking influence by switching to a more prestigious Anglo-Protestant church, as had several prominent Lutherans before him, Schmucker hoped to transform his own tradition into a more respectable American evangelical denomination.[30] In one of his first published works, he noted the "intellectual greatness" of Lutheran universities in Germany but lamented that he could not point "to some Wittenberg, to some Helmstadt [*sic*], among us." If only Lutherans could build up better institutions, he believed, "then, also, should we see more of our men high in the offices of our country, guiding the civil and political destinies of our land."[31] According to his biographer Abdel Ross Wentz, shortly after finishing his studies at Princeton in 1820, Schmucker identified four "great needs for Lutherans in America": an organized system of church government, an academically demanding seminary, a similarly rigorous college, and theological works in English.[32]

In less than fifteen years, Schmucker had accomplished all four goals. In 1823, the talented young pastor "came to the rescue of the General Synod," saving the fledgling federation from dissolution.[33] He was also the chief architect of the *Formula for the Government and Discipline of the Evangelical Lutheran Church,* formally adopted by the General Synod in 1829, which outlined its polity and constitution.[34] Over the next twenty years Schmucker helped to grow the General Synod from three member synods to sixteen, so that by 1850 it encompassed nearly half of all Lutherans in the United States. In 1826, Schmucker helped to found Gettysburg Theological Seminary, sponsored primarily by the General Synod, and was named the school's first professor.[35] The following year he established a classical academy as a preparatory school for the seminary. The institution was chartered as Pennsylvania College in 1832, with Schmucker managing its affairs until a full-time president was appointed two years later. Amid his manifold administrative and pedagogical duties, Schmucker also published several lengthy works, including his *Elements of Popular Theology* (1834), the first textbook of Lutheran theology written in English.[36] By the age of thirty-five he had established himself as the ecclesiastical, educational, and theological leader of American Lutheranism.

In addition to addressing what he saw as his denomination's institutional and academic deficiencies, Schmucker directed his organizational and intellectual gifts toward building up relations with non-German Protestants. He worked with various Anglo-evangelical associations that made up the "benevolent empire," such as the American Bible Society, the American Sunday School Union, and the American Tract Society.[37] In 1838, Schmucker pressed his desire for Lutheran inclusion in the nation's Protestant establishment even further by publishing his "Fraternal Appeal to the American Churches" in the *American Biblical Repository*.[38] Later published as a book, the *Fraternal Appeal* argued that individual denominations should collectively subscribe to one "Apostolic, Protestant Confession," participate in "sacramental, ecclesiastical, and ministerial communion," engage in cooperative mission efforts, and refer to each other as "branches" of the one "Apostolic, Protestant Church."[39] Schmucker's proposal for interchurch cooperation was a bold step beyond the Lutheran–Reformed partnership of Pennsylvania Germans. Instead of an ecumenism based primarily on ethnic heritage, he was advocating for American Lutherans to embrace a broader Protestant identity and play a leading role in evangelical unity.[40]

Schmucker was not alone in promoting what Schaff labeled "New Lutheranism" and what he and his allies would come to call "American Lutheranism." His most significant collaborator was Benjamin Kurtz (1795–1865).[41] An early advocate of the General Synod, Kurtz had visited Germany in 1826 and 1827 to solicit funds for the newly founded seminary at Gettysburg. In 1833, after serving various pastorates in Maryland and Pennsylvania, he became the full-time editor of the Baltimore-based *Lutheran Observer*, a position he would retain for more than twenty-five years. Under Kurtz's leadership, the paper quickly became the principal Lutheran publication in the United States, boasting more than three thousand subscribers and at least five times that many readers by 1839.[42] During the mid-1840s, it added editorial departments in Pittsburgh, Pennsylvania; Dayton, Ohio; and Ebenezer, Georgia.[43]

Like Schmucker, Kurtz's *Lutheran Observer* sought to bring about a convergence with other American Protestants by heralding various evangelical causes. The most prominent of these was revivalism. During its first twenty years and beyond, scarcely an issue of Kurtz's *Lutheran Observer* appeared that failed to promote the progress, theology, and practice of revivals.[44] Often, New Lutherans discussed revivalism in terms of "new measures," which David Bittle (1811–1876), an ally of the *Lutheran Observer* in Virginia, defined as "protracted meetings, revivals, anxious-seats, prayer meetings and voluntary societies."[45] Kurtz, Bittle, and others admitted that these practices were a "modern invention" but argued that their "spirit and design" were "old and venerable."[46] They cited "the authority of the apostles" as well as historical figures—both Lutheran pietists like Johann Arndt, Philip Jakob Spener, and August Hermann Francke, and Anglo-evangelicals such as Jonathan Edwards, George Whitefield, and John Wesley.[47] Kurtz was also adamant about demonstrating their propriety. The *Lutheran Observer* frequently described how revivals in Lutheran congregations "were conducted in the greatest order and solemnity, without noise or confusion of any kind."[48] In sum, New Lutherans were advocating something similar to the middle-class revivalism of Charles Finney rather than the energetic camp meetings of the western frontier.

While revivalism brought New Lutherans like Kurtz closer to American evangelical theology, temperance advocacy aligned them with Anglo-Protestant reformism. In the early republic, alcohol consumption increased at a rate that shocked the sensibilities of religious leaders and led to the formation of the American Temperance Society in 1826. Unsatisfied with merely advocating restraint, many antebellum evangelicals soon began to argue for total abstinence.[49] The *Lutheran Observer* came out firmly on the side of teetotalism, arguing that even though the use of alcoholic beverages was "lawful," the Bible taught that it is not "expedient."[50] Other Lutherans echoed these views by participating in interdenominational temperance rallies and societies.[51] Like their advocacy of "new measures," the involvement of Kurtz and other New Lutherans in the temperance cause had sincere motives but also strategic value. It allied them with influential power brokers in antebellum evangelical Protestantism, which, as Richard Carwardine notes, was "the largest, and most formidable, subculture in American society."[52]

New Lutherans also resembled Anglo-Protestants in arguing that both ministers and the church had a role to play in the nation's political life. Schmucker wrote that although a minister should avoid "mere party politics," he believed that "the Christian pulpit has an important work to perform in preserving and promoting the moral purity of our political institutions." For Schmucker, this included preaching against "all immoral, unequal and oppressive laws" and "offensive war in general, and that . . . with Mexico in particular."[53] Kurtz's *Lutheran Observer* agreed, proclaiming it "the duty of every Christian to take a decided and active part in all the great moral movements of the day and age."[54] As with many antebellum evangelicals, proponents of New Lutheranism believed that religious faith should shape one's political opinions, and at least in the northern states, they tended to support the Whig Party.[55]

On the most significant issue facing the nation—slavery—New Lutherans' views also mirrored those of other white evangelicals. Within a span of eight years, the three largest American denominations divided on account of slavery. In 1837, the Presbyterian church split into New School and Old School factions. Though the schism was officially due to the issues of revivalism and interdenominational cooperation, regional differences on slavery played a significant role in the division. The 1844 and 1845 schisms of Methodists and Baptists, by contrast, were explicitly about the slavery issue and along sectional lines.[56] For American evangelicals in both sections, a shared biblicist hermeneutic and mutual commitment to revivalism and social reform could not thwart the overwhelming influence of regional culture.[57] Though Lutherans never split denominationally on the issue prior to the Civil War, their opinions on slavery and race, like those of other U.S. Protestants, were divided primarily along geographic rather than strictly doctrinal lines.[58]

The *Lutheran Observer,* based in the slave state of Maryland, attempted to chart a moderate course. In the pages of his church paper, Kurtz called attention to the American Colonization Society and urged Lutherans to support this venture.[59] On the subject of "abolition," however, Kurtz declared an editorial policy of "neutrality," since in his view the question was "not essential" and because "we know a conflict of opinion to prevail in the Lutheran Church."[60] As some readers pressured him to take a more definitive stance, Kurtz resolved in 1837 that "the question of Abolition shall not even be mentioned in our columns in any connection whatever."[61] The editor's conservatism on the slavery issue represented sentiments widely shared in Greater Pennsylvania, where most Lutherans resided.[62]

Schmucker took a stronger antislavery position than the *Lutheran Observer* but was also sympathetic to the situation in the South. As a young pastor, he had served parishes in Virginia with members who held slaves. When he remarried after the death of his first wife, he became a slaveholder himself through his second wife's estate.[63] In the 1834 edition of his *Elements of Popular Theology*, the Gettysburg professor wrote that he was "convinced that those who advocate entire, immediate abolition, do not understand the subject" and instead supported both colonization and the "*gradual* and *entire* abolition by legislative provision of the several States."[64] As slavery continued to expand, he dropped the rhetoric of gradualism in the book's 1846 edition, though he still cautiously supported colonization and argued that complete abolition "has difficulties more formidable than some Christians in non-slaveholding states suppose."[65] Unlike Kurtz and the *Lutheran Observer,* Schmucker was not hesitant to label those who "fail sincerely to desire and faithfully to labour for [slavery's] extinction" as "guilty of sin." Yet he also distinguished between "voluntary slaveholding," which was always sinful, and "involuntary slaveholding," which (conveniently) excused situations like his own.[66] Because Schmucker never advocated immediatism and refused to join the American Anti-Slavery Society—due to what he regarded as its "indiscriminate denunciation, and occasionally exaggerated statements"[67]— it is imprecise to characterize his views as "abolitionist," as some scholars have done. Instead, his position resembled that of antislavery moderates like Francis Wayland and Leonard Bacon.[68]

If Kurtz and Schmucker represented the center of New Lutheran opinion on slavery, the leaders of the Franckean and South Carolina synods represented the peripheries. The Franckean Synod was organized in 1837 by pastors in upstate New York. Though the synod took its name from the eighteenth-century German Lutheran pietist leader August Hermann Francke, its more immediate influence was the activist revivalism of the state's "burned-over district."[69] Dissatisfied with the insufficient response to slavery by their fellow Lutherans, the Franckeans made opposition to slavery an integral feature of their synodical platform and were among the few antebellum Lutherans who could accurately be labeled as abolitionists. In 1839, the synod ordained Daniel Alexander Payne (1811–1893), a free Black minister originally from South Carolina who had studied briefly under Schmucker at Gettysburg. Payne would later switch his ecclesial allegiance to the African Methodist Episcopal Church, but not before leading a synodical proposition that condemned slavery in unambiguous terms: "American Slavery brutalizes man—destroys his moral agency, and subverts the moral government of God."[70] Three years later, the Franckean Synod issued a "fraternal appeal" to their fellow Lutherans, demanding "uncompromising ACTION" against slavery.[71] The church body earned plaudits from William Lloyd Garrison's *Liberator*, who praised it as "the only Lutheran ecclesiastic association that has taken decisive action in relation to the abolition of slavery."[72]

Just as the Franckean Synod reflected the abolitionism of its region, the South Carolina Synod mirrored the racial paternalism of southern proslavery evangelicalism. Under the leadership of John Bachman (1790–1874), pastor of St. John's Lutheran Church in Charleston and chief spokesman for New Lutheranism in the South, the synod denounced abolitionists as "enemies of our beloved country" and argued that their antislavery agitation is "contrary to the precepts of our blessed savior, who commanded servants to be obedient to their masters."[73] Despite being the most explicitly proslavery Lutheran synod, the South Carolinians were also the most active in evangelizing Blacks. Both Payne and Jehu Jones (1786–1852), the pastor of the first Black Lutheran church in Philadelphia, came to Lutheranism through Bachman's church.[74] By 1850, African Americans, almost all of whom were enslaved, accounted for about one-sixth of the synod's members.[75]

Though the Franckean and South Carolina synods were small minorities—by 1850, each numbered about three thousand members—their divergent stances on slavery revealed the prevailing attitudes within antebellum Lutheranism as a whole. The Franckean Synod, despite being New Lutheran in its theology, was barred from membership in the General Synod on account of its abolitionism.[76] The South Carolina Synod, by contrast, was welcomed into the federation in 1835, the same year it issued its defense of slavery. Despite the existence of some antislavery sentiment among New Lutherans, most prioritized appeasing their proslavery coreligionists in order to preserve church unity.

New Lutherans also reflected the more conservative end of the American Protestant spectrum on the subject of women's roles.[77] The *Lutheran Observer* fully embraced the view, prominent in the antebellum United States, that "the female sex are the most pure and enlightened of all the human species."[78] Rather than pressing for political "rights" or seeking to "lead in public prayer and teaching," the paper's writers argued, women should devote their superior moral virtue toward those activities befitting their "exalted station."[79] As with other evangelicals, New Lutherans saw the "sphere" of woman as being primarily in the home, but they also believed that "well-educated, pious females" could "assist" in mission work, temperance advocacy, and other "practical duties of charity, beneficence, and love." With this understanding, male leaders such as Bittle and Kurtz encouraged their denomination to participate in the wider Anglo-evangelical effort to create educational institutions for the "proper intellectual, moral and physical education of the [church's] daughters."[80] By the end of the 1850s, Lutherans connected to the General Synod operated twelve "female seminaries" throughout the United States.[81] Yet despite these gestures toward a larger role for women, their voices were mostly absent from the debates and discussions affecting the church.

Perhaps the most important component of New Lutherans' quest to align themselves with Anglo-Protestants was their effort to refute the widely held assumption that, in the words of Charles Buck's influential *Theological Dictionary,* "of all Protestants, [Lutherans] are said to differ least from the Romish church."[82] Buck and others were especially critical of Lutheran teachings on the sacraments, particularly Christ's real presence in the Lord's Supper and baptismal regeneration. New Lutherans responded by modifying or rejecting those traditional doctrines. When a Presbyterian paper repeated Buck's criticism, Kurtz declared that most Lutherans in the United States no longer held to their church's historic positions on the sacraments. "The Lutheran churches of the present day," he concluded, "are just as far from the Romish church as any other denomination of Protestants."[83] Others went even further. Bachman, the leading spokesman for New Lutheranism in the South, not only argued that those "doctrines are unscriptural" but also claimed—seemingly out of ignorance—that they "are not contained in the articles of our Church or in the writings of the Reformers."[84]

Of course, the allegation of Catholic tendencies entailed more than a theological critique. Most Anglo-Protestants viewed "papism" as antithetical to the American ideals of republicanism and religious liberty.[85] Because of this, New Lutheran leaders attempted to quell any close association with Catholicism on this front as well. One strategy was to go on the offensive against "Romanism." In the pages of the *Lutheran Observer,* Kurtz faithfully reported the "awful disclosures" of the Hotel Dieu Nunnery, and during the public school controversy in New York City, he sternly warned his readers that "the Catholics would rule the nation and subject it to the darkness of popery."[86] Other New Lutherans echoed these conspiratorial views, accusing priests of undemocratic beliefs and immoral behavior.[87]

In addition to espousing a virulent anti-Catholicism, proponents of New Lutheranism sought to demonstrate that their church was compatible with, and even the source of, their nation's values. In his widely circulated book *Why Are You a Lutheran?*, Kurtz argued that American Lutheranism's liturgy, polity, and practice of church discipline avoided all hierarchical tendencies and stood "in lovely harmony with the principles of our liberal and republican government."[88] Others went further. Schmucker, in a lengthy treatise, asserted that the Lutheran Reformation was the wellspring of "liberty of conscience" and "delivered the civil government . . . from papal tyranny."[89] In a similar vein, Bachman claimed that "our venerable Church is the mother of Protestants," which established "those principles which in the process of time, would give religious toleration to the human race."[90] By asserting their church's quintessential Americanness, New Lutherans not only were countering accusations of "Romish" sympathy but also were seeking to assimilate their denomination into Anglo-evangelicalism.

In their boldest attempt to do so, Schmucker, Kurtz, and three other New Lutherans traveled to London in the summer of 1846 to participate in the meeting of the World Evangelical Alliance. This organization aspired to bring about church unity among Britons, Americans, and a few continental Europeans along much the same lines that Schmucker had outlined in his *Fraternal Appeal.* The New Lutheran professor played a leading role in the American delegation, which included such luminaries as Lyman Beecher and Sidney Morse, and solidified his reputation as "the most significant ecumenical leader among American evangelicals."[91] The buildup to the trip received extensive coverage in the *Lutheran Observer,* where Kurtz evinced high hopes for the meeting and trumpeted Lutherans' central role in "break[ing] down the high partition walls which bigotry had erected."[92] The Alliance, however, would fail to bring about a united world-wide evangelicalism, largely because British evangelicals, who represented about 85 percent of the delegates, insisted that the organization exclude slaveholders. Instead, the meeting resulted in separate British and American associations, with the U.S. version disbanding in 1850. Despite the London meeting's failure, New Lutherans' participation in the venture marked a new high point in their efforts to become part of the American Protestant mainstream.

By the mid-1840s, Lutherans like Schmucker, Kurtz, and Bachman were becoming respectable insiders in the minds of the Anglo-evangelicals who shaped antebellum American politics and society. In 1844, Robert Baird, Schmucker's former roommate at Princeton, published a landmark survey of religion in the United States that separated the "evangelical churches" from the "unevangelical" ones. He placed the Lutheran church squarely in the evangelical category, noting its "rapid progress . . . since the Revolution" and declaring it to be "much more sound than it once was." In particular, he praised the Lutherans of the General Synod for "abolish[ing] the remains of papal superstition" and making a "systematic adjustment in its doctrine."[93] Such recognition was precisely what New Lutherans were working toward. Yet in his short summary, Baird overlooked antebellum Lutheranism's other factions, who had a much different idea about what it meant to be both Lutheran and American.

OLD LUTHERANISM

In November 1838, five ships departed from the German port of Bremerhaven, carrying nearly seven hundred Lutherans from Saxony known as the Stephanites. Fervent adherents of what they considered to be "the old, pure, Lutheran faith," the voyagers were journeying to America to establish what historian Walter Forster called a "semiautonomous theocratic community." The emigrants were named after their charismatic leader Martin Stephan (1777–1846), a pastor in Dresden who had gained a loyal following not only in his congregation but also among several young clergymen. As his influence grew during the mid-1830s, Stephan attracted the attention of the civil and ecclesiastical authorities, particularly for his unusual practice of holding "nocturnal meetings" with both male and female followers. In November 1837, he was placed under house arrest and lost his pastoral position. As his self-described "persecution by powerful enemies" mounted, Stephan became convinced that his and his disciples' only course of action was to leave Germany. They chose the United States, "a land," they believed, "where complete religious and civil liberty prevails."[94] Over the course of the nineteenth century this zealous sect would drastically alter the development of American Lutheranism.

The Stephanites were one of the most radical groups to come out of the German *Erweckungsbewegung* (Awakening Movement), or simply *Erweckung*.[95] Following the upheavals of the Napoleonic Wars, "awakened" Protestants worked to reform and revive their churches through mission work, social action, parish renewal, and orthodox doctrine. Though they shared a common emphasis on individual salvation and heartfelt piety, the movement was hardly united. Proponents of the *Erweckung* advocated both the emerging liberalism that culminated in the revolutions that took place throughout Europe in 1848 and 1849 and the throne-and-altar conservatism that squelched those democratic uprisings. Some supported the Reformed–Lutheran ecumenism of the Prussian Union, while others emphasized confessional particularism. However, the vast majority of the awakened believed that reform should occur through the German state churches. What made the Stephanites unusual was their conviction that "pure and unadulterated" Lutheranism could not be preserved in Germany.[96] Like the *Mayflower* pilgrims more than two hundred years before, Stephan and his followers were the separatist fringe of a broader reform movement in their homeland.[97]

After four of the ships arrived in New Orleans in January 1839 (the fifth was lost at sea), the Stephanite clergy invested their "spiritual father" with the office of bishop, and shortly thereafter, while traveling by steamboat up the Mississippi River, they pledged to submit themselves to him in "both ecclesiastical and community affairs." The immigrants founded a colony of four congregations in Perry County, Missouri, as well as a congregation in St. Louis, about eighty miles to the north. But the Saxons' holy experiment quickly began to unravel. Stephan's despotic leadership and profligate spending soon antagonized his followers. The final straw occurred when two women confessed that they had engaged in adultery with Stephan and several others claimed that he had made advances toward them. In May 1839, less than five months after their arrival in America, the Stephanites banished their leader from the colony, exiling him to the Illinois side of the Mississippi River. These tumultuous events provoked a profound crisis. The immigrants had considered Stephan to be "the last, unshakeable pillar on the ruins of the now devastated Lutheran Church." Now, with their "bishop" revealed to be a fraud, many of the colonists were beginning to question the legitimacy of their congregations, the validity of their pastors' authority, and whether their emigration had been a sinful act. Several laypeople returned to Germany and many clergy resigned their positions.[98]

During this time of upheaval and uncertainty, Carl Ferdinand Wilhelm Walther (1811–1887) emerged as the new leader of the immigrants.[99] Walther had come under the influence of Stephan while studying at the University of Leipzig. After serving less than two years as a pastor of a small parish, he resigned his position to join the Stephanite migration. The youngest clergyman in the group, Walther took the lead in exposing and deposing Stephan. Following his spiritual mentor's banishment from the community, however, he entered a period of deep distress. In a letter written in May 1840, he called the emigration "an abominable undertaking" and wondered, "Are our congregations truly Lutheran congregations? . . . Do we still belong in Germany?"[100]

Walther's breakthrough came the following year, after an intense period of personal study. In a debate held in the Stephanite settlement of Altenburg, Missouri, the young pastor laid out eight theses on the nature of the church. The central claim of Walther's argument was that "the orthodox church is chiefly to be judged by the common, orthodox, public confession" rather than the faithfulness of its leaders or members. His words convinced the majority of the community's clergy and laity that despite the actions of Stephan their congregations and pastors were still members of "the true Church" and that they should remain in the United States.[101] Besides resolving the colonists' inner turmoil, the Altenburg Debate had two lasting effects: It established Walther as the unquestioned leader of the remaining Stephanites and it confirmed "pure doctrine" as their principal emphasis.

In 1844, shortly after moving to St. Louis to pastor the city's Stephanite congregation, Walther founded *Der Lutheraner* (The Lutheran), a fortnightly paper dedicated to rallying others to the banner of "true Lutheranism." According to the young pastor, every particularity of his church's historic teachings was a nonnegotiable: "A true Lutheran and a true Christian, the Lutheran church and the Christian church, God's word and Luther's doctrine, all of this is one and the same for us."[102] Walther also strove to define the boundaries of the "true church" by warning his readers against "heresy." He was especially critical of the Methodists, who represented everything he believed was wrong with religion in the United States: revivalism, antisacramentalism, and "build[ing] practically all of their Christianity . . . upon their uncertain, changing emotions."[103] According to the *Lutheraner,* "false teaching" was the evidence needed to prove that a group of Christians was a "sect" that true Lutherans should avoid.[104] In stark contrast to the evangelical ecumenism of Schmucker and the New Lutherans, Walther believed that the Lutheran church was the sole possessor of the "old pure doctrine."[105]

For all his invective against various American "sects," however, Walther's understanding of Lutheranism bore a resemblance to the primitivist movements that arose in the antebellum United States.[106] Espousing a view similar to that of the Landmark Baptists, he claimed, "So long as there has been an orthodox church on earth, there has also been the Lutheran Church. She is (as strange as that sounds) as old as the world, for she has no other doctrine than the patriarchs, prophets, and apostles."[107] His theological project also shared an affinity with the restorationism of Alexander Campbell, another early nineteenth-century immigrant.[108] According to Walther, Martin Luther was "the chosen and sanctified instrument of God, through whom the old apostolic doctrine and church were restored in their original form."[109] Now, after decades of decline, he was urging his fellow Lutherans to "join together and rally around the banner of the old, unchanging doctrine of our church."[110] Though Walther's views were initially that of a tiny minority, several other German Lutherans in the United States came to embrace his positions.

One such person was Friedrich Wyneken (1810–1876).[111] Deeply influenced by the *Erweckung,* Wyneken came to America in 1838 as a missionary to German immigrants in the vicinity of Fort Wayne, Indiana. However, the young pastor was scandalized by religious life on the American frontier, and after three years he fell ill and moved back to Germany. Upon his return, Wyneken toured Europe promoting a tract he had composed during his time in Indiana, *Die Noth der deutschen Lutheraner in Nordamerika* (The Distress of the German Lutherans in North America).[112] His broadside painted a bleak picture. Along with the "morass of vulgarity" and "gross indifference" among the immigrants, Wyneken criticized the "swarming pests" of Methodists and other revivalists. More ominously, he warned that "the misleading interpretation of freedom" he had witnessed in the United States was spreading to Europe. "If the struggle is not settled in America," he predicted, "the flood will soon enough flow across the Atlantic toward our German fatherland."[113] He urged orthodox Lutheran pastors to emigrate and stem the tide of heresy. In 1843, he took his own advice and returned to America.

Before leaving Germany for a second time, Wyneken had become affiliated with other conservative churchmen who would play critical roles in antebellum Old Lutheranism. The first of these was Wilhelm Löhe (1808–1872), a pastor in the Bavarian village of Neuendettelsau and leader of German Neo-Lutheranism, a submovement of the *Erweckung* that emphasized confessionalism, churchliness, and cultural traditionalism.[114] Influenced by Wyneken's characterization of the challenges facing Lutheranism in America, Löhe founded a mission society dedicated to sending theologically conservative Lutheran pastors to the New World. By 1853, the Bavarian pastor had commissioned eighty-two missionaries to the United States.[115] Another key figure was Wilhelm Sihler (1801–1885). A former Prussian military officer and holder of a doctorate from the University of Jena, Sihler was initially a devotee of the rationalist theology of Friedrich Schleiermacher but converted to the *Erweckung* in 1830. In the spring of 1843, while working as a private tutor, he read Wyneken's pamphlet. "It struck me like lightning to my soul," he later recalled.[116] By September, he had obtained pastoral credentials, secured funding from the Dresden Missionary Society, and departed for America.

Upon their arrival in the United States, Wyneken, the Löhe missionaries, and Sihler all failed to find satisfactory Lutheran synods with which to affiliate. After a brief return to his old church in Fort Wayne, Wyneken became pastor of a congregation in Baltimore. Both churches were connected with the General Synod, whose New Lutheran leaders Wyneken described as having "completely broken away from the faith of their fathers."[117] The Löhe missionaries and Sihler spread throughout Ohio, Michigan, and Indiana. At first, many joined the Ohio Synod (discussed later), but they soon severed their connections because they deemed it insufficiently orthodox.[118] As these conservative missionaries struggled to find similarly minded Lutherans in the United States, Walther's *Lutheraner* presented what they were searching for. When Wyneken first read the paper, he reportedly commented, "God be praised! There are still more Lutherans here in America."[119] Both he and Sihler quickly became regular contributors to the *Lutheraner*, and it transformed from Walther's personal paper into the mouthpiece of a movement.

As the *Lutheraner* expanded its readership, its principal polemical targets became the New Lutherans of the General Synod. For the paper's writers, Lutherans like Schmucker and Kurtz were especially dangerous because they combined the errors of the German Union churches and the Methodists under the guise of the name Lutheran. As one correspondent wrote, by rejecting doctrines such as baptismal regeneration and the real presence in the Lord's Supper, these "pseudo-Lutherans" were sowing "soul destroying weeds."[120] Wyneken accused New Lutherans of engaging in "whoredom with the sects" through their use of revivals, prayer meetings, and other "Reformed-Methodist inventions."[121] Walther summarized his and his colleagues' accusations: In the General Synod, "apostasy . . . is being praised as progress."[122]

New Lutherans soon responded in kind. Ironically, Kurtz and the *Lutheran Observer* initially had welcomed the Saxon immigrants to the New World. During his trip to Germany in the late 1820s, Kurtz had met Stephan and had been impressed by the Dresden pastor's battle against "infidelity" and (ironically) "looseness of morals." In 1833, the two ministers had corresponded about the viability of emigration. When the Saxons arrived five years later, Kurtz expressed confidence that "christians of every orthodox denomination, who are properly acquainted with this people, will join us in welcoming the 'STEPHANITES' to 'the asylum of the oppressed of all nations.'"[123] Yet after he became more "properly acquainted" with these immigrants' style of Lutheranism, his praise turned into criticism. Kurtz saw the Stephanites' theology as resembling that of Roman Catholicism and high-church Anglicanism. Their claim to be "the true sons of the church," he wrote in the *Lutheran Observer,* was "a mistake which has been quite common from the days of the first Pope to the modern Pusey."[124]

In their criticism of the *Lutheraner,* Kurtz and the New Lutherans referred to their opponents as "Old Lutherans." At first, Walther and his allies pushed back against this name. For them, the term signified a specific faction of Lutheranism in Germany, the *Altlutheraner* of Prussia, represented in the United States by another immigrant group led by Johannes Grabau (1804–1879). Equally punctilious about doctrinal exactitude, Grabau and his followers had become embroiled with the Stephanites in a heated dispute over church polity in the early 1840s and would go on to found their own church body, the Buffalo Synod, in 1845.[125] Yet most fundamentally, those associated with the *Lutheraner* disputed the term because true Lutheranism, in Sihler's words, "remains above the temporal distinctions of old and new."[126] Blaming the rise of this "oxymoronic designation" on the "Schmuckerites [and] Kurtzites," he argued that "there are not any Old or New Lutherans, but rather only Lutherans, that is orthodox, and non-Lutherans, that is heretical."[127] Yet the label stuck. New Lutherans continued to use the term, and those associated with the *Lutheraner* came to accept the designation.[128]

In contrast to their boisterous theological claims, Old Lutherans' political views were mostly muted. In part, this was due to the mutual suspicion between themselves and the German American political press, which was dominated during the early 1840s by the liberal and mildly anticlerical intellectuals known as the Dreissiger. The relationship between the Old Lutherans and the St. Louis–based *Anzeiger des Westens* was particularly testy. After mocking the initial Stephanite immigration and continuing to criticize their churches, the paper accused Walther in 1844 of harboring undemocratic political views.[129] His congregation responded with a letter defending their minister: "We can assure you that Pastor Walther has never made a political public address. . . . He believes that such political activities are not in keeping with the dignity of his ministerial office."[130] As the letter indicates, Old Lutherans' political ambivalence stemmed not only from their estrangement from German American political leaders but also from a principled opposition to mixing religion and politics. As Walther wrote in 1849, "Our church teaches according to God's Word that temporal and spiritual powers are to be strictly divided."[131] Because of these factors, Walther and his associates avoided endorsing particular parties or candidates and steered clear of the contentious issues of American political culture in the 1840s, especially slavery.

Yet the Old Lutherans were not complete political quietists; they paid frequent homage to the blessings of "this wondrous land of freedom."[132] Those associated with the *Lutheraner* enthusiastically participated in the rituals of American civil religion, celebrating the Fourth of July and observing days of thanksgiving and repentance. On one such occasion, Walther hailed the United States' founding as ordained by God: "Who gave the framers of the Constitution . . . the wisdom to invent such a thing? Is it not the Lord . . . from whom comes all wisdom? Who gave victory in the War for Independence? Is it not . . . the Lord of Hosts, who is the true warrior?"[133] More than anything, Old Lutherans praised their adopted nation's religious liberty. Some, such as Wyneken, had initially blamed the "destructive elements" in U.S. Christianity on "the complete freedom in religious matters granted by the American Constitution."[134] However, under

Walther's guidance, Old Lutherans came to embrace the idea that the American doctrine of the separation of church and state reflected the Lutheran teaching of the two kingdoms. In a Fourth of July lecture, he argued that while religious freedom is often misused, it alone allows for "true religion" to prevail. Because of this, Walther called upon his fellow Lutherans to "courageously battle and, when necessary, gladly shed our blood, that this land not only remain a free land, but above all retain the golden crown of its freedom, that is, its religious liberty."[135] The remnant of the Stephanites had not only birthed a religious movement but also embraced American national identity.

In 1847, the movement became an organization. The idea of forming an Old Lutheran synod had been discussed for some time in private correspondence and informal meetings.[136] In September 1846, the *Lutheraner* published a proposed constitution for a new Lutheran church body that was endorsed by twenty-two clergymen, including former Stephanites as well as Sihler and several Löhe missionaries.[137] (Wyneken would support the venture but did not join until 1850.) Walther conceived of the proposal in grand terms: "We obviously stand at the portals of a most significant and ... most decisive time for our church."[138] Seven months later, representatives of fourteen congregations from Missouri, Illinois, Indiana, New York, and Ohio convened in Chicago. The delegates elected Walther as their new synod's first president, designated the *Lutheraner* as its official publication, and chose the unwieldy name The German Evangelical Lutheran Synod of Missouri, Ohio, and Other States.

Rather than a replication of European Lutheranism, the newly founded Missouri Synod, as the church body quickly became known, was distinctly American. Though "German" was used in its official title, this word was meant to contrast with "English," not "American." Leaders of the new synod described themselves with phrases like "our American Lutheran church," "the American German Lutheran church," or "our precious Evangelical Lutheran Zion in this our new homeland."[139] Outside commentators also recognized the Missouri Synod's Americanness. As the *Lutheran Observer* noted, "They transact and record their business pretty much as we Americans do. ... In the Fatherland, this sort of synod is wholly unknown."[140] The *Lutheran Standard* (discussed later) offered a similar evaluation, describing the new church body's constitution as "truly scriptural and eminently American."[141]

What these papers were primarily referencing was the Missouri Synod's adoption of congregational polity. In the wake of Stephan's scandals, Walther and other Saxon leaders had emphasized the rights of laymen as a safeguard against the potential abuse of clerical power. Initially, other constituents of the Old Lutheran movement—Wyneken, Sihler, and the Löhe missionaries—had expressed skepticism about this form of ecclesiastical governance, believing that it yielded too much to the spirit of American liberty. However, after discussions with Walther, their fears were assuaged.[142] The Old Lutheran leader summarized the new synod's principles in his first address as Missouri Synod president: While it would be a mistake to place "a restriction on the freedom of the congregations, especially in a free state such as ours," he trusted that by asking "nothing . . . except submission to the Word," they would "*use* this power rightly" and confess "the pure doctrine of our dear Evangelical Lutheran Church."[143]

Denominational historians have long debated the extent to which the Missouri Synod's form of governance was influenced by the environment of its immigrant founders' new home.[144] Undoubtedly, it played a role, as Walther himself admitted.[145] Even the acts of writing a synodical constitution and electing a president were indebted to American conceptions of republicanism.[146] Yet congregationalism was hardly the chief way in which Walther and his followers engaged in Americanization. For many other denominations—Episcopalians, Methodists, and Presbyterians—alternative forms of church polity fit just as well into the nation's democratic milieu. The more genuinely "American" aspects of Old Lutheranism were its biblicist primitivism, its emphasis on church-state separation, and, more broadly, its ability to craft a unique identity in the nation's religious marketplace. Like other "American originals" and "religious outsiders," this novel form of Lutheranism would blossom in the land of freedom.[147]

Of course, the Old Lutherans did not consider their views to be unique or novel. Rather, they believed that they had recovered the pure doctrine of authentic Lutheranism. In order to counteract their New Lutheran opponents, they had founded a national church body with a church paper circulated throughout the country. By the end of the 1840s, they had also established rival educational institutions: Concordia College in St. Louis, headed by Walther, and a "practical seminary" led by Sihler in Fort Wayne. Yet despite their grand designs, Old Lutheranism was a minority movement. At its founding, the Missouri Synod numbered about five thousand members, less than 5 percent of all Lutherans in the United States. Nevertheless, Walther expressed confidence in the Old Lutherans' divine calling: "Compared to those they battle, those who fight now for the re-establishment of the Lutheran church in her original form . . . are still just a drop in the bucket. . . . Yet the Lord has arisen to aid his church once more."[148]

MODERATE LUTHERANISM

In his 1854 assessment of American Lutheranism, Philip Schaff described Moderate Lutherans not as a "party" or "faction" but as a "tendency." What united members of this "school" was a discomfort with the New Lutherans' theological modifications and embrace of revivalism, on the one hand, and an aversion to the rigidity and harshness of Old Lutheranism, on the other. Though he was sympathetic to their viewpoint, Schaff could be critical. Most Moderate Lutheran pastors, he wrote, "have few firm convictions, are poorly educated, stagnant, and are much more concerned about building programs . . . than theology and church affairs." Yet he believed that this group possessed "many promising young theologians" and "has the oldest American Lutheran tradition on its side."[149]

Schaff noted that the synods most closely associated with Moderate Lutheranism were the Pennsylvania Synod (as the Pennsylvania Ministerium was commonly known) and the Joint Synod of Ohio (usually called the Ohio Synod), two church bodies with an intertwined history.[150] Lutherans had been migrating to Ohio even before the territory achieved statehood in 1803. After being served by preachers mostly from the Pennsylvania Synod, the Ohio congregations and ministers organized their own church body in 1818. But the ties between the two synods persisted. Soon after the Ohio Synod founded its own seminary in Columbus in 1830, the Pennsylvania Synod chose to support this institution rather than the General Synod's school in Gettysburg. When Lutherans of the Ohio Synod established their own paper, the *Lutheran Standard,* twelve years later, the new venture also received an endorsement from their counterparts in Pennsylvania.[151] Though it failed to match the circulation of the *Lutheran Observer,* by 1854 the paper had grown large enough for Schaff to label it as the "organ" of Moderate Lutheranism.[152]

In the inaugural issue, its first editor Emmanuel Greenwald (1811–1885) cited the two issues on which the *Lutheran Standard* differed from its New Lutheran counterpart.[153] The first centered on the Augsburg Confession of 1530. Unlike those associated with the *Lutheran Observer,* Greenwald believed that everything contained in this oldest Lutheran confession, including its teachings about the sacraments, was "preeminently biblical." "To explain and meekly to defend those doctrines," he wrote, "will be our business and our pleasure." The editor cited "new measures" as the second point of disagreement. He believed that these re-vivalist practices were causing "most of the evils of division and strife, that now unhappily afflict the Lutheran Church." Yet despite his criticisms, Greenwald insisted that "we are determined to have no controversy on the subject." Instead, he hoped that by raising this issue "we may still be enabled to journey on harmo-niously together."[154]

Kurtz, at the *Lutheran Observer,* also initially tried to strike a cordial tone. After praising the new paper's first issue, he commented on Greenwald's inaugu-ral editorial: "In essentials we entirely *agree* with him; in non-essentials we most cheerfully award to him the same *liberty* we claim for ourselves; and in all things we desire to exercise *charity.*" Yet after a few more articles directed against the New Lutherans' doctrine and practice, Kurtz began to criticize the *Lutheran Standard* for its "spirit of jealousy" and "want of manly candor." "If we must have an opponent," he complained, "we prefer that he should be an open, above-board, courageous and honorable one."[155] Throughout the 1840s, the papers oscillated between friendly disagreement and outright hostility.

Further inflaming the controversy between the two Lutheran papers was their divergent reactions to the 1843 publication of *The Anxious Bench* by John Williamson Nevin (1803–1886), who served with Philip Schaff as a professor of theology at the German Reformed seminary in Mercersburg, Pennsylvania. Nevin's book has been hailed by many historians of nineteenth-century American religion as an incisive critique of the Finneyite revival system. Yet many of these same scholars overlook the more specific target of Nevin's polemic: the advance of revivalist practices into the "German Churches." The Reformed professor sin-gled out the *Lutheran Observer* as the chief object of his criticism. He claimed that "the Anxious Bench, after having enjoyed a brief reputation, has fallen into discredit," but he lamented that Kurtz and his New Lutheran associates were breathing "new life" into the "system of New Measures." After scrutinizing the emotionalism, superficiality, and disorder of revivalism, Nevin urged "our Ger-man Zion" to rededicate itself to "the system of the *Catechism.*"[156]

Both the *Lutheran Observer* and the *Lutheran Standard* responded to Nevin's diatribe. Kurtz criticized the book as "erroneous and in some instances glaringly so" and predicted that its "effect will be evil, only evil, and disastrous to the salvation of many immortal souls."[157] Over the course of four months, the New Lutheran editor wrote a thirteen-part rebuttal, using the same arguments for revivalism that he had been promoting for the previous ten years.[158] Even more irksome to Kurtz was that the *Lutheran Standard* and other Moderate Lutherans endorsed Nevin's views. Greenwald praised the book's "correct sentiments" and printed excerpts in his paper.[159] Another Ohio Synod pastor published a complete German translation.[160] The *Lutheran Standard* printed several letters that took aim at Kurtz and the *Lutheran Observer*, with one accusing New Lutherans of viewing new measures as "the sine qua non for the existence of the church" and alleging that "the anxious bench with all its accompaniments operated like a magic charm upon their imagination and feelings."[161]

Besides heightening the tensions between the two periodicals, the controversy over Nevin's publication also signaled an important realignment in American Lutheran ecumenism. Lutherans in the early republic had collaborated with the Reformed out of a shared commitment to Pennsylvania German culture, but for most Lutherans theological issues were now beginning to supersede ethnic concerns.[162] New Lutherans like Kurtz and Schmucker rejected the antirevivalism of Nevin, Schaff, and other German Reformed leaders. Instead, they sought alliances with more theologically revivalist (and more culturally and politically connected) Protestants. Moderate Lutherans, particularly those associated with the Pennsylvania Synod, would hold on to their ethnic solidarity with the Reformed for a longer time, particularly in their opposition to the certain aspects of the common school system.[163] Yet as confessional distinctiveness became more important to their sense of Lutheran identity, the alliance began to fade.

Further widening the rift between New and Moderate Lutherans were their differing assessments of the Tennessee Synod. In 1820, six pastors and their congregations, led by David Henkel (1795–1831), had split off from the North Carolina Synod over the proposed General Synod and founded their own church body. Like other critics of the new federation, Henkel couched his opposition in terms of liberty, expressing fears of centralized authority, but he went further in insisting that the Augsburg Confession alone should be the marker of Lutheran unity.[164] As the new synod began attracting members from not only Tennessee but also Virginia and the Carolinas, it drew considerable ire from New Lutherans in the South. For John Bachman, the Tennessee Synod's insistence on baptismal regeneration and the real presence of Christ in the Lord's Supper was "directly opposed to the Gospel of Christ" and put them outside the bounds of true Lutheranism. "No Synod in our country has ever acknowledged, or given countenance, to this sect," he declared.[165] Kurtz agreed with Bachman's assessment. Though "claiming to be Lutheran," the editor of the *Lutheran Observer* wrote, the Tennessee Synod is "not admitted to be so by many who are better acquainted with its members."[166] Despite this opposition, the church body continued to grow, accounting for somewhere between 15 and 25 percent of all southern Lutherans in the 1850s.

This high level of animus explains why, in 1846, the *Lutheran Standard,* now under the editorship of Christian Spielmann (1810–1895), received such a harsh response when it innocuously referred to the Tennessee Synod as an "Ev. Lutheran body." One reader wrote to cancel his subscription, asserting that "every person that is acquainted with [the synod], knows it to be a disgrace to the cause of Christianity."[167] Another letter writer criticized "the Henkelites" for their "divisive spirit, moral laxity, and refusal to participate in Sabbath Schools, Bible, Tract, Missionary and Temperance Societies."[168] Over the next few years, however, as Moderate Lutherans, particularly those in the Ohio Synod, became more acquainted with the Tennessee Synod's positions—and as this southern church body's leaders tempered their more pugnacious rhetoric—the two groups grew closer together.[169] In 1852, the *Lutheran Standard* began publishing news and opinions from this church body in its "Tennessee Department," an act unthinkable a decade before.[170] Over the course of the 1850s, the two synods became de facto partners, with the Tennessee Synod regarding the *Lutheran Standard* as its "organ."[171] Such collaboration drove an even deeper wedge between the Moderate and New Lutherans.

Ultimately, their chief locus of dispute was the General Synod itself. The Pennsylvania and Ohio synods, the two chief Moderate Lutheran church bodies, initially balked at joining this national federation out of fears of centralization. Adding to the tension was the decision of several congregations during the 1830s and 1840s to break away from those synods in order to form the East Pennsylvania, Allegheny, and English Ohio synods, new church bodies founded for the purpose of joining the General Synod. Over the course of the 1840s, the *Lutheran*

Standard gave voice to various frustrations with this federation. Some writers lamented the General Synod's promotion of the theology of Samuel Schmucker and other New Lutherans, particularly their rejection of certain traditional doctrines found in the Augsburg Confession.[172] Yet the most frequent complaint from Moderate Lutherans was that the federation presumed to speak for all Lutherans in the United States. The "so called [*sic*] Gen. Synod," the *Lutheran Standard* griped, has "covertly and publicly stigmatized the large portion of our church, embracing many of our oldest, most intellectual, pious and self-sacrificing ministers, who could not and *cannot* affiliate with it." Whereas the Old Lutherans of the Missouri Synod accused the General Synod of being "pseudo-Lutheran," the Moderate Lutherans of the Ohio and Pennsylvania synods criticized this federation of synods for being "pseudo-General."[173]

Therein lay the chief difference between the Moderate Lutherans and the Old Lutherans. The *Lutheran Standard,* which in 1848 came under the editorship of a committee of Ohio Synod pastors, regarded the writings of Walther and other Missouri Synod leaders to be "valuable."[174] However, while "we commend their orthodoxy and respect their piety," the paper's editors wrote, "we do not like their exclusiveness." In fact, they saw "the same unlovely trait of character" in both Old Lutheranism and New Lutheranism. Each faction, they argued, "arrogates to itself all the truth and all the piety that exist in the church" and "anathematizes all who do not sympathize with it."[175] Thus, while Moderate Lutherans were sometimes sharply critical of various aspects of the General Synod, they were not willing to declare it outside the bounds of Lutheranism. "Although some diversity exists as to doctrines and measures," wrote one Ohio Synod clergymen, "we are one church."[176]

Because of this, the boundaries between the Moderate Lutheran synods and those associated with the General Synod were often fluid. Since its founding in 1826, several members of the Gettysburg seminary's board of directors had been clergymen from the Pennsylvania Synod. In 1848, the church body resolved to sponsor a "German professor" at the seminary, an arrangement that finally materialized in 1855, when Charles F. Schaeffer (1807–1879) was appointed.[177] Clergymen frequently changed synodical affiliations with little friction. William Reynolds (1812–1876) was ordained by the Pennsylvania Synod but became an instructor at the General Synod's Pennsylvania College. Before joining the faculty at the Gettysburg seminary, Schaeffer had served as a pastor in the General

Synod–affiliated West Pennsylvania Synod and had taught at the Ohio Synod's seminary in Columbus.[178] Both of these leaders had Moderate Lutheran leanings, but collaborating with the General Synod was not seen as a contradiction.

Further evidence of this cooperative spirit was the establishment of the *Evangelical Review,* the first Lutheran theological quarterly in the United States. With Reynolds serving as editor and other critics of New Lutheranism, including Greenwald and Schaeffer, serving as assistant editors, the periodical had a decidedly Moderate Lutheran bent. Yet the journal was hardly launched as a conservative counteroffensive.[179] In his inaugural editorial, Reynolds insisted that the journal "belongs to no particular school or party in the Lutheran church" and expressed his belief that "the church is still essentially one." He envisioned the *Evangelical Review* as a "remedy," where "all parts of the church should meet each other as upon neutral ground." In a retrospectively prophetic analogy to the political realm, the editor wrote, "In civil life the collision of opposite parties . . . does not tend to the destruction of our national union. On the contrary, the first step towards disunion or civil war would be the separation of the different parties into different conventions." Reynolds also expressed an irenic view of other denominations: "We do not wish to be understood as occupying a hostile position toward any other part of Christendom."[180] Conservative dogmatism this was not.

New Lutherans reacted favorably to the journal. Kurtz enthusiastically promoted the buildup to its publication and published an article in the inaugural issue.[181] During its first year, correspondents to the *Lutheran Observer* praised its "moderate tone" and "dignified style" and proclaimed it to be "especially adapted to the present wants our church."[182] Schmucker, the intellectual head of New Lutheranism, offered both public and private approval of the new journal. In a two-part review, he expressed confidence that "by adherence to the editor's excellent motto, [it will] prove itself suited to the times, and worthy of general patronage."[183] To his son, he wrote, "With the Ev. Mag. of Mr. R. I am in general pleased, & if I can find time, I will occasionally write for it."[184] Even after Schmucker and Reynolds engaged in a tendentious exchange of articles over the nature of the Augsburg Confession, New Lutherans, including Schmucker, continued to support and publish in the journal.[185] Their hope was that the *Evangelical Review* would, in the words of one correspondent to the *Lutheran Observer,* help to "harmonize and consolidate our church."[186]

A major step in this direction came in 1853, when the largest Moderate Lutheran church body, the Pennsylvania Synod, joined the General Synod. In the *Lutheran Observer*, Schmucker lauded the decision. Though he acknowledged that doctrinal disagreements existed within the federation, he considered those differences to be "non-essential" and believed that such a union would work because "they are willing to concede to us the same liberty which we extend to them."[187] As they prepared to align with the General Synod, the leaders of the Pennsylvania Synod asked their fellow Moderate Lutherans in the Ohio Synod to join them.[188] But the delegates to its 1853 convention refused because they regarded the General Synod's doctrinal position as inadequate. Nevertheless, the Ohio Synod's leaders still expressed their "hope that, the Gen. Synod may, ere long, place itself in such a position as that we may be able to co-operate with it in the important work of uniting the church."[189] Shortly after the Pennsylvania Synod's decision, the *Evangelical Review* voiced the sentiments of the vast majority of American Lutherans: "The day is not far distant, when the whole Evangelical Lutheran church of this country . . . will labor together to extend the reign of *peace on earth and good will to men.*"[190]

★ ★ ★

Philip Schaff was also optimistic about the future prospects of Lutheranism. In his 1854 lectures in Berlin, he praised the Pennsylvania Synod's union with the General Synod as an important step in allowing Moderate Lutherans to accomplish what he believed was their mission: to "consolidate the different elements in the Lutheran church of America." Schaff was convinced that a moderate and irenic position would emerge as the primary form of Lutheranism in the United States. A truly American Lutheranism, he argued, not only would be true to its "heritage and history" and its "dogmatic and religious identity" but also would work with other denominations in shaping the "entire development of Anglo-American Christianity."[191]

Over the course of the nineteenth century, Schaff's prognostication would prove to be inaccurate. Less than twenty years after his Berlin lectures, the principal type of Lutheranism in the United States would be inward-looking and polemical, rather than outward-looking and ecumenical. Schaff, however, should be forgiven for getting it wrong. When he forecasted the future of the Lutheran church in America, only the Old Lutherans, still a tiny minority, were insisting on dogmatism and separatism. By the early 1850s, the vast majority of Lutherans were at home in the nation's Anglo-evangelical milieu and confident that a more united Lutheranism would contribute to the shaping of American culture.

TWO

★ ★ ★ ★ ★ ★ ★

The Crises of the 1850s

I N 1852, the New Lutheran minister Simeon Harkey addressed members of various evangelical denominations in Springfield, Illinois, and declared, "I believe that the Lutheran Church has a special mission and a distinct work in this country." For Harkey, Lutheranism's American errand was two-pronged. Its first duty was to evangelize and educate the "immense multitudes" of German and Scandinavian immigrants. He argued that because of its origins in these European nations, the Lutheran church was best suited to this task. Lutheranism's second purpose, Harkey continued, was theological. Just as the Declaration of Independence and the U.S. Constitution were the "mother" of political liberty, he contended, so also "Luther and his coadjutors of the Augsburg Confession" established the great "fundamental principles of Protestant Christianity," namely *"the supremacy of the Bible"* and *"the right of private judgment."* Thus, the theological mission of the Lutheran church, was to "take her proper position" and serve as a mediator in American Protestant disputes. The key to realizing this vision, he believed, was for the Lutheran church in the United States to remain united. Though he admitted that we "occasionally have a man among us" who insists on complete agreement in "non-essential" matters, the majority regard such a person as an "intolerant bigot." Most American Lutherans, according to Harkey, recognized that "'in union there is strength" and that "all our interests are one, whether in the north, south, east or west."[1]

46

Harkey's ideas about his church's mission highlighted the three chief crises facing Lutherans during the 1850s: debates about newly arriving immigrants from Northern Europe, quarrels over the boundaries of true Lutheranism and church unity, and somewhat obliquely, disagreements over slavery and sectionalism. In many ways, these debates reflected the disputes that strained and reconfigured the nation's political system during this decade. Like U.S. political parties, Lutheran synods responded to the unprecedented numbers of Northern European immigrants both with nativism and by seizing the opportunity to increase their constituency. Additionally, the heated rhetoric of national politics mirrored the impassioned theological and ecclesiastical quarrels within American Lutheranism. Finally, as in the rest of the nation, the moral and political conflict over slavery strained the sectional unity of Lutherans.

Yet despite these parallels, the American nation and the Lutheran church were on different trajectories. By 1860, the central issue of slavery would lead the republic to the brink of disunion. American Lutheranism, meanwhile, save for a few holdouts, stood more unified than ever before. Contrary to other historical accounts, the 1850s was not a time of escalating intra-Lutheran tensions leading inexorably to theological conflict.[2] Instead, by the end of the decade, most Lutherans had united around the institution of the General Synod, a commitment to liberty of conscience in matters of "nonessential" doctrine, and the vision of making their denomination a respectable branch of the American evangelical establishment. Rather than dreading the prospect of an ecclesiastical house divided, on the eve of the Civil War most Lutherans, like Harkey, were boundlessly optimistic of their church's future.

ANTEBELLUM IMMIGRATION

From 1846 to 1860, the influx of nearly 3.5 million immigrants shaped the United States in a variety of ways.[3] The first was the changing ethnic and religious composition of the American people. Largely due to the approximately 1.5 million migrants from Ireland, Roman Catholicism became the largest denomination in the United States. The era also saw the arrival of a variety of other Northern European peoples and faiths, as well as a significant minority from China. Immigration also influenced the American political system. While Democrats successfully courted many of these newcomers, especially Irish Catholics, other native-born Americans reacted with hostility. This nativist backlash led to the creation of the American Party, or Know-Nothings. Yet this new party never gained the mass support needed to overtake the slowly collapsing Whigs. Instead, the Republican Party arose as the somewhat more immigrant-friendly challenger to the increasingly powerful Democrats.[4]

For Lutherans, the most consequential aspect of antebellum immigration was the arrival of about 1.25 million people from Germany. The most prominent newcomers were the forty-eighters, ideological refugees of the 1848 and 1849 revolutions in Europe. These intellectuals overtook the Dreissiger as the leaders of the German American press, overwhelmingly supported the Republican Party, and established the image of the "freedom-loving" German immigrant. The vast majority of new arrivals, however, were ordinary people who came to the United States for economic opportunity and held a variety of political positions. Most arrived as adherents to one of the three main branches of German Protestantism: Lutheran, Reformed, or Evangelical (United Protestant).[5] Because the state churches in Germany offered little institutional support to those who moved to the United States, the religious life of these antebellum immigrants was shaped by the circumstances of their new homeland.

Some newly arriving German American Protestants founded their own church bodies. The Church Society of the West, later renamed the Evangelical Synod of the West, sought to replicate the model of the United Protestant churches in Germany. Ironically, despite its ecumenical principles, this church body forged few relationships with other American denominations, including Lutherans.[6] Because of this, the Evangelical Synod of the West and its successor, the German Evangelical Synod of North America, stands outside the story of nineteenth-century American Lutheranism.

Other immigrant-led synods, while open to interchurch cooperation, were established as explicitly Lutheran. These included the Wisconsin Synod, founded in 1850, and the Texas Synod, founded in 1851. In the schema of Philip Schaff, these new church bodies are best categorized as Moderate Lutheran. William Julius Mann (1819–1892), a friend of Schaff and a key leader in the Pennsylvania Synod, described the Wisconsin and Texas synods as belonging to the "centre" of the American Lutheran church. According to Mann, these church bodies were "not strictly Symbolical" and rejected the "exclusivism" of the Old Lutherans, but they also were skeptical of the New Lutherans' departures from traditional Lutheran doctrine and practice. The Texas Synod followed the example of the Pennsylvania Synod and joined the General Synod, while the Wisconsin Synod followed the example of the Ohio Synod and did not.[7]

For the most part, if antebellum European Lutheran immigrants joined a church, they attached themselves to already extant denominations. Throughout the late 1840s and 1850s, American Lutheran writers published numerous petitions urging ministers to establish congregations for these new immigrants. Like Harkey, they saw their church as the natural home for incoming Germans and Scandinavians. However, many New, Moderate, and Old Lutherans also saw this influx of nominal Protestants as a potential menace that needed to be domesticated. Like the rest of the American nation, those Lutherans already present in the United States approached immigrants with a mixture of hospitality and trepidation.

The New Lutherans were the most ambivalent about the new arrivals. Harkey, in his exposition of the Lutheran church's mission, saw Protestant immigrants from Germany and Scandinavia as "the most hopeful class of foreigners." Yet he also warned that they "must be *Americanized,* must be educated in the principles of our government and laws, and be brought under the influence of the religion of the Bible, or they will most assuredly destroy us."[8] The *Lutheran Observer,* in equal parts, pleaded for missionaries to the new immigrants and warned of their lawlessness, infidelity, and religious indifference.[9] Some General Synod pastors who served the German immigrant population commented on their lack of response to revivals and their lax morals in terms of alcohol.[10] Yet others, such as Samuel Schmucker, praised those "enlightened" immigrants who "have not only learned to love the freedom and wisdom of our well-balanced civil institutions; but have also attained a consciousness of the fact, that one grand part of the vocation of the American churches is, to throw off the shackles of traditionary, patristic, and symbolic servitude."[11] In the view of New Lutherans, German immigrants were to be Americanized, which meant embracing the nation's culture and institutions, and evangelized, which meant accepting the beliefs and practices of Anglo-evangelicalism.

Moderate Lutherans saw more promise in German Protestant immigrants, as long as they were of the right sort. For these Lutherans, many of whom were still clinging to their Pennsylvania German heritage, churchmen from Germany commanded a certain level of respectability. Professorial appointments at the Ohio Synod's seminary and pastoral positions at the Pennsylvania Synod's most prestigious churches were often held by German immigrants. Like the *Lutheran Observer*, the Moderate *Lutheran Standard* called for missions to the immigrant population. But instead of merely regarding them as a foreign people needing to be assimilated, they also expressed hope that these new arrivals would help in the "diffusion of the German spirit and culture" in America.[12] As long as German immigrants were ministered to by pastors "of the right kind"—meaning both pious and theologically sound—Moderate Lutherans believed that these new American Lutherans would contribute to the building up of both the church and the nation.[13] Judging by synodical statistics, Moderate Lutherans were the most successful in attracting these new immigrants.

The Old Lutherans of the Missouri Synod, despite being German immigrants themselves, forged few bonds with the new arrivals from Europe, whom they deemed insufficiently orthodox. One of their chief charges against other immigrant churches was that they were guilty of "unionism," a term used by C. F. W. Walther and his colleagues to describe interchurch relations not based on full doctrinal agreement. The *Lutheraner* leveled this accusation against not only the Evangelical Synod of the West but also Lutheran church bodies such as the Wisconsin Synod.[14] Old Lutherans' criticism extended even to the newly arrived immigrants who joined their own church body. Friedrich Wyneken, who became president of the Missouri Synod in 1850, hoped to oversee an increase in his church's membership, but he also worried that "the state of general ignorance and lack of discipline renders our path of building congregations a slow and difficult one."[15] Despite these worries, the church body grew at a fairly rapid pace, from less than five thousand members at its inception in 1847 to about twenty-five thousand in 1860.

In addition to their reluctance to connect with other immigrants, the Missouri Synod was also becoming alienated from Lutherans in Germany, including from their chief supporter, Wilhelm Löhe. According to Löhe, the Missouri Synod's congregational polity had been formed "not out of Christian concern, but an American desire and inclination for worldly freedom in churchly things."[16] In 1851, Walther and Wyneken traveled to Germany to heal the growing division. In Walther's telling, Löhe alleged that "our Synod had succumbed to the rampant deception of liberty," while the Missouri Synod ministers believed that Löhe had "embraced hierarchical principles and begun to Romanize his teachings."[17] The two parties reached a temporary accord, but the breach between them soon reopened when, in 1852, Walther published his first book, *Die Stimme unserer Kirche in der Frage von Kirche und Amt* (The Position of our Church on the Question of Church and Office). This work formalized his church body's congregationalism and received a stern rebuke from Löhe.[18] Two years later, the German pastor officially renounced the Missouri Synod and sent missionaries to found a new church body, the Iowa Synod. Led by the brothers Sigmund (1833–1900) and Gottried Fritschel (1836–1889), the new synod, because of the unique circumstances of its founding, remained more closely connected to Europe than any other Lutheran church body in the United States.[19] By the mid-1850s, the Old Lutherans of the Missouri Synod stood almost completely isolated from other Lutherans, both in America and in Europe.[20]

Compared to the large waves of German and Irish immigrants, Scandinavians were a drop in the ocean. Between 1845 and 1860, fewer than forty thousand Swedes, Norwegians, and Danes moved to the United States, about 3 percent of the total number of Germans.[21] (The large-scale arrival of immigrants from these nations, particularly from Sweden and Norway, would not come until after the Civil War.) Nevertheless, the ecclesiastical institutions formed and the theological decisions made by the first generation of Scandinavian American Lutherans would have a critical impact on future developments. Like their German counterparts, Scandinavian immigrants were mostly devoid of institutional support from their state churches. Consequently, like other Lutherans in the United States, they were shaped by the assumptions and circumstances of their new homeland. Largely due to key intellectual leaders, Swedish and Norwegian Lutherans quickly sorted themselves into the American categories of New, Moderate, and Old Lutheran.

The early history of Swedish Lutheranism provides a stark example of how the American experience often made Lutheran immigrants more self-consciously conservative. Influenced by the pietist awakenings in Scandinavia, most early immigrants from Sweden resembled New Lutheranism specifically, and American evangelicalism more generally, in their commitments to revivalist preaching, temperance, and freedom of conscience. This shared outlook produced partnerships. Two early missionaries, Tufve Nilsson Hasselquist (1816–1891) and Lars Paul Esbjorn (1808–1870), initially received funding from the evangelical

American Home Missionary Society and later partnered with English-speaking New Lutherans to form the Northern Illinois Synod, a church body affiliated with the General Synod.[22] However, over the course of the 1850s, many Swedish Lutherans came to adopt a more confessional theological position. In a letter to his protégé Eric Norelius (1833–1916), Esbjorn wrote that he had found it "necessary to once more read through the symbolical books, due to the many meetings and conflicts here [in America]." Once eager to partner with the General Synod, Esbjorn now lamented "the loose, unsymbolic spirit" of the "New-Lutherans."[23] Rather than the Gettysburg seminary, he encouraged Norelius to enroll in the Ohio Synod's seminary in Columbus, and instead of the *Lutheran Observer,* he recommended the *Lutheran Standard* and *Evangelical Review.*[24] Other Swedish Lutherans followed a similar trajectory. By the end of the 1850s, the Swedes of the Northern Illinois Synod represented a small portion of the growing number of Moderate Lutherans within the General Synod who sought to reform the federation from within.[25]

Most Norwegian Lutheran immigrants, guided by leaders such as Herman Amberg Preus (1825–1894) and Ulrik Vilhelm Koren (1826–1910), adopted an even more conservative posture than their Swedish coreligionists.[26] Though a minority tried to transplant the Haugean revivalism that had swept through Norway in the early nineteenth century, and a few others joined with their fellow Scandinavians in the Northern Illinois Synod, the majority came together to form the Norwegian Synod in 1853. Nearly all of its founding ministers had been trained at the University of Christiania (Oslo), and many were influenced by one of its professors, Gisle Johnson (1822–1894), whose combination of confessionalism and pietism resembled many of the *Erweckung* theologians in Germany.[27] Despite this theological connection, Norwegian Lutheran immigrants were still largely on their own institutionally. Because of this, they aimed to partner with other conservative American Lutherans, especially in the realm of pastoral education. In 1857, the synod commissioned two ministers to scout the seminaries of the Missouri, Ohio, and Buffalo synods. The pair recommended the Missouri Synod's school in St. Louis on account of its doctrinal rigor and heartfelt piety.[28] The following year, the two church bodies formalized the relationship by establishing a Norwegian professorship at the seminary. The Norwegian Synod became the exception to the Missouri Synod's ecclesiastical isolation.

Despite the immense numbers of Northern European immigrants and the expressed desire of Lutherans in the United States to bring them into their churches, the large-scale immigration of the late 1840s and the 1850s did not transform American Lutheranism as much as many had anticipated. The membership in Lutheran churches nearly doubled, from less than 150,000 in 1850 to more than 250,000 in 1860. Yet this growth, when compared to the approximately 1.3 million German and Scandinavian immigrants who arrived between 1846 and 1860, was quite small. (The much larger increase would come in the final three decades of the nineteenth century.) The majority of Lutherans remained native-born and the principal language of Lutheran publications continued to be English. Rather than demographic or linguistic changes, the more significant effects on American Lutheranism during the 1850s were theological and political.

CONFESSIONAL ADHERENCE AND CHURCH UNITY

Two interrelated questions animated American theological debates during the 1850s. First, to what extent were ministers and church bodies bound to the historic confessions, or symbols, of the Lutheran church contained in the *Book of Concord,* particularly the Augsburg Confession of 1530? Second, on what basis should Lutheran synods unite with one another? Both questions were intrinsically important to American Lutherans, but they also had broader ramifications. How one regarded the authority of the Lutheran confessions and approached the issue of ecclesiastical unity crystalized how one viewed the church's mission in the United States.

By the early 1850s the positions of the New, Old, and Moderate Lutherans were mostly defined. The New Lutheran view had remained consistent since the 1820s, when Samuel Schmucker helped to devise the founding documents of the General Synod. Though the federation's constitution required no confessional pledge for its member synods, the *Formula for the Government and Discipline of the Evangelical Lutheran Church* asked all ministers to affirm that "the fundamental doctrines of the word of God are taught in a manner substantially correct in the doctrinal articles of the Augsburg Confession." Schmucker expounded on the meaning of this formula in his 1851 book, *The American Lutheran Church:* Though General Synod minsters must profess their "fundamental agreement" with their church's oldest confession, they were allowed "liberty of difference on minor points." According to Schmucker, this "doctrinal basis" balanced "unalienable rights" with "unalienable duties." The New Lutheran leader was prepared to extend the hand of fellowship to strict confessionalists, as long as they were "willing to regard their peculiarities as non-essential." But if they insisted on complete adherence to books "which contain numerous errors and Romish superstitions," he warned, "we desire no ecclesiastical communion with them." Schmucker believed that his principles represented a truly "American Lutheranism," which stemmed from "the unrestricted liberty of following the scriptures" and "the influence of our free civil institutions."[29]

Old Lutherans greatly differed in their understanding of these issues. The Missouri Synod's constitution, ratified in 1847 and reaffirmed in 1854, stipulated the "conditions under which a congregation may join Synod and remain a member." This included an affirmation that the entire *Book of Concord* was "the pure, unadulterated explanation and presentation of the Word of God." It also meant not "taking part in the service and Sacraments of heretical or mixed congregations" or participating in "any heretical tract distribution and mission projects."[30] However, as C. F. W. Walther had argued in his first presidential address, these stipulations were not antithetical to American liberty. Though individual congregations were required to assent to the Missouri Synod's membership requirements, they were otherwise "free to govern themselves." Such a view, Walther believed, struck the proper balance: "In a republic, as the United States of America is, . . . a restriction of freedom and independence beyond that drawn by God himself, no matter how well-intentioned, would provoke resistance" and "we would lose sight of our beautiful aim of building the true Church."[31] For Old Lutherans, the nation's liberty allowed for the establishment of a pure Lutheranism unified around a strict interpretation of its historic confessions.

Moderate Lutherans mostly agreed among themselves on the nature of confessional authority, but they differed on its implications for church unity. Many members of the Pennsylvania and Ohio synods shared a belief in the complete truthfulness of the Augsburg Confession, though their constitutions did not impose a stringent test like that of the Missouri Synod.[32] Despite this shared doctrinal outlook, the Pennsylvania Synod joined the General Synod in 1853, whereas the Ohio Synod refused (see chapter 1). The leaders of the Pennsylvania Synod regarded the General Synod "merely as an association of Lutheran Synods entertaining the same views in regard to the principal doctrines of our church." By becoming a member, it would still retain its "rights to manage its own internal affairs," including "in regard to church doctrine."[33] Those in the Ohio Synod believed that the General Synod's "confessional basis" was too ambiguous. Though they did not rule out a future union, the editors of the *Lutheran Standard* first wanted the General Synod to consider itself "an association of Lutheran Synods entertaining similar views in regard to the doctrines set forth in [the Augsburg] Confession."[34] Both groups of Moderate Lutherans cherished their liberty to set their own doctrinal standards, but they disagreed about whether those rights could be maintained within the General Synod.

The issues of confessional allegiance and church unity had been simmering for many years and briefly reached a boiling point in September 1855 when the pastors of the General Synod were mailed an anonymous tract titled *Definite Platform, Doctrinal and Disciplinarian, for Evangelical Lutheran District Synods.* The publication's anonymity and means of delivery almost guaranteed that it would provoke contention—recipients were even asked to send a contribution of twenty-five cents if they wished to keep the unsolicited mailing. But it was the content of the forty-two-page booklet that occasioned the most consternation. The *Definite Platform* purported to give "a more specific expression of the General Synod's doctrinal basis." Its most audacious proposal was for each of the federation's member synods to adopt the American Recension of the Augsburg Confession, which removed certain passages that "have long since been regarded by the great mass of our churches as unscriptural, and as remnants of Romish error."[35] The controversial tract occasioned one of the most misunderstood episodes in American Lutheran history.

Contrary to the impression given by many scholars, the *Definite Platform* did not advance any novel theological arguments.[36] The "Romish errors" that the American Recension sought to purge from the Augsburg Confession, such as "baptismal regeneration" and "the real presence of the body and blood of Christ in the Eucharist," had been rejected by New Lutherans for decades.[37] Because of this, most readers correctly assumed that Schmucker was one of the anonymous document's writers. The other coauthors were Benjamin Kurtz, the editor of the *Lutheran Observer,* and Samuel Sprecher (1810–1906), a professor in Ohio. Rather than its theology, what made the *Definite Platform* so contentious was its threat to disrupt the growing unity of American Lutheranism.[38]

The reaction against the *Definite Platform* was swift and decisively negative. The tract's most controversial passage was the resolution to "not receive into our

[General] Synod any minister who will not adopt this Platform."[39] For most Lutherans, both Moderate and New, such a proposal contradicted the General Synod's long-standing position of liberty of conscience. In the most sustained critique of the *Definite Platform*, W. J. Mann of the Pennsylvania Synod defended the doctrines of the Augsburg Confession attacked by Schmucker, Kurtz, and Sprecher. But he criticized them first and foremost for "produc[ing] contention and strife in our Lutheran Church" by attempting to "*unlutheranize* every one who could not or would not coincide with their views."[40] Lutherans more sympathetic to the doctrinal views of the tract's authors also took issue with their proposal. The West Pennsylvania Synod, Schmucker's ecclesiastical home, declined to accept the American Recension because such "tests of fellowship" were "inimical to the peace and harmony of the church." Kurtz's Maryland Synod took a similar stance. In the end, only three synods adopted the *Definite Platform*.[41] Even so, its widespread rejection by General Synod Lutherans did not represent an avowal of the truthfulness of the Augsburg Confession. Instead, both Moderate and New Lutherans were affirming the right of private judgment and the importance of preserving church unity.

Though it provoked intense debate, the tumult over the *Definite Platform* actually changed very little in the General Synod during the late 1850s. Less than six months after the tract's publication, thirty-nine leaders on different sides of the controversy, including Schmucker and Kurtz, signed the Pacific Overture. The statement asserted that "the points of difference entertained among us, are nonessential" and urged that "the harmony and peace of our church" be preserved.[42] Though Schmucker would later retract his endorsement of this statement and continue to defend the *Definite Platform,* he remained committed to preserving the principle of "individual judgment" that "pervades the Constitution of the General Synod."[43] Kurtz, too, would withdraw his signature from the Pacific Overture, and shortly afterward he would spearhead the formation of the Melanchthon Synod, a new church body in Maryland dedicated to propagating the theology of the *Definite Platform.* However, this new synod quickly joined the General Synod, and its leaders, including Kurtz, pledged themselves to the federation's constitution.[44] The only Lutherans to withdraw from the General Synod in the aftermath of the controversy were the Swedes and Norwegians of the Northern Illinois Synod, who formed the independent Scandinavian Augustana Synod in 1860. However, this division had as much to do with issues of ethnic identity as with doctrinal disagreements.[45] In short, despite plenty of sound and fury, the General Synod experienced no major institutional ruptures and made no changes to its constitution or doctrinal basis.

In view of this, the publication of the *Definite Platform* was not the "last stand" of New Lutheranism, as several historians have claimed.[46] New Lutherans retained control of the church's educational institutions, including the flagship seminary at Gettysburg, and its most widely circulated periodical, the *Lutheran Observer.* Moreover, the larger theological project of Schmucker and Kurtz continued to persist, almost as strongly as before. Aided by the Great Revival of 1857–1858, New Lutherans continued with renewed vigor to promote revivalism, social reform, anti-Catholicism, and cooperation with Anglo-evangelicals.[47] The promoters of the *Definite Platform* may have overplayed their hand, but they continued to believe, with quite a bit of justification, that their version of Lutheranism was the American church's future.[48]

Nevertheless, the controversy surrounding the *Definite Platform* had important long-term ramifications: Along with sowing seeds of distrust among different parties within the General Synod, it also affected Lutherans outside of it. For the Moderate Lutherans of the Ohio Synod, the publication confirmed that their decision not to join the federation had been the correct one. The editors of the *Lutheran Standard* called attention to the fact that two synods could remain in the General Synod despite holding completely different views on the Augsburg Confession. This, they believed, was why the federation was doomed to failure. They also vehemently denied that the American Recension was truly American, labeling its proponents "self-styled American Lutherans."[49] At the Ohio Synod's meeting in 1856, the delegates resolved to acknowledge only those church bodies that "avow the unaltered Augsburg Confession in the spirit and sense of the collected symbolical creeds of the Evangelical Lutheran Church."[50] Essentially, they were arguing that many New Lutheran synods stood outside the bounds of Lutheranism. The conflict over the *Definite Platform* was pushing the Ohio Synod closer to the position of Old Lutheranism.

For C. F. W. Walther and the Missouri Synod, the controversy signaled that the situation in the American Lutheran church was perhaps not as dire as they had thought. In January 1855, Walther founded *Lehre und Wehre* (Doctrine and Defense), a monthly theological journal. The title alone indicated that this periodical did not share the same ecumenical purpose as the *Evangelical Review.* In the *Lutheraner,* Walther explained that the journal would not be a "playground" for those who attack the "true-believing church." Instead, "the Holy Scriptures and the Book of Concord will be the norm of all its recorded essays."[51] Yet in the wake of the conflict surrounding the *Definite Platform,* Walther penned an editorial in *Lehre und Wehre* expressing his surprise at the nearly unanimous rejection of the proposed American Recension: "The number of those who have not bowed, or will no longer bow, their knees to the Baal of the so-called progress and so-called higher enlightenment of the nineteenth century is undoubtedly greater than our weak faith and faintheartedness had imagined." He proposed a "free conference" dedicated to "ultimately achieving one Evangelical Lutheran Church of North America" and invited all Lutherans who "acknowledge and confess without reservation the Unaltered Augsburg Confession of 1530" to participate.[52]

Walther's proposal, however, failed to produce the results he intended. Though a few clergymen from Pennsylvania and New York answered his call, no church body from the General Synod sent a delegation to the conference. Instead, the meeting that took place in October 1856 in Columbus, Ohio, was principally a discussion between the Missouri and Ohio synods.[53] Despite the poor turnout, Walther emerged confident that the conference had "clear[ed] the way for the eventual formation of an Evangelical Lutheran Church of North America united in faith, doctrine, and confession."[54] The editors of the *Lutheran Standard* likewise declared this meeting of "true Lutherans" to be "a rich blessing."[55]

These hopeful signs led to further meetings—in 1857 in Pittsburgh, in 1858 in Cleveland, and in 1859 in Fort Wayne, Indiana. But in the course of the proceedings, leaders of the Ohio Synod found the Missouri Synod's views to be too "extreme."[56] The dialogue between the two church bodies came to an end following a dispute over a Missouri Synod pastor who transferred his membership to the Ohio Synod. The editors of the *Lutheran Standard* saw a "pharisaical" spirit in the "Missourians" and admonished them "to resign [their] assumed supervisory generalship of all other Lutheran Synods, and attend better to their own concerns."[57] The next free conference, scheduled for the summer of 1860, never occurred.

The failure to bring about more confessional unity among American Lutherans provoked a period of soul-searching for Walther. At the urging of his colleagues and with the blessing of his parishioners, he left St. Louis in February 1860 for a six-month trip to Europe. Before his departure, he penned a letter to his congregation, asking them to pray that God "grant that I again become strong to undertake His ministry for our poor American Zion, which is bleeding from a thousand wounds."[58]

The trip reinvigorated Walther. Before traveling back to the United States, he penned an open letter to the interim editor of *Lehre und Wehre*, giving a passionate reaffirmation of his church body's position: "Our dear Evangelical Lutheran Church, as she has set forth her doctrine in her confessions . . . is the continuation of the old, apostolic church; in short, at the present time the only orthodox church." In Europe "this treasure seems to have been lost entirely," he wrote, but it could be found in "our synod in America." Having been "renewed in strength," he resolved to resume the fight for "true unity in doctrine and faith."[59] When Walther returned in August 1860, his Missouri Synod accounted for about 10 percent of the Lutheran population in the United States and stood almost completely isolated from other churches in both America and Europe. Remarkably, twelve years later his understanding of confessional allegiance and church unity would be the predominant view among Lutherans in the United States.

THE CONFESSIONAL MOVEMENT IN THE GENERAL SYNOD

The controversy over the *Definite Platform* led to one more significant development: it catalyzed a nascent confessional movement within the General Synod. This movement was led by four Lutheran clergymen who were a generation removed from that of Samuel Schmucker, Benjamin Kurtz, and John Bachman. Each grew up in the German American culture of Greater Pennsylvania, was educated at the theological seminary in Gettysburg, and began his career as a committed New Lutheran. By the end of the 1850s, this quadrumvirate of young intellectuals had come to question several tenets of their spiritual fathers'—and, in some cases, their actual fathers'—theology.

William A. Passavant (1821–1894) was born and raised in western Pennsylvania.[60] His parents were immigrants from Germany but raised their children as English-speaking Americans. At the age of fifteen, Passavant enrolled at the Presbyterian-run Jefferson College, where he participated in revivals and developed an interest in missions. As a young man, he also became acquainted with and developed a deep admiration for the *Lutheran Observer*, calling the paper "invaluable."[61] In 1840, he began his studies at Gettysburg under Schmucker. In a letter to his sister, he described the professor as "a profound thinker," though he was also put off by his demeanor "in the lecture room," where he has "a vinegar and repulsive aspect."[62] Two years into his studies, he was persuaded by Kurtz to cut his seminary education short in order to accept a position as assistant editor for the *Lutheran Observer.* After being licensed and ordained by the Maryland Synod and serving a congregation on the outskirts of Baltimore, Passavant accepted a call in 1844 to First English Lutheran Church in Pittsburgh. The city would serve as his home base for the rest of his life.

When, precisely, Passavant began to move away from New Lutheranism is difficult to determine. In 1845, he helped to found the Pittsburg Synod, a new church body that initially did not join the General Synod. Three years later, he founded the *Missionary,* a church paper dedicated to promoting inner, home, and foreign missions. Yet neither event represented a major shift in his outlook. For example, in the inaugural issue of the *Missionary,* which his mentor Kurtz commended, Passavant printed the minutes of a special meeting of the Pittsburg Synod, which stated that the Augsburg Confession "possesses in itself no confessional authority."[63] Over the course of the early 1850s, however, his position slowly changed. In January 1852, after the *Lutheran Observer* accused the *Missionary* of expressing insufficiently New Lutheran sentiments, Passavant responded that his paper "is the organ of no party, school, or section of the Church."[64]

But it was not until the controversy over the *Definite Platform* that the tone and contents of Passavant's paper began to shift decidedly. In 1856, he turned the *Missionary* from a monthly into a weekly publication and pledged to "not shrink from confessing, explaining, and defending the faith of our Church."[65] Kurtz lamented the change: "We would, indeed, have preferred that he should have ranged himself among the American Lutherans, and become a coadjutor of the Lutheran Observer."[66] Another contributor to the *Lutheran Observer* was even more surprised: "I knew [Passavant] once as an ultra new measure man, but . . . he is now at the opposite pole. . . . The reader will find in [his paper] . . . the most decided and ultra symbolists."[67]

One of the contributors to Passavant's revamped *Missionary* was Charles Porterfield Krauth (1823–1883).[68] His father, Charles Philip Krauth (1797–1867), spent the majority of his career as a professor, serving at both Pennsylvania College and the Gettysburg seminary and, from 1850 to 1861, coediting the *Evangelical Review.*[69] Though the elder Krauth had some confessional leanings, he was "adverse to controversy" and is best characterized as a Moderate Lutheran. The younger Krauth studied under his father at both institutions, but his early views were nearer to those of his father's colleague in Gettysburg, Schmucker. While serving a church in Baltimore from 1842 to 1847, he wrote to his father about holding "protracted meetings" and preaching at the Presbyterian and Methodist churches.[70] Krauth also became a close associate of Kurtz. In 1846, he served as the guest editor of the *Lutheran Observer* while the General Synod's delegation to the Evangelical Alliance traveled to London. In his early years, Krauth exhibited all the traits of a typical New Lutheran.

Like Passavant, Krauth slowly began to move away from this position. The key issue on which his theological development turned was the real presence of Christ in the Lord's Supper. During his first years as a pastor, Krauth read deeply and widely in the Lutheran tradition and slowly became convinced of the Augsburg Confession's teaching that "the Body and Blood of Christ are truly present, and are distributed to those who eat the Supper of the Lord." In June 1849, while serving congregations in northern Virginia, he wrote a pseudonymous article for the *Lutheran Observer* contending that this doctrine was just as "fundamental" to the Augsburg Confession as any other.[71] A few months later, in an article for the *Evangelical Review,* this time published under his own name, he criticized New Lutherans' anti-creedalism and disputed their characterization of strict confessional adherence as "Romanism."[72] One colleague later remarked that by the time Krauth published these articles, his "change of view and conviction were substantially complete."[73]

By the early 1850s, Krauth was becoming the widely acknowledged intellectual leader of a growing confessional movement within the General Synod.[74] The young pastor published numerous articles in the *Evangelical Review,* as well as sermons and essays as stand-alone publications. In 1855, he accepted a call to a congregation in Pittsburgh, where he became a frequent contributor to Passavant's *Missionary.* Five years later he became the pastor of a church in Philadelphia, the city he would call home for the remainder of his days. Shortly after his arrival, Krauth helped to establish a semimonthly paper, the *Lutheran and Home Journal.*

Krauth's coeditor of the new periodical, and perhaps his closest friend, was Joseph A. Seiss (1823–1904).[75] Seiss grew up in northern Maryland and was confirmed in the Moravian church. He made his way to Lutheranism through the influence of Ezra Keller (1812–1848), a prominent New Lutheran who pastored congregations near Seiss's hometown and would later found Wittenberg College in Ohio.[76] At Keller's urging, Seiss enrolled at Pennsylvania College in 1839. After a year of study, in which he also attended Schmucker's lectures at the Gettysburg seminary, he abruptly dropped out of school and returned to Maryland. After two years of teaching at a local school, he was licensed by the Virginia Synod to preach and was ordained by the same body two years later. After serving churches in Virginia and Maryland for fifteen years, Seiss moved to Philadelphia in 1858, where he lived for the rest of his life.

Seiss's theological development followed a trajectory similar to that of Passavant and Krauth. After being a proponent of "new measures" in his first years as a pastor, he published a critique of the practice in 1845. As with Krauth's first printed criticism on the subject, Seiss wrote pseudonymously. In his four-part article, he critiqued Simeon Harkey's popular book *The Church's Best State: Constant Revivals of Religion*. Mirroring many of the arguments of John Williamson Nevin's *Anxious Bench,* Seiss argued that an overemphasis on revivals resulted in a neglect of catechesis.[77] Seiss also began to emphasize the importance of creeds and confessions. In 1852, he published an article in the *Evangelical Review* that defended the practice of confessional subscription.[78] Like Krauth, Seiss was prolific, publishing numerous articles as well as stand-alone sermons and essays, many of which sought to push Lutheranism in a more confessional direction.

Perhaps the most symbolically significant figure of this confessional movement was Beale M. Schmucker (1827–1888), the son of New Lutheranism's founding father.[79] Schmucker grew up in Gettysburg with Charles Porterfield Krauth, and the two remained lifelong friends and correspondents. Both shared a deep interest in exploring the "glorious old Lutheran books." In 1849, Schmucker wrote to Krauth that he wished the seminary "would appoint me librarian." Rather than the "new books printed by steam," Schmucker preferred the "books of the olden time . . . whose mighty ponderous piles of thought bind earth and heaven together."[80] Instead of becoming a librarian, he entered the pastoral ministry, serving churches in northern Virginia and Pennsylvania.

Unlike his fellow confessionalists, Schmucker published very little, making the precise course of his theological journey difficult to determine. The best evidence comes from his father's letters to him. Already in 1849, the elder Schmucker was expressing concern about his son's penchant for reading the "older divines" of Lutheranism. Their "spirit," he counseled, "is rather too polemic and intolerant." He also warned his son about "falling into the tide of Puseyism and Romanism." When his father was debating with William Reynolds about the Augsburg Confession, the younger Schmucker evidently took the side of Reynolds, which prompted the elder Schmucker to write a lengthy rebuttal to his son's views.[81] Despite being on different sides of the theological issues facing the Lutheran church, the father and son never became estranged, and they corresponded throughout their lives. Still, the fact that the son of Samuel Schmucker had moved away from New Lutheranism lent additional clout to the emerging confessionalism within the General Synod.

The movement led by Krauth, Passavant, Seiss, and Beale Schmucker, despite some resemblances to various European confessional movements, was the product of particularly American circumstances.[82] None of its intellectual leaders studied in Europe, and only Passavant visited there before 1860. Conversely, prominent New Lutherans such as John Bachman studied in Germany, and others, including Kurtz, traveled multiple times to Europe. To be sure, confessionalists sometimes positively referenced German writers or church news. Krauth and Seiss translated and reviewed German theological writings that they deemed valuable, while Passavant expressed confidence that a genuine revival of "evangelical religion" was taking place in Germany.[83] Yet the same selective appropriation of German theology and cautious hope for the German church could be found in the writings of New Lutherans. Samuel Schmucker referenced numerous theologians from Germany to bolster his doctrinal claims, and the *Lutheran Observer*, despite its frequent condemnations of German infidelity and high-churchism, still defended the genuine piety of many Lutherans there.[84] For English-speaking Lutherans of all persuasions, German theology and church affairs functioned as a convenient quiver of arrows to sling occasionally at opponents, but they were hardly formative in their theological thought.

Indeed, confessionalists went to great lengths to demonstrate that their understanding of Lutheranism was just as "American" as that of Schmucker and Kurtz. When Krauth first went public with his criticism of New Lutheranism, he argued that adherence to the Augsburg Confession was the truly "American Lutheran" position and that confessional allegiance and American identity "excite no conflict but blend harmoniously together."[85] More than a decade later, he echoed the same themes. "Lutheranism in this country," he wrote, "must be

American, bringing hither its priceless experiences in the old world, to apply them to the living present."[86] In Krauth's view, New Lutherans misunderstood how Christian liberty should operate in the American context. Rather than individuals, congregations, or synods being able to do as they pleased, he believed that liberty needed to be "regulated" by a higher authority. In this, he saw parallels between the Lutheran church and the American Union: "We are free citizens of free States, which are bound together as a free country. The individual has liberty, the State has liberty, and our whole land has liberty; but, this liberty is regulated by one general principle—and that is the whole is greater than a part."[87] For Krauth, the unity of the Lutheran church in the United States depended upon a distinctively American conception of ordered liberty.

Despite some affinities with other critics of New Lutheranism, the movement led by Krauth was distinct from other Lutheran factions in the antebellum United States. Throughout the 1850s, the confessionalists in the General Synod insisted that their ideas starkly contrasted with those of "bigoted Old Lutheran[s]."[88] In the *Missionary*, Passavant commended the Missouri Synod for its growth but denounced its "exclusiveness, which prevents them from associating or co-operating with the other Synods of our Church in this country."[89] As late as 1861, Krauth condemned Old Lutheranism in unequivocal terms: "If there be a Lutheranism which is exclusive, harsh, and repellent . . . [and] would die rather than submit to any adaptation, that is not our Lutheranism."[90] The confessional movement within the General Synod also differed from Moderate Lutheranism.[91] Its leaders had no patience for the "fanaticism" of those who clung to the German language or were content to exist in the German subculture of Greater Pennsylvania. Instead, like the New Lutherans, they were seeking to improve the quality and quantity of English-language Lutheran literature and to raise their church's level of intellectual respectability and cultural influence.[92] Rather than a subset of Moderate Lutheranism, Krauth, Passavant, Seiss, and others were forming their own distinctive movement.

A final distinction between the confessionalists, on the one hand, and the Old Lutherans and some Moderate Lutherans, on the other, was the former's ardent support of the General Synod and its principles of church unity. In 1856, Passavant wrote in the *Missionary* that while "diversity confessedly exists," he believed that "there exists a unity in diversity that justifies the fraternal declaration, 'We be brethren.'"[93] Krauth, in 1857, called the General Synod "the hope of our church in this country" and insisted that any discussion of "schism" was beyond the pale: "It would be to our church what a separation of the States would be to our Union."[94] In the inaugural issue of the *Lutheran and Home Journal,* he and Seiss pledged to represent "the interests of our church, within the bounds of the General Synod" and to avoid "every species of partisanship."[95] The reason for this position was that despite their shift in theological views, those in the confessional movement remained comfortable with much of New Lutheranism's outlook. As Krauth wrote in 1861, "We propose no sectarian hedge to our pulpits, no bar to our communion tables or abnegation of the sweet bonds of Christian fellowship."[96] Along with advocating interchurch cooperation, Krauth, Seiss, and Passavant also promoted temperance and even cautiously endorsed revivals.[97] Despite the controversy over the *Definite Platform,* the leaders of the confessional movement still shared with their New Lutheran counterparts the conviction that the General Synod should serve as an instrument for creating a unified national church, truly Lutheran and truly American.

SLAVERY AND POLITICS

American Lutherans in the 1850s were conflicted about more than theology. The increasingly irrepressible political and sectional divisions over slavery and its expansion were part and parcel of Lutherans' discourse as well. Though the various parties within the church approached the slavery question in different ways, Lutherans, like most American Protestants, continued to be shaped principally by their cultural contexts rather than by their theological differences. Yet as with their debates about confessional adherence and church unity, the disputes over the peculiar institution did not pose an existential crisis to Lutheran unity.

The leading paper of New Lutheranism, the *Lutheran Observer,* based in Baltimore, reflected the state of Maryland's conflicted views on slavery.[98] Benjamin Kurtz, though committed to an editorial stance of "neutrality" on the issue of abolition, at times broke with this policy. Sometimes he found himself defending slaveholders. He maintained that accounts of "the cruelties said to be practiced on the slaves in the South" contain "a vast amount of falsehood and slander" and countered, "How seldom do we hear of the religious and other advantages enjoyed by the slaves."[99] Yet he also criticized some biblical defenses of slavery. He wrote that the institution's morality cannot be determined simply by looking at the actions of biblical figures. This "false logic," he contended, leads to "dangerous results," such as the Mormons' practice of polygamy.[100] Throughout the 1850s, he continued to promote Liberian colonization as a solution to the problem of American slavery.[101] Yet for the most part Kurtz made good on his promise "not to allow the Observer to be used either in opposition or in vindication of slavery." For him, "to take part in this 'vexed question'" would distract from the paper's "high and holy mission."[102] This policy of "neutrality" remained even after Kurtz retired from the editorship of the *Lutheran Observer* in February 1859.

Even New Lutherans who held antislavery opinions conspicuously avoided the subject in the 1850s. The only substantive publication about slavery by a New Lutheran in the General Synod during this decade was an article on the history of the African slave trade, published in the *Evangelical Review* in 1857. Though the author, Morris Officer (1823–1874), condemned the "giant evil" of the transatlantic slave trade, he said nothing about the immorality of slavery as then currently practiced in the United States.[103] Synodical proceedings also reveal a dearth of discussion about the issue. Only one member synod of the General Synod, the Wittenberg Synod, published a condemnation of slavery.[104] Even Schmucker, perhaps the most prominent New Lutheran supporter of emancipation during the 1830s and 1840s, wrote nothing new on the subject in the decade before the war. His only public mention of slavery came in the ninth and final edition of his *Elements of Popular Theology,* published in 1860, which advocated the same moderate antislavery position as his book's previous version.[105]

The major exception to this silence was the continued advocacy of the Franckean Synod. Since its founding in 1837, the leaders of this small church body had, unlike most of their fellow New Lutherans, made opposition to slavery central to their identity. Throughout the 1850s, the Franckeans took every opportunity afforded by the nation's political events—the Compromise of 1850, the Kansas-Nebraska Act, and *Dred Scott v. Sandford*—to condemn slavery and demand immediate emancipation.[106] Yet theirs was a lonely voice. When in 1857 the members of the General Synod decided to allow the synod to reapply for membership, the Franckeans refused, citing the federation's toleration of slavery.[107] Apart from the principled abolitionism of this tiny church body, the most noticeable aspect of northern New Lutherans' commentary on slavery during the decade preceding the Civil War was their silence.

Both Moderate Lutherans and the confessional movement resembled the New Lutherans in their ambivalence. Like other Lutheran church bodies, the Pennsylvania and Ohio synods passed no resolution on slavery at their meetings.[108] The *Lutheran Standard* remained largely muted on the subject in the 1850s, save for a few articles that were mildly critical of the institution's practice in the United States.[109] Similarly, confessionalists such as Charles Porterfield Krauth and Joseph Seiss published no major discussion of the subject.[110] Slavery was not a source of division between New Lutherans and their Moderate and confessional opponents, as some historians have claimed. Rather, these factions shared a general reluctance to address the issue.[111]

One of the few exceptions to this trend was the confessionalist leader, William Passavant, whose moderate antislavery views resembled those of Schmucker. One of the reasons that Passavant's church body, the Pittsburg Synod, initially refused to join the General Synod, according to the minutes of its 1852 meeting, was that by doing so it would "become implicated in the sin of slavery."[112] But like Schmucker, Passavant and other members of his synod suppressed their personal convictions, and they joined the General Synod the next year. In the early years of the *Missionary,* Passavant's habit of avoiding the topic of slavery mirrored the official policy of the *Lutheran Observer.* In October 1857, however, he changed this practice and printed a set of antislavery resolutions adopted by the Middle Conference of the Pittsburg Synod. The conference declared "slavery, as it exists in this country" to be "sinful" and asserted that "Christians are solemnly bound to make their influence tell against this evil," not only in the "ballot-box" but even in the "pulpit."[113] In a follow-up article, Passavant defended his decision to print the resolutions. Though he admitted that "the question of slavery ... is one of the most difficult of all problems to solve," he argued that "if the Church will not speak, Slavery will."[114] Over the next three years, he made frequent comments on the subject in his paper.[115]

Passavant's decision to open up the *Missionary* as a forum to discuss slavery prompted a rejoinder from John Bachman. In addition to being the leader of New Lutheranism in the South, the Charleston minister had also become a prominent figure in South Carolina's scientific community.[116] His response, which was published in Passavant's paper, reflected the proslavery paternalism of other southern intellectuals.[117] Bachman claimed that slavery had raised up Africans "from a state of the lowest barbarism," contended that the spiritual care of the enslaved was superior to that of the "laboring classes in the Northern States," and argued that their "mild servitude" was necessitated by the inferiority "marked on them by their Creator." He also expressed surprise that those "who read the same Bible" could think that slavery was sinful, when Scripture clearly sanctioned and even "enjoined" the practice. While Bachman's defense of slavery was unremarkable, his commentary on the pertinence of the slavery question to the Lutheran church was distinctive. Just as Martin Luther was "ardently devoted to preserving harmony among his followers," Bachman believed that it was the "high and holy mission" of the reformer's American descendants to remain united. By doing so, he opined, they would play a key role in "preserving that blessed Union of States which should be dear to every American heart."[118]

Passavant responded with his own interpretation of the subject. He began by defending his publication of Bachman's letter: "Thinking men in the North are anxious to know the views of good men in the South on this great subject." He then expressed his regret that Bachman had avowed "the inherent rightfulness of American slavery" and had defended "it from the Scriptures of God." American slavery, he asserted, differed from the "mild and humane servitude" of the Old Testament. He further argued that the "apostolic directions" found in the New Testament were "no more an approval either of the principle and practice of Roman slavery" than the call to obey the imperial government was "an approval of the tyranny of the Neroes." Above all, he contended, a loving God could not endorse such as system. Passavant even made a tepid defense of racial equality by denying the inherent inferiority of African Americans. While he believed that there were "a few worthless negroes" in the North, he considered the free Blacks of Pittsburgh to be "incomparably above the thousands of low Irish."[119] Like Bachman's proslavery apology, Passavant's views on slavery and race were hardly extraordinary, reflecting those of other northern moderates.

What was unusual was that the two ministers were discussing the subject at all. Historian Mark Noll has written that the 1844 exchange between the Baptist theologians Richard Fuller and Francis Wayland was "one of the United States' last serious one-on-one debates where advocates for and against slavery engaged each other directly, with reasonable restraint, and with evident intent to hear out the opponent to the extent possible."[120] Yet thirteen years after these Baptists' debates, two Lutherans were engaging in a similarly measured exchange of arguments. Though Bachman made a few veiled threats of the southern synods withdrawing in reaction to antislavery agitation, the articles in the *Missionary* actually demonstrated the surprising strength of the General Synod's unity. Whereas Fuller and Wayland's denomination split the year after their debate, as the Presbyterians and Methodists had done before them, Bachman and Passavant's church remained united. In part, this was due to the lack of a sizable Lutheran presence in the South. (As of 1860, only one-sixth lived in slave states.) But it was also due to the firmly held belief among native-born Lutherans in both sections that the key to their denomination's growth in membership and prestige was the preservation of a united church. If a schism over slavery was to happen in the General Synod, it would be precipitated by external events rather than internal disagreements.

Immigrants from Sweden and Norway were less circumspect about addressing slavery and other political questions. Over the course of the 1850s, Scandinavian Americans, almost all of whom settled in the Upper Midwest, adopted the practice of publishing two types of newspapers, religious and political. Both types of publications were usually edited by Lutheran clergymen. For example, in 1851, Claus Lauritz Clausen (1820–1892), a Dane by birth, helped to found the *Kirkelig Maanedstidende* (Monthly Church News), a periodical affiliated with the Norwegian Synod. A year later he founded the *Emigranten* (Immigrant), a Norwegian paper in Wisconsin exclusively devoted to political issues. In 1855, T. N. Hasselquist founded the first Swedish American newspaper, the Illinois-based *Hemlandet* (Homeland). A year later, he began the *Rätta Hemlandet* (True Homeland) as the explicitly religious counterpart to his other publication.[121]

Over the course of the 1850s, Scandinavian Americans moved from a general loyalty to the pro-immigrant Democrats to a nearly unanimous support of the newly formed Republican Party.[122] A key reason was their opposition to slavery. The *Emigranten*, now under the editorship of the layman Carl Solberg (1833–1924), opposed the Kansas-Nebraska Act and the *Dred Scott v. Sandford* decision and promoted Black suffrage in the North.[123] Swedish Lutherans were even more explicitly antislavery. In the inaugural issue of the *Hemlandet*, Hasselquist declared slavery to be "ungodly in its very foundation" and unable to "stand the test of Christianity."[124] Yet Scandinavian Lutheran opposition was more the product of their American circumstances than the result of "freedom-loving" principles brought with them from Norway and Sweden. The few Scandinavians who immigrated to the state of Texas came to defend slavery just as quickly as their northern counterparts embraced emancipation.[125]

The only Lutherans whose geographic location was not predictive of their views toward slavery were the Old Lutherans of the Missouri Synod. Most members of this national church body lived in the free states of Ohio, Michigan, Indiana, and Illinois, and those who resided in the slave state of Missouri were too poor to afford slaves. Despite those circumstances, most Old Lutherans would come to defend slavery as sanctioned by Scripture. Before the Civil War, however, few Missouri Synod theologians commented publicly on the subject. C. F. W. Walther, for example, wrote nothing on slavery during the 1850s.[126] The most comprehensive treatment came from August Biewend (1816–1858), Walther's colleague at the seminary in St. Louis. In a *Lehre und Wehre* article, which Walther published only reluctantly, Biewend contended that slavery was compatible with the Bible. His argument resembled the defense of slavery by other conservative Christians, such as Old School Presbyterians and Roman Catholics: the institution itself was neither inherently good nor sinful; instead, its morality hinged on how slaveholders treated the enslaved. Though he claimed to address slavery from a biblical standpoint rather than a political one, the Old Lutheran professor, like other American intellectuals, could not conceptualize slavery apart from its racialized practice in the United States.[127]

Biewend's attempt to limit his discussion of slavery to purely moral considerations reflected Old Lutherans' reluctance to mix religion and politics. However, the leaders of the Missouri Synod were hardly apolitical. Walther believed that although church and state should be "strictly divided," Christians also had a responsibility as citizens.[128] Throughout the 1850s, he and other members of the Missouri Synod were fierce critics of German American political leaders, particularly Heinrich Boernstein, the new forty-eighter editor of the *Anzeiger des Westen*. Though the Old Lutherans' relationship with this paper had been tenuous already, the appointment in 1850 of the openly anticlerical Boernstein convinced several Missouri Synod leaders of their need to counteract what Walther called "the German satanic press."[129] For a brief period, they believed the solution lay in allying with the *Saint Louiser Volksblatt* (Saint Louis People's Paper), a Democratic daily, which declared itself to be "neither irreligious nor unchristian."[130] The *Lutheraner* endorsed the paper, and Walther even recruited a Missouri Synod pastor be its editor.[131] Yet in 1857, the *Saint Louiser Volksblatt,* after falling on hard times, changed ownership and was now edited by Walther's nemesis, Boernstein. The *Lutheraner* promptly retracted its endorsement.[132]

A more successful Old Lutheran enterprise for addressing the secular realm was the *Illustrirte Abend-Schule* (Illustrated Evening School).[133] Founded in Buffalo in 1854 and relocated to St. Louis in 1856, the biweekly paper's mission was to educate the German American public on a wide variety of subjects, including history, law, geography, nature, culture, and politics. Though it was edited by various Missouri Synod clergymen, the *Illustrirte Abend-Schule* sought to appeal to a broadly Christian audience as an alternative to the publications of irreligious or antireligious forty-eighters. Given this mission, it both deemphasized confessional particulars and steered clear of party politics. For example, during the run-up to the election of 1856, the paper endorsed no candidate and urged its readers to vote their conscience, even though the *Saint Louiser Volksblatt* had backed the National Democrats.[134] The paper also largely avoided the issue of slavery, except for a few descriptive accounts of its abuses.[135] Rather, its highest goal was to make its readers better citizens of their new homeland. In the words of the paper's prospectus, which Walther heartily approved, "We do not want to be American Germans, but Americans, German Americans."[136]

Despite the *Illustrirte Abend-Schule*'s moderate stance, most members in the German American intellectual class regarded Old Lutherans as on par with Roman Catholics because of their justification of slavery and support for the Democratic Party. One forty-eighter in Michigan wrote home to Germany in 1856 that the Democrats' constituency consisted of "the bulk of the German riffraff, certainly all the Catholics, and everyone who is entangled in the Bible," including "the Old Lutherans (the mere word is a disgrace)."[137] In reality, Old Lutherans were not politically monolithic, save for their unwavering dedication to preserving the "great, precious blessing" of "religious freedom."[138] For example, Francis Hoffmann (1822–1903), one of the first clergymen to join the Missouri Synod, resigned his pastorate near Chicago in the early 1850s and became a lawyer. An opponent of the Kansas-Nebraska Act, Hoffmann became a prominent member of the newly formed Republican Party. In 1860, he was elected lieutenant governor of Illinois.[139] Though Old Lutherans were more likely to defend slavery and vote Democratic, they shared with other American Lutherans an aversion to sowing division in the church over issues considered to be political.

* * *

In 1859, Simeon Harkey once again took to the podium to discuss the American Lutheran church's mission, this time before a joint meeting of the General Synod. Though the occasion was different than that of his 1852 address, Harkey's optimistic vision remained the same. The New Lutheran minister noted the growth in numbers and "brotherly love" within the General Synod and expressed his belief that the different nationalities and parties within the Lutheran church would become even more unified. Though he acknowledged "great and exciting questions of doctrine, discipline, policy and morals," Harkey believed that this union would be preserved by a commitment to "liberty of conscience" and the "fundamentals" of the Augsburg Confession. He urged the General Synod to continue to "evangelize and Americanize the larger foreign Lutheran population of this country" and to build up its institutions, benevolent work, and missions. In the United States, where "she is free," Harkey concluded, the Lutheran church is "ready for her great mission."[140]

Other Lutherans shared his optimism—and for good reason. In a striking divergence from the Baptists, Methodists, and Presbyterians, who had divided over the issue of slavery, Lutheran unity was increasing. By 1860, almost two-thirds of Lutherans in the United States belonged to the General Synod, whereas ten years before the figure stood at less than 45 percent. In an 1858 article, the Moderate Lutheran editors of the *Evangelical Review* condemned those who, like the Old Lutherans of the Missouri Synod, "discard from fellowship all who do not receive every jot and tittle of the symbols" and praised the General Synod's policies of "substantial agreement in faith and practice" and "freedom of thinking and inquiry." If such a position is maintained, they argued, then "our union, like the great union of our country, notwithstanding diversity of views, [will] be preserved."[141] Leaders of the confessional movement in the General Synod expressed similar sentiments in an 1860 editorial in the *Lutheran and Home Journal:* "A calm review of the history of our church in this country up to this hour, impresses us with a deeper conviction that she is a daughter of God, and destined to do much for his glory in this modern world."[142] By the end of the 1850s, most Lutherans believed that a more unified church would aid in allowing their denomination to becoming members of the Anglo-Protestant establishment.

To be sure, lurking beneath this optimism were doubts about the future of intra-Lutheran unity and an inferiority complex when it came to Lutherans' relationship with mainstream American Protestants. In a lengthy series of articles in the *Lutheran Observer,* one pseudonymous writer boasted that "the Lutheran church is just as rich in mental, moral, and pecuniary resources as any other church in America" but worried that other Protestants were not taking notice because American Lutherans lacked "uniformity in *belief,* in *experience,* and in *practice.*"[143] Another correspondent lamented, "Although the Lutheran Church in America has, during the last fifty years, rapidly and widely extended her borders and largely increased her membership, . . . [she] has often been treated by some journals of sister denominations . . . as *almost a non-entity.*"[144]

Yet most Lutherans repressed such worries and anxieties. At the General Synod's convention in 1859, twenty-six leaders from the church body's various factions submitted a joint statement on "the State of the Church." They cheerfully reported that American Lutherans are "becoming more intelligently united than at any former time." While they acknowledged that "the slavery question, the church or symbolic question, and other very delicate points were extensively debated at this meeting," these discussions were done "in the very best spirit." They expressed "our decided conviction that at no former period of her history has [the American Lutheran church] been so fully and so generally aroused to her great mission and work as at the present."[145] On the eve of the Civil War, Lutherans stood more united and confident of their place in American culture than ever before.

THREE

★ ★ ★ ★ ★ ★ ★

Lutherans and
the Union, 1860–1863

O N OCTOBER 31, 1861, Charles Porterfield Krauth and William Passavant, two leaders of the confessional movement in the General Synod, published the first issue of a new weekly church paper based in Philadelphia. Appearing on the anniversary of the Protestant Reformation and during the first year of the Civil War, the *Lutheran and Missionary* advanced the dual goals of preserving Lutheran unity and saving the American Union. In church affairs, the editors promised to "rise above every species of partisanship" and "heartily sustain the General Synod in all its efforts to unite and strengthen our beloved Church."[1] In the civil realm, however, they saw no room for compromise. "This war, like every truly great war, is a war of ideas," they asserted. "Nothing but the maintenance unconditionally of the Constitution, and of the Union, could justify this war, and on this issue our government must stand, or by it must fall."[2]

Krauth's and Passavant's inaugural editorials reflected the concerns shared by many other Lutherans. During the first years of the Civil War, members of American Lutheranism's various parties discussed and disputed a host of political, moral, and theological issues related to the conflict. The result of these debates was the exacerbation and magnification of the tensions that had been repressed during the 1850s.

Lutherans, of course, were not alone among American Christians in being shaped by the Civil War. Over the past twenty-five years, scholars have shown how the conflict was a crucial turning point in the nation's religious history, just as much as it was the fulcrum of change in politics, economics, and race. Among the many developments explored by historians are the strengthening of civil religion and religious nationalism, clashing views about the role of preachers in politics, and a "theological crisis" over the central moral issue of slavery.[3] Lutherans fully participated in these debates. Yet despite being the fifth-largest religious group in the United States by 1860—with more than 250,000 communicant members (and perhaps as many as 1 million adherents)—they are almost completely absent from this growing corpus of scholarship. Lutheran denominational histories have reciprocated this neglect by treating the war as extraneous to intra-Lutheran developments.[4]

The Civil War, however, played a crucial role in shaping American Lutherans' identity and their church's history. During the secession crisis and first year of conflict, Lutherans were sharply divided in their reactions, as the outbreak of war strained and broke ecclesiastical partnerships. By the war's second year, most had embraced the cause of their respective sections and become ardent promoters of Christian patriotism. Yet despite being largely united in their endorsement of religious nationalism, different factions within the church espoused contrasting understandings of the relationship between religion and politics. The war also forced Lutherans to cease their circumvention of the issue of slavery, which drove and exposed further divisions. On the eve of the Civil War, Lutheranism in the United States had stood more united than ever before, with about two-thirds of American Lutherans belonging to a national federation, the General Synod. By 1863, that unity had begun to fracture.

THE NATION AND THE CHURCH

American Lutherans differed substantially in their reactions to the Civil War's outbreak. Most Lutherans in the Confederate states quickly and fervently championed secession. Lutherans in the loyal states, by contrast, were divided. Some embraced the Union cause immediately and with great enthusiasm, others were more cautious in their support, and a few others held views that resembled those of the Copperheads. As historians such as Paul Kleppner and Robert Swierenga have shown, these divergent views, at least in the northern states, were in part the product of ethnoreligious factors. The New and confessional Lutherans of the General Synod, who tended to align themselves with the nation's evangelical establishment, were more likely to support the Republicans, while Moderate and Old Lutherans, who were more averse to Anglo-Protestantism, tended to vote Democratic. By contrast, Scandinavian Lutherans almost uniformly supported the party of Abraham Lincoln.[5] Even more significant than ethnicity or theology, however, were regional differences. During the secession crisis and onset of armed conflict, Lutherans were principally shaped by the political and cultural climate of the various states in which they lived. These differences would have important ramifications for church unity.

Lutherans in the southern states reflected their sectional milieu, none more so than John Bachman of South Carolina. Before the war, Bachman proclaimed himself a "union man" to his northern associates in the General Synod.[6] However, to his friends in elite southern society, he expressed much different sentiments. After John Brown's raid on the federal arsenal at Harpers Ferry in October 1859, the South Carolina minister encouraged his friend Edmund Ruffin, the prominent southern Fire-Eater, to stoke the flames of secession in "our sister Virginia."[7] Following the election of Lincoln, Bachman broke from his usual custom of avoiding politics in the pulpit and preached a sermon to his Charleston congregation that called for "a peaceful separation."[8] The next month he offered the invocation at South Carolina's secession convention. In his prayer, Bachman asked for wisdom in the face of northern "fanaticism, injustice and oppression" and the ability "to protect and bless the humble [African] race, that has been confided to our care." He hoped that "this division of the government in our land" might "be effected in peace" but implored his "gracious Father," if war should come, "to spread thine arm of protection over those who are contending for their liberties."[9] When the secession crisis turned into armed conflict, Bachman would lead his fellow southern Lutherans in the direction of Confederate nationalism.

As the chain reaction following South Carolina's secession moved the country inexorably to war, Lutherans throughout the rest of the nation reacted to the political turmoil. Of particular consequence were the responses of those living in Maryland. Though the two Lutheran synods in this border state comprised only about ten thousand members, or less than 6 percent of the total membership of the General Synod, Baltimore was home to American Lutheranism's most widely circulated periodical, the *Lutheran Observer*.[10] Following the retirement of longtime editor Benjamin Kurtz in 1859, the paper went through a series of

editorial changes. (In February 1861 alone the paper was managed by three different groups of ministers.) Despite these frequent changes, the opinions about the
national crisis expressed by the *Lutheran Observer* remained consistent throughout the war's first year.

Drawing on its long-standing practice of attempting to remain "neutral" on
topics of political controversy, the paper sought to be a proponent of peace. On
February 15, shortly after seven states met to form the Confederate States of
America, its editors wrote, "If we must have two confederacies, let the separation
of states be conducted and consummated in peace."[11] After President Lincoln
called for seventy-five thousand troops to put down the rebellion following the
Confederate attack on Fort Sumter in April, the paper declared that it was "the
duty of christians" to unite "in desiring an amicable adjustment of our present
difficulties."[12] In May, the editors finally decided that it was "time for every true
American to show his undying loyalty to the government," but confessed that
their support for the Union was mixed with "feelings of unuttered sadness."[13]
This tragic view of the war continued during the summer of 1861. Following the
Battle of Bull Run in July, the paper's editors blamed the "rabid political press"
for "kindl[ing] the flame of civil strife."[14] Even into the early months of 1862, the
Lutheran Observer continued to oscillate between praying for a swift victory and
advocating a negotiated ceasefire.[15] Like many other Marylanders, those who
managed the oldest and most widely read Lutheran paper in the United States
never supported secession but were indecisive in their support of the Union.[16]

The stance of the *Lutheran Observer* during the early stages of the war was
due not only to its location in a border state but also to its being the flagship
publication of New Lutheranism, the school to which most southern Lutherans belonged. Consequently, the paper's editors desired peace not only in the
nation but also in their church party. Following the secession of South Carolina,
they worried "what the effect of this agitation will be upon the Lutheran church
south" and hoped to avoid "a division in our church."[17] Even after war was declared, the *Lutheran Observer* persisted in its advocacy for intra-Lutheran unity.
Rather than "furnishing an excuse for dividing the church," its editors argued,
the "evils" of national conflict "constitute a very powerful motive for a closer and
more vital union of all sections of our beloved Zion." Drawing on rhetoric similar
to Lincoln's first inaugural address, they wrote that "the memories of the past, the
association of the present, and the bright hopes of the future should constrain all

to promptly dismiss the thought of dividing." Lutherans of the General Synod, they insisted, "should unite in hearty efforts of 'keeping the unity of the Spirit in the bond of peace.'"[18] The paper's editors feared ecclesiastical schism even more than national disunion.

Despite the numerous olive branches that the *Lutheran Observer* extended to its southern readers, the relationship between New Lutherans in the Union and those in the Confederacy soured quickly.[19] In June 1861, the paper published excerpts of several angry letters from correspondents in the South who lambasted the paper for its supposedly pro-Union viewpoint. One writer, a Lutheran pastor from Georgia, told the editors that "if the Lutherans of the north hold the views presented in the Observer, there is an absolute, an inevitable necessity for a division."[20] By mid-July, all southern Lutherans had canceled their subscriptions to the *Lutheran Observer*, costing the paper one thousand subscribers.[21] The following month, Confederate Lutherans formed their own paper, the *Southern Lutheran*. As various synods in the South began to withdraw from the General Synod, the paper encouraged them to "meet in Convention for the more perfect organization of our Southern Lutheran Church."[22] The meeting took place in Salisbury, North Carolina, in May 1862. Though poor attendance due to the difficulties of traveling during wartime forced the delegates to postpone the new organization's official formation, Lutherans in the seceded states had become united around a shared Confederate identity.[23] The efforts of the *Lutheran Observer* to preserve sectional unity in their church had failed.

The Maryland paper's stance also drew fire from the other papers associated with the General Synod. The most pointed criticism came from William Passavant's *Missionary*. At first, during the early months of 1861, the Pittsburgh-based weekly echoed the *Lutheran Observer* by expressing hope that a "general civil war will be averted."[24] Following Fort Sumter, however, Passavant's paper began to beat the war drum: "Secessionists have taken the sword, and by the sword they will perish."[25] When its Maryland rival failed to voice the same sentiments, readers of the *Missionary* voiced their disapproval. One correspondent went so far as to ask, "Is the 'Observer' in League with the Great Civil Rebellion?"[26] Even after the *Lutheran Observer* declared its official support for the Union's war effort, Passavant continued to criticize the paper's "former Secession proclivities" and its "sudden conversion to loyalty."[27] The *Lutheran and Home Journal*, edited by a committee of clergymen led by Charles Porterfield Krauth and Joseph Seiss and headquartered in Philadelphia, also made no concessions to any form of southern sympathizing.[28] As the war commenced, Krauth and Seiss laid the blame for the conflict squarely on the shoulders of the "seceding States" and proclaimed that God would judge the "wicked ambition" of southern "demagogues."[29] Their paper approvingly quoted the resolutions adopted by the delegates of the Pennsylvania Synod, the representative of Moderate Lutheranism within the General Synod, who pledged their "unalterable fidelity to the Union; a conscientious obedience to the lawfully constituted authorities; and a heartfelt willingness and readiness to aid to the utmost of our ability, in preserving and protecting our glorious Union."[30]

The disagreements between the *Missionary* and *Lutheran and Home Journal,* on the one hand, and the *Lutheran Observer,* on the other, were not merely the result of their respective locations in Pennsylvania and Maryland; ecclesiastical concerns were also a factor. Because the former papers' editors belonged to the confessional movement in the General Synod, they had little reason to placate the numerous New Lutherans in the South and every incentive to disparage the *Lutheran Observer* for doing just that. Passavant was particularly fierce in his criticism. He accused the New Lutheran paper of bowing to the wishes of its "masters in the South" by excluding from its pages "every thing having the most remote bearing to loyalty and liberty."[31] Those associated with the *Lutheran Observer* were deeply offended by these accusations of disloyalty and responded in kind. One writer defended the paper's initial advocacy for "an amicable adjustment to our national troubles," and when that failed, its attempt "to save our church from being sundered." He laid the guilt for "rending and wounding the body of Christ" squarely at the feet of "firebrand" Lutherans like Passavant and Krauth.[32] While the *Missionary* blamed New Lutherans' southern entanglements for bringing them perilously close to treason, those helming the *Lutheran Observer* accused the confessional movement of exalting the concerns of the nation above the mission of the church.

Nevertheless, by the end of the war's first year, the different parties of the General Synod were able to navigate these differences. In May 1862, the federation met in Lancaster, Pennsylvania to hold its first convention since the war's outbreak. With southern Lutheran synods conspicuously absent, delegates representing twenty-one synods—mostly from Pennsylvania, and Ohio, but also from New York, Maryland, Indiana, and Illinois—passed five resolutions on the

"State of the Country." The first echoed the words of Passavant and Krauth by condemning the "rebellion against the constitutional government of this land" as "wicked" and "unnatural." The second continued this belligerent tone, declaring the "maintenance of the Constitution and the Union by the sword" to be "an unavoidable necessity and a sacred duty." The fourth resolution, however, shifted to the pacifying language of the *Lutheran Observer*, asking "that God would restore peace to our distracted country" and "re-establish fraternal relations between all the States." The fifth and final declaration offered "devout thanks . . . to Almighty God for the success which has crowned our arms." (The third resolution, which addressed the issue of slavery, will be discussed later.) The delegates concluded by appointing a special commission to deliver the resolutions in person to President Lincoln.[33] Despite their conflicting views, by 1862, the northern Lutherans of the General Synod were able to unite behind the Union cause.

Those Lutherans in the North who stood outside of the General Synod also confronted the issues facing the church and the nation. During the secession crisis and early stages of the war, the stance of the *Lutheran Standard,* the biweekly paper of the Moderate Lutheran Ohio Synod, resembled that of its ecclesiastical adversary, the *Lutheran Observer,* in its advocacy for peace. Even before South Carolina had officially seceded, its editor, Daniel Worley (1829–1888), argued that the "best" option was "to separate into two or more distinct confederacies" and urged his readers to "unite our prayers for a peaceful solution of the difficulties which will be sure to arise in the process of separation."[34] When war was declared in April, the Columbus-based paper blamed "ungodly ambition, national pride, and sectional prejudices" for bringing on the conflict and prayed "that peace and unity may be restored."[35] Yet Worley's paper went even further than its New Lutheran opponent by maintaining this stance not just during the summer and fall of 1861 but also throughout the war.[36] Just as the *Lutheran Observer* reflected the border state politics of its headquarters in Maryland, the Ohio-based *Lutheran Standard* echoed the principles of the state's large number of Copperheads.[37]

Like its New Lutheran rival, Worley's Moderate Lutheran paper also had ecclesiastical reasons for urging peace. Over the course of the 1850s, the Ohio Synod had become partners with the Tennessee Synod, a church body made up of congregations that had broken away from the South's various New Lutheran synods. During the early stages of the war, the *Lutheran Standard* made an even more determined effort than the *Lutheran Observer* to maintain unity with its "Southern friends and brethren." In contrast to the General Synod, which had effectively split along sectional lines by the fall of 1861, Worley insisted as late as May 1862 that "true Lutheran Synods" like his own "know no North[,] no South, no East, no West, but only a universal Christian brotherhood."[38]

The realities of war, however, gradually eroded the two synods' fellowship. In August 1862, the *Lutheran Standard* ceased listing agents for distributing their paper in the South.[39] The following November, the clergy of the Tennessee Synod, who had already thrown their support behind the Confederate cause, began contemplating their own church paper.[40] Though one correspondent hoped as late as October 1864 that the two synods might resume their fraternal connection, no reunion ever occurred.[41] By the midpoint of the Civil War, despite the efforts of the *Lutheran Standard* to preserve sectional harmony, the partnership between the Ohio and Tennessee synods had ended.

Scandinavian Lutherans' reaction to the outbreak of the Civil War was also shaped by regional politics and ecclesiastical considerations. The Moderate Lutherans of the Augustana Synod, a predominantly Swedish church body located in the Upper Midwest, had no formal ties to the South. Unsurprisingly, its leaders unreservedly condemned secession and urged loyalty to the Union. However, the Old Lutherans of the Norwegian Synod were beginning to experience an internal conflict already in the summer of 1861. Because of their partnership with the Missouri Synod, whose leaders were accused of sympathizing with the Confederacy, several prominent lay members questioned whether their church body's pastors were loyal to the Union and tolerant of slavery. Though leading clergymen denied any support of secession, the debate over slavery would threaten to tear the Norwegian Synod apart (as discussed later).[42]

Despite being accused of southern sympathy, the actual opinions of the Old Lutherans of the Missouri Synod, a church body made up of German immigrants located throughout the Midwest, were more complicated. In May 1861, C. F. W. Walther wrote to a fellow pastor that "our congregation [in St. Louis] is split," but "the largest part seems to be Republican." As for him and his colleagues at the synod's seminary, Walther wrote that "we are . . . naturally for the Union," but he also noted that "we cannot see why the state does not have the right of secession according to the United States Constitution."[43] This ambivalence was reflected in the pages of the *Lutheraner.* During the first year of the war, the Old

Lutheran paper made no definitive pronouncements on the rightness or wrongness of either side of the conflict; instead, it urged a "general repentance for our entire American nation" in order to bring "a speedy restoration of peace."[44]

Because they viewed the war primarily as a hardship to be endured, the church body's leaders discouraged their members from joining the war effort. Shortly after the outbreak of fighting, the Missouri Synod merged its seminary in Fort Wayne with its seminary in St. Louis so that ministerial students could avoid Indiana's draft laws.[45] Walther wrote to a colleague that "we are opposed to having our Lutherans freewillingly serve in the Union military."[46] His paper, the *Lutheraner,* gave theological justification for this view, arguing that Christians could refuse military service if they deemed the cause to be "godless."[47] More than anything, the leaders of the Missouri Synod simply wanted to avoid the war entirely.

On account of such opinions and actions, Old Lutherans were viewed antagonistically by supporters of the Union. Many German American political leaders were ardent Republicans and viewed the clergy of the Missouri Synod with suspicion.[48] Walther, in particular, was labeled as a Confederate sympathizer, a charge that possessed an element of truth. Though he never publicly urged disloyalty, in letters he expressed sympathy for Missouri's Democratic government and state militia.[49] He also criticized the Lincoln administration in private conversations, calling it a "fanatical abolitionist government."[50] In the early months of 1862, Walther was among the many ministers compelled by Major General Henry Halleck, the commander of the Department of Missouri, to sign an oath of loyalty to the state and federal governments.[51]

Other Old Lutherans, however, were treated with hostility by secessionists. One congregation in western Missouri was terrorized by Confederate guerillas for their presumed support of the Union. In 1862 and 1863, bushwhackers raided the German American settlement near Cook's Store (renamed Concordia after the war), including once during a baptismal celebration, murdering several men on each occasion. As the congregation's pastor wrote to his sister, "No pleading helped. . . . They had neither Christian nor human feelings."[52] A year later, when the guerillas returned for a third attack, about one hundred German farmers gathered at the Lutheran church to defend their community. The battle resulted in a massacre. In addition to those killed during the fight, the rebels executed the wounded and several others.[53] Though most Lutherans did not experience anything resembling these atrocities, these events demonstrate how the Civil War forced all Americans—even those who, like the Old Lutherans of the Missouri Synod, wanted to be left alone—to confront the fraught questions facing the nation.

PATRIOTISM AND CHRISTIANITY

By the beginning of 1862, the majority of Lutherans had come to support the war effort of their respective sections, some more enthusiastically than others. As they did so, their church's leaders commented on the relationship between patriotic duty and the Christian faith. For the most part, Lutherans in the South wholeheartedly embraced the divine obligation of the Confederate cause. In the loyal states, opinion was more divided. General Synod Lutherans, no matter their theological persuasion, tended to mirror mainstream evangelical Protestants by championing religious nationalism. Many Scandinavians also saw the Union cause as a sacred duty. Both the Moderate Lutherans of the Ohio Synod and the Old Lutherans of the Missouri Synod, however, were more circumspect in combining Christianity and patriotism. Nevertheless, during the Civil War's first two years, most Lutherans had adopted various forms of American civil religion.

Lutherans in the South saw a clear linkage between patriotism and Christianity. This view was especially promoted by the *Southern Lutheran,* headed by John Bachman and the South Carolina Synod. The Charleston-based paper commended the sacrifice that "patriotism compels us to lay upon the altar of our country" and praised the southern war effort as a "just and holy cause."[54] Bachman compared the support of southern Lutherans for the Confederate cause to the participation of "our Lutheran forefathers" in the American Revolution. Those "heroes," he asserted, "contended for the same rights for which the South is struggling."[55] Patriotic sermons also reinforced Confederate Lutherans' sacred duties. Though "civilization and christianity demand a peaceful separation," preached one North Carolina pastor, "the North is now in arms against the South, with a view of coercing her back into an unnatural Union." Because "the war has been forced upon us," he implored his congregation to "meet our opposing foe" and "lift our heart devoutly to Almighty God . . . in defense of our rights."[56] For many southern Lutherans, the Christian faith and Confederate nationalism went hand in hand.

In the loyal states, General Synod Lutherans mirrored their southern counterparts by sanctifying the Union cause. The most fervent were the confessional
Lutherans. In October 1861, the two papers associated with their movement, the
Lutheran and Home Journal and the *Missionary,* combined to form the *Lutheran
and Missionary,* with Charles Porterfield Krauth and William Passavant serving
as editors. For the next several years, the Philadelphia-based paper devoted nearly
half of each issue to news and commentary on the war. The editors not only
zealously advocated for northern victory but also promoted Christian patriotism. As Krauth confidently asserted, "Our blessed Lord was a patriot.... Like a
true patriot the Savior had an *opinion* ... [and] not only had an opinion but he
expressed it."[57] He also believed that the military conflict had a divine purpose.
Reflecting on the one-year anniversary of the war's commencement, the editor
assured his readers that "God will use this war" to create "a nation just, tender,
and, for the first time, in the highest sense, free."[58]

The *Lutheran Observer,* the mouthpiece of New Lutheranism, also came to
champion the righteousness of the Union cause. In February 1862, Benjamin
Kurtz came out of retirement to reprise his role as editor. Under his leadership,
the paper increased its coverage of the war and became more explicit in its defense of "the best government in the world" and praise for "the fairest and happiest land that God's sun ever shone upon." Though Kurtz claimed no ability to
discern the mysteries of "providence," he knew that "one thing is certain—sin is
wrong and virtue is right, obedience to God is acceptable and will be rewarded,
while disobedience is hateful and will certainly be punished."[59] Other contributors to the paper expressed similar sentiments. "The Bible, as well as the whole
genius of our holy religion," one correspondent proclaimed, "justify the people
of the Union in destroying all rebels and traitors."[60] Like their rivals at the *Lutheran and Missionary,* writers for the *Lutheran Observer* believed that the war
to preserve the American nation had a sacred purpose.

Some northern Lutherans further demonstrated their devotion to the nation
by volunteering in the Union army. Determining the number of Lutherans who
served militarily in the Civil War and examining the thoughts and experiences
of lay Lutheran soldiers are not only beyond the scope of this study but also
present significant challenges in terms of documentary evidence.[61] Yet accurate
figures and ample sources are available on the service of pastors. At least twenty-
three Lutheran ministers served as chaplains. (This figure does not include Fer-

dinand Sarner, a German Jewish rabbi mistakenly listed by the American board of chaplains as a Lutheran pastor.)[62] For these clergymen, the war afforded the opportunity to serve both God and country, which many saw as closely linked. As one chaplain prayed before his regiment, "Bless all those have who have gone and still go forth . . . to preserve among us and to spread abroad to the remotest parts of the Earth the precious blessings of liberty and undefiled Religion."[63]

Several Lutheran deaconesses also served the Union army as nurses. This form of ministry came to the United States at the behest of William Passavant, who had discovered the German deaconess movement during his trip to Europe in 1846.[64] From 1850 to 1866, nineteen Lutheran sisters, many of whom were immigrants, served at the orphan house founded by Passavant in Pittsburgh. During the Civil War, several of them temporarily left the orphanage to serve at Union infirmaries. Two of these women, Elisabeth Hupperts (1822–1895) and Barbara Kaag (1823–1900), became the lead nurses at hospitals near the nation's capital.[65] Like their counterparts in the chaplaincy, the war presented the opportunity to demonstrate their obedience to God and their loyalty to their adopted homeland.

Northern Lutherans in the General Synod also demonstrated their patriotic commitment by promoting the United States Christian Commission. Founded in 1861 as an agency for distributing Bibles and tracts to Union soldiers, by the end of the war's second year, this interdenominational organization had expanded its mission. Volunteers visited the sick and wounded, provided food and medical supplies, and helped to identify the battlefield dead.[66] By the fall of 1863, both the *Lutheran Observer* and the *Lutheran and Missionary* devoted a portion of nearly every issue to updating their readers on the benevolent association's work and urging them to support it with their monetary contributions.[67] For General Synod Lutherans in the North, advocacy for the Christian Commission served not only as a way to minister to Union troops but also as a means to demonstrate their credentials as both mainstream Protestants and devoted Americans. As one correspondent to the *Lutheran and Missionary* enthused, "It is the embodiment of all that is true and noble in the nation's heart" and "cannot be too much contemplated and admired by Christians and patriots."[68]

The wedding of American nationalism and the Christian faith was on fullest display among General Synod Lutherans in sermons held on special days of fasting and thanksgiving. At the beginning of the war some, such as Joseph Seiss, had cautioned against "*patriotizing* Christianity."[69] Most preachers, however, ignored his warning. Sermons in Lutheran churches declared "the defence of our blood-hallowed Union" to be "a christian duty" and described the war as "baptism of blood" for "a christian people."[70] Underlying these effusions of civil religion was the premise that God had established as special covenant with the United States. As "the Jewish nation, in its ancient history, is known as God's chosen people," preached one Pennsylvania Lutheran, "just thus did God deal with us."[71] Other ministers affirmed that the United States was God's "peculiar heritage" and a "Christian nation."[72] Mirroring their southern counterparts' embrace of Confederate nationalism, the vast majority of these sermons by northern General Synod ministers exalted the American Union as ordained and favored by God.

Scandinavian American Lutherans also saw the war as a way to demonstrate their loyalty to both God and country. As historian Anders Bo Rasmussen has shown, immigrants from Sweden, Norway, and Denmark not only framed their support of the Union in terms of "American values" but also "appealed to a common Scandinavian ethnicity." In doing so, they emphasized their identity as "Protestant and Lutheran as opposed to Irish or German Catholic."[73] Because of their boisterous proclamations of devotion to their adopted homeland, Scandinavian Americans acquired the self-understanding as "the Union's most loyal citizens."[74] In actuality, as Rasmussen has documented, many of these immigrants were ambivalent about the war effort and resisted enlistment.[75] Nevertheless, at least in their rhetoric, Swedish, Norwegian, and Danish Lutherans saw patriotic duty as intimately connected to their religious faith.

A very different approach came from the Moderate Lutherans of the Ohio Synod. Throughout the war, David Worley's *Lutheran Standard* advocated a position of neutrality. This posture stemmed from a firmly held belief that a Christian should not allow "his patriotism to run away with his religion" and that ministers should seek to "quell the storm and quiet the excitement" of political controversy.[76] However, this opposition to mixing Christianity and patriotism rested less on a principled opposition to religious nationalism and more on the conviction that Lutherans were "free to choose their own political opinions."[77] Moreover, Worley's supposedly neutral stance implied that Copperheadism—or even secession—were legitimate viewpoints. In a telling article, the Ohio Synod editor asserted that "the government, as an instrumentality ordained of God[,] demands the absolute obedience of the Christian citizen," but also insisted that "the special applications" of this doctrine "we must leave to each Christian reader."[78] Though it never openly criticized the Lincoln administration or advocated for Peace Democrats, throughout the Civil War the *Lutheran Standard* maintained a studied detachment toward the Union cause.

By contrast, the Old Lutherans of the Missouri Synod, despite their initial ambivalence about the rightness of the Union cause, came to voice support for the northern war effort. Though they were sharply critical of "preaching patriotically," they nevertheless argued that "good Lutherans are also good citizens" and should stand by their government.[79] One clergyman, Friedrich Richmann (1820–1885), served as a chaplain in the 58th Ohio Regiment, describing his duty as performed "in God's name."[80] Missouri Synod publications also promoted the Union. The *Illustrirte Abend Schule*—renamed the *Abend Schule* in 1863, when financial pressures forced the paper to no longer print pictures—supplied news and commentary on political and military matters, written from, in their estimation, "an unpartisan, truthful" perspective.[81] Though coverage of the war itself was sparser in the *Lutheraner* and *Lehre und Wehre,* these periodicals commented on a variety of issues surrounding the conflict.

Like other American Lutherans, the leaders of the Missouri Synod were not hesitant to offer interpretations of the war's theological meaning. C. F. W. Walther expressed these views in two sermons on national days of repentance. Rather than a conflict caused by southern traitors, Walther saw the war as a tragedy brought on by the nation's transgressions, including its tolerance of "false prophets," "fanatical sects," and "unbaptized Christians."[82] In Walther's telling, God had made the United States "the sanctuary for the poor and oppressed of every nation" and had granted it "all the blessings of religious and civil liberty." The result was that "our America stood out as a wonder before the eyes of every nation." But rather than thanking God, "our nation has committed idolatry with itself, its freedom, its might, its wealth" until "finally, God decided to overlook this no longer."[83] Though Walther's particular list of sins and his refusal to cast blame on the South were somewhat atypical, his overarching rhetoric was hardly unique among Lutherans and other Christians in the loyal states. Both in his evocations of American exceptionalism and his claim that the war was a visitation of God for the nation's sins, he espoused the widely held belief in the divinely ordained "destiny" of the United States.[84] Even Old Lutherans could not avoid the pull of American civil religion.

POLITICS AND RELIGION

Though most Lutherans were united in their belief that it was the duty of Christians to defend their government, they were divided over the extent to which religious leaders should engage in "political preaching." Historian Timothy Wesley has usefully sorted the wartime approaches to this question into three categories. On one extreme were those like Old School Presbyterian Stuart Robinson, who divided religion and politics into two entirely "separate spheres" and argued that the preacher's obligation was to focus solely on church affairs. At the other pole were those such as Congregationalist Henry Ward Beecher, who saw religion and politics as "separate components of an all-encompassing Christian ministry" and openly advocated for politicians and parties. Occupying the centrist position were those who believed that religious instruction and political commentary were "separate duties," equally legitimate but distinct.[85] Variations of each of these approaches could be found among Lutherans in the Union.

The New Lutherans' *Lutheran Observer* exemplified the "separate duties" position. On the one hand, the paper was sharply critical of Christian leaders becoming "political agitators."[86] "We cannot for a moment open up our columns to the discussion of partisan politics," declared one editorial, "and we repudiate the low and vulgar slang often employed by truckling politicians, as a defilement of any religious paper."[87] Yet the paper also criticized political quietism. In an article that explicitly denounced Robinson and his paper, the *True Presbyterian*, the *Lutheran Observer* asserted that the "theory of the separation of spiritual from secular matters . . . is in antagonism to the spirit and teaching of christianity."[88] As one contributor to the paper wrote, Lutheran pastors "have duties to our God and our country." He argued that while preachers should refrain from "electioneering for office" or "making stump speeches," they still should "denounce everything which is injurious to christianity," such as the sale of "intoxicating drinks" and "political corruption."[89] Exempt from his list of sins, however, was slavery.

The confessional movement's *Lutheran and Missionary*, by contrast, exhibited a more expansive approach toward political preaching. William Passavant, the paper's coeditor, was an admirer of Henry Ward Beecher, and his outlook resembled the famous preacher's comprehensive view of Christian political engagement. Yet Passavant principally saw the role of ministers, including religious editors, as standing separate from "party connections"—or, more accurately, above them. "We care not a farthing for the names or platforms of parties," he announced. "Our business as an Editor is with Christian principles. Whatever conflicts with these, we oppose; whatever agrees with these, we advocate."[90] Krauth, the paper's general editor, endorsed a more conservative view. Citing the Gospel of Matthew, he argued that Jesus "places before us two spheres, the sphere of Caesar, of human government, and the sphere of God, or of divine government" and that "we are not to give one what is due to the other."[91] However, "while the sanctuary is no place for the discussion of the partisan questions that divide good men," Krauth also contended that "at proper times and under proper circumstances, controlled by charity and prudence," church leaders "may utter what they believe."[92] Though Krauth saw a somewhat more constrained political role for ministers than did Passavant, both agreed that preachers had the duty to speak to the most pressing issues of the day.

Much less reticent about opining on political matters were the small numbers of Scandinavian American Lutherans. The Swedish and Norwegian immigrant political press had close ties to the Lutheran church, and some papers even were edited by Lutheran ministers. The Swedish *Hemlandet,* edited by T. N. Hasselquist, a pastor, openly advocated for the Republican Party throughout the war and published pro-Union articles written by other clergymen.[93] The Norwegian *Emigranten,* edited by Carl Solberg, a layman, likewise supported Lincoln and the Republicans, though it also evinced the growing divide between the Norwegian clergy and the laity over the issue of slavery. Papers dedicated principally to the work of the church, such as Hasselquist's *Rätta Hemlandet* and the Norwegian Synod's *Kirkelig Maanedstidende,* however, offered commentary on the war, but not from an explicitly partisan perspective.[94]

In contrast, the *Lutheran Standard* of the Moderate Lutheran Ohio Synod resembled the "separate spheres" approach. Under the editorship of Daniel Worley, the paper drew a bright line "between religion and worldly policy" and warned against "desecrating the pulpit" with "political war preaching."[95] Even as battles increased and casualties mounted, Worley tried to keep its pages free from discussion of the war. However, Worley at times let slip his own political preference for a swift return to the status quo ante bellum. In 1863, he boasted that throughout the war his paper had "carefully abstained from bringing to our columns anything which might even have borne the suspicion of our taking sides in any way, in the political questions, out of which our present troubles have mainly arisen." Yet in the same article he advocated "a return to peace and unity."[96] As was the case with similarly minded American Protestants, the *Lutheran Standard*'s avowal to keep religion and politics completely distinct betrayed a political ideology.[97]

A more thoroughly thought-out "separate spheres" view came from the Old Lutherans of the Missouri Synod. Rather than deriving their position from the southern doctrine of the spirituality of the church, these conservative Lutherans espoused an American version of their church's historic teaching of the two kingdoms. An address given at the meeting of the Missouri Synod's Western District distilled their stance: "State and church . . . are two completely different kingdoms at the same time. One is spiritual, the other secular. One is maintained and ruled by the sword and force, the other . . . through God's Word alone. Every alliance between the two is unnatural and can only result in damage to the church."[98] Yet for Old Lutheran leaders, this separation of church and state did not imply that Christians, even pastors, must remain neutral on questions of politics. When the Civil War erupted, one contributor to the *Lutheraner* listed ten principles to guide his fellow Lutherans "in this time of political confusion and agitation of minds." The writer distinguished between matters "purely of a political kind," which had no place in the pulpit, and "political opinions . . . aris[ing] from false doctrine," which pastors and theologians had a duty to denounce.[99] In the Old Lutheran view, the earthly and spiritual kingdoms were distinct but ministers had the responsibility to speak when those two realms intersected.

With such an understanding, the leaders of the Missouri Synod offered extensive commentary on the political issues surrounding the war. For Walther and other Old Lutherans, the great sin unleashed by the Civil War was a false conception of liberty. This assessment was in part a reaction to German American political newspapers, which those in the Missouri Synod continued to label as the "satanic press."[100] Walther saw the views of forty-eighters and other radical Republicans as resembling the "spirit of the French Revolution" and the "Anabaptists" of the Peasants' War during the Reformation era. "This spirit," he wrote, "confuses Christian liberty with civil equality" and claims that the "the voice of the people is the voice of God." According to Walther, democratic radicalism that subverts the rightly ordained authorities in both church and state was the "idol of this new spirit of the times" and was beginning to take hold of the American citizenry.[101]

Though Walther's particular assessment of the war's meaning was unusual among American Lutherans, his lack of hesitation in commenting on public affairs was not. In the years following the Civil War, however, this approach to political engagement would shift, as Lutherans became increasingly—but not completely—quietist. What would persist in the long term would be the aversion to political and social radicalism, expressed in its most extreme form by Walther. In the short term, the disagreements over the relationship between faith and politics would intensify intra-Lutheran disputes over the central issue of the war.

SLAVERY AND THE BIBLE

Before the Civil War, Lutherans had done their best to avoid arguments over slavery. While "other denominations attempted to legislate on the subject of slavery . . . and were rent asunder," the *Lutheran Observer* boasted in May 1861, "the Lutheran church always confined itself to the legitimate work of preaching the Gospel."[102] However, amid a war fought over questions surrounding that very issue, the subject was inescapable. Even after southern Lutherans had severed bonds with their northern coreligionists, Lutherans in the loyal states engaged in debates about the morality of slavery and its place in their nation. These quarrels heightened the already existing tensions between the church's theological divisions.

From the outset of the war, virtually all northern Lutherans in the General Synod declared slavery to be the reason for southern secession. A July 1861 article in the *Evangelical Review* was representative. "Slavery," the author wrote, "is undoubtedly, the great problem, the great source of irritation, and that which distinguishes the one section from the other."[103] Nevertheless, despite recognizing that the peculiar institution was central to the Confederate cause, most did not view emancipation as the purpose of the Union war effort. In this, their opinions resembled those of many other white northerners. As historian Gary Gallagher has shown, "Maintenance of the Union . . . always ranked first among war aims for most citizens in the United States."[104]

Yet despite sharing the same basic outlook, General Synod Lutherans in the loyal states were divided over the particulars of this "Union war" stance. The New Lutherans associated with the *Lutheran Observer* were the most conservative. In January 1862, one of the editors of the Maryland-based paper reminded his readers that "the Lutheran church has never made any deliverances on the subject of slavery" and criticized "the feeling which this war has developed in the free states against all who are connected with slavery."[105] The following month, Benjamin Kurtz wrote plainly that "the abolition of slavery . . . is not the object of the war; its great aim is to crush out rebellion, and restore the integrity of the Union."[106] The view of Charles Porterfield Krauth's *Lutheran and Missionary* was more moderate. Echoing the statements of President Lincoln, Krauth wrote, "We are as remote in our convictions from the class who would destroy the Constitution and the Union to remove slavery as we are from those would destroy both to uphold it." Yet he also held out hope that the war would bring about "a change in the convictions of men" so that slavery could be extinguished by constitutional means.[107] While many New Lutherans believed that the subject of slavery should be kept out of discussions about the war, Krauth and others associated with the confessional movement viewed emancipation as a salutary, if ancillary, outcome of the conflict.

These divisions were exposed at the General Synod's May 1862 meeting in Lancaster, Pennsylvania, during a debate over the convention's resolutions on the state of the country. According to a local newspaper report, four of the five statements were "unanimously adopted," but the remaining resolution, which addressed the issue of slavery, "produce[d] an animated discussion." The leading skeptics against its adoption were various New Lutheran representatives. Samuel Sprecher of Ohio "did not think it became ecclesiastical bodies to make declarations as to political measures," while Simeon Harkey of Illinois believed that a statement on slavery should be "calculated to give the least offence." Other New Lutherans urged "extreme caution," warned that emancipation "interfered with the onward course of the government," and questioned the propriety of discussing the matter without the presence of "our southern brethren." However, William Passavant, a leader of the confessional movement, argued that the Lutheran church had a responsibility to support "the emancipation of those for whom Christ died" and that "now the time was come for her to speak."

After a lengthy debate, the resolution finally carried. However, as the report noted, "the ayes and noes were called for, but not taken."[108] The adopted statement read:

Resolved, That, while we recognize this unhappy war as a righteous judgment of God, visited upon us because of the individual and national sins, of which we have been guilty, we nevertheless regard this rebellion as more immediately the natural result of the continuance and spread of domestic slavery in our land, and therefore hail with unmingled joy the proposition of our Chief Magistrate, which has received the sanction of Congress, to extend aid from the General Government to any State in which slavery exists, which shall deem fit to initiate a system of constitutional emancipation.[109]

Though hardly radical, this was the first official proclamation on slavery by the General Synod in its more than forty-year history.

The papers representing the federation's different factions responded as expected. The New Lutherans of the *Lutheran Observer* viewed the resolution negatively. One contributor claimed that "like the abolitionists of Congress," the convention's delegates were guilty of "taking advantage of the absence of representatives from the southern Synods." The writer then declared, "The avowed object of the Federal government . . . is the restoration of the Union and Constitution as they were."[110] Benjamin Kurtz, the paper's editor, believed that the General Synod's slavery resolution was "unnecessary, inexpedient, and calculated to effect little or no good, while, on the other hand, it might do harm."[111] This assessment reflected this New Lutheran leader's views on race and politics. In the early stages of the war, he and others associated with the *Lutheran Observer* had abandoned their support of colonization, citing its "great difficulty."[112] However, Kurtz still worried about setting free "four millions of such rude and helpless creatures," and argued that "if slavery is to be abolished, it must be done gradually."[113] Even after the General Synod's resolutions, New Lutheran leaders remained opposed to making emancipation part of the war effort.

By contrast, the confessional Lutherans of the *Lutheran and Missionary* praised the delegates' actions. Krauth boasted that the war resolutions "put our General Synod, and through it our church, in the true attitude to the great question of the hour." He lauded the delegates for speaking "firmly and moderately" and remarked, quite credulously, that the General Synod "has demonstrated that its long silence gave no consent to the system of slavery."[114] Two months later, Krauth was still elated: "Our General Synod's action in regard to the State of the Country, was, in some respects, the wisest and noblest work it has ever done." Yet he reminded his readers that the convention's resolution mentioned "not one word . . . of abolition, of violent, unconstitutional, or dubious, modes of overthrowing slavery."[115] Though they were more antislavery than their New Lutheran counterparts at the *Lutheran Observer,* those associated with the *Lutheran and Missionary* still saw emancipation as subordinate to the Union cause.

American Lutherans not connected with the General Synod also reacted to the Lancaster convention's resolutions on the war. The *Lutheran Standard* of the Ohio Synod condemned the decision: "The General Synod has made a great mistake in meddling at all in public affairs." Such a reaction reflected the paper's stated principle that church leaders should avoid political questions. This included a complete silence on the subject of slavery throughout the war. Yet just as its policy of "neutrality" masked a political agenda, the paper's editor, Daniel Worley, let slip his true feelings when commenting on the debates at the Lancaster meeting: "It struck us a little strange that so many of the radicals in a churchly view [the New Lutherans], were upon these questions the real conservatives, and that many from whom better things might have been expected [the confessional Lutherans], were here perfectly rabid."[116] In the estimation of the *Lutheran Standard,* even the General Synod's mild condemnation of slavery was a sign of radicalism.

Another group affected by the resolutions were the abolitionist Lutherans of the Franckean Synod, the tiny church body based in upstate New York that had boycotted the General Synod on account of its toleration of slavery. During the first months of the Civil War, the statements of the Franckeans differed starkly from those of other Lutherans. The synod reacted swiftly and decisively to the outbreak of the conflict, calling the southern cause "a crime against the civilization of the world."[117] In a sermon on November 28, 1861, Nicholas Van Alstine (1814–1900), one of the synod's leading ministers, contended that if the choice was "either the nation must die or slavery," he preferred that "the latter" would perish.[118] Following the Lancaster convention's resolutions, however, the Franckeans began to reconsider their refusal to join the General Synod. Though they viewed the statement on slavery as "moderate," they believed it represented a "very marked change." In 1863, the Franckean Synod officially reapplied for membership to the federation.[119] Nevertheless, this small synod was singular among Lutherans in viewing the destruction of slavery as the war's chief objective.

For most other northern Lutherans, however, the preservation of the Union was paramount, a stance further demonstrated by their subdued reactions to the Emancipation Proclamation. The *Lutheran Observer* reprinted both the preliminary and final proclamation, but its editors offered no analysis.[120] Krauth at the *Lutheran and Missionary* followed a similar course, printing both proclamations but making no editorial remarks.[121] The one exception to this trend came from Krauth's coeditor, the more stridently antislavery William Passavant, who claimed that the president's declaration "boldly sets the Government before the world on the side of liberty for all men" and "secures for our nation the approbation of Heaven."[122] Yet aside from this singular laudatory article, Lutherans in the General Synod greeted the proclamations with little fanfare. In this, they reflected Gallagher's observation that most white northerners viewed emancipation mainly as a "tool to help restore the Union and protect it against future slavery-related threats rather than as a grand moral imperative."[123]

Like their dearth of commentary on emancipation, General Synod Lutherans made almost no serious attempt to reckon with slavery's depiction in the Bible. The most conspicuously silent voice was that of Samuel Schmucker, the leading New Lutheran theologian. The Gettysburg professor had been his church's most prominent antislavery voice in the 1830s and 1840s but had published nothing new on the subject in the 1850s. His silence continued during the Civil War.[124] Scholars of Schmucker have overlooked this change, presuming instead that his antislavery advocacy remained consistent throughout his life.[125] Instead, with his ecclesiastical fate linked to Kurtz, Sprecher, and other New Lutherans who either refused to condemn slavery in unequivocal terms or viewed the subject as too politically volatile to discuss, Schmucker curbed his activist rhetoric. Some contemporaries noticed a change. One minister expressed the view that Schmucker and other "professors at our Gettysburg institutions who, in former days wrote and spoke against the sin of slavery, had in these latter times wheeled about and at least were 'winking' at this evil now." Schmucker, for his part, "denied the truth of such reports."[126] Nevertheless, even if his personal views remained unchanged, when the question of slavery brought the nation to the breaking point, the public witness of the most well-known antislavery Lutheran in the United States was strangely muted.[127]

Other Lutherans within the General Synod were not completely silent, but serious treatments of the issue were rare. The *Evangelical Review* (renamed the *Evangelical Quarterly Review* in 1862) published only two articles on the subject during the war, neither of which made a serious attempt to wrestle with the relevant biblical passages.[128] Krauth and Passavant's *Lutheran and Missionary* condemned slavery as sinful but published only one article of any depth on the topic, a two-part essay submitted by a guest contributor (discussed later). Krauth, who unlike Passavant had never commented on the morality of slavery before the war, was perhaps unwittingly honest when he wrote in the summer of 1862 that "God has forced even upon the mildest the conviction that slavery is the sin of all sins, and the curse of all curses."[129] Such a view was confirmed several months later when Kurtz finally admitted in the pages of the *Lutheran Observer* that "slavery is a great evil." However, in making this claim, he offered no biblical justification for his change of viewpoint.[130] Most northern Lutherans' views on slavery, like those of many other white Protestants, were shaped primarily by the pressures of war rather than by theological reasoning.[131]

As was the case in other areas, on the issue of slavery the Old Lutherans associated with the Missouri Synod were an important exception. Though they also were influenced by the exigencies of the Civil War, these conservative immigrants, more than any other Lutherans, attempted to wrestle with the question of slavery's treatment in the Bible. Before the war, Missouri Synod publications had been ambivalent about the subject. What scarce commentary they had offered actually resembled their theological rivals at the *Lutheran Observer,* claiming that the institution of slavery was not in and of itself sinful but condemning abuses against the enslaved themselves. Mostly they avoided the issue. For example, C. F. W. Walther, Old Lutheranism's foremost leader, published nothing on the subject in the 1840s or 1850s. Yet by the midpoint of the Civil War, Walther and other Old Lutherans were marshaling a defense of American slavery as robust as that of some southern apologists.

The first major Old Lutheran argument for slavery's biblical permissibility came not from the German Americans of the Missouri Synod but from their partners in the Norwegian Synod. By and large, Scandinavian immigrants were antislavery. T. N. Hasselquist, a prominent pastor in the Augustana Synod and the editor of the Swedish-language *Hemlandet,* declared in 1861 that the war was "God's plan to blot out slavery."[132] Similarly, the *Emigranten,* the leading paper among Norwegian Americans, decried the institution as "an absolute enemy of our republican institutions."[133] These realities help to explain the outcry when several clergy of the Norwegian Synod introduced a resolution at the church body's convention during the summer of 1861 that stated, "According to God's Word, it is not in and by itself sin to own slaves." The pastors' statement provoked a counter-resolution, backed by many laypeople, which argued, "Slavery considered as an institution can only exist by definite law, and since the laws on which it is based are in direct conflict with God's Word and Christian love, it is sin."[134] The terms of the debate had been set: A largely lay contingent argued that slavery was inherently sinful, while a mostly clerical faction contended that it was not fundamentally sinful to hold slaves.

These disagreements led to a protracted conflict. Taking up the cause of the Norwegian Synod's antislavery party was C. L. Clausen, a former editor of the *Emigranten* who was now serving as a pastor in Iowa. Clausen had initially signed the pastors' resolution but later became convinced that the clergy was "'pull[ing] the wool over the eyes' of the laity." After examining "the various Scripture passages," he concluded that slavery "must be sinful" and began to advocate against his fellow pastors.[135] The proslavery party was led by H. A. Preus, the Norwegian Synod's president. Preus worked to quell the opposition from Clausen and the synod's laity by appealing to the theological faculty of the University of Christiania. After a two-year delay, the faculty replied that slavery, as currently practiced in the United States, was sinful. Unsatisfied, the Norwegian Synod pastors wrote back to the faculty in an attempt to refute their position. After the professors replied by curtly referring to their original statement, the incensed American clergymen wrote a final rebuttal to their counterparts in Norway. For Preus and his fellow pastors, the stakes of the debate could not be higher. Antislavery agitation, he argued in 1864, "is merely a single paragraph in the present-day anti-Christian program" and "one step toward ultimate and absolute carnal emancipation, when government shall be overthrown and man shall rule in God's stead."[136] Among the Norwegian Synod, the disputes over the slavery question would persist even after the Civil War concluded (see chapter 5).

The views of Preus and other Norwegian Synod pastors mirrored those being developed by their colleagues in the Missouri Synod. Public conflict among the Missourians over the Bible and slavery began in 1862 when Friedrich Craemer (1812–1891), Walther's colleague at the seminary in St. Louis, wrote a short article for the synod's theological journal, *Lehre und Wehre*.[137] In it, Craemer reprinted portions of an essay on the "slavery question" by Ernst Hengstenberg, a leading conservative churchman in Germany. Even though the Old Lutherans of the Missouri Synod did not consider Hengstenberg to be a true Lutheran, due to his affiliation with the Prussian Union church, Craemer claimed that on the issue of slavery, the German pastor possessed "more light and sound judgment than hundreds of so-called Lutheran theologians." In his essay, Hengstenberg appealed to both Scripture and various church fathers to argue that the "testimony of the whole Christian church throughout the ages" stands opposed to the "agitation against slavery." Significantly, the Prussian minister also grounded his argument in the "curse of Canaan" (sometimes referred to as the "curse of Ham"), which many European and American theologians had interpreted to mean that God had cursed Africans with a status of inferiority.[138] By recommending Hengstenberg's article, Craemer was endorsing not merely slavery in the abstract but also the race-based slavery practiced in the American South.

Responding to this Old Lutheran defense of American slavery was Gustavus Seyffarth (1796–1885). A former professor of archaeology at the University of Leipzig and an adherent of "strict Lutheranism," Seyffarth had joined the faculty of the Missouri Synod's seminary in St. Louis in 1856.[139] Three years later he left his professorship in order to accept a position at the Astor Library in New York. However, the available evidence suggests that his departure had nothing to do with disagreements with other faculty members over the issue of slavery.[140] Because of this, Walther expressed complete surprise when he received a letter from Seyffarth, condemning Craemer's "antichristian article" and threatening to write a public reproof.[141]

Several months later Seyffarth made good on his threat and published a two-part article in the New York–based *Lutherische Herold*. His central—and most original—contention was that because African slaves had come to the New World as a result of "man-stealing," the entire American institution rested on a "deadly sin." Even those not directly involved in kidnapping were guilty, Seyffarth argued, because "whoever knowingly appropriates stolen property" becomes a participant in theft.[142] In addition, he rebutted appeals to the curse of Canaan and demonstrated how southern slaveholders' treatment of the enslaved differed from the prescriptions outlined in the Bible.[143] Seyffarth published two more articles on slavery in 1863, including in Krauth and Passavant's *Lutheran and Missionary*.[144] The crux of his argument was that the Old Lutherans of the Missouri Synod ignored the historical context in which American slavery originated and the actual realities of the institution as practiced in the United States.

Seyffarth's articles prompted rejoinders from leaders in the Missouri Synod. Walther devoted the foreword to the 1863 volume of *Lehre und Wehre* to defending slavery's biblical sanction. While he previously had expressed private opinions on the subject and had taken passing swipes at abolitionists in his periodicals, this was the first full statement of his views on the subject. In his article, Walther cited numerous church fathers and the "unambiguous words" of Scripture but did nothing to rebut Seyffarth's argument about the specific evil of slavery as practiced in America. Instead, he chose to lambast abolitionism as a "child of unbelief" and "brother of modern socialism, Jacobinism, and communism."[145]

An even lengthier exposition came from Wilhelm Sihler of Fort Wayne, Indiana. In a four-part essay in the *Lutheraner,* subsequently published as a tract, Sihler went through various "irrefutably clear" biblical verses to show that participation in the institution of slavery was not sinful—and avoided those passages, such as those mentioning "man-stealing," that might counteract his arguments.[146] Like his colleague in St. Louis, Sihler condemned "fanatical abolitionists" and "professional politicians" for distorting the Christian gospel and the true meaning of freedom.[147] Yet Sihler went even further than Walther by explicitly defending the race-based slavery practiced in the American South. Along with the curse of Canaan, he cited the colony of Liberia as evidence that Africans were unfit for civilization "on their own and without connection to the white race."[148] For Sihler, both slavery in the abstract and the peculiar institution in the United States were sanctioned by God.

Old Lutherans' full-throated apology for slavery prompts the question of why Midwestern immigrants, who had no economic interest in its perpetuation, came to defend the institution with nearly the same vigor as southern slaveholders. The answer is twofold. First, along with some conservative Episcopalians and many Roman Catholics, Old Lutherans saw the abolition of slavery as representing the broader collapse of societal order and the elevation of a false conception of liberty.[149] As Walther wrote, "The abolitionist dreamers of our modern world" falsely claim that "the gospel demands civil equality" and "contains a revolutionary element which overturns the external orders in the world."[150] Second and even more fundamentally, Old Lutherans defended slavery because, in one of the most telling signs of their Americanization, they believed it was clearly taught in the Bible. Seyffarth's challenge to examine a moral problem within its historical context had gone unheeded. Instead, Walther and Sihler believed that the "plain meaning" of Scripture was easily apprehended and could be applied directly to their contemporary setting. In reality, they were oblivious to how political concerns and racial prejudice informed their interpretation. Though they were far apart from other Protestants in the United States on a host of theological matters, Old Lutherans shared with them all the hallmarks of the distinctively American hermeneutic of "common sense" reasoning.[151]

★ ★ ★

Lutherans in the Confederacy, with some rare exceptions, were also convinced of slavery's biblical sanction.[152] The *Southern Lutheran,* edited by John Bachman and other South Carolina ministers, worked under the assumption that the institution was not only biblically permissible but also a positive good. Though the paper never mounted the same extended defense of slavery that Bachman had made in the antebellum era, it unsparingly condemned abolitionism and took for granted that "liberty" meant the freedom to claim ownership of other human beings.[153] In the spring of 1863, the paper endorsed and reprinted the *Address to Christians Throughout the World,* a publication signed by more than one hundred prominent southern ministers, including David Bittle, a Lutheran from Virginia. The tract demonstrated the intimate connection between Confederate nationalism and slavery, announcing that the "separation of the Southern States is universally recognized by our people as final" while simultaneously declaring the enslavement of Africans to be "Providential" and "Scriptural."[154] For Bachman, Bittle, and others, advocacy for southern independence was inseparably linked to their support for the region's peculiar institution.

On May 20, 1863, more than two years after the Civil War commenced and after several delays, southern Lutherans met in Concord, North Carolina, to officially organize the General Synod of the Evangelical Lutheran Church in the Confederate States of America. The twenty delegates represented five synods: Georgia, North Carolina, South Carolina, Virginia, and Western Virginia.[155] (Not present were the members of the Tennessee Synod, which refused to join for theological reasons, and the Texas Synod, a church body primarily made up of German immigrants who tended to support the Union and which remained connected to the northern General Synod.)[156] Following an opening sermon by Bittle, the representatives moved to the matter at hand. After indicting northern Lutherans for believing "it to be the duty of the government to prosecute this war even to our subjugation," the convention's participants declared, "We renounce them as brethren."

Over the course of the weeklong meeting, the delegates drafted a constitution, designated the *Southern Lutheran* as their church body's official paper, and elected John Bachman to be their first president. Bachman's election was fitting. Having prayed over the convention that began the process of sundering the American nation, he now presided over a new federation of synods that had divided the Lutheran church. In his first presidential address, Bachman declared "this withdrawal to be a final act" with "no provision for any renewal in the future of the intimate relations which have existed between the Northern and Southern sections of the Church in the past."[157]

Despite being the first major reversal to American Lutheranism's growing unity, the organization of a separate southern church body did little to curb the predictions of many northern Lutherans about their church's future prospects. In part this was due to the small size of the Lutheran church in the South. The synods that joined the Confederate federation numbered only about twenty thousand communicants, or a little over 10 percent of the General Synod's membership.[158] Additionally, some Lutherans in the North predicted that the sectional division would bolster their church's reputation among mainstream American Protestants. As Krauth wrote in the *Lutheran and Missionary,* the secession of the southern synods left the General Synod only a "little injured," but it threw "into relief the almost universal loyalty of our Lutheran people."[159] At the start of the Civil War's third year, Lutherans in the General Synod, flush with patriotism, still believed that a glorious destiny of increasing unity, numerical growth, and cultural prestige was awaiting their church.

The high-water mark of that patriotism came in the wake of the Battle of Gettysburg, in the late summer and fall of 1863. That the war's pivotal battle had taken place in the town that housed their church's preeminent educational institutions filled General Synod Lutherans with a poignant sense of pride. One correspondent to the *Lutheran and Missionary* lamented the devastation caused to the college and seminary, which were the "very heart of the church," but praised them for "sending their life blood into every section of the union."[160] The *Lutheran Observer* commended the people of Gettysburg for showing "great liberality and the most self-sacrificing generosity in their kindness to the wounded," including the use of the two Lutheran campuses as makeshift hospitals, and declared that "the hand of God was strikingly manifest in giving us the victory."[161]

Lutherans also participated in shaping the battle's memory. At the dedication of Gettysburg National Cemetery on November 19, 1863, Henry Lewis Baugher (1804–1868), the president of Pennsylvania College, gave the benediction. Almost three years after Bachman had sanctified the cause of southern secession, another Lutheran minister now blessed the war's most famous speech. In a prayer as short as Abraham Lincoln's address, Baugher asked the "King of kings and Lord of lords" to "bless this consecrated ground" and implored that "this great nation be delivered from treason and rebellion."[162] The outpouring of patriotism by General Synod Lutherans following the events at Gettysburg signified their aspirations to become members of the nation's Protestant establishment. It also reflected the broader embrace of American exceptionalism among Lutherans throughout the United States.

Yet the intra-Lutheran disputes over slavery, political preaching, and the meaning of the Union were preparing the ground for a much larger upheaval. Three years after the break between the northern and southern synods, the Lutheran church in the United States would undergo an even great schism, as competing theological factions split the General Synod in two. Though their disagreements were officially over issues relating to the church's historical confessions and the boundaries of ecclesiastical unity, the Civil War—particularly different interpretations of its origins and meaning—would frame and shape these doctrinal battles.

FOUR

★ ★ ★ ★ ★ ★ ★

The Lutheran Civil War, 1863–1866

IN JULY 1865, Charles Porterfield Krauth announced an important change. In the past, he and his fellow members of the confessional movement had endorsed the General Synod's position that Lutherans could differ on the "nonfundamental" doctrines in the Augsburg Confession. But now, following four years of civil war and theological conflict, Krauth admitted to his readers, "Time and experience have modified our earlier views." In order to ensure "the true unity of the Church," he had become convinced that every Lutheran must confess, "without reservation or ambiguity," that "the doctrinal articles of the Augsburg Confession are all articles of faith, and all articles of faith are fundamental."[1]

This was a stunning transformation. Krauth and others had founded the *Lutheran and Missionary* in October 1861 to promote a Lutheranism "moderate in its tone" and "free from the spirit of false exclusiveness."[2] While they hoped to bring about theological reform, they also had pledged to "sustain the General Synod in all its efforts to unite and strengthen our beloved Church."[3] However, the paper now in 1865 argued that unless the controversy over confessional adherence and church unity was settled, the Lutheran church in the United States "never can have peace."[4] One year later, the General Synod would fracture and intra-Lutheran unity, which had been steadily building since the 1830s, would be inalterably reversed.

In addition to being the defining event of nineteenth-century American Lutheranism, the breakup of the General Synod was the fourth-largest denominational schism of the Civil War era and the only major church division to occur in the aftermath of the war.[5] As such, it serves as an important contrast with the antebellum ruptures among Presbyterians, Methodists, and Baptists. Unlike these other denominational upheavals, the General Synod schism in 1866 was not sectional in character. (As detailed in chapter 3, southern Lutherans had already formed their own separate federation in 1863.) Instead, the split that occurred just after the Civil War was between rival schools of northern Lutherans who held to competing views on their church's historic confessions and the basis of denominational unity. Due to the lack of regional divisions between the opposing parties and the definitively theological character of their disagreements, most scholars who have examined the fracture of the General Synod have assumed that the larger issues consuming the American nation were peripheral or inconsequential.[6]

In fact, they were central and decisive. Throughout the war and its immediate aftermath, the factions of the General Synod—increasingly designated "Old School" and "New School"—developed differing interpretations of the Civil War and applied those interpretations to the conflict facing their church. According to Krauth and other Old School Lutherans, the war was a contest over constitutional principle, with the North seeking to defend the American republic against southern traitors. Consequently, they came to see the struggle to sustain the U.S. Constitution as analogous to the battle to uphold the Augsburg Confession. Krauth himself noted the overlap of the theological and political realms just after the war concluded: "In Church and State the last years have wrought changes, deep and thorough, in every thinking man, and on no point more than this, that compromise of principle, however specious, is immoral."[7] New School Lutherans, by contrast, believed that the war resulted from an unwillingness of both North and South to compromise. The Confederacy was wrong not because of its ideology but because its leaders had chosen disunion over sectional harmony. Like their Old School rivals, they saw an inextricable connection between the upheavals in the American nation and the trials facing the Lutheran church. "The most enlightened congregations," wrote one contributor to the New School–affiliated *Lutheran Observer,* "consider any secession, either ecclesiastical or political, as a sin."[8]

The General Synod schism then was not the result of strictly doctrinal debates. Rather, competing understandings of the Civil War inflamed, framed, and drove the theological quarrels that resulted in Lutheran disunion.

OLD SCHOOL VERSUS NEW SCHOOL

During the first two years of the Civil War, Lutherans in the General Synod had reopened debates about the theological questions that had been tentatively resolved in the late 1850s: the extent to which Lutherans should adhere to the church's historic confessions, particularly the Augsburg Confession of 1530, and the basis on which Lutheran churches should unite with one another and cooperate with other denominations. These doctrinal disputes had two effects. First, they solidified a partnership between Moderate Lutherans and the confessional movement. Second, they set the pattern for interweaving theological quarrels with arguments about the war. By 1863, the General Synod was divided into two distinct parties, each with competing views on the nature of Lutheranism and the meaning of the Union.

The realignment in the General Synod was driven by changes within the Pennsylvania Synod. Even before the Civil War began, leaders of this Moderate Lutheran church body, such as W. J. Mann, were beginning to make common cause with Charles Porterfield Krauth, William Passavant, and other leaders of the confessional movement.[9] This alliance was confirmed with the formation of the *Lutheran and Missionary*. Shortly after its publication in October 1861, the *Lutheran Observer* stated that the appearance of this new Philadelphia-based paper signaled "the existence of two parties in the church."[10] Less than a year later, the Pennsylvania Synod formally recommended the *Lutheran and Missionary* to its members.[11] The emergence of two distinct factions within the General Synod, each represented by a different church paper, had officially come to pass.

Assigning labels to these two competing parties is a difficult task, not only because both groups went by a variety of names but also because they often rejected each other's designations. Those associated with the *Lutheran Observer* most commonly called themselves "American Lutherans." But the party connected to the *Lutheran and Missionary* refused to concede that term to their opponents, arguing that their own form of Lutheranism was not any less American.[12] The *Lutheran Observer* indiscriminately called their adversaries "symbolists," "high-churchmen," "hyper-Lutherans," and even "Old Lutherans." But once again, the

Lutheran and Missionary did not accept those names as representative of their viewpoint. The party affiliated with this paper preferred to be known as "true Lutherans" or simply "Lutherans," but their adversaries at the *Lutheran Observer* wanted the same thing.[13]

Ultimately, the most accurate terms for each group are quite familiar to scholars of religion in the nineteenth-century United States: New School and Old School. While not precisely equivalent to the divisions in American Presbyterianism, the theological divisions between the two parties within the General Synod bore a noticeable resemblance, as even the Lutherans involved in the controversies recognized.[14] Though the participants used other names more frequently, those were the only labels that each party came to accept as accurately characterizing both their own position and that of their opponents.[15] Moreover, the terms "New School" and "Old School" best reflect the realignment of the various factions within the General Synod during the late 1850s and early 1860s.

The theology of New School Lutherans during the Civil War was essentially the same as that of antebellum New Lutheranism. Those associated with the *Lutheran Observer* persisted in their support of revivalism, temperance, and other facets of American evangelicalism and continued to believe that the historic confessions of the Lutheran church contained "anti-Scriptural" errors.[16] In particular, they regarded the Augsburg Confession's doctrines of baptismal regeneration and the real presence of Christ in the Lord's Supper as "antiquated superstitions" inherited from Roman Catholicism—or in the more colloquial phrasing of one correspondent, these teachings were "all moonshine."[17] Yet following the negative reaction to the *Definite Platform,* which the *Lutheran Observer* originally had promoted, the paper had distanced itself from the idea that all Lutherans in the United States needed to adopt their views. Chastened by the negative reaction to the proposed American Recension of the Augsburg Confession, New School Lutherans committed themselves to the "basis of the General Synod," which allowed "freedom of thought" in "non-essentials."[18] When Kurtz asserted in February 1862 that he and the paper he had edited for nearly thirty years were standing "in statu quo, or where we always stood," he was mostly correct.[19]

Old School Lutherans were critical of various aspects of this New School Lutheran program, but their chief disagreement was over the doctrines of their church's confessions. Though "neither in lip nor in heart opposed to revivals of religion," those associated with the *Lutheran and Missionary* were wary of some practices associated with the Anglo-evangelical style.[20] Old School Lutherans also were more inclined to emphasize the importance of liturgy and vestments, though they still mirrored their New School opponents in their rejection of "formalism" in worship.[21] Rather than being about revivals and rituals, the principal quarrel between the two schools centered on doctrine. In stark opposition to their New School counterparts, leaders of the Old School believed every teaching in the Augsburg Confession, including its teachings on the sacraments, to be true. This confessional theology was not derived from European romanticism or traditionalism, as some historians have asserted.[22] Instead, as Krauth contended in a seminal article for the *Lutheran and Missionary,* the confession simply presents "the truth set forth in the Word."[23] Like other American Protestants, Old School Lutherans believed that the doctrine they professed was plainly taught in the Bible.[24]

These theological disagreements were inflamed by the differing reactions of the leading Lutheran church papers to the outbreak of the Civil War. During the conflict's first months (as shown in chapter 3), the papers associated with the Old School, the *Missionary* and the *Lutheran and Home Journal,* supported the Union war effort with greater rapidity and vigor than did the *Lutheran Observer,* the chief paper of New School Lutheranism. Throughout the summer of 1861, Old School editors mingled their condemnation of their New School counterparts' reluctance to embrace the war effort with an increased criticism of their theology. After the *Lutheran Observer* officially expressed its support for the Union after several weeks of trying to remain neutral, William Passavant insinuated that the paper's "conversion to loyalty" might be, like the type of revivalism it promoted, "too sudden to be permanent."[25] A few weeks later, Charles Porterfield Krauth and Joseph Seiss brought up the New School leaders' past support for the American Recension of the Augsburg Confession. Though they admitted that "agitation" over the *Definite Platform* "has long since passed away," Krauth and Seiss felt the need to remind their readers of this former act of churchly "treason" in light of the current war "to maintain every article intact in our national Constitution."[26]

The *Lutheran Observer* also conflated disputes about the war with arguments over doctrine. In March 1861, the editors of the New School paper wrote that the different views of "our symbolical brethren" should "be peacefully tolerated" and "not be made a cause or occasion of strife."[27] Just a few months later, however, the paper was calling "high-churchism or symbolism" a "distorted, intolerant and bigoted thing." Benjamin Kurtz expressed his fear that just as political extremism had divided the nation, "our good Lutheran Zion is in danger of being riven into fragments," and he blamed this situation on "the mischievous working of symbolism."[28] The *Lutheran Observer* saw the Old School papers' theology as stemming from the same "spirit of intolerance" that was gripping "those who are actively participating in the war that afflicts our country."[29]

Yet even though tensions between the two parties were strained during the war's first year, both schools insisted that ecclesiastical schism would be just was as wrong as national division. The *Lutheran Observer* condemned those who advocated the "loose and dangerous principles" of "the right of secession [and] the right of revolution" as injurious to peace and harmony in both "church and state."[30] Similarly, the *Lutheran and Missionary* believed that the doctrinal disagreements within the General Synod did not warrant division. Krauth condemned any talk of disunion as "Ecclesiastical Secessionism," seeing it as stemming from the same attitude of "licentious liberty" that had caused the southern states to rebel against the federal government.[31] Though holding to differing theological and political positions, each school shared a desire to avoid disunion in the church.

The uneasy alliance between the Old School and New School was on display at the General Synod's 1862 convention in Lancaster, Pennsylvania. The most contentious issue was the debate over the resolutions on the state of the country. These pronouncements (as discussed in chapter 3) were more in accord with the political views of Krauth and Passavant's *Lutheran and Missionary* than Kurtz's *Lutheran Observer*. Yet in the realm of theology, the General Synod took a decided turn in the direction of the New School. In the run-up to the meeting, Krauth had expressed increasing dismay with the General Synod's "somewhat vague" mode of confessional subscription. Fearing that the wide diversity of interpretations of the Augsburg Confession could "rend the church into fragments," he urged the church body to "set forth a statement of facts" about what the confession actually teaches.[32] However, the convention took no action on the questions posed by Krauth, a de facto reaffirmation of the General Synod's doctrinal basis. And in an even greater endorsement of the New School, the delegates replaced the outgoing president, Old School clergyman Charles W. Schaeffer (1813–1896), with none other than Benjamin Kurtz.[33]

The results of the meeting produced mixed reactions from both schools. Kurtz was honored by his election and encouraged by his church's prospects. Though he disagreed with some aspects of the war resolutions, particularly their harsh condemnation of slavery, he was pleased that no attempt had been made "to assail the doctrinal basis of the General Synod, and bring it into perfect conformity to every item of the Augsburg Confession." In contrast with the nation divided by war, "the harmony and unity of our beloved Zion" had been preserved.[34] Krauth, meanwhile, despite the seeming setbacks at the meeting, remained hopeful about the General Synod's future direction. Though he believed the convention's resolution against slavery could "have gone much further," he still praised its wisdom and moderation.[35] In the realm of ecclesiastical politics, Krauth spun the election of Kurtz as merely a "tribute of kindliness to an old and influential minister." However, he insisted that by choosing his New School rival as president, the General Synod's delegates "did not mean to endorse his theology."[36] Though disappointed at the lack of action on the Augsburg Confession, Krauth believed that "changes are sure to come." He declared, "Our Synods are now in a lax confederation in the General Synod; but the day is coming, when Confederations will everywhere be superseded by Union."[37]

As they continued to issue their confident pronouncements, the leaders of the New School and the Old School increasingly applied the political lessons they were learning in the national conflict to the disputes in the General Synod. The war, in the view of Kurtz and the *Lutheran Observer,* would have been averted if not for the "the machinations of ambitious and unscrupulous men." Discord in the church, they believed, stemmed from the same fractious spirit.[38] For the editors of the *Lutheran and Missionary,* however, the struggle to preserve the Union demonstrated the importance of standing on constitutional principle, not just in the nation but also in the church. "The Augsburgh Confession is at once the banner and the Constitution of our great Lutheran Confederation throughout the world," Krauth argued. "Like the flag and Constitution of our land, when it falls our distinctive life falls with it."[39] The Old School editor also claimed that the New School's advocacy of wide doctrinal leeway ultimately led to "sectarian" divisions. This "sectarianism in the Church," he wrote, "is, in its principles and tendencies, what secessionism is in the State."[40] While the New School paper repeatedly urged Lutherans to "keep the unity of the spirit in the bond of peace,"

Krauth and the Old School saw a different lesson in the Civil War: "We must first be pure, then peaceable."[41]

The tensions between Old School and New School Lutherans briefly cooled when control of the *Lutheran Observer* once again changed hands in the fall of 1862. The new editors and proprietors were three clergymen led by Frederick W. Conrad (1816–1898).[42] Conrad, a pastor in the Pennsylvania Synod, had led the effort to recommend the *Lutheran and Missionary* to the members of that church body.[43] He was also a vocal proponent of the Union cause.[44] Because of these factors, Krauth believed that the *Lutheran Observer* was being imbued with a "new spirit."[45] The Old School editor expressed delight that Kurtz, the paper's "old monarch," had been dethroned, and he claimed that these "friends will strive to make the Observer what the *Lutheran and Missionary* confessedly is."[46] Conrad and his fellow editors, however, declined Krauth's offer of companionship. They thanked him for "his warm expressions of friendliness and approval" but made it clear that their positions "are substantially those which the Observer has always held."[47]

At first, Krauth did not take the hint, even insisting that Conrad's paper only "supposes itself to differ from us."[48] However, after the two editors engaged in a series of heated debates about worship—and when it became clear that Kurtz would continue to write frequent guest columns—Krauth finally accepted that his reappraisal of the *Lutheran Observer* had been incorrect. In his paper's final issue in 1862, he once again took up the imagery of war to frame the confessional conflict facing American Lutheranism: "As the glory or shame of a nation is read upon its battle fields . . . , so may the glory or shame of a Church be determined when we know what it fought for and what it fought against."[49]

Though Krauth's martial language at the end of 1862 seemed to signal a looming period of controversy between Old School and New School Lutherans, the first two-thirds of the new year actually saw a period of relative peace between the two parties and their respective papers. During the spring and summer of 1863, the rising swell of patriotism among Lutherans in the General Synod, culminating after the Battle of Gettysburg (see chapter 3), submerged their theological squabbles. Though the *Lutheran Observer* and the *Lutheran and Missionary* continued to present their distinctive versions of Lutheranism, the simmering theological conflict was placed on the back burner as Old School and New School Lutherans rallied around the Union cause.

"AN IRREPRESSIBLE CONFLICT"

However, beginning in the fall of 1863, the peace between the Old School and the New School gave way to renewed hostility, as a series of ecclesiastical and theological controversies reignited the firestorm of words between the factions. One correspondent to the *Lutheran Observer*, writing in the spring of 1864, captured the mood. Just as "every discerning mind must see now" that "the present war, was inevitable," he worried that the American Lutheran church was also facing an "irrepressible conflict between truth and error."[50] Previously, Lutherans in the General Synod had been able to reconcile the tensions between the competing theological parties. But during the final two years of the Civil War their disagreements became increasingly intractable.

Two episodes in particular helped to intensify the disputes between the two schools. The first involved the always provocative Benjamin Kurtz. As the guest preacher at the September 1863 meeting of the West Pennsylvania Synod, Kurtz delivered a sermon that contrasted "true experimental religion" with "ritual religion." Its hearers immediately recognized this as an attack on the Old School.[51] One eyewitness, a young pastor in the synod, wrote to the *Lutheran and Missionary*, chiding Kurtz for voicing "the old tirade against the peculiarities of our beloved Zion." According to the correspondent, the "condemnation" of the sermon was "universal," so much so that the minister assisting Kurtz left the church service during the middle of his sermon. The writer saw the reaction as a sign that "an indignant and outraged church is rising up" against the New School.[52]

Unsurprisingly, Kurtz had a different perspective on the affair. In the *Lutheran Observer*, he responded that "the sermon was adapted to the occasion." He contrasted the negative reaction of "the high-church or symbolic" ministers with the positive response "of my lay-hearers" and condemned the "defamatory remarks" of the "inflated young man" who "was still peeking in his nurse's arms, while I was standing in the very front of the conflict . . . for sound doctrine and revived religion in the Lutheran church." Kurtz then lambasted Krauth for "giv[ing] publicity to such vile abuse" in the pages of the *Lutheran and Missionary*. He believed that his sermon and the reaction to it had exposed a wide rift between the "American Lutheran and revival Synod[s]" and the "high-toned Old-Lutheran, real presence" ones.[53]

The second controversy stemmed from an article by Levi Sternberg (1814–

1886) in the *Lutheran Observer.* Sternberg, a professor at Hartwick Seminary, the small General Synod seminary in upstate New York, argued that the doctrine of the real presence of Christ in the Lord's Supper was "superstitious," "Romish," "unsustained by Scripture," and "the one dark spot" in the "Lutheran system of theology."[54] Sternberg was expressing boilerplate New School Lutheranism, but Krauth believed that the wording of the article had crossed a clearly defined line of propriety. In the *Lutheran and Missionary,* he called the article a "flagrant assault" on "one of the acknowledged doctrines of the Lutheran church" and "treacherously un-Lutheran." Though the editors of the *Lutheran Observer* claimed that they did not necessarily "endorse its positions" but merely thought that the article deserved to be "spread before the people," Krauth had no patience for such fine distinctions. Likening his opponents to the rebels who were seeking to abolish the nation's Constitution, he wrote, "Ministers of the church who are spending their energies in overthrowing its doctrines are traitors."[55]

In the minds of many New School Lutherans, Krauth's words had broken one of the chief terms of the compromise in the General Synod: not to "un-Lutheranize" one's opponents. According to the editors of the *Lutheran Observer,* the "bitter invective" of the *Lutheran and Missionary,* particularly the accusation of ecclesiastical treason, had exposed the Old School paper's "true spirit and character" as one of fractiousness and, worse, that of a "Romanist." In response to the denunciations issued by Krauth in the *Lutheran and Missionary,* the New School paper pronounced its own anathema: "Now we say in the face of the whole church, that a paper calling itself Lutheran ... [but] denying the right of an appeal from the Confessions to the Bible ... is '*a disgrace to the name it bears.*'"[56]

At issue were differing interpretations of freedom of conscience and the right of private judgment. For the New School editors of the *Lutheran Observer,* "the assumption that we are bound irrevocably by the decisions of the church in past generations" was "both un-Lutheran and un-Protestant." An essential feature of the movement begun by Martin Luther, in their view, was "the right of every generation of the church to re-examine and re-judge, in the light of the Bible, the decisions of former generations."[57] Kurtz, in his controversial sermon, put the matter more boldly, claiming that the Lutheran church fathers "knew full well, that in aftertimes men would arise ... with increased light and additional and improved facilities for interpreting God's Word."[58] Krauth, however, insisted that the Old School position did not deny the right "to test every doctrine by the word of God." "We not only concede the right," he declared, "but maintain it to be a sacred duty of every man."[59] Rather, the editor was arguing, once a person has "reached the conclusion that our church confesses any doctrine in conflict with that Word," he is "bound to leave her communion." Just as Luther ceased to regard himself as "a Papist and Romanist" once he became convinced that the Catholic Church was in error, those who believed certain doctrines of the Augsburg Confession to be false should stop calling themselves Lutherans and switch denominations.[60]

Both schools considered their understanding of freedom of conscience to be not only the "purest and truest type" of Lutheranism but also the one that best reflected American values. According to the editors of the *Lutheran Observer*, the views of the "hyper-Lutherans" or "extreme symbolists" are "not adapted to the active, progressive character of the American people."[61] By contrast, the New School's "American Lutheranism," they asserted, produced "true piety" instead of doctrinal rigidity and was responsible for the institutional growth of the Lutheran church in the United States.[62] For Krauth, such claims were "clap-trap." The Lutheranism promoted by the New School, he wrote, was neither American nor Lutheran: "Its fundamental principles" were those of European "errorists," such as Ulrich Zwingli and "the Anabaptist fanatics," and its leaders were "spending their energies in misrepresenting the doctrines of our Church." Instead, the Old School editor argued, "the life and hope of our Church in this country are with the men who are firm in the faith of the Church."[63]

The General Synod had sought to chart a middle course between those two opposing understandings of the place of private judgment in the Lutheran church. Its *Formula for the Government and Discipline of the Evangelical Lutheran Church* asked ministers to confess that "the fundamental doctrines of the Augsburg Confession were substantially correct." On the one hand, by grounding membership in the church's oldest confession, this formula conceded that Lutheran identity was not infinitely elastic. On the other hand, by only stipulating an adherence to that confession's fundamental doctrines, it allowed leeway on those teachings that provoked widespread disagreement. As the May 1864 convention of the General Synod approached, this "doctrinal basis" emerged as the key issue facing the convention.

In the immediate run-up to the meeting, however, both the New School and Old School toned down their condemnatory rhetoric and even expressed cautious optimism. The *Lutheran Observer,* convinced that the General Synod "can afford to tolerate some degree of diversity on non-essentials," asked the convention's delegates to keep "the bond of union on its old, liberal basis." Desiring "love, and harmony, and brotherly courtesy," the New School paper resolved to cooperate with "the brethren with whom we have held some controversial discussion."[64] Unsurprisingly, the *Lutheran and Missionary* had a different goal for the meeting. Though Krauth did not propose an amendment to the General Synod's doctrinal basis, he expressed his desire that the delegates rebuke "the public assailing of the doctrines taught in the Augsburg Confession" by the likes of Kurtz, Sternberg, and the *Lutheran Observer.* At the same time, he urged "pure love for each other and just forbearance where there are conscientious differences."[65] Each school, confident that the upcoming convention would ratify its understanding of confessionalism, believed that they could be somewhat magnanimous to their soon-to-be defeated opponents.

The meeting, held in York, Pennsylvania, in May 1864, saw a decisive victory for the New School. On its first day, the delegates elected Samuel Sprecher to succeed Kurtz as the federation's president. Sprecher was the president of Wittenberg College in Ohio and an ardent proponent of the "American Lutheranism" advocated by his mentor, Samuel Schmucker. With Schmucker and Kurtz, he had coauthored the *Definite Platform,* and he belonged to one of the few synods that had adopted the proposed American Recension of the Augsburg Confession.[66] For the second convention in a row, representatives from the General Synod had elected an outspoken New School Lutheran as their leader.

A further defeat for the Old School occurred on the fourth day of the meeting, when the majority of the General Synod's delegates, after a fierce debate, voted to admit the Franckean Synod into the federation. As the sole abolitionist Lutheran synod in the United States, the Franckeans had long been a lightning rod for controversy. However, the opposition of Old School leaders to their admission did not stem from disagreements over slavery.[67] During the first years of the Civil War (as documented in chapter 3), it was the Old School Lutherans who had been vocally opposed to slavery and the New School that had avoided discussion of this contentious topic. But after three years of war, most General Synod Lutherans had come to see slavery as immoral and opposing it as a Christian duty. Sprecher, the federation's new president, reflected this change. In 1862, he had expressed discomfort with the General Synod's antislavery resolution,

believing it to be too "political." Now, two years later, in the convention's opening sermon, he condemned slavery in explicit terms and exhorted his hearers to
bring their faith to bear "upon our public councils."[68] Shortly after Sprecher's
sermon, the delegates unanimously adopted another set of resolutions on the
state of the country. Though they were careful not to mention emancipation as
an objective of the Union war effort, they denounced the "persistent efforts . . . to
prove from the Holy Scriptures the divine institution of American Slavery" and
asserted that this "system of human oppression . . . exists only by violence, under
the cover of iniquitous laws."[69] Though most General Synod Lutherans did not
share the fervent abolitionism of the Franckeans, by 1864 they no longer viewed
their activism antagonistically.

Rather than being fought over slavery, the conflict surrounding the admission of the Franckean Synod centered on theology. The church body had never
formally subscribed to the Augsburg Confession, leading members of the Old
School to question the validity of its application. However, after the Franckean
delegates pledged themselves to the "doctrinal position of the General Synod,"
their admission was accepted by a vote of 97 to 40, "with the understanding" that
their church body would officially affirm at its next meeting that the Augsburg
Confession is "a substantially correct exhibition of the fundamental doctrines
of the Word of God." In response, twenty-three Old School delegates, including
William Passavant and Beale Schmucker, signed a formal protest declaring that
the Franckean Synod could not be classified as "a regularly constituted Lutheran
Synod" and that, by granting its admission, "the General Synod has violated its
Constitution." The delegation from the federation's largest church body, the
Pennsylvania Synod, went even further. Led by Charles W. Schaeffer, they announced that along with signing the protest, they would not participate in the
rest of the meeting.[70]

In an attempt to quell the upheaval, the convention's delegates passed a series
of resolutions meant to appease members of the Old School. First, they proposed
an amendment to the General Synod's constitution, which stated that newly
applying synods must accept "the Augsburg Confession, as a correct exhibition
of the fundamental doctrines of the Divine Word." Second, they passed a resolution affirming that "the Augsburg Confession, properly interpreted, is in perfect consistence . . . with the Holy Scriptures."[71] These slight concessions to the
Old School delegates, however, hardly signaled a turn by the General Synod in a

more theologically conservative direction, as some historians have argued.[72] By qualifying the terms of confessional adherence with phrases such as "fundamental doctrines" and "properly interpreted," the convention's representatives were reaffirming the position that New School Lutherans had long been promoting. A final resolution, which reprimanded those stirring up controversy over "nonessential features in the Augsburg Confession," underscored this continuity.[73] Coupled with the election of Sprecher and the withdrawal of the Pennsylvania Synod, the 1864 convention at York was a significant reversal for the cause of the Old School.

The divergent reactions to the meeting illustrate this. The *Lutheran Observer* praised the convention as an unqualified victory: "The doctrinal basis and policy for which the Observer has contended in the face of the most determined opposition, was accepted by the General Synod with a unanimity and quiet enthusiasm that filled every heart with joy." The delegates, the paper proclaimed, had rejected "hyper-orthodoxy on the one hand" and "radicalism on the other" and had shown themselves to be "true Lutherans."[74] The *Lutheran and Missionary*, meanwhile, was uncharacteristically reserved. In the first weeks after the meeting, Krauth, who had not been a delegate to the convention but had attended its proceedings for a few days, limited himself to simply reporting on what had occurred.[75] This cautious silence was due to the Old School editor waiting to see which actions the Pennsylvania Synod would take. At its annual meeting, which occurred less than three weeks after the General Synod's convention, the members of the church body voiced their approval of their delegates' actions. Even more controversially, they voted to begin the process of establishing a new theological seminary in Philadelphia.[76]

Although the Pennsylvania Synod's resolution said nothing about the new institution being a rival to the Gettysburg seminary, the responses to it indicated otherwise. The *Lutheran Observer* queried why another theological school was needed in Pennsylvania. If its focus would be training pastors to evangelize German immigrants, the New School paper believed it would be "an undertaking worthy of praise." But if it was to have a "different theological standpoint from the General Synod's seminary [in Gettysburg]," they worried that it would disrupt the "harmony" of the church.[77] The *Lutheran and Missionary*, by contrast, expressed unqualified support for the new venture. Breaking his brief silence on the controversies in the General Synod, Krauth argued that establishing this seminary was a necessary measure against those who "make the title Lutheran a cloak for war to the death upon Lutheranism itself."[78] Though not himself a member of the Pennsylvania Synod, he offered the church body some advice: Rather than limiting itself to serving German churches, the new institution should "make itself thoroughly at home in the national and religious life of America."[79]

In July 1864, the Pennsylvania Synod held a special meeting. After minimal debate, the delegates officially approved the establishment of the Philadelphia seminary. They also elected its first three professors: Charles F. Schaeffer, who would resign from the Gettysburg seminary as the Pennsylvania Synod canceled its endowed professorship there; W. J. Mann, who would serve as the new institution's "German professor"; and in an appointment that left no doubts about the Philadelphia seminary's theological direction, Krauth.[80]

Just weeks after being chosen as a professor, the Old School editor began to use his paper to define the institution's aim and purpose. "The new Theological Seminary is imperatively needed," he argued, "for the sake of PURE DOCTRINE." Krauth claimed provocatively that at the moment, "we might more safely send our sons to Princeton or Andover to imbue them with just ideas of Lutheran doctrine" than entrust them to the seminaries of the General Synod.[81] By contrast, the "doctrinal character" of the Philadelphia school would be "unreservedly and unalterably based on the Confessions of the Evangelical Lutheran Church," as contained in the *Book of Concord*.[82] Along with promoting a "homogenousness [*sic*] of doctrinal influence," the editor of the *Lutheran and Missionary* believed that the Philadelphia seminary would supersede the Gettysburg seminary as the theological institution for "the whole Church" and bring about "true unity."[83]

The *Lutheran Observer* was outraged. Following the appointment of Krauth and the appearance of his blustering articles, the New School paper's editors dropped their ambivalence about the new seminary and condemned it unreservedly. They criticized the Old School editor's "unjust and groundless aspersions" against the Gettysburg seminary and accused his theological institution of advocating "the position of the extreme Old-Lutherans."[84] Their most serious charge was that those behind the Pennsylvania Synod's seminary were guilty of "revolution." In the months following the General Synod convention, the *Lutheran Observer* had begun to describe its position not only as liberal but also as conservative. By "liberal," the paper's editors meant toleration in "non-essentials"; by "conservative," they meant not strict confessionalism but the desire to "preserve from ruin, innovation, injury, or radical change . . . the General Synod in its present state."[85] Once again, the Civil War informed their views: Just as the Confederate cause was a "revolution" against a good and just government, the "whole movement" for the new seminary was "virtually one of secession."[86]

Another accusation hurled against Krauth was that he was acting out like a "spoilt child" because he was bitter about not being appointed to the General Synod's seminary at Gettysburg.[87] The charge had some truth to it. In the spring of 1864, Samuel Schmucker had announced his intention to retire from the seminary he had helped to establish nearly forty years before. One minister recalled how the Old School Lutherans who sat on the seminary's board were hoping to appoint Krauth as his successor and to reform the school "little by little."[88] The scheme never materialized. Shortly after the formation of the Pennsylvania Synod's seminary in Philadelphia, Schmucker officially tendered his resignation and the board selected James Allen Brown (1821–1882) to take his place.[89]

Brown was a seemingly odd choice. In 1857, he had engaged in a war of words with Schmucker, accusing the Gettysburg professor of teaching a "New Theology."[90] (Given future developments, it is ironic that one of the principal defenders of Schmucker against the these charges had been Krauth.)[91] Because this squabble occurred in the wake of the controversy over the *Definite Platform,* some historians have assumed that Brown was a proponent of "conservative Lutheranism."[92] In actuality, he was criticizing issues only incidentally related to the debates over the Augsburg Confession, and he insisted throughout the controversy that he had "no leanings toward symbolism."[93] In the years following his quarrel with Schmucker, Brown published no articles or tracts. For a brief period, he taught at Newberry College in South Carolina. After the state seceded, however, Brown resigned his professorship in order to serve as a Union chaplain, first for the Eighty-Seventh Regiment of Pennsylvania and then for the Army hospital in York, Pennsylvania.

By 1864, the two theologians apparently had resolved their past disputes. When Brown accepted the Gettysburg professorship, he wrote that "the liberal yet truly evangelical basis of the Seminary meets my cordial approbation" and that he was "one in spirit, aim, and effort" with the school's mission.[94] Shortly after his successor's arrival, Schmucker wrote to his son that Brown "is very friendly & cordial & preaches excellent discourses."[95] The *Lutheran Observer* similarly commended the new professor for "his broad views of christian truth, untrammeled by the narrow prejudices of sectarian littleness."[96] A few months into Brown's tenure, Krauth tried to walk back his harsh comments about the Gettysburg seminary by claiming that the selection of this new professor, whom "we presume, never changed his opinion as to Dr. S[chmucker]'s unsoundness," signaled a shift in the school's theological direction.[97] Brown replied that his appointment was neither meant "to pass sentence upon Dr. S., nor to bestow a tardy recognition of . . . dissertations written 'long ago.'" Such ideas, he wrote in an open letter to Krauth, are "the product of your very fruitful imagination." Instead, Brown believed that he was selected because, unlike the editor of the *Lutheran and Missionary*, "I am for unity and peace" and "utterly detest the spirit of secession, whether in state or in church."[98] Thus, rather than a turn in a more confessional direction, as some have argued, Brown's appointment represented continuity with the seminary's New School vision.[99]

The two parties of the General Synod now not only controlled their own church papers but also supported rival educational institutions. The editors of the *Lutheran Observer* recognized the gravity of the situation. In October 1864, they offered a summary of the differences between the two factions within the General Synod: The "majority," represented by their paper and the Gettysburg seminary, accepted the federation's "old, liberal, evangelical basis" and "reject[ed] the Romish doctrine of the real presence"; the "minority," represented by the *Lutheran and Missionary* and the new seminary in Philadelphia, were "tending to radicalism" by "advocat[ing] an unqualified subscription of all the Symbolical books." Though the New School editors still believed that the "church in this country" would remain "one body," they foresaw "a coming theological crisis."[100]

AMERICAN PEACE, LUTHERAN SCHISM

The following month, Abraham Lincoln defeated George McClellan to win his second term as president of the United States, setting in motion a chain of events that led to the end of slavery and victory for the Union. On January 31, 1865, the House of Representatives passed the Thirteenth Amendment to the Constitution, which, once ratified by the states, permanently abolished the institution of chattel slavery in the United States. In less than ten weeks, Ulysses S. Grant defeated Robert E. Lee at the Battle of Appomattox Court House, bringing an end to major military operations. After nearly four years of bloodshed, the American Civil War was over.

However, on April 14, Lincoln was killed by John Wilkes Booth in Ford's Theater. The assassination caused an outpouring of grief in numerous editorials, speeches, and discourses. Among the most prominent Americans to eulogize the president were northern Protestant ministers, who tried to make sense of the tragedy for their readers and hearers. That Lincoln had been killed on Good Friday added extra solemnity to the event, and also provided material for allegorizing the president's death.[101] Lutheran clergymen also participated in this public ritual of civil religion. The editors of the *Lutheran Observer* and the *Lutheran and Missionary* proclaimed the president to be a Christlike figure, having "died for the nation" as a "substitute" and "sacrifice" and having endured "suffering and death for righteousness' sake."[102] Additionally, several ministers, including Krauth, published sermons on the president's death, extolling the president as an exemplar of Christian patriotism and biblical morality.[103]

The president's assassination also prompted Lutherans of both schools to reflect on the war's purpose and the nation's future. Though the passage of the Thirteenth Amendment had received little notice from either the *Lutheran Observer* or the *Lutheran and Missionary,* following Lincoln's murder the editors of both papers began to trumpet emancipation as inextricably linked to the Union cause.[104] According to Frederick Conrad of the *Lutheran Observer,* the Civil War's "baptism of blood," which culminated in the president's death, had "re-consecrated the nation to the maintenance of universal freedom during all coming time."[105] Krauth wrote that the impending death of the "Demon-Spirit of Slavery" would be the "one grand consolation" for the mourning nation.[106] The papers of both schools also agreed that the United States should honor the fallen president by pursuing a policy of reconciliation. For the *Lutheran and Missionary,* showing "compassion" and "tenderness" to the defeated South would be the nation's "second victory."[107] Similarly, the *Lutheran Observer* implored that "judgment may be tempered with mercy, and that persistent prodigals may be kindly received back to their forsaken father's house."[108] In the wake of Lincoln's assassination, both Lutheran papers considered the causes of union, emancipation, and reconciliation to be inseparably connected components of the nation's sacred purpose.

Despite their mutual outpouring of patriotism and shared hope for the reunited nation, however, the confessional dispute between the two papers continued unabated. The differing doctrinal bases of the seminaries of Gettysburg and Philadelphia remained at the center of their disagreement. One contributor to the *Lutheran and Missionary* identified the crux of the matter: "Gettysburg thinks that the doctrinal character of the church is something fluctuating; Philadelphia thinks that it is not."[109] In contrast, the *Lutheran Observer* argued, "If no change can ever be made in the doctrinal principles of the Lutheran church, as embodied in the Symbolical Books, then it must be because their authors . . . were infallible in all their conceptions and expressions of divine truth."[110] For the Old School, all of the doctrines set forth in the Augsburg Confession were an unchangeable expression of "true Lutheranism"; for the New School, the confession's "nonfundamental" teachings were subject to reexamination.

By the summer of 1865, Krauth had had enough of this "aimless battle." Following a series of polemical articles by Conrad, the Old School editor threw down an italicized gauntlet to the New School: "*The doctrinal articles of the Augsburg Confession are all articles of faith, and all articles of faith are fundamental. Our church can never have a genuine internal harmony, except in the confession, without reservation or ambiguity of these articles, one and all.*" In addition to this ultimatum, Krauth made the following announcement: "We hereby retract before God and his Church, formally . . . every thing we have written or said in conflict with this our present conviction."[111]

Once again, the Civil War helped to bring the terms of this theological conflict into sharper relief. Despite the seeming consensus in the wake of Lincoln's death, New School and Old School Lutherans still retained subtle but important differences in their interpretations of the conflict's meaning and lessons. The New School editors of the *Lutheran Observer* continued to blame a stubborn unwillingness to compromise for causing the war. In their view, the restoration of "peace" and "reconciling parties long estranged" should be the preeminent postbellum goals. Likewise, in the conflict within the church, their chief critique of their Old School opponents was that these "symbolical hair-splitters" were disturbing "the peace of Zion."[112] Those associated with the *Lutheran and Missionary*, by contrast, continued to argue that the war was primarily a struggle over constitutional principle. For Krauth, the Union victory represented the triumph of the "great principles of humanity, right, freedom, and law." Consequently, he proposed a harsher policy of reconstruction: Though the "deluded masses" of the South should be shown leniency, the "voluntary leaders in this unparalleled crime" deserved "the award of strict justice."[113] Likewise, in the battles facing the

Lutheran church, he and other Old School Lutherans believed that principle must precede peace.

Despite these important differences, both the New School and Old School agreed that Lutherans in the North should reunite with their counterparts in the South. According to the *Lutheran Observer*, "there should be no difficulty" for "our Southern churches" to "return to their former relations." The editors noted that the "Lutheranism in those States was emphatically of the General Synod type," in that it promoted revivals and did not bind "the conscience to all the minutiae of the confessional writings." Now with the war concluded, they believed that "the only cause of irritation has been removed."[114] The *Lutheran and Missionary* was slightly more circumspect. In a series of editorials, Krauth argued that based on the General Synod's constitution, there was no reason to exclude the southern synods. If they requested to reunite with their northern brethren, "that petition will be sufficient evidence that God has given a better mind and heart touching these [political] questions."[115] The reconciliationist perspective promoted by the two papers was not universally held by its readers. Correspondents to the *Lutheran Observer* and the *Lutheran and Missionary* voiced their disagreements, arguing that southern Lutherans should present sufficient proof of "having repented of their treason" and "renouncing and forsaking their evil ways."[116] Yet the editors of both papers continued to insist that reuniting the Lutheran church along sectional lines was the duty of the General Synod.[117]

Nonetheless, this northern Lutheran push for reconciliation was rendered irrelevant when southern Lutherans, led by John Bachman, rejected any prospect of ecclesiastical reunion. In a lengthy letter published in the *Lutheran and Missionary,* Bachman recounted the "wholesale system of plunder, insult, blasphemy and brutality" carried out by William Tecumseh Sherman's army in his home state of South Carolina. Embittered by the "heathen barbarity" of Union troops and outraged by "vindictive, malicious, and unmitigated falsehoods" coming from the northern Lutheran press, Bachman declared that among Lutherans in the South, "there is not one in a thousand who would for a moment entertain the slightest idea of a reunion with the Northern General Synod."[118] In the increasingly intractable quarrels between the Old School and New School, sectional reconciliation was one of the few areas of agreement. With Bachman's declaration, that potential rallying point of harmony had been forestalled.

Instead, the disputes over Lutheran confessional identity in the General

Synod continued unabated, though neither faction was willing to call for an end to denominational unity. The Pennsylvania Synod had withdrawn from the 1864 convention in protest and had founded their own seminary, but at its 1865 meeting the synod resolved to remain within the General Synod and to send delegates to its next convention.[119] Krauth had declared the leaders of the New School and the seminary in Gettysburg to be doctrinally unsound, but his church paper remained devoted to "the interests of the General Synod."[120] Similarly, though many associated with the *Lutheran Observer* believed the Pennsylvania Synod and its seminary in Philadelphia to be "de facto out of the General Synod" and the New School and Old School to be "practically . . . *two denominations,*" they considered the prospect of actual disunity to be unthinkable.[121] As one lay correspondent to the *Lutheran Observer* wrote, "The old symbolists now denounce us as un-Lutheran, and we in turn denounce them as formalists and romanistic, but this is only a family quarrel. . . . The Lutheran church is not divided, and is not going to be divided."[122] During the first year after the Civil War's conclusion, these unresolved contradictions continued to build up.

The dam finally burst at the General Synod's May 1866 convention in Fort Wayne, Indiana. On the meeting's first day, Samuel Sprecher, the federation's New School president, preached a sermon which claimed that "the church can be held in subjection to no decision of the church, in the past," a clear swipe at the Old School.[123] Immediately thereafter, during the meeting's roll call, Sprecher refused to seat the delegation from the Pennsylvania Synod until "the General Synod can receive a report of an act restoring her practical relations." The convention sustained this decision by a vote of 77 to 24 and appointed a special committee, headed by Samuel Schmucker, to study the Pennsylvania Synod's status. In the meantime, J. A. Brown, the new professor at the Gettysburg seminary, was elected as the General Synod's next president.

After two full days of debate, the convention delegates resolved to receive the representatives of the Pennsylvania Synod, but for these Old School Lutherans, this action was not good enough. Led by Krauth and Joseph Seiss—both of whom had joined the Pennsylvania Synod in 1865—the church body's delegation stated that they would not accept their seats unless the convention declared Sprecher's actions to be unconstitutional. After this counterproposal was rejected by a nearly two-thirds majority, the synod's representatives left the meeting in protest, while other Old School delegates, led by William Passavant, signed a petition against the convention's actions.[124] Three weeks later, the Pennsylvania Synod formally announced its withdrawal from the General Synod and resolved to begin making plans to form a new "general ecclesiastical body representing the true faith."[125]

Quite aware that this action resembled the one taken by southern states in the formation of the Confederacy, the Old School Lutherans of the *Lutheran and Missionary* went to great lengths to demonstrate that their actions were consistent with the antisecession constitutionalism they had espoused during the Civil War. As one of the paper's correspondents contended, it was the leaders of the New School who had violated the "noble design" of the General Synod's founders and thus were guilty of a "revolutionary rupture" and "semi rebellion."[126] Krauth also tried to characterize those remaining in the General Synod as the ones guilty of disunion. "The General Synod, by the action of a majority," he declared, "has violated its Constitution in such a manner as to destroy itself." The Pennsylvania Synod's only choice, he argued, was to pursue "the ultimate union of all the genuine Lutheran elements in this country, for the securing of the ends which the General Synod had failed to secure."[127]

For New School Lutherans, this argument was self-evidently absurd. According to the *Lutheran Observer*, "it is a principle universally admitted, (always excepting rebels,) that the right and the power of those who are loyal to a Union, to exercise the functions of Government, cannot be impaired or destroyed by the withdrawal of the disloyal."[128] The parallels between the General Synod's conflict and the American Civil War were readily apparent to the New School paper. One writer, citing the Pennsylvania Synod's complaint about how the new president of the General Synod was elected, wrote that just as "the attempt to destroy the Federal Union was based on the plea of the Unconstitutional election of a sectional president," so also "the disunionists in our church have only seized on this pretext to carry out a previous design."[129] Conrad, the paper's editor, accused Krauth and the *Lutheran and Missionary* of operating from the same principles as "Jefferson Davis and his secession associates." He asserted, "What South Carolina has done in the sphere of the State ... the Pennsylvania Synod has done in the sphere of the Church."[130] In the view of New School Lutherans, their predictions about the Old School's "hyper-Lutheranism" had been vindicated: Just as southern rebels' unwillingness to compromise had plunged the nation into war, "symbolists" had stubbornly insisted on "non-essential" doctrines and broken the bonds of Lutheran union.[131]

REACTIONS AND REALIGNMENTS

Closely following the controversy in the General Synod were those American Lutherans who stood outside of it. In the antebellum era, various Moderate and Old Lutheran church bodies, mostly located in the Midwest and primarily led by immigrants, had refused to join this federation, largely on account of its lack of confessional rigor. However, as the controversy between the Old School and New School ramped up during the latter stages of the Civil War, spokesmen for these Midwestern synods—several of which were themselves moving in a more conservative theological direction—reacted positively to the arguments of the *Lutheran and Missionary* and the protests of the Pennsylvania Synod. At the same time, the native-born leaders of the Old School were coming to view these largely immigrant church bodies as potential allies. The result was a convergence between the Moderate and Old Lutherans of the Midwest and the Old School Lutherans of the East.

This realignment was seen in the actions of the Augustana Synod. In 1860, immigrants, chiefly from Sweden but also from Norway, had broken away from the General Synod–affiliated Northern Illinois Synod and formed their own more confessional church body. Over the course of the Civil War, leaders from this Scandinavian synod reengaged with English-speaking Lutherans, this time with the spokesmen for the Old School. In 1864, the church body passed "a unanimous resolution" that "warmly commended" the *Lutheran and Missionary* "to their members who read English."[132] After the events at the General Synod's 1866 convention in Fort Wayne, delegates for the Augustana Synod "unanimously" supported the Pennsylvania Synod's proposal to establish "a new General Synod, on a true Confessional basis." As Eric Norelius, one of the synod's leaders, wrote to the editors of the *Lutheran and Missionary,* "the object of the Convention" met the approval of "all true Lutherans."[133]

Even more dramatic changes were occurring in the Wisconsin Synod. Though this Moderate Lutheran church body was not officially a member of the General Synod, it maintained close ties with the federation's institutions, particularly those of the Pennsylvania Synod. Over the course of the Civil War, however, this Midwestern synod made a sharp "turn to the right," largely thanks to two young leaders, Johannes Bading (1824–1908) and Adolph Hoenecke (1835–1908).[134] Bading was elected president of the church body in 1860 and remained in that position for nearly thirty years. In 1864, he declared that "our Wisconsin Synod adheres not only to the Augsburg Confession but to *all* the confessional writings of the Lutheran church."[135] Two years later, the church body's paper pledged to support "like-minded people within the General Synod in the fight for truth."[136] Following the events of the 1866 convention in Fort Wayne, leaders in the Wisconsin Synod applauded the decision of the "old Pennsylvania mother synod" and praised their plans to form "a new General Synod of the Old School."[137]

Also moving in a more conservative direction was the Ohio Synod, for which the label Moderate Lutheran was becoming increasingly anachronistic. Key to this development was the leadership of Matthias Loy (1828–1915). The son of nominally Catholic immigrants from Germany, Loy became Lutheran under the influence of Samuel Sprecher. During the 1850s, however, the young pastor came to reject his mentor's New Lutheranism and played a leading role in preventing the Ohio Synod from joining the General Synod. In 1860, Loy was elected president of this church body, and four years later he was appointed editor of its paper, the *Lutheran Standard*. He would serve in both positions until the 1890s and be, in the words of his biographer, the Ohio Synod's "guiding spirit."[138] In this leadership role, Loy began to move his church body toward the position of Old Lutheranism. He expressed favorable opinions of the "brethren" of the Missouri Synod and penned writings that mirrored their views, especially on "unionism," or interchurch cooperation.[139] The leaders of the Missouri Synod, however, continued to view the Ohio Synod as insufficiently orthodox, particularly because of "the unionistic practice in many of their congregations."[140] Nevertheless, despite their inability to unite in church fellowship, the Ohio and Missouri synods were growing closer theologically.

The leaders of these two church bodies were also converging in their assessment of the Old School Lutherans associated with the Pennsylvania Synod and the *Lutheran and Missionary*. In the late 1840s and the 1850s, the Ohio and Pennsylvania synods, once close partners, had drifted apart, chiefly over the issue of membership in the General Synod. But during the final years of the Civil War, as Old School Lutherans battled against the New School, leaders of the

Ohio Synod began issuing calls to rekindle their former friendship. In 1864, Loy praised the founding of the Philadelphia seminary as "the dawning of brighter days in the East."[141] After the Pennsylvania Synod officially withdrew from the General Synod in 1866, he was even more elated, calling the schism an occasion at which "all true Lutherans must rejoice."[142]

An even more striking reevaluation was occurring in the Missouri Synod. As the disputes within the General Synod became increasingly heated, leaders of this Old Lutheran church body began to offer tempered praise for the "true and resolute witness" of the *Lutheran and Missionary* and other Old School Lutherans.[143] Though the Pennsylvania Synod was "not yet truly Lutheran," asserted one article in 1864, "we recognize ourselves fraternally connected to individual members of the synod."[144] When the General Synod schism occurred two years later, C. F. W. Walther, the Missouri Synod's leading theologian, was effusive: "Scarcely any event within the bounds of Lutheranism has ever afforded us greater joy."[145]

Spokesmen for the Old School began to reciprocate the kind words coming from the various Lutherans in the Midwest. The *Lutheran and Missionary* was especially complimentary of the "zealous" Scandinavians of the Augustana Synod, not only for preaching the "pure faith" but also for sending "their noblest sons by scores and hundreds to struggle and die for their country and for liberty."[146] The Old School paper also heaped praise on the "worthy brethren" of the Wisconsin Synod, celebrating their newly founded college as "connected with the great mission of our beloved Zion in this country" and applauding their growing conservatism as contributing to "the onward progress of Christ and the truth."[147] Those connected with the *Lutheran and Missionary* were even softening in their views toward the Ohio Synod, despite this church body's past disagreements with the Pennsylvania Synod. The paper praised Loy's "thorough fidelity to the Word of God and to the faith of the church" and approvingly reprinted several articles from the paper he edited.[148] In the months following the 1866 General Synod convention, the *Lutheran and Missionary* happily reported about these Midwestern church bodies' interest in partnering with the Pennsylvania Synod.[149] Old School leaders were increasingly looking beyond the General Synod for potential allies.

The most stunning shift was Old School Lutherans' reevaluation of the Missouri Synod. In his inaugural editorial for the *Lutheran and Missionary*, Charles Porterfield Krauth had emphatically declared, "We are not 'Old Lutherans.'" This "fossil Lutheranism," he warned, was unable to "discriminate between essence and accident, between truth and her clothes."[150] Yet as the debates within the General Synod became increasingly heated, the Old School editor began to revise these former judgments. In 1864, he wrote that "the spirit of the Synod of Missouri," in comparison with the New School, "is a model of candor and moderation."[151] One year later, Krauth praised the "brethren of the Missouri Synod" for producing "pure theological and religious literature" and recanted his previous condemnation of the label associated with the church body: "It was a reproach to be called an *old* Lutheran; it is no longer so; it is an honor."[152]

This growing convergence was vividly demonstrated at the General Synod's 1866 convention in Fort Wayne. On Sunday, several leaders of the Old School, including Krauth, attended worship at the Missouri Synod congregation pastored by Wilhelm Sihler. In a significant gesture of unity, Sihler invited them to partake of the Lord's Supper. As the *Lutheran and Missionary* reported, "Three of the Pennsylvania Synod's delegation rose, and went forward.... They thanked God not only for the privilege of coming to His table, but also for this pleasant meeting of brethren, striving for the same faith."[153] The divisions within the General Synod were producing realignments unthinkable just a few years before.

What made this convergence all the more remarkable was that it was occurring despite significantly different approaches to the issues of the Civil War. Of the various factions among northern Lutherans, the Old School leaders associated with the *Lutheran and Missionary* had been among the most vocally committed to the Union cause and the most ardently opposed to slavery. Though the Scandinavian Lutherans of the Augustana Synod shared similar sentiments, the leaders of other Midwest-based synods refused to make definitive pronouncements in favor of the Union. Under Loy, the Ohio Synod's *Lutheran Standard* continued its policy of urging neutrality on "political issues" and criticizing those who preach on "subjects of temporal concern."[154] In a similar way, Wisconsin Synod presidents declined to take a stand on "political problems"; instead, they portrayed the war as a "judgment of God" to be endured.[155]

The Old Lutherans of the Missouri Synod were even more conservative. Walther, in particular, adopted an especially reactionary view of the war in its final year. In an August 1864 sermon, he blamed its protraction on "wicked people" who "want the war to continue in order to attain certain party goals ... [and] to make themselves rich" and condemned "the inexpressible spiritual corruption which has descended upon . . . our deeply fallen American nation."[156] Additionally, the periodicals he edited continued to defend the biblical sanction of slavery, even after the passage of the Thirteenth Amendment.[157] However, in their increasing praise for the theology of these conservative Lutherans in the Midwest, the Old School writers for the *Lutheran and Missionary* made no mention of their political differences.

The reason for this was twofold. First, those associated with the *Lutheran and Missionary* were themselves beginning to change. Already during the conflict's final years, the paper's coverage of the war was decreasing and their commentary was becoming more circumspect. Though still committed supporters of the Union and in no way proslavery, some Old School leaders were beginning to question the extent to which the church should engage in political matters and to shrink back from the more radical implications of democratic equality. Because of this, during the first years of Reconstruction (as chapter 5 will show), Krauth and others would adopt an increasingly conservative posture toward the issues facing the American nation.

But there was another reason for Old School Lutherans' seeming disregard of the political differences between themselves and the leaders of these Midwest-based synods. For Krauth and those associated with the *Lutheran and Missionary,* the war had demonstrated the central importance of standing on constitutional principle. So also in the church, they believed, doctrinal purity must take precedence above all other concerns. Ironically then, it was the lessons they had learned from their commitment to the Union cause that were leading Old School Lutherans to seek theological partnerships with those who did not share that same commitment.

★ ★ ★

In August 1866, three months after the tumultuous General Synod meeting in Fort Wayne, the Pennsylvania Synod issued a "fraternal address" that officially invited all American Lutherans to meet together and form a new "general organization" devoted to the "maintenance of unity in the true faith." The document, written by Charles Porterfield Krauth and other Old School leaders, once again framed the issues at stake in terms of the Civil War. The representatives of the New School, they argued, were engaged in "warfare with the Confession of our Church" and had violated the General Synod's constitution. Because of this, Krauth and his coauthors claimed that the federation had "ceased to be such a Body as that Constitution defines." Appealing to the "Providential guidance whose history is too recent and familiar to all to need repetition here," the leaders of the Pennsylvania Synod concluded that their only choice was to form a new "union of Lutheran Synods." Just as the North had fought to preserve the American nation and to uphold its constitution, Old School Lutherans believed that they were struggling to establish "true unity" and to defend the Augsburg Confession as the Lutheran church's "unchangeable confessional foundation."[158]

Unsurprisingly, New School Lutherans saw the justifications for this newly proposed Lutheran union as self-contradictory. As numerous articles in the *Lutheran Observer* pointed out, the behavior of the Pennsylvania Synod was a paradigmatic example of "secession" and exhibited "the spirit of discord and division in the Church and in the State."[159] The New School paper urged the leaders of other synods to reject the "revolutionary advice" of the Old School and to remain "loyal" to their church: "To become rebellious against the General Synod, would be to compromise their characters as Christian gentlemen and Lutherans."[160] Yet even if the "schismatics" should persuade others to follow them "into secession," the *Lutheran Observer* predicted that the General Synod would persist as "the largest and most vigorous organization in our Church" and that its New School vision would continue to represent American Lutheranism's "glorious future."[161]

Both predictions would prove to be false. At the beginning of the Civil War, the General Synod had encompassed almost two-thirds of the Lutheran church in the United States. Seven years after the war's conclusion—due to the withdrawal of Old School Lutherans, the continued separation of the southern synods, and the growth of immigrant-led church bodies—the federation represented less than a quarter of the nation's Lutherans. The years following the General Synod schism would also witness a sharp conservative turn in American Lutheranism. During the first years of Reconstruction, the confessionalism and separatism that New School leaders lamented would continue to make headway. However, in a stunning turn of events, it would not be Krauth and the *Lutheran and Missionary* that emerged as the leading voice of Lutheranism in the United States. That role would instead fall to C. F. W. Walther and the Missouri Synod.

FIVE

Conservative Reconstruction, 1866–1872

I N MAY 1869, Frederick Conrad, the New School editor of the *Lutheran Observer*, called attention to a word that "has been incorporated into our national nomenclature and [whose] significance is well-known." That word, wrote Conrad, is "RECONSTRUCTION." In the political realm, "it expresses the great work . . . of restoring the seceded States to their rightful place in the Union, healing the wounds and cementing the divisions caused by the war, and re-establishing, on the enduring foundations of truth and justice, the political fabric reared by our fathers."[1] However, Conrad also believed that the same word could be applied to the situation facing his church. Lutheranism in the United States, he wrote, "must be, to a considerable extent, *re-constructed*." The editor listed two requirements for this to occur: "It must prove itself the faithful guardian of Lutheran doctrine" and "it must . . . maintain unity in the faith." He concluded, "Thus only can it inaugurate a new era, accomplish its true mission, become a blessing to America, and a praise and glory throughout the world."[2]

Conrad was not alone in seeing the years following the Civil War as a cru-cial moment. Between 1866 and 1872, Lutherans of all geographic sections and theological schools debated the status of the southern states, the citizenship of freedpeople, and the future of the nation. At the same time, they sought to chart a new course for their church, to make a Lutheranism that was pure, unified, and truly American.

The aims of Lutherans during Reconstruction mirrored those of other white Protestants. Several scholars have demonstrated how, during the first years following the Civil War, many Christians prioritized the goals of reunion and reconciliation over the prerogatives of racial justice and equality. This played out in both the state and the church. In the political sphere, many northern evangelical leaders became "apostles of forgiveness," urging northern and southern whites to move past their sectional divisions and forge a new, more unified republic—at the expense of the rights of Black Americans. In the ecclesiastical realm, several Protestant denominations reunified. The Episcopal Church, which separated along sectional lines in 1861, quickly reconciled in 1865. In the northern states, Old School and New School Presbyterians, who had split in part over the issue of slavery in 1837, resolved their differences and reunited in 1869. Baptist and Methodist leaders also worked to repair their antebellum divisions. Though separate sectional organizations persisted, these and other northern and southern evangelicals did unite around a shared conception of the United States as a "Christian nation." As with white Americans more generally, many religious leaders sacrificed the promise of a more free and equal nation on the altar of the Union and white nationalism.[3]

Though most Lutherans espoused these goals of reunion and reconciliation, both in the state and in the church, the first several years after the Civil War actually resulted in the intensification of their theological debates and further fragmentation. In 1866, the Old School Lutherans who had withdrawn from the General Synod began the process of forming a rival organization, the General Council, which its leader Charles Porterfield Krauth believed would unite all American Lutherans in "the pure faith of our church."[4] Yet six years later, the General Council was eclipsed by another, even more conservative federation, the Synodical Conference. Headed by the Old Lutherans of the Missouri Synod, leaders of this new Lutheran union believed that their church's future lay in reestablishing what C. F. W. Walther called the "old, good, pure doctrine" in the United States.[5]

It is difficult to overstate the magnitude of this realignment. At the beginning of Reconstruction, Walther's Missouri Synod stood on the fringe of American Lutheranism, numbering just above 10 percent of the nation's Lutherans and possessing few allies. By 1872, this church body headed the largest organization of synods. Moreover, the Lutheran church as a whole, especially Krauth and the

General Council, was moving toward its theological position. Seven years after the Civil War's conclusion, the predominant ethos of Lutheranism in the United States had been altered in ways that would have made it unrecognizable to many antebellum observers.

POLITICAL CONTEXTS

American Lutheranism's conservative transformation took place in the context of Radical Reconstruction. During these years, Lutheran political commentary reflected the views of those who, to use the formulation of historian Mark Wahlgren Summers, prioritized "security" over "justice."[6] Such an emphasis was a logical outcome of the primacy placed on the preservation of the Union throughout the Civil War. The more dramatic change among Lutheran leaders was their growing reticence to comment on the issues facing the nation. In part, this quietist stance derived from a theological conviction about the dangers of mixing religion and politics, but it also stemmed from worries about re-inflaming national tensions, disgust with political corruption, and an apathy about the plight of Black Americans. As they would become in theology, from 1866 to 1872, Lutherans became much more conservative politically.

This shift was particularly acute among Old School Lutherans. Throughout the Civil War, those associated with the *Lutheran and Missionary* were much more willing to denounce rebellion and condemn slavery than their New School rivals at the *Lutheran Observer.* Yet during the early years of Reconstruction, they quickly embraced reconciliation. A frequent feature of Old School commentary was the elicitation of sympathy for the South. The *Lutheran and Missionary* published several letters telling tales of the region's "subjugation," "destitution," and "suffering," with the hopes that its readers would provide pecuniary support for "our brethren South."[7] Undergirding this reconciliationist viewpoint was the conviction that, as one correspondent wrote, "the causes which produced the alienation of feeling during the war, have ceased to exist."[8] With the Union restored and the constitution preserved, Lutherans should work to "wipe out existing animosities" and to "restore former fraternal relations."[9] Unsurprisingly, then, the Old School paper made almost no editorial comments on the struggle for justice and equality facing the 4 million recently emancipated African Americans.[10] Sympathy for the South meant sympathy for southern whites.

Coinciding with these calls for sectional reconciliation was the growing refusal of Old School Lutherans to engage in "political preaching." During the Civil War, the pages of the *Lutheran and Missionary* had been filled with coverage of the conflict, and its editors had defended the moral imperative of preachers to address the crucial issues of the day. Already in the early months of 1866, this situation began to change. The section "Our Country," a staple of each issue of the paper throughout the war, appeared only infrequently, and political commentary all but vanished.[11] Crucial to justifying this change of policy was a distinction between "patriotism" and "partisanship." In one editorial, Charles Porterfield Krauth wrote that it had not been "political preaching" to express "loyalty to the Constitution" and "love of the Union" or to denounce "treason." But now that "our country's awful struggle" is over, he argued, "ministers of Christ [should] be cautious," especially when "loyal citizens differ on political questions."[12]

Others, such as Joseph Seiss, took this quietist posture even further. In 1867, Krauth retired from his position as editor of the *Lutheran and Missionary* and the paper came under the editorship of a group of Philadelphia clergymen principally headed by Seiss.[13] The new editor revealed his political views in an open letter to a southern clergyman. Though he "had not the least sympathy with the doctrines of Southern secession" during the war, he wished to assure the "Southern people" that he was no "rabid politician." Seiss confessed, "I have so little respect for politicians in general, and so little confidence in the way political matters are conducted, that, for the last fifteen years, I have refused so much as to vote at political elections, holding that my citizenship is in heaven, and that I am only an ambassador in this corrupt earthly country, in whose squabbles I have no very important concern."[14] Other contributors to the paper also lamented what they saw as the growing prevalence of political "corruption," even as they decried "meddling in politics."[15] Over the course of the late 1860s and early 1870s, the Old School Lutherans associated with the *Lutheran and Missionary* were becoming increasingly apolitical, and in some cases, antipolitical.

One exception to this trend in the early years of Reconstruction was John G. Butler (1826–1909).[16] Butler, a pastor in Washington, DC, had prioritized the cause of emancipation throughout the Civil War. At the outset of Reconstruction he argued that Lutheran ministers should preach that "in the eye of the law and before Heaven, no man's interests are prejudiced by the color of his skin." Though Butler was personally New School in theology, he made these arguments in the pages of the Old School's *Lutheran and Missionary,* presumably because it was more antislavery than the *Lutheran Observer.*[17] Butler continued to promote the cause of racial equality throughout Reconstruction, declaring in sermons that "the revolution must yet go on" and resolving to preach "a Gospel of justice and equity and righteousness between man and man."[18] In 1869, he was appointed as chaplain of the U.S. House of Representatives, serving in that position for six years, and in 1871 he accepted a position as professor at Howard University, where he taught for two decades.

Yet over this same period the Old School Lutherans of the *Lutheran and Missionary* became disaffected with Butler's radicalism. As late as 1867 the paper still lauded the pastor for calling upon the nation to "reconstruct our Government upon the principles of eternal truth, justice, and right."[19] But two years later, the editors condemned Butler for "identify[ing] his political opinions with the message Christ has given him to preach" and "transmut[ing] his pulpit into a place for political harangue." They concluded their criticism with a scoffing statement representative of the Old School's increasing political conservatism: "Our genuine Lutheran communion . . . finds something higher in the world than Dr. Butler's 'Gospel of Justice, Equity, and Freedom.'"[20]

Owing to his rejection by the *Lutheran and Missionary*—and, of course, due to the schism in the General Synod—Butler began to publish exclusively in the *Lutheran Observer.* However, the New School paper's viewpoint on the political issues surrounding Reconstruction was closer to their Old School rivals' than to Butler's. A telling parenthetical observation in a November 1865 editorial encapsulated this conservatism: "This country had its great political issues . . . in 1861, (all of which have now been settled, excepting some of the details of reconstruction and some particulars of the status of the freedmen)."[21] With peace restored, the *Lutheran Observer* worked to promote the cause of sectional unity by drawing attention to the South's "prostrate condition," "extreme destitution," and "well known impoverishment," and by urging their fellow Lutherans to send aid and relief.[22] After the election of Ulysses S. Grant in 1868, the paper's chief editor, Frederick Conrad, implored "Republicans and Democrats, Northern men and Southern," to "forget past differences" and "meet in the sanctuaries of the most High, as brethren." Conrad believed that the new president would "heal the festering relics of the war" and restore "peace, plenty, and prosperity" to southern states.[23] Like the *Lutheran and Missionary,* the chief aim of Reconstruction in the view of the *Lutheran Observer* was reconciliation between northern and southern whites.

However, perhaps owing to the influence of Butler, the New School paper was more attentive than its Old School counterpart to the struggles of Black southerners—at least during the initial years of Reconstruction. In the late 1860s, interspersed with pleas to relieve the South's suffering were supplications to "elevate," "Christianize," and "educate" freedpeople.[24] Often these appeals were equivocal on the subject of equal rights, and blatantly paternalistic. As one correspondent wrote, "I don't care whether you give them the power to vote, or withhold it"; what mattered is that these "four millions of precious immortal souls" were raised up from "all the ignorance, degradation and feebleness that slavery had entailed upon them."[25] Yet by the early 1870s, even these tepid calls for racial uplift largely faded away.[26] Instead, the *Lutheran Observer* lamented the "masses of colored men" who "put one another into office with all their unfitness still clinging to them," and it even reverted to its antebellum position of endorsing voluntary colonization.[27] Even Butler came to avoid the issue of racial equality in the pages of the paper.[28] New School Lutherans exemplified the widespread "retreat from Reconstruction" among white northerners.[29]

A similar trajectory could be found in the paper's views on political preaching. During the first years of Reconstruction, the *Lutheran Observer*, under the leadership of Conrad, sought to differentiate itself from the increasingly apolitical *Lutheran and Missionary*. The editor argued that Christians "should make themselves felt in political circles" in order to "correct political evils and maintain the liberty and happiness of the people."[30] One way his paper pursued this objective was by continuing its support, already begun during the final months of the Civil War, of the "Christian Amendment," a proposal that attempted to add a recognition of "Almighty God" to the preamble of the U.S. Constitution.[31] Writers for the New School paper contended that "every Christian patriot" should endorse this idea, and they continued their support into the early 1870s.[32] During this same period, however, those associated with the *Lutheran Observer* became more and more disillusioned with this positive assessment of Christian political involvement. Along with his revulsion at the "general corruption of party politics in our country," Conrad was particularly aghast at the "persistent falsehood and personal slander" in the presidential election of 1872.[33] Though they were not as apolitical as the spokesmen of the Old School, by 1872 New School Lutherans were beginning to distance themselves from political commentary—save, of course, for their promotion of sectional unity.

Other groups of northern Lutherans expressed similar sentiments. Scandinavian Lutherans, many of whom were vocally antislavery before and during the Civil War, showed little interest in the plight of freedpeople during Reconstruction. According to Anders Bo Rasmussen, Swedish and Norwegian newspapers, many of which were Republican in political orientation, promoted "economic concerns . . . at the expense of racial equality." For most Scandinavian Americans, Rasmussen writes, "the work to ensure political and civil rights for freedmen was done" following the formal end of slavery.[34] Even the Franckean Synod, the lone abolitionist voice in antebellum American Lutheranism, moderated its social activism. Already in the summer of 1866, the church body adopted a resolution to "exhort the members of all our church to extirpate every root of bitterness" in order to become "a more united and happy nation."[35] Throughout the postbellum era, the synod issued no statements on the rights of freedpeople; instead, its leaders turned their focus toward temperance advocacy, "systematic benevolence," and mission work.[36] Along with many other white Americans in the Mid-Atlantic and Midwestern states, the vast majority of northern Lutherans viewed the primary objectives of Reconstruction as being reconciliation and reunion.

Lutherans in the South also shared the predominant ethos of their region. The *Lutheran Visitor,* the principal church paper among southern Lutherans during Reconstruction, was representative. Though appreciative of charitable gestures, the editors still believed that "the North sits in judgment upon us" and lays "all of the sin of the war . . . at our door."[37] A frequent criticism from the southern paper was that northern ministers, including Lutheran ones like John Butler, were guilty of "political preaching." If "the first Lutheran chaplain of the U.S. Congress" had his way, one correspondent grumbled, southern preachers would have to "favor equality of races, female suffrage, reconstruction upon his interpretation, 'moral ideas,' puritanism, and for aught I know, *miscegenation* included."[38] Yet despite their determination to avoid any discussion of politics in their paper's pages, the editors of the *Lutheran Visitor* occasionally broke from this policy. In the run-up to the 1872 presidential election, the paper lamented that "in the South we are ruled by a faction, over-taxed, [and] governed by incompetent and unprincipled demagogues" and asserted that "unless a change of men and measures is speedily effected, the South will not only be ruined, but become a wilderness."[39] Like other white southerners, Lutherans in the former Confederacy mostly rejected the reconciliatory advances coming from the North.

Of course, not all southern Lutherans were white. At the beginning of the Civil War, more than one thousand African Americans were members of Lutheran churches in the Confederate states. During Reconstruction, southern synods took two different approaches to retaining Black members. The South Carolina Synod tried to keep freedpeople under the auspices of white congregations; unsurprisingly, African American membership dwindled to nothing. The Tennessee and North Carolina synods, conversely, encouraged separate Black congregations and commissioned at least six African American preachers, yielding very modest results. When these Lutherans eventually formed their own church body, the Alpha Synod, in 1889, it encompassed five congregations and 180 members.[40] Meanwhile, Lutherans in the North mostly ignored the plight of Black Americans. During the first years of Reconstruction, whites from various Protestant denominations traveled to the South under the auspices of the American Missionary Association to provide education, humanitarian aid, and spiritual care to the formerly enslaved. However, no Lutherans participated in this venture or in similar ones.[41] Although they were not alone among white Christians in their prioritization of sectional reconciliation over racial justice, Lutherans were exceptional in their abject failure to reach out to freedpeople in the aftermath of the Civil War.

An even more conservative outlook on Reconstruction came from the Old Lutherans. Continuing a trajectory begun during the war, the periodicals of the Missouri Synod adopted an especially reactionary tone. Writers for the *Lutheraner* and *Lehre und Wehre* criticized preachers who involved themselves in politics as "worthless abusers of their office."[42] Yet the clergymen who edited these periodicals often did this themselves, railing against secular newspapers that they believed to be "satanic" and "antichristian" and criticizing politicians they deemed "unscrupulous."[43] Echoing this inconsistent position was the *Lutheran Standard* of the Ohio Synod, which under the leadership of Matthias Loy had been moving in the direction of Old Lutheranism during the final years of the war. Loy both complained about preachers who "seek to impose their opinions upon the people in the name of the Lord Jesus" and lamented that "Christian statesmen are scarce among us."[44] C. F. W. Walther, the leading Old Lutheran theologian, tried to rectify this seeming contradiction by arguing that when political leaders utter "blasphemy" or "misuse God's Word," then "we theologians cannot remain silent."[45] What Walther failed to acknowledge, however, was that this same principle was espoused by many of the "political preachers" he and his colleagues were lambasting. The difference, of course, was that Walther saw theological error in concepts such as "inalienable human rights" and "abolitionist, socialist zealotry."[46]

Nowhere was this reactionary posture among Old Lutherans more evident than in the continuing disputes over slavery. During the Civil War, figures such as Walther and Wilhelm Sihler of the Missouri Synod and H. A. Preus of the Norwegian Synod had adopted a position, formulated in response to the antislavery views within their ranks, that argued that the institution was sanctioned by the Bible (see chapter 3). Rather than letting the matter rest after slavery was abolished, however, the controversy picked up with renewed vigor during the late 1860s.

The most contentious debate occurred in the Norwegian Synod. At the church body's 1866 meeting in Madison, Wisconsin, slavery was among the chief topics of discussion. A faction led by Preus demanded that C. L. Clausen and other antislavery pastors recant their "blasphemous and ungodly" views.[47] Unable to resolve their disputes, both Preus and Clausen headed to Norway to plead their respective cases. In February 1867, each pastor met with Gisle Johnson, a leading conservative theologian at the University of Christiania.[48] Both believed that Johnson stood mostly on their side and returned to the United States more convinced of their positions than before. In 1868, the Norwegian Synod's pastoral council, led by Preus, drew up ten theses on slavery, reaffirming their belief that the "forced servitude mentioned in the New Testament" was "not in and by itself sinful" and that an enslaved person "has no right to demand the abolition of his servitude and procure his own freedom."[49] The debate over this proposal became so heated that proslavery pastors barred Clausen from participating in their celebration of the Lord's Supper.[50] At the Norwegian Synod's convention in Chicago later that year, the church body adopted Preus's ten theses on slavery. Clausen, along with several congregations, withdrew from the Norwegian Synod and joined the Scandinavian Augustana Synod, its less conservative rival.

Though the slavery issue never produced a similar level of strife in the Missouri Synod, Walther followed the events in the Norwegian Synod closely and corresponded with several of its pastors. In one such letter, Walther wrote that it was vital to hold the position that slavery "was not a sinful institution," because it counteracted what he saw as the modern tendency in the United States to raise political and social liberty above the clear teachings of Scripture. It was the divine mission of Lutherans, he argued, "to be a threshing machine for America." He warned, "We dare not shirk this responsibility. America, drunk with freedom, needs people such as we are, lest unwarned it should go to destruction."[51] Over the course of the nineteenth century the disputes over the slavery would fade, but the underlying skepticism about some of the nation's liberal, democratic principles would persist.[52] Though most Lutherans did not follow Preus and Walther, these Old Lutherans' unremitting insistence on the biblical permissibility of slavery was just the most extreme manifestation of the conservative trajectory in American Lutheran political thinking during Reconstruction.

Paralleling Lutherans' increasing political conservatism was their declining religious nationalism. During the Civil War, numerous thanksgiving discourses and fast-day sermons by Lutheran ministers had been printed in church papers and as stand-alone tracts. Over the course of Reconstruction, however, the number of such publications decreased substantially. The few sermons that were published, as well as the announcements for Thanksgiving Day celebrations, contained fewer boisterous exclamations of Christian patriotism.[53] To be sure, Lutherans of the various theological schools continued to regard the United States as divinely favored. The New School's *Lutheran Observer* was the most forthright, declaring that "our government is doubtless the best ever ordained of God for any nation."[54] Old School and Old Lutherans used similar language, describing the United States as a "Protestant country," a "Christian nation," and the "final refuge . . . of the inestimable jewel of religious freedom."[55] But overall, Lutherans' enthusiasm for the nation's civil religion was diminishing. Joseph Seiss was not fully representative of his church's opinion, but he demonstrated the general trend when he asserted that while he was "not wholly indifferent to this world's affairs," he had "sworn allegiance to the Kingdom which is not of this world."[56]

Yet Seiss's claim was illusory. No matter how often Lutheran leaders expressed skepticism about "political preaching" or insisted that they stood apart from the political fray, they still voiced opinions and pronounced judgments on the pressing issues of civic life in the postbellum United States. When they exhibited a preference for sectional reconciliation over racial justice, when they denounced corruption in government while ignoring the plight of freedpeople, when they continued to debate the legitimacy of slavery, or when they articulated a proud but cautious patriotism, these supposedly quietist churchmen were staking out *political* positions. In the end, religion and politics could never be fully separated. Lutherans, often in ways that they themselves did not fully recognize, would be profoundly influenced by the political contexts of Reconstruction.

SEEKING A MORE PERFECT LUTHERAN UNION

In the summer of 1866, the Pennsylvania Synod had withdrawn from the General Synod and issued a "fraternal address" to other American Lutherans, asking them "to unite with us in a Convention for the purpose of forming a new Union of Lutheran Synods" (see chapter 4). The choice of wording was intentional. For Lutherans during Reconstruction, the image of the Union continued to exert a powerful influence. According to the leaders of the Old School, members of the New School had carried out a "revolution" inside the General Synod and had "by contrivance and partisan organization . . . made it the instrument of their will."[57] Because the General Synod had violated its constitution, they argued, "all genuine Lutherans in this country" were compelled to acknowledge that "the old General Synod . . . is a dead failure" and to "seek another Union," one that would be free from the "false spirit of conciliation and compromise."[58] Mirroring their vision for the American nation, Old School Lutherans were seeking to reconstruct an ecclesial union that would ensure "a future, great and glorious."[59]

In the months building up to the Pennsylvania Synod's proposed meeting, leaders of the various Lutheran church bodies, both inside and outside the General Synod, debated whether to participate in this new venture. Of the twenty-three synods remaining in the federation, nineteen refused to participate. However, the four that chose to send delegates included the Pittsburg and New York synods, two of the largest in the federation. Many church bodies outside the General Synod also sent representatives, though several had misgivings. Leaders of the Missouri and Ohio synods believed that the Pennsylvania Synod was moving too quickly. Walther suggested that a series of meetings "for the purpose of exchanging views" would be preferable to trying to accomplish "great things" right away.[60] Meanwhile, the Old Lutherans in the Norwegian Synod expressed reservations because the organizers of the meeting seemed to favor their Moderate Lutheran rivals and fellow Scandinavians in the Augustana Synod.[61] Nevertheless, the Missouri, Ohio, and Norwegian synods, along with several other

Midwest-based church bodies, chose to send delegates. All told, the thirteen synods represented at the meeting together comprised more than half of all Lutherans in the United States.[62]

The convention took place in Reading, Pennsylvania, from December 12 to December 14, 1866. Though the meeting was organized by the Pennsylvania Synod, the church body's leaders made a concerted effort to widen the circle of participation. For example, Matthias Loy of the Ohio Synod preached the opening sermon, and Gottlieb Bassler (1813–1868) of the Pittsburg Synod was elected president of the new organization. But ultimately the convention was dominated by Charles Porterfield Krauth of the Pennsylvania Synod. The bulk of the proceedings consisted of discussing two sets of theses he had composed: "Fundamental Principles of Faith and Church Polity" and "Of Ecclesiastical Power and Church Polity." Krauth wrote that for "true Unity" to exist among American Lutherans, all must "accept and acknowledge the doctrines of the Unaltered Augsburg Confession in its original sense" and profess the church's other confessions to be "in the perfect harmony of one and the same scriptural faith." Both documents were adopted unanimously. On the final day, a committee proposed an "outline constitution," which used Krauth's theses as its doctrinal basis, and resolved to hold its first official convention the following November. The delegates also proposed a name for the new union: The General Council of the Evangelical Lutheran Church in North America.[63]

Though Krauth acclaimed the convention in Reading as demonstrating "unanimity of principle" and being "one of the ... most harmonious meetings ever held on these shores," many Lutherans from around the nation reacted with a mixture of hostility and skepticism.[64] Predictably, New School Lutherans were condemnatory. The *Lutheran Observer* described the Old School's actions as "insubordination" and "rebellion" and labeled the proposed General Council an "Ecclesiastical Confederacy."[65] Old Lutherans, despite supporting the increasing conservatism of the Pennsylvania Synod, continued to regard the newly emerging union with suspicion. Both Walther and Sihler had been slated to represent the Missouri Synod at the meeting, but instead the two clergymen sent a letter that declared "an immediate union" to be "improper."[66] The synod's lone delegate, as well as the representative from the Norwegian Synod, voted against the new constitution because "the right time ... had not yet come."[67] Many in the increasingly conservative Ohio Synod also were hesitant to embrace the new union. Loy, the church body's president, had praised the Reading convention's "unflinching devotion to the faith of the Church," though he was not ready to endorse the proposed General Council until it formally "declare[d] itself against all un-Lutheran doctrines and practices." At a meeting in June 1867, a special committee of the Ohio Synod decided that "a formal connection cannot now be effected."[68] In response to the actions of the Missouri, Norwegian, and Ohio synods, the *Lutheran Observer* triumphantly announced, "Neither unity nor harmony exists among the Synods dragged together . . . by the cord of a common hatred of the General Synod."[69]

Undeterred by the snubs of the Old Lutherans and the polemics of the New School, the leaders of the Old School pressed on to create a new Lutheran union. Though they were disappointed in the decisions of our "beloved brethren of Missouri and Ohio," the editors of the *Lutheran and Missionary* were still confident that their differences could be resolved: "We look for the day . . . when they will form a part of the General Council."[70] As for the criticism coming from the *Lutheran Observer,* those associated with the Old School paper continued to defend their actions. One writer, "an esteemed clergyman in Ohio," characterized the formation of the General Council as consistent with well-established American principles: The Old School was justified in forming a new union, just as "when the thirteen Colonies of this Country were deprived of their rights, they found it necessary to dissolve the political bonds which connected them with England."[71] Another correspondent from Illinois lauded the new Lutheran fellowship for setting the church on the path toward "forming a more perfect union."[72]

The first official convention of the General Council took place from November 20 to November 26, 1867, in Fort Wayne, Indiana. The choice of location was significant. As one correspondent to the *Lutheran and Missionary* reminded the paper's readers, "On this very spot, a year and a half ago, the venerable Synod of Pennsylvania was thrown out of the General Synod," but now it "witnesses the consummation of a new organization [that] will unite in name and spirit the whole of the Lutheran Church in this land."[73] Over the course of the weeklong meeting, the participants formalized the new Lutheran union.

Once again, Krauth dominated the proceedings. In the convention's opening sermon, he outlined the challenges facing "our union," namely its ethnic, linguistic, and regional diversity. "The Council will meet this difficulty," he asserted, by "avoiding all sectional and political questions" and "represent[ing] that true and genuine Lutheranism which is the servant of no nationality, language or section."[74] Krauth's vision of "genuine Lutheranism" was expressed in the General Council's official constitution, which declared the "Principles of Faith and Church Polity," which he had authored, to be "fundamental and unchangeable."[75] All told, eleven synods, representing about one-third of all American Lutherans, assented to the constitution and agreed to become members. These included former members of the General Synod, such as the Pennsylvania, Pittsburg, and New York synods, as well as others with no previous affiliation, such as the Scandinavian Augustana Synod and the predominantly German-immigrant Wisconsin Synod. Flush with optimism, the *Lutheran and Missionary* predicted that the General Council "would become that great central bond of union which would finally unite all true Lutherans in our land."[76]

Yet despite the high hopes articulated by leaders of the Old School, the new Lutheran fellowship would experience dissension and discord. These issues were already apparent at the November 1867 convention in Fort Wayne. Both the Missouri and Norwegian synods, despite being promised "all the privileges of fraternal counsel and discussion," refused to send representatives.[77] The delegates from the Ohio Synod, who were only attending as "advisory members," raised questions about where the General Council stood on four points: "Chiliasm" (that is, millennialism), "Mixed Communion," "the exchanging of pulpits with Sectarians," and "Secret, or unchurchly Societies." In response, a committee headed in part by Krauth was formed to study the matter. Following less than a day of deliberation, the committee issued a short report that concluded that the Ohio Synod's objections lacked "official evidence" but promised that if "un-Lutheran doctrines or practices" were found to exist, they would be removed "as speedily as possible." The delegates from the Iowa Synod, another German-immigrant church body, also voiced misgivings about the final three issues and proposed amendments to the constitution. After another committee politely brushed aside their concerns, the Iowa Synod representatives also refused to join the new Lutheran union.[78]

Following the meeting, the editors of the *Lutheran and Missionary* tried to control the damage: "We desire no controversy with . . . any of our more rigorous brethren. We feel that we ought to be one, and that it is our solemn duty to avoid troubling Israel further." The paper predicted "that a few years of earnest, honest, and brotherly co-operation would enable us to see eye to eye in all respects."[79]

Instead, the conflict over the Four Points would prove to be the stumbling block in the way of the General Council's growth and unity.

The controversy also provided an opening for the Missouri Synod to extend its influence. Even before the General Council's convention in Fort Wayne, leaders of this Old Lutheran church body had been engaging in theological discussions with other Midwestern Lutherans. In March 1868, representatives from the Missouri Synod, led by Walther, met in Columbus with Loy and other members of the Ohio Synod to discuss the possibility of union. At the meeting, the delegates declared that they "mutually recognize each other as orthodox bodies" and agreed that their synods' pastors could freely move from one congregation to another.[80] The editors of the *Lutheran and Missionary* evinced a sense of betrayal, complaining that the Ohio Synod had rejected the "earnest and solid union" offered by the General Council in order to gain doctrinal "recognition" from the Missouri Synod. "Perhaps," they wrote with not a little bitterness, "after a while they will discover that the General Council is also orthodox."[81]

As the next convention of the General Council approached, its Old School proponents could feel their project slipping away. As one editorial in the *Lutheran and Missionary* lamented, "these four points" were preventing "the harmonious co-operation of the great mass of Lutherans in this country" and obstructing this "great work of Union."[82] Meanwhile, their rivals at the *Lutheran Observer* predicted that after the upcoming convention of the General Council, "there will be nothing left but the Pennsylvania Synod, with its small satellites." The new union as originally conceived, the New School paper's editors concluded, "will have been dissolved."[83]

The meeting itself, held in Pittsburgh in November 1868, was consumed with debates about the Four Points. After several days of discussion, a committee headed by Krauth presented a report.[84] The first and fourth issues were fairly easily resolved. The delegates reaffirmed the teaching concerning "the Last Things" in the Augsburg Confession and denounced "all connection with infidel and immoral associations." Reaching a decision proved more difficult on the second and third points: whether non-Lutherans could partake of the Lord's Supper in Lutheran churches and whether Lutheran and non-Lutheran ministers could preach in one another's congregations. Ultimately, Krauth's committee asserted that "the purity of the Pulpit should be guarded with the most conscientious care" and that "the principle of a discriminating as over against an indiscriminate Communion is to be firmly maintained."[85] Unsurprisingly, the *Lutheran and Missionary* hailed the convention as a great success: "There has probably never been an ecclesiastical assembly in our country in which such importance questions were discussed with more honesty and fidelity and Christian love."[86] As the year 1868 came to a close, the paper's editors declared that "peace and union had been gained."[87]

Yet these optimistic pronouncements ignored the many voices dissenting against the decisions at Pittsburgh. Matthias Loy, whose Ohio Synod had sent no delegation to the meeting and remained unconnected to the General Council, complained that the convention's declarations only condemned "errors in general" but not "errors in particular."[88] The leaders of the Iowa Synod also declined to join the General Council on account of the Four Points, but they continued to send delegates to federation's conventions for the next several decades.[89] The most significant setback for this new Lutheran union, however, came from the Wisconsin Synod. In October 1868, just a month before the General Council's convention, delegates from this church body met in Milwaukee with leaders from the Missouri Synod. Both sides declared the other to be "orthodox Lutheran church bodies" and agreed to "practice pulpit and altar fellowship."[90] A few weeks later, the Wisconsin Synod's lone representative at the Pittsburgh meeting, Johannes Bading, signed a "minority report" that declared, "In the decisions of the General Council on these [four] points we do not find everywhere the full, unmistakable truth."[91] In June 1869, the church body officially severed its connection with the General Council.[92]

Gleefully observing this discord were the New School Lutherans of the General Synod. According to the *Lutheran Observer*, the Ohio, Iowa, and Wisconsin synods were simply carrying the General Council's principles to "their logical consequences" and revealing that "there is no tenable middle ground between an honest adoption of the doctrinal basis of the General Synod, and that of [the] Missouri [Synod]."[93] The controversy over the Four Points also proved to these New School leaders that their "broad, catholic, Scriptural, and historically Lutheran basis" was the only hope for uniting "the divided household of Lutheranism in America."[94]

Perhaps the most eloquent champion of this view was J. A. Brown, who had been elected president of the General Synod at its tumultuous 1866 meeting. Two years later, as his presidential term neared completion, Brown preached a sermon that enumerated the federation's "past and future blessings": The General Synod was the original "bond of union among the different Lutheran Synods in our land"; it restored "the Augsburg Confession to its legitimate and normal position in the church"; it awakened the "spirit of revivals"; and now it "furnishes the only basis" for both "union among Lutherans" and "co-operation with other Evangelical churches."[95] In a later article, Brown contrasted the position of the New School with that of the Old School: "The spirit of the General Synod is the spirit of Union," while the General Council's "origin" was "in the spirit of division and disunion."[96]

With criticism coming from multiple directions, those associated with the *Lutheran and Missionary* continued to claim that the General Council's "moderate, middle" position was the best hope for Lutheran unity. On the one hand, they criticized their New School rivals in the General Synod, not only denouncing them as the "extreme left" but also complaining about their presumptuousness. Even though the General Synod had been reduced to less than a fourth of all American Lutherans, the Old School paper fumed, "These 86,000 talk as if they were the Lutheran Church of this country and the only hope for the future!"[97] On the other hand, defenders of the General Council were becoming exasperated with the "extreme right" of their "Missouri [Synod] accusers," who "throw doubt upon the orthodoxy and consistency of some men."[98] These "men of strife," they argued, were chiefly responsible for convincing the other confessional synods to "stand aloof from the General Council."[99] Nevertheless, the editors of the *Lutheran and Missionary* still believed that their form of Lutheranism would eventually win the day: "The end of the long struggle will be a union of all upon an honest, moderate basis."[100]

PURSUING SECTIONAL RECONCILIATION

As proponents of the General Council were clinging to their hope for a more perfect ecclesiastical union, both they and the leaders of the General Synod were ramping up their pursuit of reconciliation with their coreligionists in the South. However, it was unclear whether southern Lutherans were interested in reunion and where the synods of the South stood on the issues of confessional adherence and church unity that had been dividing northern Lutherans.

In June 1866, the General Synod of the Confederate States of America met for the first time since the conclusion of the Civil War. The delegates resolved to remain a separate southern organization but rebranded their federation with the less sectional-sounding—but certainly overstated—name: The Evangelical Lutheran General Synod in North America. (The editors of the *Lutheran Observer* considered it a "preposterous" title for an association "representing scarcely one-twentieth portion of the Church in this country" and quipped, "Why not call it the 'Evangelical Lutheran Synod of the planet earth.'")[101] The convention also signaled that many southern Lutherans were moving in a more theologically confessional direction. The delegates revised the federation's constitution to remove any qualifying language about adherence to the Augsburg Confession, and they endorsed a new church paper, the *Evangelical Lutheran,* edited by the staunch confessionalist Gotthardt Bernheim (1827–1916).[102] A few months later, Bernheim's paper praised the Pennsylvania Synod's separation from the General Synod and predicted that the proposed General Council would "enjoy the confidence of all true Lutherans."[103]

This seeming turn toward confessionalism was befuddling to the New School Lutherans of the General Synod. For decades, the majority of southern Lutherans had been proponents of revivalism and opponents of strict adherence to the Augsburg Confession. Because of this, the editors of the *Lutheran Observer* considered it "inconceivable" that "the most Methodistic portion of our Church, should inculcate Missouri, or even Philadelphia Lutheranism."[104] They also found it unlikely that Lutherans in the South would unite with the General Council, when many of its leaders were "the most rabid abolitionists before the war."[105] The only explanation, in their view, was that this new theological direction was due to the scheming of a "few leaders in the Southern Church" and that "a majority of our ministers at the South" held to the New School view.[106] Convinced of this, writers for the *Lutheran Observer* insisted on "the duty of the Church, North and South, to take earnest steps at once to bridge the gulf that separates those Southern Synods from the old General Synod."[107] At its 1869 convention the General Synod officially proposed a reunion of the two sections.[108]

The Old School Lutherans of the General Council, on the other hand, believed that the movement toward confessionalism was widespread throughout the South. During the late 1860s, the *Lutheran and Missionary* printed numerous letters and reports from southern Lutherans, attempting to prove that their coreligionists were embracing "the faith once delivered to the saints." The paper's editors were confident that "God is himself leading the South in the way of truth" and that soon "they will unite with all who love the same truth."[109] After several years of observing "the new life, spirit, and energy . . . developing in the Southern Lutheran churches," they believed that the time had come to act. In November 1870, the editors of the *Lutheran and Missionary* proposed a "free conference" to "meet with our Lutheran brethren of the South" and to discuss "the great interests of our common Lutheran Church in America."[110]

As they pushed for union with southern synods, the competing factions of Lutherans in the North sought to outdo each other in their rhetoric of sectional reconciliation. The Old School editors of the *Lutheran and Missionary* brought up an article, written by a New School leader in 1865, that had argued for southern Lutherans to be barred from the General Synod until "they have repented of their wickedness." By contrast, their position since "the termination of the late war" was that "it was not proper to make the political differences which had separated the Lutheran churches North and South a barrier to their re-union."[111] New School Lutherans, however, recalled how Old School leaders had forcefully condemned southern Lutherans during the war. The editors of the *Lutheran Observer* asked whether their rivals at the *Lutheran and Missionary* intended to "recant, repudiate, and renounce" their past words. As for their own views on "the course proper to be pursued in Church and State," they wrote, "it is the common Christian duty of *all* our people, North and South, as speedily as possible, to heal every wound, extirpate every root of bitterness, remove every occasion of sectional alienation, and thus obliterate all traces of the war."[112] Spokesmen for both the General Council and the General Synod were not only certain of their theological compatibility with southern Lutherans but also confident that they exhibited the most generous spirit of reconciliation.[113]

In the midst of these northern overtures, Lutherans in the South were themselves divided, not only on the question of sectional reconciliation but also on the issue of confessionalism. The North Carolina–based *Evangelical Lutheran*, despite being endorsed at the 1866 meeting of the southern General Synod, was soon eclipsed by the *Lutheran Visitor*, principally edited by Anton Rude (1813–1883) of Columbia, South Carolina.[114] Rude's paper aspired to chart a distinctive course for southern Lutheranism. When news reached him of the growing circulation of the *Lutheran Observer* in the South, he accused this northern paper of "appeas[ing] the gnawings of hunger, by feeding in the Southern fields."[115]

However, Rude insisted that his chief opposition to sectional reunion was theological: "We hold views and principles . . . not held by any of the organizations North."[116] As he described it, "In doctrine, we are with the Old [School]," but "new measures [revivals] . . . should be employed."[117] Members of the North Carolina Synod, however, found Rude's combination of confessionalism and revivalism to be incoherent. They also indicated a willingness to cooperate with northern Lutherans. At its 1870 convention, after the *Evangelical Lutheran* had been discontinued due to lack of support, the synod's delegates endorsed the *Lutheran and Missionary* as its "official organ" and threatened to separate from the southern General Synod unless it became "one in faith and practice."[118]

It was in this context of intrasectional divisiveness that southern Lutherans debated the offers of reconciliation coming from the North. One of the leading proponents of reunion was John Bachman—a remarkable position, given the leading role he had played in urging secession, in both church and state, and the vehemence with which he had rejected reconciliation shortly after the Civil War. Unable to attend the 1870 meeting of the southern General Synod because of his failing health, the aging pastor forwarded a "fraternal letter" that urged "the Southern Church" to take the lead in reuniting "all the Lutheran synods of this country."[119] Yet for many other Lutherans in the South, reconciliation with their northern coreligionists was unthinkable. The *Lutheran and Missionary*'s proposal for a free conference, in particular, stirred up passionate feelings. Rude opposed the idea, and his *Lutheran Visitor* filled up with articles condemning it. One writer, "Sic Semper," questioned the sincerity of northern Lutherans, who during the Civil War had "denounced Southern Synods and ministers as guilty of *treason* . . . for doing what the great and good Washington and our own sainted Muhlenberg did—dar[ing] to do what they believed to be right."[120] Another correspondent saw the conference as a "disgusting" plot, designed by those who "have for their ultimate object the dismemberment and ruin of our [southern] General Synod."[121] Numerous others echoed similar sentiments.[122]

Despite these southern rebuffs, many northern Lutherans continued to hold out hope that reconciliation would prevail. Joseph Seiss of the *Lutheran and Missionary* was convinced that the idea for a free conference was "largely approved by our Southern ministers and people," who had overcome "all sectional jealousies and mere political bitternesses," and was opposed only by a minority led by

"Brother Rude," who "invokes against us the rancorous feelings of a past political struggle."[123] Those associated with the (northern) General Synod, meanwhile, believed that Lutherans in the South were coming to see the errors of the General Council. When Rude accused Seiss of being "too exclusive" and an advocate of "extreme Symbolism," the editors of the *Lutheran Observer* saw his criticisms as "a good omen in [*sic*] the ecclesiastical horizon" and "an olive branch that augurs peace." Soon, they declared, "it will be seen that he endorses the conservative position of the General Synod North."[124]

Nevertheless, Rude and the *Lutheran Visitor* remained hostile toward any talk of reunion, believing that northerners intended "the destruction of the Southern Church and the dissolution of our General Synod."[125] In June 1871, Seiss made one last attempt to organize a free conference, traveling to Virginia to hold informal discussions with several southern ministers in the town of Salem.[126] Afterward, Rude invoked the specter of the famous witch trials held in the Massachusetts town of the same name—both events, he said, were instances of "ignorant zeal"—and reported that the meeting was a "failure."[127] In September, the two editors met in person and agreed to "bury" any further talks of a free conference.[128] Having successfully warded off the reconciliatory advances of the General Council, Rude restated his commitment to a separate southern church: "We have taken our stand. We are of the General Synod, South. . . . It survived the lost cause. It is God's work. And shall we now, while Northern men attempt to destroy God's work, unite and cooperate with them[?] Forbid it God!"[129]

Rude's fear of a northern conspiracy to sow disunion in his church was seemingly confirmed when the North Carolina Synod withdrew from the southern General Synod in the summer of 1871, with delegates citing "the un-Lutheran tendencies of said body."[130] Shortly thereafter, leaders from North Carolina entered into negotiations with the independent and ardently confessional Tennessee Synod, with the hopes of forming an alternative southern union—a plan that failed to materialize.[131] As its 1872 convention approached, the optimistically named General Synod in North America totaled just five synods and fewer than twelve thousand communicant members, not even half of all Lutherans in the southern states. One disheartened correspondent to the *Lutheran Visitor* wondered whether it was even worthwhile for the meeting to take place.[132] Meanwhile, leaders of the (northern) General Synod continued to suggest that the best solution was for Lutherans in the South to accept their standing offer of reunion.[133] To that end, they appointed a delegate to attend the upcoming southern convention.

In response, Rude and the *Lutheran Visitor* once again stirred up hostility against any suggestion of sectional reunion. One writer argued that giving up on the southern General Synod would be as disastrous as "when General Lee surrendered at Appomattox."[134] Another issued a not-so-veiled threat to the delegate being sent by the (northern) General Synod: "I wonder if the good brother has ever heard of Ku Klux."[135] Urged on by these sentiments, representatives at the May 1872 meeting, held in Charleston, South Carolina, unanimously adopted an "emphatic declaration," which argued that a separate southern Lutheran federation was "a necessity, and will be so for years to come." Though the statement "disavow[ed] any sectional, political or ecclesiastical animosity," those claims were belied when the convention delegates rejected the credentials of the (northern) General Synod's representative.[136] A frequent contributor to the *Lutheran Visitor* summed up the meeting's import. "Our [southern] General Synod," he asserted, "has become a fixed fact."[137]

The pursuit of Lutheran sectional reconciliation had foundered, though not for lack of effort on the part of northern Lutherans. Leaders of both the General Council and the General Synod had been eager to remove all enmity lingering from the Civil War, almost to the point of obsequiousness. Yet among Lutherans in the South, sectional loyalty proved decisive, both during Reconstruction and beyond. In 1876, the General Synod in North America dropped the pretense of being a national union and changed its name to the General Synod of the Evangelical Lutheran Church in the South. Five years later, the leaders of the North Carolina Synod overcame their theological qualms and reunited with their fellow southerners. In 1886, the Tennessee Synod followed suit and, along with seven other synods stretching from Virginia to Mississippi, joined together to form the United Synod of the Evangelical Lutheran Church in the South, an organization that would last until 1918.

DEFINING THE "TRUE CHURCH" IN AMERICA

Amid this denominational disunion, it would be easy to miss the theological convergence that was taking place. During the first years after the Civil War,

American Lutherans continued to debate the central issue that been animating their disputes since the antebellum era: what constituted the most authentic expression of their faith. Yet while their arguments and rhetoric remained as contentious as before, they were approaching their debates from an increasingly confessional perspective. As with the quests for ecclesiastical union and denominational reconciliation, this growing emphasis on doctrinal rectitude was shaped by the larger political and cultural context of Reconstruction. In an era of perceived "radicalism" and "extremism," fidelity to the church's historic confessions offered a sense of order and certainty.

No Lutheran theologian in the United States was more convinced about his church's doctrinal position than C. F. W. Walther of the Missouri Synod. In 1867, he published perhaps his most influential and certainly his most provocative work, *Die evangelisch-lutherische Kirche, die wahre sichtbare Kirche Gottes auf Erden* (The Evangelical Lutheran Church, the True Visible Church of God on Earth). In twenty-five theses, Walther rigorously defined the nature of true Lutheranism. "The Evangelical Lutheran Church," he wrote, "is the sum total of all who without reservation profess the doctrine which was restored by the Reformation of Luther." Based on this principle, he and his fellow Old Lutherans resolved to "reject every fraternal or ecclesiastical fellowship with such as reject its Confession, either in whole or in part." In his final thesis, he made his boldest claim: "The Evangelical Lutheran Church thus has all the essential marks of the true visible church of God on earth; since they are found in no other church body, it is therefore in no need of any doctrinal reformation."[138] Though this book was stating his position more audaciously than before, the content of Walther's views had been mostly consistent throughout his career: The Lutheran church was the sole possessor of pure scriptural truth and only those who affirmed that belief could join together in church unity.[139] What changed in the late 1860s and early 1870s was the widespread embrace of his outlook by other Lutherans in the United States.

This transformation was particularly evident in the Ohio and Wisconsin synods. Both church bodies had been considered Moderate Lutherans during the 1850s but had been moving in the direction of Old Lutheranism throughout the Civil War. During the first years of Reconstruction, both came to embrace fully the Missouri Synod's position. In the Ohio Synod, the influence of Matthias Loy's *Lutheran Standard* was decisive. Shortly after the publication of Walther's book, the church paper approvingly reprinted its twenty-five theses.[140] After the Missouri and Ohio synods agreed to terms of fellowship, the *Lutheran Standard* translated Walther's entire book into English and increasingly made its own assertions about Lutheranism as the "true church."[141] The Wisconsin Synod moved more slowly toward the Missouri Synod. As late as April 1868, leaders of the two church bodies were engaging in a heated war of words over the Wisconsin Synod's continued acceptance of money from joint Reformed–Lutheran mission societies in Germany. However, at its convention during that summer, the Wisconsin Synod officially broke off ties with these organizations.[142] After representatives from the church body met with Missouri Synod leaders in October and agreed to terms of fellowship, Walther proclaimed, "Our suspicions against the dear Wisconsin Synod have not merely disappeared but also have been put to shame."[143] Over the next years, the synod's paper, the *Evangelisch-Lutherisches Gemeinde-Blatt,* came to resemble the periodicals of the Missouri Synod in its promotion of doctrinal "truth and purity."[144]

Even more remarkable was the movement of Old School Lutherans toward the position of Walther and Old Lutheranism. Writers for the *Lutheran and Missionary,* though frustrated by the Missouri Synod's refusal to join the General Council, frequently found themselves defending this church body and noting the similarity in their theological positions.[145] An important sign of this growing convergence was the Old School's use of the language of the "true church." In a telling article, Joseph Seiss responded to the accusation that "we consider the Lutheran Church the only true Church" by arguing that "the proper answer to the inquiry is well embodied in ... Dr. Walther's *Theses.*" After quoting Walther's book, as well as several Lutheran church fathers, he concluded, "In so far as [non-Lutherans] do not receive and hold the great doctrines confessed by our Church, we regard them as in error from the pure and full truth of God's holy word, and to that extent beclouded in their title to be accounted pure parts of the One Holy Christian Church."[146] Despite their inability to fully agree on doctrine, leaders of the General Council increasingly mirrored the claims of those in the Missouri Synod.

The most comprehensive expression of this escalating confessional rigor came from Charles Porterfield Krauth. In 1870, Krauth was elected president of the General Council, a position he would hold for the next decade. The year after his election, he published his eight hundred–page "magnum opus," *The Conservative*

Reformation and Its Theology. The central argument of Krauth's weighty tome was that Lutheranism was "the purest Protestantism" and "the most perfect form of Christianity." These and other assertions bore a striking resemblance to those advanced by Walther. Like his Missouri Synod counterpart, Krauth viewed the Lutheran church as "the pillar of the truth in the church universal" and saw the Lutheran confessions as the definitive statement of "the one, pure, and unchanging faith of the Christian Church." In one of the book's most quoted passages, Krauth declared, "We do not claim that our Confessors were infallible. We do not say they could not fail. We only claim that they did not fail."[147] Though he never repeated Walther's precise formulation of the Lutheran church as the "true visible church," Krauth was using similar language to describe his communion's exalted status in Christendom.

However, despite this growing theological convergence, the General Council and the synods associated with the Missouri Synod could not find unity on precisely what constituted the "true church." The leaders of each group acknowledged that Christians need not agree on absolutely everything—both Krauth and Walther recognized a difference between "fundamental" or "essential" doctrines, on the one hand, and "nonfundamentals" or "unessential matters," on the other.[148] Where they disagreed was on the boundaries.[149] Walther and his colleagues believed that the Lutheran confessions "agree with the written Word of God on all points." Consequently, the Missouri Synod required assent to the entire *Book of Concord* "without reservation."[150] Krauth and the General Council, by contrast, distinguished among the different Lutheran confessions. The Augsburg Confession was the "primary confession," which should be accepted "without equivocation or mental reservation," while the others, such as the Formula of Concord, were "secondary confessions," which should be subscribed to "inasmuch as they set forth" the Augsburg Confession's teachings.[151]

Both groups also disagreed on how to approach issues not explicitly discussed in the Lutheran confessions. This had been the chief issue in the controversy over the Four Points. The Missouri Synod and its allies claimed that their opposition to millennialism, secret societies, and altar and pulpit fellowship with non-Lutherans rested on "the fact that our standard authors [the Lutheran church fathers], with great unanimity, condemn these things as unscriptural and un-Lutheran."[152] As Walther wrote, "Our Confessions do not claim to be a complete system of all doctrines taught by our church."[153] Seiss and other defenders of the General Council labeled this position "extraordinary *nonsense*," because it "depend[s] for its vindication on *something outside the utterances of the Lutheran Church, as such.*" Such "*extra*-confessional" views, he asserted, were evidence of "*anti*-Lutheran unsoundness, not to say heresy."[154] Even though the leaders of the Missouri Synod and the General Council concurred that Lutheranism constituted the "true church," they differed on how to define it.

The New School spokesmen of the General Synod, despite rejecting the views of both the Missouri Synod and the General Council, also believed that the Lutheran church occupied a privileged place in Christian history. Writers for the *Lutheran Observer* continued to claim that Lutheranism was "the Queen of Protestantism" and that the Augsburg Confession served as the "model Confession" for other denominations.[155] True Lutheranism, in their view, was neither "exclusive" nor "intolerant" but should play a leading role in Protestant unity.[156] According to Samuel Sprecher, the president of Wittenberg College in Ohio, there are "two methods for the attainment of truth and unity": one "would preserve orthodoxy by rigidly enforcing a creed," while "the other strives first for the unity of the spirit, . . . and earnestly labors for revivals of religion." According to Sprecher, the latter method, which had been adopted by the "friends of the General Synod," represented "the Protestant—the true—the Lutheran ideal of the Church."[157] Though they were uncomfortable designating their denomination as the "true church," leaders of the New School believed that their branch of Protestantism was the "mother of the Reformation" and were not hesitant to describe themselves as the defenders of "true Lutheranism."[158]

The advocates of the General Synod were also adamant that their opponents' views were "un-Lutheran" or "anti-Lutheran."[159] According to the editors of the *Lutheran Observer,* the positions of the General Council and the Missouri Synod were indistinguishable in their "Extreme Symbolic tendencies"—the former's "basis," they claimed, "is not a whit behind the basis of Missouri."[160] This "rigid Symbolism," declared Sprecher, was a "hindrance in the way of the complete apprehension, development, and application of the original and true idea of the Reformation."[161] Others went one step further. The principles of the General Council and Missouri Synod, wrote one New School theologian, were "papistical" and "not Lutheran," because they make "human creeds a binding authority for the Church."[162] One author, writing in the wake of the First Vatican Council, was especially aghast at Krauth's statement that "our Confessors . . . *did not fail.*"

Such an assertion of "confessional infallibility," he warned, "is claimed . . . for the Infallibility of the Pope."[163] For these General Synod leaders, the high elevation of the Lutheran confessions by the General Council and the Missouri Synod violated the true spirit of the Reformation.

Yet for all of the New School's denunciations of the "un-Lutheran" and "papistical" elevation of creeds, the General Synod was subtly being pulled in a more confessional direction. At its 1864 meeting, the delegates had proposed an amendment to the federation's constitution, which required its member synods to receive and hold "the Augsburg Confession, as a correct exhibition of the fundamental doctrines of the Divine Word" (see chapter 4). In 1866, that amendment was ratified.[164] Though this was essentially the General Synod's previous position, the formal nature of the change had consequences. As the editors of the *Lutheran Observer* acknowledged, "The General Synod, judged by the only legitimate criterion, its constitution and its official acts, . . . is a *symbolical* body, in distinction from such religious societies as reject the use of any creed."[165] Rather than condemning "symbolism" as such, leading spokesmen for the New School increasingly attacked the "extreme symbolism" of both the Missouri Synod and the General Council and referred to their own position as "moderate" or "conservative."[166] According to J. A. Brown, the General Synod's "conservative Lutheranism" stood between those who wished to "cut loose from all historical and doctrinal connection with the Lutheran Church of the past" and those who insisted on "a rigid adherence to everything in the Symbolical Books."[167] Though the General Synod's leaders were convinced that they had not changed, they were admitting more and more that their church's confessions possessed some measure of authority.

As these competing groups vied to define the nature of the "true Lutheranism," each also sought to demonstrate that their understanding best reflected the values of the United States. The leaders of the New School felt especially confident in making that case. Their doctrinal principles, contended the *Lutheran Observer*, were the product of the nation's "free and unrestricted development" and balanced the American ideals of "freedom" and "restraint."[168] Samuel Sprecher made an even grander claim: "The General Synod . . . is the most complete realization of Luther's idea of the Church."[169] New School Lutherans also argued that their opponents represented a foreign invasion. In the words of Frederick Conrad, the Missouri Synod was "indigenous to Europe," has been "transplanted to America," and now "attempts to overspread the land."[170] His evaluation of the General Council was similar: "Its birth took place on American soil," but "the child is nevertheless an alien."[171] According to the General Synod's leaders, their rivals' "extreme symbolism" was both "un-Lutheran" and "un-American" because it violated individual liberty. This principle, Conrad wrote, "was in the brain and heart and words of Luther, when he uttered his heroic protest at Worms," and "America, with her Republican institutions, was in his . . . noble declaration of personal liberty, as the oak is in the acorn."[172] The mission of the General Synod, its defenders believed, was to conserve and promote the spirit of the Protestant Reformation and American freedom.

The leaders of the General Council also were certain that their form of Lutheranism reflected the nation's ideals. Krauth adamantly denied that the General Synod's version of the faith should be called "American Lutheranism." First, he wrote, "it is not *American*" but "an adoption and adaptation of European error." Second, he continued, "it is not *Lutheran*" because "its whole distinctive life turns upon the denial of the Lutheran faith."[173] General Council Lutherans also criticized the Missouri Synod and its allies as insufficiently American. According to Seiss, they had "gone too far in the direction of legalistic rigors and exclusiveness" because of their "language, nationality, and indisposition to come under the influences of American society."[174] In contrast to these rivals, the proponents of the General Council saw themselves as the true Americans. In his *Conservative Reformation and Its Theology,* Krauth summarized his vision: "The Lutheranism of this country . . . must be American. It must be conformed in accordance with its own principles to its new home, bringing hither its priceless experiences in the old world, to apply them to the living present in the new."[175] The vocation of the General Council, its advocates argued, was to balance fidelity to the Lutheran heritage with assimilation into the nation's culture.

Despite being denounced as "foreign," the Old Lutherans also believed that they had a distinctive American calling. Two interrelated evaluations of the United States shaped their understanding of that mission. On the one hand, as Friedrich Schmidt (1837–1928) of the Norwegian Synod wrote, the nation's "ruling religious spirit" was "radically opposed" to "the Lutheran cause." The duty of "true Lutherans," then, was to fight "against the countless sects and their mischievous errors" and to produce "a thorough and permanent Regeneration of our Church in America."[176] On the other hand, the United States was, in the words of Walther, a refuge of "complete freedom of religion," where "God has opened the gates wide for the arrival of the church of the Reformation" to "build, unhindered, upon the old foundations." The "present task of the Lutheran church in this country," therefore, was to use "this glorious freedom" to create a "newly awakened church of the true confession."[177] Those associated with the Missouri Synod hoped to refound the Lutheran church in its purity. Only in the United States, the divinely ordained land of religious liberty, they believed, was such a mission possible.

Along with their mutual aspiration to represent the most authentic expression of American Lutheranism, the leaders of the Missouri Synod, the General Council, and the General Synod shared another important commonality: Each group's views were shaped by the politics of Reconstruction, particularly an opposition to "radicalism." The Old Lutherans associated with the Missouri Synod saw themselves as "faithful witnesses against the radical diseases" that are found "in this country," including the "raging torrent of mammon-worship," the "antichristian character of a large portion of the public press," and "bold ungodliness."[178] Krauth claimed that Lutheranism represented "that sobriety of tone, that patience of spirit, and that moderation of manner, which are involved in Conservatism," and he stood opposed to the "revolutionary spirit" and "radical Reform."[179] Even the New School Lutherans of the General Synod saw themselves as the true conservatives, believing themselves to be a bulwark against "radicalism or extreme liberalism" and "an idolatrous worship of 'the spirit of the times.'"[180] In short, what emerged after the Civil War were three types of American Lutheran "conservatism." Each was confident that their form of the faith not only represented "true Lutheranism" and epitomized the nation's ideals but also stood as a bastion of order in an era of radicalism.

★ ★ ★

By the early 1870s, it was the Missouri Synod's version of the faith that was making the greatest inroads. The church body's leaders not only were shaping intra-Lutheran debates with their rhetoric of the "true church," but they also they were taking the lead in the formation of a new federation of synods. In January 1871, representatives from the Missouri, Ohio, Wisconsin, and Norwegian synods met in Chicago and agreed to establish a "Union of all Lutheran Synods in America in one orthodox American Lutheran Church."[181] Over the course of the year, two more church bodies, the Illinois and Minnesota synods, left the General Council to unite with the proposed union. In November, delegates from these six church bodies met in Fort Wayne, Indiana—the same city that had seen the General Synod schism of 1866 and the formation of the General Council in 1867. There they drafted a constitution, appointed C. F. W. Walther as provisional president, and agreed to hold their first official meeting the following summer. They also confirmed the official name of the new organization: The Evangelical Lutheran Synodical Conference of North America.[182]

The buildup to the Synodical Conference's first convention prompted varied responses. Leaders in the General Synod reacted with dismay. The *Lutheran Observer* predicted that the new organization "will exert a commanding influence" and worried that the Missouri Synod's "extreme symbolism" might become "the controlling power of our church."[183] Those associated with the *Lutheran and Missionary* could not help but stand in awe of "the powerful Synod of Missouri."[184] Though some expressed frustration with their "tirades" and "sectarianism," others hoped for a "brighter day" when "the new Missouri general body" and the General Council "shall be merged into one body."[185]

Spokesmen for the emerging Synodical Conference sought to justify the new Lutheran union as a necessity. In a lengthy "Memorial" composed at the November 1871 meeting in Fort Wayne, they insisted that "we take no pleasure in the existing division" and expressed hope for a future "union between all Synods bearing the Lutheran name in this country." Yet at the present time, they argued, "we cannot entertain any idea of entering into church-fellowship" with those who lacked "a truly confessional and Lutheran spirit." Convinced of their "incontestable biblical and churchly right to form a separate church-organization," representatives met in July 1872 in Milwaukee, Wisconsin, for the first official convention of the Synodical Conference.[186]

Walther preached the opening sermon. Standing before more than one hundred delegates and advisory members, the Missouri Synod's leader marveled how "just a few years ago [they] stood in array against each other, indeed, even fought as enemies," but now they were gathering "as members of one household of faith, as sons of one Church, and as cherishers of one cause." Though "our former disunion was a very sad spectacle for all friends of Zion," he declared, "our present brotherly union is undoubtedly a cause of joy to God, to all His holy angels, and to all His true children." Walther then proceeded to lay out the basis for this union:

> We are all convinced of the fact that the church of our fathers, the Evangelical Lutheran Church, as she has professed her faith before the whole world in the Unaltered Augsburg Confession and the other confessions, is the true visible church of God on earth. And we are resolved in the name of the Lord jointly to build in doctrine and practice this church, and none other, in this Western land.

"With joyful hope," he proclaimed, "we look today into the future."[187]

Such optimism was well deserved. A quarter decade after its humble founding in 1847, the Missouri Synod now headed the most numerous Lutheran fellowship in the United States. At its height in the late 1870s, the Synodical Conference accounted for almost 45 percent of the nation's Lutherans, nearly equaling the combined membership of the General Synod and the General Council. It would remain the largest American Lutheran union until 1918.[188]

Yet Walther's comment on the church's future was prescient in another respect: Lutheranism in the United States as a whole was trending toward the positions that he championed. Those who had formed the General Council embraced theological views that differed from the Synodical Conference's outlook in degree but not in kind. Southern Lutherans were affirming a reverence for the Augsburg Confession that had been unthinkable during the antebellum years. Even the New School Lutherans of the General Synod had adopted the language of "conservatism" to describe their relationship to their church's heritage. Before the Civil War, the Missouri Synod had stood virtually alone; now the majority of American Lutherans were coming to profess its rigorous confessionalism.

What Walther did not acknowledge—and most likely did not even realize— was the profound and complex ways in which this conservative transformation of Lutheranism in the United States had been shaped by the context of Reconstruction. During the years following the Civil War, Lutherans had prioritized the goal of reunion, adopted an increasingly apolitical outlook, and rejected the era's radicalism. They applied these lessons to ecclesiastical life by seeking to form a "more perfect" church union, pursuing ecclesiastical reconciliation, and attempting to ground their religious identity in the certainties of the Lutheran past.

However, their shared desire for intra-Lutheran harmony and the increasingly widespread reverence for their church's confessions were not enough to overcome the divergent views about what constituted "true Lutheranism."

The end result was both dramatic in its consequences and ironic in its outcomes. By 1872, the majority of Lutherans in the United States had come to embrace a theological and political conservatism grounded in notions of American exceptionalism. Institutionally, however, their church was more divided than it had been since the 1830s, comprising four competing unions—the Synodical Conference, the General Council, the General Synod, and the southern General Synod—as well as several independent church bodies. American Lutheranism had indeed been reconstructed, but in ways the participants never could have predicted just six years before.

SIX

★ ★ ★ ★ ★ ★ ★

The Triumph of
Confessional Conservatism,
1872–1900

I N 1882, less than thirty years after Philip Schaff had predicted that an ecumenical and united Lutheranism would play a key role in shaping "the entire development of Anglo-American Christianity" (see chapter 1), another
prominent figure in American Protestantism offered a very different assessment
of the Lutheran church in the United States. Henry Carroll was a Methodist layman and one of the editors of the *Independent,* a New York City–based religious
newspaper made famous under the brief editorship of Henry Ward Beecher. In
an article for the *Methodist Quarterly Review,* Carroll directed his energies to
profiling and analyzing American Lutheranism. The picture he painted, however, was very different from the one foretold by Schaff. "The Lutherans, though
strong in numbers, have not impressed their importance upon the people of our
country," Carroll wrote. "The great body of them have no bonds of fellowship
with other Protestants. . . . They believe that they constitute the true Church of
Christ, and that the rest of Protestantism is made up of sects more or less steeped
in error." Though Carroll expressed regret that Lutherans "have not received the
attention to which their numbers, their work, and their importance entitle them,"
he believed that this was not because Lutherans were "unwelcome [to be] in
association with the Evangelical Churches." Rather, the Methodist writer stated
bluntly, "their isolation is of their own choice."[1]

Carroll's article highlights the two key developments in American Lutheranism during the final decades of the nineteenth century. The first was the church's

exponential growth in membership and institutions. The second was the triumph of a version of the faith that sharply contrasted with the church's principal outlook during the antebellum era. This confessional conservatism had been forged during the Civil War and early years of Reconstruction, but it was solidified and expanded during the Gilded Age.

From 1872 to 1900 the United States underwent enormous technological, economic, political, and social changes.[2] Yet in terms of its impact on Lutheranism's numerical enlargement and intellectual evolution, the most significant development of this era was the growth of American pluralism, both ethnic and religious. Unprecedented levels of immigration, not only from Northern Europe but also from Southern and Eastern Europe and parts of Asia, increased the nation's cultural diversity and expanded its varieties of faith.[3] Another form of pluralization was the division of the "evangelical empire" into the "two-party system" of American Protestantism.[4] On the one side stood proponents of the new theology, the social gospel, and other expressions of liberalism or modernism; opposing these ideas were those who embraced the various streams of conservative evangelicalism that would flow into fundamentalism. Though many Americans continued to insist on Anglo-Protestant supremacy, the fin-de-siècle United States bore scant resemblance to the nation that had fought the Civil War.

In this increasingly pluralistic environment, Lutherans propagated a distinctive identity. By 1872, American Lutheranism had been split into three main federations—the Synodical Conference, the General Council, and the General Synod. These institutional divisions would persist into the early twentieth century. However, though the three fellowships continued to disagree about numerous particulars and engage in incessant infighting, the range of theological views became increasingly narrow. Historian Susan Juster's astute observation about the underlying unity of the numerous Baptist groups during the Revolutionary era applies also to Lutherans in the Gilded Age: "The extreme sensitivity toward the finer points of doctrine . . . only reaffirms our sense that these people held a common religious ethos."[5] During the final decades of the nineteenth century, the factions of the Civil War era—New School, Old School, Moderate Lutheran, Old Lutheran—gave way to a broadly shared consensus. Apart from a few notable exceptions, the majority of Lutherans in the United States came to espouse an identity united around four principles: confessionalism in doctrine, separatism in church affairs, conservatism on political and social issues, and a unique interpretation of American exceptionalism.

POSTBELLUM IMMIGRATION

From 1865 to 1900, the United States received an estimated 13.5 million newcomers, about twice the total number of immigrants in the more than 250 years between the founding of Jamestown and the end of the Civil War. About one-third of these new arrivals came from countries in which Lutheranism was the principal religion. The largest sender was Germany (which became a unified nation-state in 1871), with just over 3.3 million immigrants. An additional 1.5 million people hailed from the various Nordic nations, chiefly Sweden and Norway, but also Denmark, Finland, and Iceland. By 1900, the number of first- and second-generation immigrants from these predominantly Lutheran nations totaled about 12 million people, or more than one in every six Americans.[6]

This tremendous increase in immigration had profound effects on the demography of Lutheranism in the United States. The most obvious impact was numerical. In the three and a half decades following the Civil War, the communicant membership in Lutheran congregations grew by more than 500 percent (over twice the rate of the U.S. population as a whole), from less than three hundred thousand to more than 1.6 million. By 1900, only Roman Catholics, Baptists, and Methodists were more numerous. Another shift was ethnic and linguistic. As late as the mid-1870s, the majority of Lutherans in the United States were native-born English speakers. However, during the final decades of the nineteenth century, Lutheranism became mostly comprised of immigrants and their children who spoke and wrote in a variety of foreign languages.

A final change was geographic. The majority of these newly arriving Lutheran immigrants settled in the Upper Midwest and the Great Plains. By 1900, nearly 50 percent of all Americans born in Germany and Scandinavia lived in eight states: Illinois, Iowa, Michigan, Minnesota, Nebraska, North Dakota, South Dakota, and Wisconsin. In three of these—Minnesota, North Dakota, and Wisconsin—first- and second-generation German and Nordic Americans made up more than half of the population. Consequently, American Lutheranism's geographic center shifted during the postbellum era from the Mid-Atlantic to the Midwest.

In 1865, less than 20 percent of Lutherans lived in these eight states; thirty-five years later, that figure was more than 50 percent.[7]

The massive influx of German and Nordic immigrants, principally to the Midwestern states, also reshaped the size and makeup of the various American Lutheran church bodies in the United States. Southern synods were the biggest losers in this demographic transformation. In 1865, the church bodies that would make up the United Synod of the South totaled about twenty-seven thousand members, or roughly 10 percent of Lutherans in the United States. By 1900, that figure was less than thirty-nine thousand, representing less than one in forty American Lutherans. (These statistics do not include Texas Lutherans, who partnered with northern synods both during and after the Civil War and, due to the state's growing German immigrant population, increased at roughly the same rate as Lutherans in the North.)[8] By the end of the nineteenth century, many southern Lutherans were still clinging to their ecclesiastical autonomy, but they were becoming numerically insignificant.

The immigration of the postbellum era also led to the creation of several independent church bodies. In 1872, more than 90 percent of Lutherans in the United States belonged to one of the three major federations—the Synodical Conference, the General Council, or the General Synod. By 1900, there were sixteen independent synods totaling nearly a half million members, or about 30 percent of American Lutherans. These church bodies were primarily led by recent arrivals from Europe. Seven were German, four were Norwegian, two were Danish, one was Finnish, and one was Icelandic.

Despite this proliferation of new immigrant-led synods, most German and Nordic newcomers joined church bodies that belonged to one of these three largest Lutheran unions. The two federations located primarily in the Mid-Atlantic states, the General Synod and the General Council, each made concerted efforts to reach out to the newly arriving Lutherans by creating German-language periodicals and forming immigrant-led congregations. Their success, however, was varied. From 1870 to 1900, the size of the General Synod doubled while the General Council's membership tripled. This disparity can be partially explained by the already substantial presence of foreign-born Lutherans in the General Council prior to the immigration surge of the Gilded Age. Indeed, the fastest growing member synods of the federation were the Pennsylvania and New York synods, both of which already possessed a sizable German-speaking population, and the Augustana Synod, which was not only led by Swedish Americans but also based in the Midwest.[9]

Undoubtedly the greatest beneficiaries of postbellum immigration were the church bodies of the Synodical Conference. When it was founded in 1872, the fellowship numbered 191,000 members; by 1900, that figure had swelled to 581,000. This tremendous growth is even more impressive when considering that two of the conference's original members, the Ohio and Norwegian synods, withdrew during the Predestination Controversy of the 1880s (discussed later). The second-largest remaining church body, the Wisconsin Synod, grew from about 23,000 members in 1872 to more than 140,000 in 1900. Over that same period, the Missouri Synod, the dominant partner in the Synodical Conference, increased at a similar rate. In 1882, Henry Carroll marveled at how this church body, which accounted for less than 10 percent of Lutherans during the Civil War, had "become the strongest and most influential synod in the United States."[10] By the end of the nineteenth century, the Missouri Synod totaled more than 413,000 members, or roughly one in four American Lutherans.

Because the growth of Lutheranism in the United States was fueled by the arrival of German and Nordic immigrants, many historians have assumed that the conservatism that came to dominate the church was the product of Europe.[11] Yet this common explanation overlooks two crucial facts. First, the shift to a more confessional and separatist faith had already occurred before the influx of immigrants during the late nineteenth century. This conservative transformation had been driven both by native-born Lutherans and by those who had moved to the United States in the antebellum era. It was the ideas of those leaders—and the periodicals, seminaries, and synods they founded before and during the Civil War—that remained the most influential during the Gilded Age.

Second, the religious situation from which the majority of these new arrivals came differed starkly from the type of Lutheranism that came to reign in America. The intellectual leaders of European Lutheranism, especially in Germany, were the pioneers of modern liberal theology. Though some parish pastors and a few university faculties were more conservative, a strict adherence to the Lutheran church's historic confessions and a disavowal of interchurch cooperation was the position of a small minority.[12] The vast majority of German and Nordic immigrants arrived in the United States with little conception of the strict confessionalism and separatism espoused by the leading Lutheran church bodies in their new homeland. Rather than importing a European Lutheranism, postbellum immigrants assimilated into a distinctively American form of the faith that had been shaped during the debates of the Civil War era.

CONFESSIONALISM AND SEPARATISM

In his 1882 article, Henry Carroll noted that two of the defining characteristics of Lutherans in the United States were their "strict adherence to the doctrines of the Church" and their "denominational exclusivism."[13] Though these positions already had been staked out during the Civil War and early years of Reconstruction, the Gilded Age witnessed not just a continuation but even an expansion of this confessional and separatist identity. In each of the three major federations of American Lutheranism—the Synodical Conference, the General Council, and the General Synod—leaders strengthened their commitment to their church's historic teachings and drew sharper boundaries between themselves and other Protestants. They also rejected, in varying degrees, the ideas associated with the "new theology," which sought to reconcile the Christian faith with modern science and biblical criticism. By the end of the nineteenth century, the Lutheran church was an outlier among other major branches of American Protestantism in its nearly wholesale embrace of confessionalism and separatism and its almost complete repudiation of theological modernism.

Leading the way in the rigorous promotion of this confessional conservatism was the Synodical Conference. As the inheritors of Old Lutheranism (though the term largely fell from use during the 1870s), the federation's leaders continued to insist on the necessity of accepting every particular of their church's historic doctrine. In a landmark series of lectures, C. F. W. Walther, the Synodical Conference's principal theologian, asserted that "the Lutheran religion is the only true one" because "all its teachings exclusively give all glory to God." Like other biblicist Protestants, Walther maintained that "everything man needs to know for salvation is recorded in Scripture; we need nothing additional." Yet he also believed that the doctrine espoused by "that precious chosen vessel Dr. Martin Luther" and "other well-known theologians of our church" was identical to the teachings of the Bible.[14] With this understanding, Walther and other Synodical Conference leaders demanded assent on a wide variety of theological judgments, sometimes quite obscure, that they believed to be based on Scripture and found in the Lutheran tradition. Throughout the late nineteenth century, for instance, they issued condemnations of the practice of "usury," the purchase of life insurance, and the marriage of in-laws.[15] For Walther and others, the Bible and the Lutheran church fathers provided decisive verdicts on even the most abstruse theological questions.

Mirroring the demand for strict adherence to seemingly minor doctrinal matters was the call for complete separation from those who did not share their views. Synodical Conference leaders' condemnation of interchurch cooperation extended beyond the sharing of pulpits and altars with those outside of their fellowship. One Missouri Synod writer listed the various activities in which "Christians who do not agree in Doctrine" cannot participate together: "Foreign Mission, Home Mission, Bible Societies, Sunday School Unions, Ministers' Institutes, Prayer-Meetings, Young Men's Christian Associations, Hospitals and Orphanages, Church Dedications and Burials."[16] Also included in their denunciations of "unionism" was participation in "secret societies."[17] This prohibition applied not only to groups such as the Freemasons and the Odd Fellows, which were censured by other conservative Protestants, but also to any voluntary organization that promoted "misuse of God's Word" or encouraged "fellowship with the ungodly," such as Farmer's Alliances, *Turnvereine* (German athletic clubs), and others.[18] This separatism even extended to daily interactions. One former Missouri Synod teacher recalled how "many, perhaps most" of the church body's pastors "considered it a divine command" to not greet or shake hands with Christians of other denominations. "As soon as a 'false teacher' approached on the street," he recalled, "they puffed themselves out like a turkey and proud as a king marched past the 'heretic.'"[19]

Synodical Conference Lutherans reinforced these strict confessional boundaries through an extensive system of parochial schools. In 1872, the congregations of the Missouri Synod supported 472 elementary schools with 30,320 pupils; by 1897, those figures had risen to 1,603 schools and 89,202 students.[20] Over the same period, the Wisconsin Synod experienced a similarly high rate of growth in this area.[21] According to leaders in the Synodical Conference, congregational schools were a necessary bulwark against the dangers emanating from public education: textbooks that contained "the leaven of false teaching," disciplinary practices that were "unchristian and pernicious," and "godless, unbelieving, and immoral" teachers.[22] By contrast, parochial schools were the "blessed means for the spreading of pure doctrine" and, in the words of Walther, "next to the public office of preaching, the chief means of our preservation and progress."[23]

The zealous confessionalism within the Synodical Conference, however, did not ensure lasting ecclesiastical harmony. During the late 1870s and early 1880s, the fellowship was ripped apart by a protracted and bitter controversy over the doctrine of election, or predestination.[24] The basic disagreement centered on the following question: Did God predestine to eternal life those whom he "foresaw would persevere in the faith," or did he elect believers according to his "unfailing necessity"? Arguing the latter position was a group headed by Walther. Opposing him was a faction led at first by Friedrich Schmidt of the Norwegian Synod and soon also by Matthias Loy of the Ohio Synod. Both accused Walther of teaching "crypto-Calvinism," a charge he vehemently rejected. Walther responded that his adversaries were making God's saving grace dependent on human merit, which they also denied. Both argued that their ideas represented the "true Lutheranism" taught by their church's forefathers.[25] These complex debates about high theology were not confined to clerical leaders; according to one participant, they also were "discussed on streets and in lanes, in stores and in saloons."[26] Eventually the disputes led to the withdrawal of the Ohio and Norwegian synods from the Synodical Conference in the early 1880s. Among Norwegian Lutherans, the controversy continued throughout the remainder of the nineteenth century, as they splintered into pro- and anti-Missouri Synod church bodies.

C. F. W. Walther died a few years after the Predestination Controversy concluded, regretful about his inability to unite the American Lutheran church but unwavering in his beliefs. His legacy was continued by several fervent disciples, most notably Francis Pieper (1852–1931), who served as professor at Concordia Seminary for fifty-three years and as president of the Missouri Synod from 1899 to 1911.[27] Yet Walther's impact on the conservative confessionalism of American Lutheranism extended beyond those who were completely loyal to his theological interpretations. In fact, the fierce polemics and ecclesiastical schisms of the Predestination Controversy actually illustrated the successful dissemination of his understanding of Lutheranism. As Abraham Lincoln had observed about northern and southern Christians' appeals to the Bible during the Civil War, both sides of this intra-Lutheran conflict read the same confessions and invoked the same church fathers. Indeed, it was their shared theological assumptions that made their quarrels so acrimonious.

That the Synodical Conference's principles of doctrinal rigor and ecclesiastical separatism were gaining ground was demonstrated by developments in the General Council. This theological convergence manifested itself in several ways. One was the oft-repeated claim that Lutheranism represented the "true church" and alone presented "pure doctrine." These phrases, originally associated with the Missouri Synod, appeared frequently in the writings and sermons of the General Council's leaders.[28] Another example was the growing emphasis on the importance of the Lutheran church fathers. Henry Eyster Jacobs (1844–1932), a rising theological star in the General Council, exemplified this trend. Jacobs sought to demonstrate the "symbolical authority" of the entire *Book of Concord*. In an 1881 article, he argued that the later Lutheran confessions, such as the Formula of Concord, were "ampler and more explicit" summaries of "the scriptural doctrines maintained in the Augsburg Confession" and that "the truth confessed by these creeds is living truth."[29] Jacobs also worked to revive the study of the sixteenth- and seventeenth-century Lutheran dogmaticians, describing their writings as "an exhibition of pure Lutheran theology."[30] Though his rhetoric did not reach the same level of stridency as that of Walther or Pieper, Jacobs's commitment to the Lutheran past matched that of his Missouri Synod counterparts.

The most conspicuous example of the General Council's movement toward the position of the Synodical Conference was in their statements about the permissibility of non-Lutherans and Lutherans partaking of the Lord's Supper together (altar fellowship) or preaching at one another's churches (pulpit fellowship).[31] At the center of these decisions was Charles Porterfield Krauth, the professor at the Philadelphia seminary who served as the General Council's president from 1870 to 1879. Initially, Krauth favored a latitudinarian approach, arguing in 1868 that no firm rule should be made on these matters.[32] Yet over the course of the 1870s, he moved in a more conservative direction. He became the leading proponent of the General Council's 1875 Galesburg Declaration (named after the Illinois city where the convention that passed the resolution was held), which read, "Lutheran pulpits for Lutheran ministers only—Lutheran altars for Lutheran communicants only."[33] In 1877, Krauth offered 105 theses on the subject, defending the rule as "derived from the Word and Confessions." Though he acknowledged that exceptions could be made in times of "urgent and exceptional necessity," he insisted that Lutheran "pulpits and altars" should be kept "as pure as we can."[34]

Krauth's strict interpretation of the Galesburg Declaration, however, was not universally accepted within the General Council. A few weeks after the 1875 convention, Krauth's longtime friend and fellow Philadelphian Joseph Seiss wrote him a letter, lamenting the upheaval caused by the decision: "Friends have turned away from my church. . . . It is simply impossible to maintain ourselves on the Missouri [Synod] ground."[35] At the 1877 convention, Seiss led the opposition against Krauth's 105 theses (which were never officially adopted or rejected), and offered twenty-four propositions of his own. Yet even in his dissent, Seiss was at pains to point out his basic agreement with his colleague. In the *Lutheran and Missionary,* he approvingly quoted another pastor: "The Theses of Dr. Krauth are able, and conceived in good spirit. With many—with most of them—there will be common consent. But . . . the extreme limitation given to the kind of 'exceptions' contemplated in the Galesburg Declaration, I think cannot be sustained." Seiss concluded by praising Krauth's theses as "a vigorous contribution in the line of needed correctives to a proscriptive and domineering Unionism."[36] The approving use of the word "unionism" was telling, as it was term coined by Walther and the Missouri Synod to describe interchurch relations not based on full doctrinal agreement.

Yet despite the General Council's movement toward the confessional conservatism of the Synodical Conference, the two fellowships remained divided. The chief criticism from leaders of the Missouri Synod was that despite the "holy earnestness" of Krauth and others, "many pastors . . . defend pulpit and communion fellowship with the heterodox."[37] Another point of difference concerned congregational schools. Whereas the Synodical Conference saw these institutions as essential to the Lutheran church's mission, the General Council, despite the efforts on the part of some leaders, was not able to build an extensive system of parochial education.[38] Further driving a wedge between the two federations was the Predestination Controversy. General Council theologians criticized the Missouri and Ohio synods for going beyond the Lutheran confessions and seeking to penetrate the "mystery of election."[39] Nevertheless, despite their disagreements, many clergymen of the General Council retained a deep respect for the Synodical Conference. As Krauth wrote to a colleague in 1876, "The Missourians . . . have helped us to see the great principles involved in this discussion. . . . They are men of God, and their work has been of inestimable value."[40]

Charles Porterfield Krauth passed from the scene in 1883. As Walther had been for the Synodical Conference, Krauth was the central figure in forming the General Council's theological identity. And like his counterpart in the Missouri Synod, he left behind a host of successors. The two most significant were Adolph Spaeth (1839–1910), Krauth's son-in-law and biographer, who succeeded him as the president of the General Council from 1880 to 1887 and taught at the Philadelphia seminary for thirty-seven years, and Henry Eyster Jacobs, who took over Krauth's professorship in 1883 and served in that position until 1931.[41] Thanks to Spaeth, Jacobs, and others, by the end of the nineteenth century the General Council's confessional conservatism was more firmly established than it had been at its founding thirty years before.

An even more profound shift occurred in the General Synod. In the two decades following the Old School's withdrawal, the New School Lutherans who controlled the federation sought to counteract their opponents' accusations that they were indifferent or hostile to their church's historic teachings, while also maintaining that certain doctrines in the Augsburg Confession were "nonfundamental." Such a stance was articulated by the General Synod's representatives at a series of "free Lutheran diets." At the 1878 colloquium, J. A. Brown, president of the Gettysburg seminary, praised this "grand old Confession" as one of the Lutheran church's "chiefest glories" but argued that Lutherans are not bound "to every jot and tittle."[42] At the following year's meeting, another General Synod representative claimed that the Lutheran symbols "embody all the essential truths of the Divine Word," but he also called for "mutual toleration" on "the doctrines peculiar to our Confessions," namely baptismal regeneration and the real presence of Christ in the Lord's Supper.[43] Similarly, in an 1883 summary of "the State of the Church," Simeon Harkey, a stalwart of the New School, cheerfully reported to the General Synod's annual convention that "our people are . . . becoming better acquainted with the history and doctrines of their own Church." Yet Harkey also made sure to emphasize that this "clearer and stronger Lutheran consciousness" was "not in the direction of bigotry and exclusiveness" or "hairsplitting distinctions in non-essential matters."[44]

Over the course of the 1880s and 1890s, however, many within the General Synod, particularly of the younger generation, began to challenge the distinction between fundamental and nonfundamental doctrines within the Augsburg Confession. Subtle but perceptible changes came to the Gettysburg seminary via new professors such as Milton Valentine (1825–1906) and James W. Richard

(1843–1909).[45] Though both continued to uphold the "catholic Lutheranism" of the General Synod over against the "particularity" of other Lutheran fellowships, these leaders insisted on adherence to the *entire Augsburg Confession*."[46] This shift was even more evident at the General Synod's Wittenberg Seminary in Ohio, where Luther A. Gotwald (1833–1900) taught that "every doctrinal article" of the Augsburg Confession was "fundamental" and that the other Lutheran symbols should be held in "high esteem." In 1893, three members of the seminary's board of directors charged Gotwald with heresy, alleging that these views were "contrary to the historic spirit . . . of the General Synod."[47] However, in a clear indication of the increasingly confessional direction of this branch of American Lutheranism, Gotwald was unanimously acquitted of all charges.[48]

This growing confessionalism was gradually codified at various conventions of the General Synod. The chief source of contention was the federation's constitution, which had been amended in 1866 to require its members synods to recognize the Augsburg Confession as a "correct exhibition of the fundamental doctrines of the Divine Word" (see chapter 5). The growing conservative contingent in the General Synod worked to bolster this doctrinal basis. In 1895, the delegates passed a resolution that proclaimed the unaltered Augsburg Confession to be "in perfect consistence" with the Bible.[49] Six years later, the convention clarified that "any distinction between fundamental and so-called non-fundamental doctrines in the Augsburg Confession is contrary to that basis set forth in our formula of confessional subscription."[50] Finally, at the 1913 convention, the delegates voted to amend the General Synod's constitution. It now affirmed the "Unaltered Augsburg Confession" as "a correct exhibition of the faith and doctrine of our Church as founded upon the Word" and declared the rest of the church's symbols to be "expositions of Lutheran doctrine of great historical and interpretive value."[51] Nearly fifty years after the schism of 1866, the General Synod had moved decisively away from the doctrinal position of New School Lutheranism.

With a greater allegiance to the Lutheran confessions came a waning interest in interchurch cooperation. This shift, like the movement toward a more rigorous confessionalism, was gradual but perceptible. Before the Civil War, Samuel Schmucker, the leading theologian of the General Synod, had been at the forefront of Protestant ecumenism. In his last major initiative, the aging churchman helped to revive the defunct American Evangelical Alliance in 1866. He also republished his influential *Fraternal Appeal* in anticipation of the World Evangelical Alliance's meeting in New York, which was held, after some delays, in 1873. Schmucker, however, died shortly before the meeting took place.[52]

Though General Synod Lutherans continued to participate in the Evangelical Alliance, as well as in organizations such as the Young Men's Christian Association, the years following Schmucker's death witnessed a decline in optimism about the prospects of inter-Protestant unity. Speaking before the Evangelical Alliance in 1877, J. A. Brown lamented "the existence of divisions" but argued that "it is useless to expect to find the divine ideal of the Church perfectly realized," and he even endorsed "a healthy rivalry between different denominations."[53] Ten years later, the convention of the General Synod issued a resolution that acknowledged "the evils which so largely mark the divisions of the Christian church" but also declared, "We deem the restoration of the organic unity of the Church, at the present period, neither desirable nor practicable."[54] Though the federation never adopted anything resembling the restrictions on interchurch cooperation authorized by the Synodical Conference or the General Council, its turn away from the hopeful ecumenism of Schmucker reflected the increasing separatism of Lutheranism in the United States.

A similar trajectory occurred on the issue of revivalism. During the antebellum era, General Synod Lutherans had vigorously promoted various "new measures," not only as methods of conversion and spiritual renewal but also as ways to bring their denomination closer to the practices of Anglo-evangelicalism. Their insistence on the importance of revivals persisted in the first two decades after the Civil War. The General Synod's "State of the Church" reports extolled the value of "revivals of religion," and the *Lutheran Observer,* the church paper associated with the federation, devoted significant space to accounts of revivals taking place at congregations, colleges, and seminaries.[55] However, by the mid-1880s, signs of a shift in practice were becoming evident. In 1885, the General Synod dropped the category of "prayer meetings" from its statistical report.[56] Two years later, the *Lutheran Observer* noted that "some pastors . . . regard all special efforts to promote revivals as of doubtful utility."[57] At the same time, many General Synod Lutherans were promoting a more liturgical form of worship.[58] By the beginning of the twentieth century, the president of the General Synod could declare, "The New School men . . . [of] the new measure party . . . belong to a departed generation."[59]

The key leader of that "departed generation" had been Samuel Simon

Schmucker. His institutional legacy was impressive. The General Synod, Gettysburg Theological Seminary, and Pennsylvania College (later Gettysburg College) all owed their existence to his tireless work. Yet unlike the other great figures of nineteenth-century American Lutheranism, Walther and Krauth, Schmucker left few intellectual heirs. When he died in 1873, his goal of uniting American Lutheranism around the "fundamental" doctrines of the Augsburg Confession, inter-Protestant unity, and religious revivals had already been eclipsed by the confessional conservatism in the Synodical Conference and General Council. What he could not have anticipated was the rejection of his theological vision in the federation he had been so instrumental in founding.

The shared theological conservatism among American Lutherans was on full display in their condemnation of the "new theology," which sought to reconcile the Christian faith with modern thought. In the postbellum era, intellectual currents from Europe, particularly those surrounding Darwinian evolutionary theory and historical criticism of the Bible, began to take hold among many Protestant denominations in the United States. By the end of the nineteenth century, Baptists, Methodists, Presbyterians, and other Anglo-Protestants were dividing into liberal and conservative factions.[60] In American Lutheranism, however, no such cleavage occurred. Instead, virtually all Lutherans in the United States—native-born and immigrant, eastern and Midwestern—rejected these new ideas.

Unsurprisingly, the leaders of the Synodical Conference (and those synods formerly connected to it) were the most dismissive. "Darwinism," predicted one writer in the Missouri Synod's theological journal, "will be regarded . . . as a confusing episode of absurdities."[61] "Biblical criticism," wrote another, "is nothing else than blasphemy of the Scriptures and therefore blasphemy of God."[62] For Matthias Loy of the Ohio Synod, the entire edifice of modern theology rested on false foundations. "Liberalism," Loy wrote in an 1883 work that anticipated J. Gresham Machen's famous *Christianity and Liberalism* forty years later, "is a system claiming for darkness and error and doubt a full equality of right in the Church with light and truth and faith."[63] This antimodernism sometimes manifested itself in extreme directions. In 1873, for example, one Missouri Synod pastor published a book calling into question the heliocentric universe.[64] For the most part, however, Lutherans in the Synodical Conference simply did not engage with the intellectual developments of the late nineteenth century. Content to label evolution, higher criticism, and other modern developments as self-evidently unbiblical, they instead focused their energy on an increasingly narrow range of theological issues.[65]

Like their mostly foreign-born counterparts in the Synodical Conference, the primarily native-born Lutherans in the General Council rejected any incursions of theological liberalism into their churches.[66] Most saw a fundamental contradiction between Darwinian evolution and higher criticism, on the one hand, and the "good confession of our Lutheran church," on the other. Typical was the assessment of one writer for the *Lutheran Church Review*—the General Council's theological journal, founded in 1882—who saw "two fiercely hostile parties" battling for supremacy, "one clinging to the faith of our fathers and the other championing an aggressive 'religion in the age of Darwin.'"[67] Theodore Schmauk (1860–1920), another prominent General Council Lutheran, argued that modern "negative criticism" rests on evidence that "is almost entirely internal and circumstantial," and even more fundamentally, on "the ever-present and ever-pressing Desire of the intellect to Deny the existence of the supernatural in history."[68] Seiss, in a sermon before a meeting of the Pennsylvania Synod in 1896, summed up his church body's hostility to the "skeptical theorizings" of higher criticism: "Stick to the Bible *as it is*. . . . Cling to the old Faith—the faith of prophets, apostles, and our own honored confessors."[69]

Mirroring their looser understanding of confessional adherence and church unity, the leaders of the General Synod were less strident in their opposition to modern science and biblical criticism. Representative was the outlook expressed by Milton Valentine in his inaugural address at Gettysburg Theological Seminary. Confident that "the oft-talked of conflict between Christianity and science is a figment," he urged students to approach "the crowding hypotheses and shifting theories" with neither "hasty and timid modification of theology, nor fierce and denunciatory polemics." Instead, they should remain assured "that no truth of the gospel is going to suffer overthrow." Valentine showed less irenicism toward "the Higher Criticism," disparaging this "present form of speculation and agitation" as full of "baseless assumptions, blunders, and contradictions." Nevertheless, he still argued that students should not "ignore these agitations which sweep around us" but pursue "straight-forward examination."[70]

Over the course of the postbellum era, a few General Synod writers made attempts to harmonize some aspects of evolutionary theory with the Bible and granted minor concessions to biblical criticism. Yet their accommodations differed little from those offered by the conservative evangelicals who would publish the *Fundamentals* in the 1910s.[71] Though constituting the "liberal" end of American Lutheranism, on the spectrum of late nineteenth-century Protestantism in the United States, the General Synod, like the Synodical Conference and General Council, was fundamentally conservative.

POLITICAL AND SOCIAL CONSERVATISM

Reinforcing American Lutheranism's confessionalism, separatism, and rejection of theological modernism was a conservative attitude toward politics and society. This outlook had its origins in the early years of Reconstruction, as many Lutherans became increasingly suspicious of Christian political involvement and wary of radical change. During the Gilded Age, these instincts hardened into two interlocking principles. On the one hand, most Lutherans expressed skepticism about, if not outright antagonism toward, efforts to address moral problems through the political process. On the other hand, the church's leaders critiqued and often opposed ideas and movements that they considered "revolutionary." These views, of course, were not universally held by all Lutherans in the Unites States. Some Scandinavian Lutheran clergymen, for example, supported temperance laws and continued to play an active leadership role in Midwestern ethnic politics.[72] Nevertheless, this dual form of conservatism—resistance to "moral legislation" and opposition to various forms of "radicalism"—was broadly shared by leaders of the American Lutheran church's three major federations: the Synodical Conference, the General Council, and the General Synod.

As in theology, the most stridently conservative on political and social issues were the Lutherans of the Synodical Conference. The publications of the Missouri Synod upheld a "complete, thorough, political separation of church and state."[73] Though they acknowledged that the government could "foster religion in general" and that it was "the duty of each Christian" to "seek the good of the state," they also were convinced that issues of morality and conscience "have nothing to do with the power of the state" and disavowed "mixing the spiritual and secular."[74] Nevertheless, Synodical Conference ministers believed that they had the responsibility to counteract "heretical" ideas in national life. C. F. W. Walther summarized this principle in a popular lecture against communism and socialism. "Politics does not in the least concern us theologians," he wrote. "But when those who pretend to be politicians, meddle with *religion*, we cannot keep silent without sacrificing the truth."[75] Given these commitments, Synodical Conference Lutherans frequently adopted the seemingly contradictory posture of condemning "the agitating spirit of mixing church and politics" and staking out positions against various forms of "Revolutionism" in public affairs.[76]

Like their convergence in the areas of confessionalism and interchurch unity, Lutherans in the General Council increasingly reflected the political and social views found in the Synodical Conference. They, too, affirmed that "church and state must move in their appropriate sphere in perfect governmental independence of each other."[77] Though the state may "advance [the nation's] moral and religious interests," one article argued, it should not "compel men to be religious by force of law."[78] Yet even though they were skeptical about combining the spheres of politics and religion, these primarily Pennsylvania-based Lutherans resembled their Midwestern counterparts in their willingness to voice their opinions on a variety of issues. As Charles Porterfield Krauth put it, "While it is true that the pulpit is no place for partisan politics, it is equally true that the whole counsel of God is not to be held back in any part."[79] For Krauth, this meant continuing the theme, begun during the early years of Reconstruction, of condemning the era's politics as "a wretched system of snares and falsehoods" filled with "partisans" of "mischievous character."[80] Others focused their attacks on the "principles of Materialism, Agnosticism, [and] Atheism" espoused by "the social agitators of our times."[81] In the view of General Council leaders, Lutherans should both uphold the separation of church and state and refute radical ideas that undermined the nation.

Spokesmen for the General Synod adopted similar principles with regard to the relation between religion and politics and the role of preachers in addressing the ills of modern society. Though "Church and State . . . are by no means absolutely independent of each other," lectured one Philadelphia minister at the Gettysburg seminary, "the Church can be faithful to her calling in her own sphere."[82] An article by another General Synod clergyman put the matter more succinctly: "The general rule taught us in our seminary days, and which has always been quite commonly accepted as well grounded in reason and scripture, is, that the Church has nothing to do, directly, with politics."[83] Like their counterparts in the Synodical Conference and the General Council, the leaders of the General Synod saw manifold problems in Gilded Age America. One minister listed them as "the evils of intemperance," "the ever-widening chasm between rich and poor," "godless socialism," and "political corruption." However, while preachers should "teach men the proper application of Christian principles to daily life," he argued, "this is altogether different from 'intermeddling *directly* with secular and political matters.'" When it came to addressing "great social problems," he wrote, "there can therefore be but one remedy—that furnished by the Sacrifice of Calvary."[84]

Of course, though Lutheran leaders spoke against the direct involvement of their church in politics, members of their congregations still participated in elections. Some historians, such as Richard Jensen and Paul Kleppner, have argued that religious commitment was the key factor in determining political affiliation during the Gilded Age, with the key divide being between "pietistic" Protestants such as Methodists and Congregationalists, who mostly voted Republican, and "liturgical" or "confessional" Christians, especially Roman Catholics, who largely supported the Democrats. The voting patterns of American Lutherans, however, do not neatly fit their analysis. True, immigrant German Lutherans in the Midwest tended to vote for Democrats, though not overwhelmingly so. But Swedish and Norwegian Lutherans, the majority of whom were just as "liturgical" and "confessional" as their German coreligionists, supported the Republicans in high numbers. Meanwhile, Lutherans in the Mid-Atlantic states, the majority of whom were native-born English speakers, were split between the two parties.[85] Lutherans' political affinities during the final decades of the nineteenth century, it seems, were driven primarily by the ethnic and regional loyalties inherited from the Civil War era.

Though their religious views did not consistently manifest themselves in particular party affiliations, Lutherans' conservatism shaped their reactions to the era's various reform movements. One of the most prominent of these was the temperance movement. Motivated by sincere concerns about the effects of intoxicating drink as well as nativist hostility toward immigrants, many Anglo-evangelicals increasingly demanded not only voluntary abstinence but also the banning of alcohol through law.[86] Another development was the rise of the social gospel. In response to the growing problems of economic inequality, poor working and living conditions, and tensions between capital and labor, various Protestants, typically of a more modernist theological persuasion, sought to Christianize society by reforming the nation's political and economic structures.[87] Finally, the Gilded Age witnessed the continued advocacy by female and Black citizens for civil and political equality. On the whole, Lutherans—no matter their ecclesiastical home or party allegiance—opposed these movements, with their assessments ranging from mild criticism to overt hostility.

This range could be seen in Lutheran reactions to the postbellum push for temperance. The spokesmen of the Synodical Conference were the most vehement in their opposition. A widely circulated tract called the movement the "outgrowth of wild fanaticism" and likened the abstinence pledge promoted by revivalist Francis Murphy to the selling of indulgences by John Tetzel. Yet its most basic criticism was that "we cannot legislate men to be good"; only the gospel could combat the sin of drunkenness.[88] General Council Lutherans, some of whom had advocated for temperance in the antebellum era, were more limited in their critiques. Though temperance and other "so-called reforms" might possess a "noble aim," declared Charles W. Schaeffer, their "tendency" is to use "a system of operations not connected with the doctrine of the Gospel."[89]

Even in the General Synod, many leaders came to reject the predominant views of evangelical reformers. As late as the 1870s, New School Lutherans continued to promote the cause of temperance, including the use of state power to address the "most important social problem of the age."[90] Yet as the advocacy of prohibition increased during the Gilded Age, some began to issue cautious warnings that "the Church is not to legislate for the State" and that Christian ministers should primarily seek to change "the sentiment of the people."[91] By the early twentieth century, even though some General Synod Lutherans continued to support prohibition as "perfectly legitimate," others argued that even in the "great moral interest" of alcohol abuse, "it does not follow that the Church should directly promote any particular piece of temperance legislation."[92] Though scattered calls for temperance could still be found among Lutherans, the vast majority opposed the Anglo-Protestant cause of prohibiting the sale of alcohol.

Lutherans' growing skepticism about Christian political participation and opposition to various forms of "radicalism" also produced a nearly wholesale rejection of labor activism in general and the social gospel in particular.[93] The leaders of the Synodical Conference were especially vociferous. Walther accused labor unions of being "schools of communism and socialism" and using Christian-sounding rhetoric to mask an anti-Christian agenda.[94] An 1886 article in the *Lutheraner* condemned Washington Gladden and others for "endorsing riots" and the "boycotting system."[95] Though Walther and others were not afraid to criticize "the tyrannical oppression on the part of the rich," they believed that harmony between capital and labor could only come when "the true Christian religion takes possession of the human heart."[96]

Lutherans in the General Council and General Synod voiced similar sentiments. While they sometimes made gestures toward the plight of workers, the papers associated with each church body more often criticized unions, denounced strikes, and condemned socialism.[97] Similarly, though they were not completely dismissive of the ideas put forth by social gospelers, leaders in both Lutheran fellowships expressed skepticism on two fronts: its leading thinkers were too optimistic about human nature and they elevated social reform above the church's chief work of preaching the gospel.[98] Typical was the assessment of Milton Valentine, president of the General Synod's seminary in Gettysburg: "All the enormous activity and colossal work of recent progress, have no healing"; instead, "social regeneration" can only come "by the old truths of a divine Saviour, through a vicarious atonement, justification by faith, and *regeneration* by the Holy Ghost."[99]

Lutherans' opposition to "radical" reform efforts could also be seen in their general resistance to women's rights. The most hostile were those in the Synodical Conference.[100] Francis Pieper described female suffrage as a violation of the "clearest order of God" and an idea that "turns all natural order upside down."[101] Rather than "giving speeches for political or social agitation," wrote August Graebner (1849–1904), another prominent Missouri Synod clergyman, "if we ask where . . . woman can primarily prove to be a useful member of society, the answer will have to be: in the home, in the family."[102] According to Synodical Conference leaders, the Bible forbid female participation in politics.

By contrast, Lutherans in the General Council and the General Synod slowly came to accept the possibility of women voting for public office. In the first years after the Civil War, the periodicals of both fellowships had expressed hostility to the idea. The *Lutheran Observer* wrote that female suffrage "would prove highly detrimental to the best interests of the State" and "highly injurious to woman herself," while the *Lutheran and Missionary* opposed "modern innovations in sentiment and action that tend to unsex woman."[103] By the end of the Gilded Age, however, some theologians were beginning to voice cautious approval. In a series of articles, Theodore Schmauk of the General Council argued that while he was "no advocate or defender" of "woman suffrage," it was incorrect to equate voting in modern society with the exercise of authority.[104] Still, Schmauk insisted that any expansion of female "rights and liberties" should not overturn "man's proper authority and rule over woman as her lord and head."[105] Even in their tentative endorsements of women's suffrage, postbellum Lutherans reflected a conservative concern for order and an opposition to radical ideas.[106]

When it came to the rights of African Americans, however, white Lutherans were almost completely silent. The researcher will search in vain for extended discussions in the church's chief periodicals of the rise of Jim Crow laws, the growth of lynching, or the various Supreme Court cases that reversed the gains in racial equality made during Reconstruction. In part, this apathy stemmed from postbellum Lutherans' apprehensions about the church addressing "political" questions. Yet it also stemmed from racial prejudice. In their few writings on the issue of race during the Gilded Age, Lutheran writers declared African Americans to possess a "peculiarly emotional nature" and "lamentably low" morals and described them as "naturalized exotic[s]" who live in a "semi-heathen state."[107]

Though scattered calls could be found to evangelize Blacks, Lutherans in the North did little to reach out across racial lines with the gospel. One exception could be found in the Maryland Synod. At the urging of John Butler, this General Synod–affiliated church body sponsored several Black students to study theology at Howard University in the 1880s.[108] The most successful of those students was Daniel Wiseman (1858–1942), an immigrant from the Danish West Indies (today's U.S. Virgin Islands). After graduating from Howard in 1884, he founded Redeemer Lutheran Church in the nation's capital and served there for nearly sixty years. However, though Wiseman's congregation was a full member of the Maryland Synod, it was one of the rare instances of interracial partnership among northern Lutherans.[109]

The only concerted Lutheran effort to reach out to African Americans in the postbellum South came from the Synodical Conference—a surprising occurrence, given their insistence, even after the Civil War, on the biblical permissibility of slavery. Predictably, their mission effort was often characterized by racial prejudice and paternalism. The federation classified its program under "heathen missions," since, as one promoter reasoned, southern Blacks' "so-called Christianity is in many ways no better than heathenism." Begun in 1877, its organizers and first missionaries seemed to have lacked any sense of the political and social situation in the South. After a fitful start, however, the mission enjoyed modest success by the end of the nineteenth century, largely thanks to the work of Nils Bakke (1853–1921). Convinced that "Negroes can ... become upright, true Lutherans," Bakke helped to establish a Black church in New Orleans in the late 1880s. In 1891, he moved to North Carolina to assist the fledgling Alpha Synod, which was soon absorbed into the Missouri Synod. By 1905, the Synodical Conference's mission to Black southerners encompassed twenty-eight congregations, a college in New Orleans, and a seminary in Greensboro, North Carolina.[110]

Yet apart from these and a few other examples, African Americans were almost entirely absent from the exponential growth of the Lutheran church during the decades following the Civil War. As late as 1950, fewer than eleven thousand of the approximately 4 million Lutheran communicants in the United States were Black.[111] Though these dismal figures have somewhat improved, Lutheranism today remains, in the apt description of one writer, "the whitest denomination in the U.S."[112]

American Lutherans' conservatism in the areas of political involvement, temperance advocacy, the "labor question," women's rights, and race was neither the necessary byproduct of their church's historic theology nor derived from their status as immigrants, as some historians have argued.[113] To be sure, Lutherans in the United States grounded some of their political ideas in Martin Luther's doctrine of the two kingdoms. However, their coreligionists throughout the world applied this teaching in a variety of other ways.[114] The claim that the conservatism of late nineteenth-century U.S. Lutheranism was attributable to the "immigrant experience" is even less convincing, as the native-born were just as likely to espouse their church's predominant ethos as those originally from abroad. (There was no stark divide between "foreign" and "Americanist" perspectives, as prevailed in Roman Catholicism.)[115]

Instead, like their embrace of confessionalism and rejection of interchurch cooperation, American Lutherans' political and social views were shaped by the culture of the Civil War era. During the first years of Reconstruction, Lutherans in the United States had already come to distance themselves from "mixing religion and politics"—which they themselves had practiced throughout the Civil War—and to reject various forms of "radicalism." In the final decades of the nineteenth century, as the nation faced a dizzying array of crises and challenges, this political and social conservatism offered a sense of surety and order. It also provided yet another way for Lutherans to propagate their distinctiveness relative to the Anglo-Protestant mainstream.

AMERICAN EXCEPTIONALISM

Despite their manifold criticisms of politics and society in the Gilded Age, Lutherans remained confident in their nation's exceptionalism and certain of their church's quintessentially American character. In fact, the four decades after the Civil War witnessed the intensification of these commitments. By the turn of the century, Lutherans were insisting not only that their church had a particular mission in the United States and stood in harmony with the nation's values but also that they, more than any other Christians, epitomized American ideals. Such grand claims went hand in hand with Lutherans' growing confessionalism and increasing separatism. Just as they represented the "true church," many also contended that Lutheranism, in contrast to other denominations, stood for "true Americanism."

Foundational to Lutherans' conception of their nation's exceptionalism was its religious freedom—a principle that they believed owed its origins to Martin Luther. This view was unreservedly proclaimed within the Synodical Conference. The Missouri Synod's Wilhelm Sihler, in a tract commemorating the United States' centennial anniversary, praised "the fundamental separation of church and state" as "indisputably the greatest" of the "countless blessings that God has shown our people."[116] The idea that "God's kingdom and the world's kingdoms should be separated things," wrote another Synodical Conference leader, was first understood by "our Doctor Luther" and then enshrined in the U.S. Constitution "under God's direction."[117]

Lutherans in the General Council and General Synod took their exceptionalist rhetoric one step further, arguing that Luther and his principles were responsible not only for religious liberty but also for civil and political freedom. In an 1886 sermon, Joseph Seiss praised the United States as "the happiest, the freest, and the most prosperous nation under all the circuit of the sun" and described this as the providential consequence of the Protestant Reformation. "American freedom," Seiss declared, "is the fullest, directest, and highest outgrowth of that mighty movement."[118] Clergymen in the General Synod invoked similar sentiments, hailing the nation's "Biblical, Christian, Protestant" character and describing the Reformation as "the true source and origin" of "our liberties." It is "certain," wrote one theologian, "that the Declaration of Independence and the American Constitution never would have been written had Luther not nailed his theses to the church door at Wittenberg and made his valorous stand at Worms."[119]

Postbellum Lutherans believed not only that their nation's greatness was indebted to the Lutheran Reformation but also that their church had a special mission in the United States. Often, they described that mission in terms specific to their own church body or federation. In an address that coincided with 1893 World's Fair in Chicago, August Graebner recounted the history of U.S. Lutheranism as the saga of "a degenerate church" renewed by the founding of the Missouri Synod. "To-day," Graebner boasted, "that synod is by far the greatest Lutheran synod not only in America, but on the face of the earth."[120] Spokesmen for the General Council also were convinced that their federation had a distinctive calling in the United States. "One of its main tasks," wrote Adolph Spaeth, was to ensure "that the different languages and nationalities of our beloved Zion should be firmly knit together in this New World in the unity of one and the same pure faith."[121] General Synod Lutherans, too, believed that they possessed a particular destiny. Samuel Sprecher, for example, continued to claim that "the true spirit of the early Lutheran Reformation" was "for the first time distinctly and fully recognized . . . in this country, and that by the General Synod."[122] Yet just as often, Lutherans' praise for their church's American vocation was of a more general character. In an 1898 sermon marking the 150th anniversary of the founding of the Pennsylvania Ministerium, Joseph Seiss recounted the growth of the "great Lutheran communion in this western world." He then looked to the future: "Like our nation, we are only at the beginning of our mission and destiny on this continent."[123]

Variations of these themes—the providential blessings of the nation's liberty, the special mission of Lutheranism in the United States, and the distinctively American character of the Lutheran church—had already been voiced in the years before, during, and immediately after the Civil War. What changed among Lutherans in the Gilded Age was the rise of the claim that other religious groups were "un-American." To be sure, such assertions were not completely new. Lutherans had joined the nativist chorus against Roman Catholics in the antebellum era and continued to label "papism" and "Romanism" as opposed to the nation's liberties throughout the postbellum years.[124] However, during the final decades of the nineteenth century, Lutherans began to extend this criticism to other Protestants, arguing that their own church stood as the most consistent advocate of American freedom.

Such assessments could be found in both the General Council and the General Synod. One article in the Philadelphia seminary's *Lutheran Church Review,* for example, sought "to place our Church in her true light over against other Protestant communions." Contra those who "contemptuously" described Lutheranism "as a foreign sect," he argued, it "was among the first Protestant Churches to be transplanted on these shores" and is "the author of civil and religious liberty in modern Europe and America."[125] A similar argument could be found in the General Synod's *Lutheran Quarterly.* One writer challenged George Bancroft's claim that the "influence of Lutheranism on America was inconsiderable" by examining the historical record. Instead of Martin Luther's defense of "individual rights," the Puritans, as well as other English colonists, adopted the "theocratic" system of John Calvin. By contrast, the German Lutherans of Pennsylvania "pursue[d] their individual development without clamoring for control in civil matters" and "were the first communion to exemplify in America the doctrine of liberty of conscience." Their "conservative, unobtrusive, steady way of self-culture and industry, and non-interference with others . . . kept calming the turbulent waters until the nation's doctrines merged into their own." These distinctively Lutheran "principles," the article concluded, represented "the spirit and culmination of American Liberty."[126]

The most forceful arguments about Lutheranism's exemplification of the nation's ideals, however, came from the Synodical Conference. Often, leaders asserted such claims when they believed that their liberty was under attack, as in the case of the Bennett Law in Wisconsin and the Edwards Law in Illinois. In 1889, the legislatures of these two states passed bills that required all schools, public and parochial, to teach in English. Lutherans in the Missouri and Wisconsin synods reacted swiftly. Church papers denounced the laws as "unconstitutional" and "tyrannical," and ministers mobilized congregants to elect new state representatives. In their political activism, spokesmen for these church bodies not only proclaimed that Lutherans were "true Americans" who stood for "the rights of the people" but also attacked the Anglo-Protestants who supported the bills as "un-American" promoters of the "spirit of Puritanism."[127] Synodical Conference Lutherans also applied this criticism to the leaders of various moral reform efforts. The "fanatics" who promote "Christian" legislation and the "tiresome temperance women," wrote August Graebner, "are storming against . . . religious freedom." By contrast, he argued, Lutherans sought to uphold "our fatherland" and "keep it *unabridged* in its liberty."[128]

Bringing these various arguments together was Graebner's colleague at the Missouri Synod's seminary in St. Louis, Friedrich Bente (1858–1930). In a short article published just after the turn of the century, Bente sounded many familiar notes: that the "most precious jewel" of religious freedom is the nation's "heart and soul"; that American liberties are "dependent" on ideas first put forward by Martin Luther; and that other Christians, both Catholic and Protestant, hold to principles that are "the very opposite of true Americanism," namely "the amalgamation of Church and State." Yet though his arguments had been well-trodden by others before him, Bente's culminating statement best captured the essence of the Lutheran version of American exceptionalism that emerged in the postbellum era: "Lutheranism and Americanism dwell in perfect harmony, and, other things being equal, a Lutheran makes the best American: the consistent representative of American liberty."[129]

★ ★ ★

Lutherans in the United States approached the twentieth century beset by a variety of ironies. The most noticeable centered on the church's size and influence. In 1830, American Lutheranism had encompassed three seminaries, one periodical, and less than fifty thousand communicant members. Seventy years later, the church operated 142 academies, colleges, and seminaries; ran 91 orphanages, hospitals, and homes for the aged; published 159 journals, magazines, and newspapers; and numbered more than 1.6 million members.[130] Yet despite this tremendous growth in people and institutions, Lutherans at the end of the Gilded Age were just as intellectually and organizationally isolated from mainstream Protestants as they had been during the early republic. The situation within their church was also ironic. By 1900, American Lutherans exhibited more unity in how they viewed their church's historic confessions than at any time in the previous seven decades, but they were even more institutionally divided than they had been in 1830. But perhaps the sharpest irony revolved around the question of American identity. As they had throughout the Civil War era, the vast majority of Lutherans believed that their church and its teachings exemplified American ideals. But by the end of the nineteenth century, they stood as conservative outsiders in the nation's culture, occupying, in the assessment of Henry Carroll, "a position apart ... from the current of Protestant life."[131]

One Lutheran who lamented the conservative transformation of his church during the decades after the Civil War was John H. W. Stuckenberg (1835–1903).[132] The son of immigrants from Germany, Stuckenberg was educated at the General Synod's Wittenberg College in Ohio, where he became an ardent disciple of New Lutheranism. In the years following his graduation, he pastored congregations in Iowa, Pennsylvania, and Indiana; served a brief stint as a Union army chaplain; and studied at the universities of Halle, Göttingen, Berlin, and Tübingen. After returning from his final studies abroad, he was appointed to teach theology at his alma mater. There, he sought to preserve the New School vision of a church that was ecumenically active, politically engaged, and culturally consequential. Of particular importance to Stuckenberg was working with other denominations in the realm of social reform. In 1880, he published *Christian Sociology,* a work that anticipated many of the arguments of the social gospel. His wife, Mary Gingrich Stuckenberg (1849–1934), was an active reformer in her own right, who advocated for women's rights and held various leadership positions in the Women's Christian Temperance Union.[133] Yet despite his many accomplishments, John Stuckenberg felt that his career was a lonely endeavor. Near the end of his life, he wrote to a friend about his isolation amid his church's growing conservatism. "Other denominations open their churches and institutions and heartily welcome me," he lamented. "But my own Church is closed to me because I am not doing its work!"[134]

Because of his disagreements with the trajectory of Lutheranism in the United States, Stuckenberg turned instead to Europe. In 1880, he and Mary moved to Berlin and would remain there for fourteen years, with John serving as a chaplain for American expatriates and Mary leading a European affiliate of the Women's Christian Temperance Union. During his time abroad, Stuckenberg discovered that the "narrow, exclusive, and bigoted confessionalism" of the Missouri Synod and the General Council "is regarded in Germany as an Americanism." Even conservative European Lutherans, he realized, had a much more broad-minded approach to the subjects of confessional adherence and church unity than what prevailed in the United States. Before his return from Europe,

Stuckenberg published several tracts that tried to convince his fellow General Synod Lutherans to avoid the "contagion" of the "American Missourians." Rather than being found in "this new, unhistoric, exclusive Lutheranism," he argued, "the hope of our Church in America" lies in "the deep, broad, historic Lutheranism of Germany."[135]

Stuckenberg's career reveals one more important irony of American Lutheranism in the postbellum era: By the end of the nineteenth century, the only Lutherans in the United States who maintained any serious connection to European theology were the last remnants of the New School, those whom historians have labeled "American Lutherans."[136] By contrast, the leading confessionalists, those who have been characterized as "European," were harshly critical of most theology from the Old World and instead embraced the conservative outlook that was distinctive to Lutheranism in the United States.[137]

C. F. W. Walther personified this paradox. The German-born leader of the Missouri Synod wrote almost exclusively in his native language and was largely isolated from the main currents of theology in the United States. Yet he was definitively American. "The Church of the Reformation, in the land of her birth," Walther claimed, "is like a rotting corpse."[138] Because of this, Lutherans in the United States had a distinctive mission, which he laid out in a sermon celebrating the three hundredth anniversary of the Formula of Concord:

> Arise, you Lutherans of America! Let us use the glorious freedom that we enjoy here, so that the old confessional banner, which in our old fatherland lies in decay, is hoisted here once again. . . . Our young American Lutheran church . . . is called to salvage and rescue the pure gospel here in the New World. . . . Oh then arise! Arise, American Lutheran Zion, and shine![139]

For Walther and many others, the future of Lutheranism was to be found in the United States.

★ ★ ★ ★ ★ ★ ★

Epilogue

O N JANUARY 29, 1905, President Theodore Roosevelt made a prediction: "The Lutheran Church . . . is destined to be one of the two or three greatest and most important national churches in the United States." The occasion for his remarks was a speech given at the rededication of Luther Place Memorial Church in Washington, DC. In his assessment of Lutheranism's potential, Roosevelt noted its "peculiar function," namely to bring "the immigrant of Lutheran faith from the Old World . . . into fellowship with the existing bodies." If Lutherans in the United States fulfilled this "prime duty," he anticipated that their church, which already was "of very great power numerically," would "grow steadily to even greater power." Writers in various Lutheran periodicals responded to their president's words with pride and enthusiastic assent. In this bold forecast of numerical growth, however, it was easy to overlook Roosevelt's revealing description of Lutheranism's place in the nation's culture: "The Lutheran Church in this country," he declared, is "one of the two or three churches most distinctly American."[1]

By the end of the nineteenth century, that "distinctly American" identity consisted of four components. The vast majority of Lutherans adhered to a strict confessionalism and rejected the incursions of theological liberalism. In the realm of church affairs, they had isolated themselves from other Protestants, either by shunning all forms of "unionism" or by limiting participation in interdenominational organizations. Most rejected all forms of political and social radicalism while also insisting on a thorough separation of church and state. Finally, Lutherans in the United States praised their exceptional nation as the bastion of religious liberty and argued that their faith was uniquely suited to the republic's free institutions. This synthesis of ideas had been forged in the debates and disputes of the Civil War and the early years of Reconstruction and had been cemented during the Gilded Age. At the time of Roosevelt's speech, Lutherans in the United States had made their own distinctive faith.

During the first decades of the twentieth century, that identity was subject to challenges and modifications. The First World War, in particular, was a watershed event for American Lutheranism. The anti-German sentiments promoted by old-stock Americans and the Woodrow Wilson administration, as well as the general campaign against "hyphenated-Americanism" (promoted by leaders such as Roosevelt), strained many Lutherans' sense of patriotism and compelled many second- and third-generation immigrants to move away from the use of their native language.[2] The immigration restrictions that followed the war reduced the already declining number of newly arriving German and Scandinavian Lutherans. By the end of the 1920s the Lutheran church in the United States was once again predominantly English-speaking, and some Lutherans were seeking to abandon their posture of ethnic and ecclesiastical isolation.[3] Additionally, as the fundamentalist–modernist controversy raged in various Protestant denominations, Lutherans were drawn into these theological debates. Many remained ardent proponents of biblical inerrancy and staunch opponents of evolutionary theory, but a few others began accepting ideas that resembled those of mainstream, liberal Protestants.[4]

Important as these developments were, they did not produce a major change in Lutheranism's relationship with American culture. As of 1930, the Lutheran church in the United States, in the apt description of one contemporary observer, still fell into three theological camps: "ultra conservative," "conservative," and "mildly so."[5] The first of these camps was represented by the Synodical Conference, the Missouri Synod–led federation founded in 1872; the second by the American Lutheran Conference, an association of mostly Midwestern church bodies established in 1930; and the third by the United Lutheran Church in America, a 1918 merger of the General Synod, the General Council, and the United Synod of the South. Yet even "mildly" conservative Lutherans remained wary of theological modernism, interdenominational cooperation, and political and social innovation.[6] For example, shortly after its founding, the United Lutheran Church in America refused to join the Federal Council of Churches—though it agreed to maintain a "consultative relationship"—due to its lack of "any definite recognition of the necessity or importance of unity in faith" and "its failure properly to distinguish . . . between the true functions of the State and those of the Church."[7] During the interwar years, Lutherans by and large remained comfortably insulated in their confessional conservatism.

Amid this theological and ecclesiastical isolation, the American Lutheran population continued to increase. But in contrast to the booming growth in the half-century following the Civil War, immigration was only a minor factor in the church's post–World War I ascendancy. Between 1920 and 1960, fewer than 1.5 million immigrants came to the United States from Germany and the various Nordic nations.[8] Nevertheless, during that same period, the baptized membership in Lutheran congregations increased at a faster rate than most other denominations, growing from under 2.5 million to more than 8 million.[9]

In 1958, Lutherans found their increasingly prominent church on the cover of *Time* magazine. The article highlighted their teachings on the sacraments and their adherence to the historic confessions found in the *Book of Concord,* particularly the Augsburg Confession. The journalist documented how Lutherans' "exclusive attitude put [them] in a special position among U.S. Protestants": they were "protected" from "revivalism" and had been "barely touched" by "theological liberalism." He also noted how their "position apart" left them "snug, smug and embattled in their mighty fortresses called synods," where they "looked down not only on their fellow Christians but on fellow Lutherans as well." Though the circumstances were different, Lutheranism's place in mid-twentieth-century American culture would have seemed quite familiar to those involved in the controversies and debates of the century before.[10]

But the *Time* article also reported that a "new tendency" was sweeping the church: it was "emerging from isolation" by pursuing the twin goals of "interdenominational understanding" and "denominational unity." Lutherans' movement toward interdenominational cooperation had been occurring since the end of the Second World War as the United Lutheran Church in America and a few other Lutheran church bodies joined the World Council of Churches and the National Council of Churches. The second objective noted by *Time,* denominational unity, had been a perennial concern among American Lutherans but would pick up in earnest during the early 1960s with the formation of two new church bodies: the Lutheran Church in America, which leaned in the direction of mainline Protestantism, and the more moderate American Lutheran Church.

The exception to this trend was found among Lutherans in the Synodical Conference. During the 1950s and 1960s, the Lutheran Church—Missouri Synod (LCMS) (the church body's official name as of 1947) became divided between "moderates," who sought to increase intra-Lutheran cooperation and introduce aspects of modern biblical criticism, and "conservatives," who opposed these innovations. Distressed by these incursions of "unionism" and "liberalism" into the LCMS, the Wisconsin Evangelical Lutheran Synod (WELS), the other major member of the Synodical Conference, suspended fellowship with its nearly one-hundred-year-old partner in 1961. Meanwhile, the LCMS experienced its own internal upheaval. A conservative resurgence led moderates to break away and, in 1976, to form a new church body, the Association of Evangelical Lutheran Churches. The vast majority, however, remained in the LCMS, which positioned itself as standing apart from the trends of the other major Lutheran church bodies.[11]

This movement toward ecumenism and intra-Lutheran unity would culminate in the 1988 merger of the Lutheran Church in America, the American Lutheran Church, and the Association of Evangelical Lutheran Churches to form the Evangelical Lutheran Church in America (ELCA). Though the LCMS, WELS, and various small church bodies refused to join, the ELCA brought together nearly two-thirds of U.S. Lutherans, the highest percentage since the General Synod on the eve of the Civil War. The new church body's vision was to be both an active participant in mainline Protestantism and true to its confessional heritage. In some ways, the establishment of the ELCA represented the long-awaited culmination of the project of Samuel Schmucker and his fellow New Lutherans. At last, Lutheranism would emerge from its isolation, unite various portions of the church together in a single body, and embrace its role as a leader in interdenominational cooperation.

Rather than taking its place as a major player in the nation's religious culture, however, over the past six decades American Lutheranism has experienced fractiousness and declining membership. Though it was founded with "high expectations," the ELCA has been plagued by internal divisions, including the breakaway of the Lutheran Congregations in Mission for Christ in 2001 and the

North American Lutheran Church in 2010.[12] Since the upheavals of the 1960s and 1970s, the LCMS and WELS have not experienced any major schisms, but they have been internally divided over questions of Lutheran identity, particularly the extent to which they should embrace facets of modern evangelicalism.[13] Meanwhile, the number of Lutherans in the United States has plummeted from more than 9 million members in the late 1960s to fewer than 6 million today, even as Baptists, Roman Catholics, and many other denominations have continued to grow in membership.[14]

Perhaps the most trenchant analysis of Lutheranism's recent history can be found in two articles written by Mark Noll. In these essays, Noll analyzes the "second coming of American Lutheranism after World War II" in light of its "first coming," from the nation's founding to the Civil War. In his telling, the nineteenth-century disputes between Samuel Schmucker, on the one hand, and Charles Porterfield Krauth and C. F. W. Walther, on the other, was a "struggle between 'American' and 'European' Lutherans." The triumph of the Lutheranism represented by Krauth and Walther, Noll argues, preserved Lutherans' theological distinctiveness but "turned [them] back to Europe."[15] However, in the late twentieth century, the opposite occurred: "Lutherans began to engage the larger American culture," but "yield[ed] to Americanizing pressures," with the ELCA "becoming less and less distinguishable from older mainline Protestant denominations" and the LCMS and the WELS "taking on the colors of American fundamentalism." According to Noll, "The decisions that faced the generation of Schmucker, Krauth, and Walther, are ... still confronting Lutherans at the start of the twenty-first century."[16] In order to make an impact on the nation's religious life, he suggests, today's Lutherans must "find out how to speak Lutheranism with an American accent."[17]

Noll's articles contain many astute observations and his prescriptions have been echoed by some of American Lutheranism's internal critics.[18] However, his analysis rests on a standard interpretation of the church's defining decades—one that this book has sought to challenge. The Lutheran identity forged in the Civil War era was *not* a European importation but a distinctively American creation. Throughout the nineteenth century, Lutherans *did* "engage the larger American culture," but they adapted and responded in their own unique way. By the beginning of the twentieth century, Lutherans *had* learned to "speak Lutheranism with an American accent," but it was not comprehended by the Anglo-Protestants who presumed to represent the nation's religious culture. Though the resulting confessional conservatism did lead to isolation and parochialism, from the Civil War era until the 1960s the church experienced numerical growth at a rate that outpaced most other denominations. Over the past sixty years, however, as Lutherans have sought either to unite with mainline Protestantism or to mimic aspects of evangelicalism, their share in the U.S. religious marketplace has dropped precipitously.

Those who attribute this declining membership to the forces of "Americanization" misunderstand the church's history. Lutheranism in the United States has always been distinctively American. The question facing American Lutherans in the twenty-first century is whether they will remain distinctively Lutheran.

GLOSSARY

Augsburg Confession: The primary Lutheran confession of faith. Prepared by Martin Luther's colleague Philip Melanchthon, this statement of beliefs was presented to the Holy Roman emperor on June 25, 1530, in the German city of Augsburg. Along with Martin Luther's Small Catechism, its twenty-eight articles became the standard expression of Lutheran doctrine in sixteenth-century Europe. During the first half of the nineteenth century, many American Lutherans came to disagree with some of the confession's teachings, chiefly concerning the sacraments of baptism and the Lord's Supper.

Book of Concord: A book of creeds and confessions adopted by the Lutheran churches of the Holy Roman Empire. Its publication in 1580 sought to bring peace, or concord, after decades of theological infighting following Martin Luther's death in 1546. The book contains the three ecumenical creeds—the Apostles, the Nicene, and the Athanasian—and seven Lutheran statements of faith—the Augsburg Confession (1530), the Apology of the Augsburg Confession (1531), the Smalcald Articles (1537), the Treatise on the Power and Primacy of the Pope (1537), Martin Luther's Small Catechism (1529), Martin Luther's Large Catechism (1529), and the Formula of Concord (1577).

Confessionalism: The belief in the importance of adhering to a church's historic confessions or creeds. Throughout the nineteenth century, American Lutherans debated the extent to which ministers and church bodies should subscribe (or pledge one's assent) to the confessions contained in the *Book of Concord,* particularly the Augsburg Confession. New Lutherans (later called New School Lutherans) believed that expressing agreement with the "fundamental doctrines" of the Augsburg Confession was sufficient. Old School Lutherans came to believe that all of the teachings in this confession were "fundamental" and insisted that they be accepted "without equivocation." However, they also contended that several of the other confessions in the *Book of Concord* were "secondary" and must only be accepted "inasmuch as they set forth" the doctrines in the Augsburg Confession. Old Lutherans required "unconditional subscription" to each of the confessions contained in the *Book of Concord.*

General Council: The General Council of the Evangelical Lutheran Church in North America was a federation of Lutheran synods founded in 1867. It comprised Old School Lutherans who had separated from the General Synod as well as several formerly independent church bodies. For the first five years after its founding, it was the largest American Lutheran federation. In 1918, the General Council merged with the General Synod and the United Synod of the South to form the United Lutheran Church in America.

General Synod: The Evangelical Lutheran General Synod of the United States of America was a federation of Lutheran synods founded in 1820. Throughout the antebellum era, it was dominated by the New Lutheran party. At its height, in 1860, the General Synod encompassed almost two-thirds of all Lutherans in the United States. It endured two major schisms. The first came in 1863, when five southern synods formed the General Synod of the Confederate States of America. Three years later, Old School Lutherans withdrew from the federation and soon after formed the General Council. In 1918, the General Synod merged with the General Council and the United Synod of the South (the successor of the Confederate General Synod) to form the United Lutheran Church in America.

Lutheran and Missionary: The church paper that represented the position of the Old School Lutherans during the Civil War and early years of Reconstruction. Founded in 1861, this Philadelphia-based paper was a merger of the *Missionary,* edited by William Passavant, and the *Lutheran and Home Journal,* edited by Charles Porterfield Krauth. After the founding of the General Council in 1867, the paper was edited by a committee of clergymen from that federation.

Lutheran Observer: The church paper affiliated with New Lutherans during the antebellum era and New School Lutherans during the Civil War and early years of Reconstruction. The paper was based in Baltimore from its founding in 1831 until 1867, when its headquarters was relocated to Philadelphia. During the nineteenth century, it primarily had two editors: Benjamin Kurtz, who served in that role from 1833 to 1859 (and as coeditor in 1861 and 1862), and Frederick Conrad, who edited the paper from 1863 to 1898. After Old School Lutherans broke away from the General Synod to form the General Council, the paper described its position as "devoted to the principles and interests of the General Synod."

Lutheran Standard: The church paper associated with the Moderate Lutherans. It was founded in 1842 and edited by various clergymen of the Ohio Synod. During the antebellum era and early years of the Civil War, its editorial position stood against both the *Lutheran Observer* and the *Lutheraner.* However, after Matthias Loy became its editor in 1864, the paper, as well as the Ohio Synod, moved toward the position of the Old Lutherans of the Missouri Synod. It became the chief English-language paper associated with the Synodical Conference until the Ohio Synod withdrew from that federation in the 1880s.

Lutheraner: The church paper that represented the position of the Old Lutherans. Established in 1844 and based in St. Louis, it became the official paper of the Missouri Synod when this church body was formed in 1847. For its first twenty-one years, the paper was edited by C. F. W. Walther. Beginning in 1865, the paper came under the joint editorship of the faculty at the Missouri Synod's seminary in St. Louis, which was headed by Walther until his death in 1887.

Moderate Lutherans: The faction of American Lutherans in the antebellum era who sought to be a middle ground between the New Lutherans and Old Lutherans. Moderate Lutherans were skeptical of the innovations of the New Lutherans, particularly their rejection of some of the teachings found in the Augsburg Confession and their embrace of revivalism. However, they were even more critical of the Old Lutherans for their doctrinal rigidity and "exclusiveness" in interchurch relations. Several Moderate Lutheran church bodies, such as the Ohio Synod, refused to join the General Synod. However, in 1853, the largest Moderate Lutheran church body, the Pennsylvania Synod, joined the federation. During the Civil War and early years of Reconstruction, Moderate Lutheran church bodies attached themselves to one of two movements. Some, such as the Pennsylvania Synod, became associated with the Old School Lutherans and helped to found the General Council. Others, such as the Ohio Synod, moved in the direction of Old Lutheranism and joined the Synodical Conference.

New Lutherans: The party of Lutherans in the antebellum United States that sought to incorporate elements of American evangelicalism into their church. Led by Samuel Schmucker and Benjamin Kurtz, proponents of New Lutheranism—sometimes called "American Lutheranism"—sought to modify historic Lutheran doctrines, chiefly surrounding the sacraments of baptism and the Lord's Supper, and encouraged cooperation with other Protestants in the areas of revivalism and social reform. Throughout the antebellum era, New Lutherans were the largest faction in the General Synod.

New School Lutherans: A term used to describe the proponents of New Lutheranism during the Civil War and early years of Reconstruction. While many New School Lutherans held to the same beliefs as the New Lutherans of the 1840s and 1850s, their leaders in the 1860s frequently defined themselves as the party of peace, which was seeking to preserve the compromises reached in the General Synod during the antebellum era. After Old School Lutherans broke away to form the General Council, the General Synod essentially became a New School federation. By the end of the nineteenth century, however, most leaders of the General Synod came to distance themselves from the New School Lutheranism of past generations.

Old Lutherans: The party of American Lutherans in the Civil War era who uncompromisingly opposed the innovations of the New Lutherans. Chiefly led by C. F. W. Walther and the Missouri Synod, Old Lutherans required strict adherence to the entire *Book of Concord,* as well as assent to other doctrines taught by Martin Luther and other historic Lutheran theologians. They also rejected unionism (cooperation with other Christians not in full doctrinal agreement) and revivalism. Though it was a small minority in the antebellum era, Old Lutheranism attracted many adherents during the first years of Reconstruction. This movement culminated in the 1872 founding of the Synodical Conference.

Old School Lutherans: A term used during the Civil War and early years of Reconstruction to describe the faction within the General Synod that wanted the federation to adopt a firmer adherence to the Augsburg Confession. Old School Lutheranism was a merger of two groups. The first was the confessional movement, formed during the 1850s by former New Lutherans like Charles Porterfield Krauth and William Passavant (see chapter 2). The second was the Pennsylvania

Synod, the Moderate Lutheran church body that had joined the General Synod in 1853. Over the course of the Civil War, Old School leaders became convinced that the compromises reached in the General Synod during the antebellum era were untenable. In 1866, after several years of controversy, the Pennsylvania Synod separated from the General Synod. The following year, several other synods associated with the Old School, together with some formerly independent church bodies, formed the General Council. In the ensuing decades, the term largely faded from use.

Symbol: A traditional name for a creed or confession. Among nineteenth-century American Lutherans, words like "symbolism" or "symbolist" were used, often pejoratively, to describe strict adherence to historic creeds and confessions.

Synod: The name for a church body in nineteenth-century American Lutheranism. These synods—some of which were also called ministeriums—were divided by geography, ethnicity, and theology. Some chose to affiliate with a larger federation, such as the General Synod or the Synodical Conference, while others remained independent. Despite often having a name that specified a state, Lutheran synods often served a wider geographic area. The Tennessee Synod, for example, was founded in 1820 to protest the involvement of other southern Lutherans in the General Synod, and its congregations were located not only in eastern Tennessee but also in the Carolina Piedmont and Shenandoah Valley. Others synods, such as the Missouri Synod and the Iowa Synod, became national church bodies with congregations in several states. Over the course of the twentieth century, "synod" came to mean, for some U.S. Lutherans, a subdivision of a larger church body. For example, the Evangelical Lutheran Church in America currently contains sixty-five synods. For others, the term remains synonymous with "church body," as with the Lutheran Church—Missouri Synod and the Wisconsin Evangelical Lutheran Synod.

Synodical Conference: The Evangelical Lutheran Synodical Conference of North America was a federation of Lutheran synods founded in 1872. Its largest member was the Missouri Synod, the leading representative of Old Lutheranism. At its founding, it was joined by five other synods, including several formerly Moderate Lutheran ones, such as the Ohio and Wisconsin synods. A controversy over the doctrine of predestination in the 1880s led to the departure of the Ohio and Norwegian synods. Nevertheless, the Synodical Conference, from its founding until the early twentieth century, was the largest federation of Lutherans in the United States. It dissolved in 1967.

United Synod of the South: The United Synod of the Evangelical Lutheran Church in the South was a federation of Lutheran synods founded in 1886. Its roots trace back to 1863, when five church bodies broke away from the General Synod to form the General Synod of the Confederate States of America. In 1866, this southern federation changed its name to the General Synod in North America. Ten years later, it adopted the more accurate title, the General Synod of the South. The name United Synod of the South was adopted after the Tennessee Synod, which had long refused to partner with other southern Lutherans, agreed to join the federation. In 1918, the United Synod of the South merged with the General Council and the General Synod to form the United Lutheran Church in America.

APPENDIX
Statistical Tables

The following tables show the communicant membership of American Lutheran synods and federations at various times during the nineteenth century. It should be noted that these figures only account for adults who passed through the rite of confirmation and were members of a congregation. They do not include children who were unconfirmed or adults who attended Lutheran churches periodically but were not official members. As noted in this book's introduction, the total number of "adherents" in nineteenth-century U.S. Lutheran synods was about three to four times the number of communicant members.

Two sources were foundational for constructing these tables. Membership statistics for 1830 are taken from an article published in the *Lutheran Observer*, while figures for 1850, 1860, 1872, and 1900 are drawn from the *Lutheran Almanac*.[1] However, the statistics found in these sources are not completely comprehensive, and in one case they are obviously inaccurate. Because of this, supplementary sources were occasionally used to help make educated estimates or to provide more accurate figures. Those instances are documented in the notes.

These tables also list the years in which various synods were founded, changed their names, or joined or left different federations. This information can be found in Robert Wiederaenders, *Historical Guide to Lutheran Church Bodies of North America*. When referencing the various national Lutheran federations, the following abbreviations are used:

GC   General Council
GS   General Synod
GSCS   General Synod of the Confederate States of America

GSNA   General Synod in North America

GSS   General Synod of the South

SC   Synodical Conference

USS   United Synod of the South

TABLE I. Communicant Membership in 1830

General Synod	12,760
Maryland and Virginia Synod (founded in 1820, joined GS in 1820)	3,807
North Carolina Synod (founded in 1803, joined GS in 1820)	1,888
Virginia Synod (founded in 1829, joined GS in 1829)	n/a[a]
West Pennsylvania Synod (founded in 1825, joined GS in 1825)	7,065
Independent synods	35,596
Hartwick Synod of New York (founded in 1830)	2,000[b]
New York Synod (founded in 1786)	1,908
Ohio Synod (founded in 1818)	8,815
Pennsylvania Synod (founded in 1748, joined GS in 1820, left GS in 1823)	19,421
South Carolina Synod (founded in 1824)	1,452
Tennessee Synod (founded in 1820)	2,000[c]
Total	48,356

[a] The Virginia Synod separated from the Maryland and Virginia Synod in 1829. However, the 1830 statistics found in the *Lutheran Observer*, as well as the 1831 statistical report published by the General Synod, appear to count the two church bodies' membership figures together.
[b] In the 1831 statistical report published by the General Synod, the Hartwick Synod is listed as having 2,332 communicants. See *Proceedings of the Sixth General Synod of the Evan. Luth. Church in the United States*, 29.
[c] Neither the 1830 article in the *Lutheran Observer* nor the 1831 statistical report published by the General Synod list membership figures for the Tennessee Synod. This estimate is based on the "parochial reports" found in the church body's 1831 proceedings. See *Report of the Transactions of the Evangelical Lutheran Tennessee Synod, During Their Twelfth Session*.

Appendix

TABLE 2. Communicant Membership in 1850

General Synod	62,818
Allegheny Synod of Pennsylvania (founded in 1842, joined GS in 1843)	5,733
East Pennsylvania Synod (founded in 1842, joined GS in 1843)	2,460
English Ohio Synod (founded in 1840, joined GS in 1841)	2,669
Hartwick Synod of New York (joined GS in 1831)	3,235
Maryland Synod (dropped Virginia from name in 1833)	9,800
New York Synod (joined GS in 1837)	7,500
North Carolina Synod	2,582
South Carolina Synod (joined GS in 1835)	3,062
Virginia Synod (left GS in 1831, rejoined GS in 1839)	2,466
West Pennsylvania Synod	15,713
Wittenberg Synod of Ohio (founded in 1847, joined GS in 1848)	1,500[a]
Five other synods	6,098
Independent Synods	81,697
Franckean Synod of New York (founded in 1837)	3,213
Missouri Synod (founded in 1847)	5,000[b]
Ohio Synod	21,200
Pennsylvania Synod	31,584[c]
Pittsburg Synod (founded in 1845)	5,700
Tennessee Synod	9,000
Wisconsin Synod (founded in 1850)	1,000[d]
Five other synods	5,000[e]
Total	144,515

[a] The *Lutheran Almanac* in 1851 lists fifteen clergy and fifty congregations for the Wittenberg Synod but does not include membership statistics.

[b] This estimate is based on the Missouri Synod's 1850 parochial report, which includes information only on the total number of souls (baptized children and confirmed adults) and voting members. See *Vierter Synodal-Bericht der deutschen evangel.-lutherischen Synode von Missouri*, 46.

[c] The *Lutheran Almanac* incorrectly lists this church body's membership as 13,362. The correct figure, here, comes from the 1850 parochial report of the Pennsylvania Synod. See *Proceedings of the One Hundred and Third Annual Session of the German Evangelical Lutheran Ministerium of Pennsylvania*, 42.

[d] This estimate is based on the congregational reports at this synod's 1850 convention. See Lehmann, "Wisconsin Synod Synodical Proceedings, 1849–1860," 4.

[e] The *Lutheran Almanac* does not list membership statistics for four of these synods. These estimates are based on the number of pastors and congregations in these synods.

TABLE 3. Communicant Membership in 1860

General Synod	164,226
Allegheny Synod of Pennsylvania	7,200
East Ohio Synod (changed name from English Ohio Synod in 1858)	3,951
East Pennsylvania Synod	12,500
Hartwick Synod of New York	4,904
Maryland Synod	6,152
Melanchthon Synod of Maryland (founded in 1857, joined GS in 1859)	4,300
New York Synod	11,516
North Carolina Synod	4,200
Northern Illinois Synod (founded in 1851, joined GS in 1853)	5,297
Pennsylvania Synod (joined GS in 1853)	40,000
Pittsburg Synod (joined GS in 1853)	8,795
South Carolina Synod	9,859
Texas Synod (founded in 1851, joined GS in 1853)	2,800
Virginia Synod	3,200
West Pennsylvania Synod	11,417
Wittenberg Synod of Ohio	2,010
Eight other synods	26,115
Independent Synods	91,500
Franckean Synod of New York	3,000
Iowa Synod (founded in 1854)	4,000
Missouri Synod	25,000
Norwegian Synod (founded in 1853)	10,000[a]
Ohio Synod	20,000
Scandinavian Augustana Synod (founded in 1860)	5,000
Tennessee Synod	5,500
Wisconsin Synod	5,000
Six other synods	12,500
Total	255,726

[a] The *Lutheran Almanac* for 1861 does not list the Norwegian Synod in its statistical table for this year. This estimate comes from Wiederaenders, *Historical Guide*, 137.

TABLE 4. Communicant Membership in 1872

Synodical Conference	191,173
Missouri Synod (joined SC in 1872)	80,000
Norwegian Synod (joined SC in 1872)	50,535
Ohio Synod (joined SC in 1872)	30,000
Wisconsin Synod (joined GC in 1867, left GC in 1869, joined SC in 1872)	23,099
Two other synods	7,500
General Council	135,517
New York Synod (majority left GS and joined GC in 1867)	21,800
Pennsylvania Synod (left GS in 1866, joined GC in 1867)	63,548
Pittsburg Synod (majority left GS and joined GC in 1867)	9,167
Swedish Augustana Synod (joined GC in 1867, renamed in 1870)	22,300
Texas Synod (left GS and joined GC in 1868)	2,700
Four other synods	16,002
General Synod	103,320
Allegheny Synod of Pennsylvania	8,350
East Ohio Synod	5,720
East Pennsylvania Synod	12,000
Franckean Synod of New York (joined GS in 1866)	3,492
Hartwick Synod of New York	4,266
Maryland Synod (Melanchthon Synod rejoined this synod in 1869)	13,220
New York and New Jersey Synod (founded in 1872)	5,340
Northern Illinois Synod	2,800
Pittsburg Synod (founded in 1867 by minority who remained in GS)	3,750
West Pennsylvania Synod	14,000
Wittenberg Synod of Ohio	4,755
Ten other synods	25,717
General Synod in North America	11,844
South Carolina Synod (left GS in 1861, joined GSCS in 1863)	4,200
Virginia Synod (left GS in 1861, joined GSCS in 1863)	3,700
Three other synods	3,944
Independent synods	42,780
Iowa Synod	12,200
North Carolina Synod (left GS in 1861, joined GSCS in 1863, left GSNA in 1870)	3,560
Norwegian–Danish Augustana Synod (founded in 1870)	2,600
Norwegian–Danish Conference (founded in 1870)	10,000
Tennessee Synod	6,370
Five other synods	10,650
Total	487,195

TABLE 5. Communicant Membership in 1900

Synodical Conference	581,029
Missouri Synod	413,101
Wisconsin Synod	140,268
Three other synods	27,660
General Council	370,409
New York Synod	60,663
Pennsylvania Synod	132,839
Pittsburg Synod	28,206
Swedish Augustana Synod	118,149
Five other synods	30,552
General Synod	199,589
Allegheny Synod of Pennsylvania	15,134
East Ohio Synod	7,366
East Pennsylvania Synod	24,485
Franckean Synod of New York	2,166
Hartwick Synod of New York	5,456
Maryland Synod	23,769
New York and New Jersey Synod	10,595
Northern Illinois Synod	3,559
Pittsburg Synod	11,938
West Pennsylvania Synod	26,953
Wittenberg Synod of Ohio	9,555
Thirteen other synods	59,723
United Synod of the South	37,152
North Carolina Synod (rejoined GSS in 1881, joined USS in 1886)	7,347
South Carolina Synod (joined USS in 1886)	8,421
Tennessee Synod (joined USS in 1886)	8,148
Virginia Synod (joined USS in 1886)	6,254
Four other synods	8,469
Independent Synods	484,509
Iowa Synod	74,058
Norwegian Synod (left SC in 1883)	66,927
Ohio Synod (left SC in 1881)	77,362
Texas Synod (merged into Iowa Synod in 1896)	n/a
United Norwegian Lutheran Church (founded in 1890)	130,000
Twelve other synods	136,162
Total	1,674,175

NOTES

INTRODUCTION

1. Niebuhr, *Social Sources of Denominationalism*, 232.
2. Ole Edvard Moe, "The European Characterization of the Three Branches of the Lutheran Church," trans. Abdel Ross Wentz, *Lutheran Church Quarterly* 1, no. 3 (July 1928): 310.
3. See Howard, *God and the Atlantic*; as well as Glaser and Wellenreuther, *Bridging the Atlantic*.
4. Smith, "Religion and Ethnicity in America," 1179.
5. Unless otherwise noted, all statements about Lutheran membership statistics are based on the information compiled in "Appendix: Statistical Tables."
6. On nineteenth-century American biblicism, see Perry, *Bible Culture and Authority*; Watkins, *Slavery and Sacred Texts*; and Noll, *America's Book*. For an important counterpoint, see Gutacker, *Old Faith in a New Nation*. On the marginalization of confessionalism in U.S. Christianity, see Hart, *Lost Soul of American Protestantism*.
7. For example, see Baird, *Religion in the United States*, 267–69.
8. See Marty, *Protestantism in the United States*.
9. On the Anglo-Protestant campaign to "legislate morality," see Foster, *Moral Reconstruction*.
10. See Lang, *Contest of Civilizations*; and Tyrrell, *American Exceptionalism*, esp. 31–140.
11. For example, see Strong, *Our Country*.
12. Hanser, *Irrfahrten und Heimfahrten*, 260.
13. "Lutheranism and Americanism," *Theological Quarterly* 8, no. 1 (January 1904): 59.
14. On Lutheranism in nineteenth-century Europe, see Conser, *Church and Confession*; Hope, *German and Scandinavian Protestantism*; Gäbler, *Geschichte des Pietismus*, vol. 3; Landry, *Ecumenism, Memory, and German Nationalism*; Ellis, *Politics and Piety*; Kloes, *German Awakening*; and Lee, *Confessional Lutheranism*.
15. See Hall, *Practice of Confessional Subscription*; and Sweeney and Hambrick-Stowe, *Holding on to the Faith*.
16. See Moore, *Religious Outsiders*; and Sarna, *Minority Faiths*.
17. In his classic study, Vergilius Ferm argued, "A developing *American* Lutheran theology was suppressed and in its place there came the rebirth of an inherited European Lutheran theology in America." Ferm, *Crisis in American Lutheran Theology*, 344. Subsequent studies have followed this interpretation. See Mauelshagen, *American Lutheranism Surrenders*; Tappert, *Lutheran Confessional*

Theology; and Gustafson, *Lutherans in Crisis.* This standard narrative, which pits "American" Lutherans against "European" Lutherans, has been repeated by prominent historians of religion in the United States. See, for example, Holifield, *Theology in America,* 408–9; and Noll, *History of Christianity,* 194–97. An important exception to this standard interpretation, discussed in later chapters, is Kuenning, *Rise and Fall.*

18. Scholarship on American Lutheran women, particularly in the nineteenth century, is sparse. For a few examples, see Albers, "Perspectives"; Lagerquist, *From Our Mothers' Arms;* and Coburn, *Life at Four Corners.* Each of these studies primarily covers developments in the post–Civil War era.

19. For example, none of the twelve women mentioned in historian L. Deane Lagerquist's "Biographical Dictionary of Lutheran Leaders" were active in public life before the 1880s. See Lagerquist, *Lutherans,* 161–242.

20. See Brekus, *Strangers & Pilgrims,* 343–45.

21. Bureau of the Census, *Religious Bodies: 1906, Part 1,* 30–31.

22. Noll, *America's God,* 18.

23. On the importance of "choice" in American religion, see Finke and Stark, *Churching of America;* and Mullen, *Chance of Salvation.*

24. On the print culture of nineteenth-century American Protestants, see Brown, *Word in the World;* and Nord, *Faith in Reading.*

25. Marsden, *Fundamentalism and American Culture,* vii, 3. A list of studies examining religion and American culture could run for pages. For two recent examples, see Kidd and Hankins, *Baptists in America;* and Voorhees, *New Christian Identity.*

26. Burton, *Age of Lincoln;* Hahn, *Nation Without Borders.*

27. Harlow, *Religion, Race, and the Making of Confederate Kentucky;* Holm, *Kingdom Divided;* Kurtz, *Excommunicated from the Union;* Oshatz, *Slavery and Sin;* Volkman, *Houses Divided.*

28. Ahlstrom, "Lutheran Church and American Culture," 331.

29. The following general histories bear mentioning at the outset: Wentz, *Basic History;* Nelson, *Lutherans in North America;* Lagerquist, *Lutherans;* and Granquist, *Lutherans in America.*

30. Noll, "Good Time for Looking Back," 318. The most complete source on the various American Lutheran divisions is Wiederaenders, *Historical Guide.*

31. Maffly-Kipp, "Burdens of Church History," 355. Holm, also quoting Maffly-Kipp, makes a similar point in *Kingdom Divided,* 4. For other recent defenses of the centrality of denominations, see Harper, *American Denominational History;* and Mullin and Richey, *Reimagining Denominationalism.*

32. Marsden, *Fundamentalism and American Culture,* 260.

33. Compare, for example, Ahlstrom, *Religious History of the American People,* with recent histories, such as Evans, *Histories of American Christianity;* and Coffman, *Turning Points in American Church History.* See also the almost complete lack of coverage in Grasso, *Skepticism and Faith;* Mullen, *Chance of Salvation;* and Noll, *America's Book.*

34. The major studies on the religious history of the Civil War are discussed in chapter 3.

35. Gjerde and Franson, "'Still the Inwardly Beautiful Bride of Christ,'" 191.

36. See Carroll, *Religious Forces of the United States,* xxxiv–xxxv. On the total Lutheran population in the United States, see George L. Kieffer, "The Difference Between European and American Methods of Calculating Church Membership," *Lutheran Church Quarterly* 1, no. 3 (July 1928): 314–19.

37. Gjerde and Franson, "'Still the Inwardly Beautiful Bride of Christ,'" 191.

38. See, for example, Charles A. Aiken, "The Comparative Value of English and German Biblical

Science," *Bibliotheca Sacra and American Biblical Repository* 11, no. 1 (January 1854): 70; and Seiss, *Ecclesia Lutherana*, 142.

39. On Northern Europeans and American "whiteness," see Jacobson, *Whiteness of a Different Color*, 39–90; Kazal, *Becoming Old Stock;* and Jackson, *Scandinavians in Chicago.* On the centrality of "whiteness" to U.S. religion, see Blum et al., "Forum: American Religion and 'Whiteness'"; Gollner, "Good White Christians"; and Gin Lum, *Heathen.*

40. Moore, *Religious Outsiders*, xi.

41. The phrase is from Smith, *Stormy Present*, 4. For other studies on northern conservatism during the Civil War era, see Ford, *Bonds of Union;* Ayers, *Thin Light of Freedom;* Phillips, *Rivers Ran Backward;* Stanley, *Loyal West;* Brodrecht, *Our Country;* Escott, *Worst Passions of Human Nature;* Furniss, *Between Extremes;* and Carwardine, *Righteous Strife.*

1. THREE AMERICAN LUTHERANISMS, 1830–1850

1. See Graham, *Cosmos in the Chaos;* and Howard, *God and the Atlantic*, 136–58.

2. Schaff, *Amerika*, 236. The first English edition abridged the section "Die deutschen Kirchen in Amerika" (The German Churches in America) to about one-fourth of its original size. All quotations come from the original German version. For a partial translation of Schaff's discussion of the Lutheran churches, see Suelflow, "Nietzsche and Schaff on American Lutheranism," 147–58.

3. Schaff, *Amerika*, 221, 223, 225–26.

4. See, for example, Nelson, *Lutherans in North America*, 211–15; Gustafson, *Lutherans in Crisis*, 28–29; and Lagerquist, *Lutherans*, 72–73.

5. For the statistics in this paragraph, see Fogleman, "Migration to the Thirteen British North American Colonies," 700–704; Wokeck, *Trade in Strangers*, 45–46; and Grubb, *German Immigration*, 2.

6. Nolt, *Foreigners in Their Own Land*, 13.

7. The most complete biography of Muhlenberg remains Riforgiato, *Missionary of Moderation.*

8. Roeber, "Henry Melchior Muhlenberg," 1. E. Brooks Holifield calls Muhlenberg a "confessional pietist." Holifield, *Theology in America*, 400. Paul Kuenning uses the label "churchly pietist." Kuenning, *Rise and Fall*, 37.

9. The literature on Halle pietism in North America is vast. For an introduction, see Grabbe, *Halle Pietism;* and Strom et al., *Pietism in Germany and North America.* On American Lutheran reactions to the Moravians and the Great Awakening, see Fogleman, *Jesus Is Female*, 135–216; and Bonomi, "'Watchful Against the Sects.'"

10. See Roeber, *Palatines, Liberty, and Property.*

11. Wellenreuther, *Citizens in a Strange Land*, 247.

12. Noll, *America's God*, 71, 410. On Helmuth, see Roeber, "J. H. C. Helmuth."

13. For statistics on German immigrants, see Grubb, *German Immigration*, 28, 343–45; and Köllman and Marschalck, "German Emigration to the United States," 518. For overall statistics on U.S. immigration, see United States Bureau of the Census, *Historical Statistics*, 105–9.

14. "Evangelical Lutheran Church in the United States: Prepared for Buck's Theological Dictionary by Rev. C. P. Krauth, of Philadelphia," *Lutheran Observer*, October 15, 1831, 87. For context, see Nolt, *Foreigners in Their Own Land*, 109–27.

15. Noll, *America's God*, 9. For a similar argument, but one that distinguishes between frontier

revivalism and the bourgeois Protestantism of eastern cities, see Haselby, *Origins of American Religious Nationalism*. Holifield, *Theology in America*, offers important contrasts with Noll but mostly agrees with him on the centrality of reason in American theological discourse.

16. Hatch, *Democratization of American Christianity*, 3.

17. For counterpoints to Hatch's argument, see Butler, *Awash in a Sea of Faith*, 225–88; and Porterfield, *Conceived in Doubt*.

18. See Baglyos, "In This Land of Liberty," 60–91.

19. See Baer, *Trial of Frederick Eberle*.

20. Nolt, *Foreigners in Their Own Land*, 5.

21. For example, see Wentz, *Basic History*, 69–72; and Gustafson, *Lutherans in Crisis*, 41–46.

22. On Quitman, see Bost, "Reverend John Bachman," 18–60.

23. For example, see Nelson, *Lutherans in North America*, 131–32; and Wentz, *Basic History*, 92–93.

24. Nolt, *Foreigners in Their Own Land*, 115; Baglyos, "In This Land of Liberty," 39–40.

25. On Franklin College, see Dubbs, *History of Franklin and Marshall College*, esp. 80–114. On Hartwick Seminary, see Wentz, *History of the Gettysburg Theological Seminary*, 64–73.

26. On the Henkels, see especially Koenning, "Henkel Press"; as well as Edmonds, "The Henkels."

27. Wood, *Radicalism of the American Revolution*, 332.

28. Baglyos, "In This Land of Liberty," 47.

29. For these statistics, see Gaustad and Barlow, *New Historical Atlas*, 22, 28, 60, 107, 219; and Hatch, *Democratization of American Christianity*, 3–4.

30. For examples of Lutherans switching to more culturally powerful churches, see Bost, "Reverend John Bachman," 67–68.

31. Schmucker, *Intellectual and Moral Glories of the Christian Temple*, 14.

32. Wentz, *Pioneer in Christian Unity*, 78. Wentz's biography is still the most comprehensive account of Schmucker's life. For insightful studies on Schmucker in his American context, see Dörfler-Dierken, *Luthertum und Demokratie*, 115–86; and Jordahl, "Schmucker and Walther."

33. Gustafson, *Lutherans in Crisis*, 57. See also Wentz, *History of the Gettysburg Theological Seminary*, 113.

34. Wentz, *Pioneer in Christian Unity*, 80.

35. Wentz, *History of the Gettysburg Theological Seminary*, 95–96.

36. Wentz, *Pioneer in Christian Unity*, 136–39, 182–83.

37. Wentz, *Pioneer in Christian Unity*, 253, 262. See also Schmucker, *Happy Adaptation of the Sabbath-School System;* and Schmucker, *Appeal in Behalf of the Christian Sabbath*.

38. S. S. Schmucker, "Fraternal Appeal to the American Churches, Together with a Plan for Catholic Union on Apostolic Principles," *American Biblical Repository* 11, no. 29 (January 1838): 86–131; and no. 30 (April 1838): 363–415. The title of the first book edition, published in 1838, was shortened to *Appeal to the Churches, with a Plan for Catholic Union*. The second and enlarged edition, published the following year, adopted the original title, *Fraternal Appeal to the American Churches, with a Plan for Catholic Union, on Apostolic Principles*. That edition was reprinted in 1965 and contains a helpful introduction by Frederick K. Wentz. All quotations come from the original (1839) second edition.

39. Schmucker, *Fraternal Appeal*, 89, 107, 117, 125, 127.

40. Nolt, *Foreigners in Their Own Land*, 115–20.

41. No full-length biography of Kurtz has been published. For short accounts of his life, see

Jensson, *American Lutheran Biographies,* 445–46; and Wentz, *History of the Gettysburg Theological Seminary,* 129–32.

42. "Lutheran Observer," *Lutheran Observer,* April 19, 1839, 3. Two years earlier, Kurtz estimated sixteen thousand weekly readers. "The Lutheran Observer," *Lutheran Observer,* January 27, 1837, 91.

43. The Pittsburgh and Dayton editorial departments began in the August 8, 1845, issue; the Ebenezer department on February 12, 1847.

44. For one comprehensive study, see Groh, "Revivalism Among Lutherans in America in the 1840s."

45. Bittle, *Remarks on New Measures,* 4. A copy of the tract is found in David F. Bittle Papers, Roanoke College Archives, Virginia. On Bittle, see Benne, "David Bittle."

46. "Defining Our Position," *Lutheran Observer,* July 9, 1841, 3; Bittle, *Remarks on New Measures,* 4. For the most comprehensive defense of Lutheran revivalism, see Harkey, *Church's Best State.*

47. "Revival Preachers: Arndt, Spener, Franke—A Glorious Trio," *Lutheran Observer,* May 29, 1840, 1; Bittle, *Remarks on New Measures,* 6–8; Harkey, *Church's Best State,* 111.

48. "Translation of Letter from the German Lutheran Magazine of Feb. 1," *Lutheran Observer,* March 1, 1832, 232. See also "Defining Our Position," 3.

49. See Tyrrell, *Sobering Up;* and Pegram, *Battling Demon Rum,* 3–42. On antebellum evangelical reform more generally, see Walters, *American Reformers.*

50. "Defining Our Position," 3.

51. Bachman, *Address Delivered Before the Washington Total Abstinence Society of Charleston;* Seiss, *Ravages of Intemperance;* Krauth, *Address Delivered on the Anniversary of Washington's Birth-day.*

52. Carwardine, *Evangelicals and Politics,* 44. See also Volk, *Moral Minorities,* 11–36.

53. Schmucker, *Christian Pulpit,* 8, 26, 29–30.

54. K[urtz], "Christians and Politics," *Lutheran Observer,* September 22, 1848, 152. See also "Religious Men Should Take Part in Politics," *Lutheran Observer,* December 13, 1844, 1.

55. Swierenga, "Ethnoreligious Political Behavior," 155–56. See also speeches given by Lutheran ministers to commemorate prominent Whig politicians, in Smith, *Ground of National Consolation and Hope;* and Anspach, *Discourse Pronounced on Sabbath Evening, July 4, 1852.*

56. The classic study remains Goen, *Broken Churches, Broken Nation.* See also Wright, *Bonds of Salvation,* 172–200.

57. On the shared theology among evangelicals in both sections, see Carwardine, *Evangelicals and Politics,* 133–74; Noll, *Civil War as a Theological Crisis;* and Daly, *When Slavery Was Called Freedom.* This is not to discount distinctive emphases in the South and North. See Snay, *Gospel of Disunion;* and McKivigan, *War Against Proslavery Religion.*

58. No monograph on American Lutheranism and slavery has been published. For short but informative studies, see Fortenbaugh, "American Lutheran Synods and Slavery," and "Representative Lutheran Periodical Press and Slavery"; and Erling, "American Lutherans and Slavery."

59. "Colonization: Important Project," *Lutheran Observer,* April 21, 1837, 138; "Colonization— Fourth July Celebration," *Lutheran Observer,* June 23, 1837, 175. See also Stange, "Lutheran Involvement in the American Colonization Society," and "Editor Benjamin Kurtz of the *Lutheran Observer.*"

60. "Neutrality," *Lutheran Observer,* July 28, 1837, 195.

61. "Abolition," *Lutheran Observer,* August 4, 1837, 199.

62. See Fields, *Slavery and Freedom on the Middle Ground;* Harrold, *Border War;* and Tomek, *Colonization and Its Discontents.*

63. Kuenning, *Rise and Fall*, 111–16.
64. Schmucker, *Elements of Popular Theology* (1834), 277–78.
65. Schmucker, *Elements of Popular Theology* (1846), 333.
66. Samuel Simon Schmucker, "Lecture on Slavery Delivered to the Senior Class of the Gettysburg Theological Seminary, August 1845," in Stange, "Dr. Samuel Simon Schmucker," 79, 81. Schmucker had presented a slightly different version of this lecture as early as 1840. See Wentz, *Pioneer in Christian Unity*, 320–22.
67. Wentz, *Pioneer in Christian Unity*, 321.
68. Kuenning, *Rise and Fall*, refers to Schmucker as an "abolitionist leader." Others use the oxymoronic terms "moderate abolitionist" or "pragmatic abolitionist." Wentz, *Pioneer in Christian Unity*, 317; Longenecker, *Gettysburg Religion*, 107. On immediatism, see Sinha, *Slave's Cause*, 195–265; and Cirillo, *Abolitionist Civil War*. On antislavery moderates, see Oshatz, *Slavery and Sin*, esp. 43–60; and Harlow, *Religion, Race, and the Making of Confederate Kentucky*, esp. 76–107.
69. On the Franckean Synod, see Stange, *Radicalism for Humanity*; and Kuenning, *Rise and Fall*, 179–219. On religion in antebellum upstate New York, see Cross, *Burned-over District*; and Sernett, *North Star Country*.
70. Stange, "Document: Bishop Daniel Alexander Payne's Protestation of American Slavery," 60. On Payne's life and work, see Thomas, *Rumor of Black Lutherans*, 25–44; and Strobert, *Daniel Alexander Payne*.
71. "A Fraternal Appeal Addressed by the Frankean Evangelic-Lutheran Synod, to the several Ev. Lutheran Synods on the subject of Slavery," in Stange, "One Hundred and Twenty-Fifth Anniversary," 47.
72. "The Right Ground," *Liberator*, March 31, 1843, 13.
73. *Extracts from the Minutes of the Twelfth Meeting of the Evangelical Lutheran Synod of South Carolina*, 8. The most extensive study of Bachman's life and theology is Bost, "Reverend John Bachman."
74. On Jones, see Thomas, *Rumor of Black Lutherans*, 1–24.
75. Johnson, *Black Christians*, 125, 127.
76. Stange, "One Hundred and Twenty-Fifth Anniversary," 43; Kuenning, *Rise and Fall*, 198–209.
77. On domesticity and "true womanhood" among antebellum evangelicals, see Dorsey, *Reforming Men and Women*; and Yacovazzi, *Escaped Nuns*.
78. Dudley, "Woman and Christianity," *Lutheran Observer*, January 10, 1840, 1.
79. "Rights and Duties," *Lutheran Observer*, August 3, 1838, 198; S. S. S[chmucker], "Is it Proper for Females to Conduct the Exercises in Any Part of Public Christian Worship, in Promiscuous Assemblies of Both Sexes?," *Lutheran Observer*, December 19, 1834, 66; Dudley, "Woman and Christianity," 1.
80. Bittle, *Plea for Female Education*, 24, 40–41; "A Female Seminary," *Lutheran Observer*, June 23, 1848, 98. For context on women's education in the nineteenth-century United States, see Turpin, *New Moral Vision*.
81. *Lutheran Almanac for 1861*, 36.
82. Buck, *Theological Dictionary*, 246. On this book's prominence among American evangelicals, see Bowman and Brown, "Reverend Buck's Theological Dictionary."
83. "'The Lutherans, of All Protestants, Differ Least from the Romish Church,'" *Lutheran Observer*, January 30, 1835, 91.
84. Bachman, *Sermon on the Doctrines and Disciplines*, 14.

85. See Gjerde, *Catholicism and the Shaping of Nineteenth-Century America;* and Farrelly, *Anti-Catholicism in America,* 134–89.

86. "Hotel Dieu Nunnery," *Lutheran Observer,* January 27, 1837, 90; "The Whole Truth in a Nut-shell," *Lutheran Observer,* December 3, 1841, 2.

87. See, for example, Giustiniani, *Papal Rome, As It Is.*

88. Kurtz, *Why Are You a Lutheran?,* 66–67, 112, 132, 138. The book went through thirteen editions from 1843 to 1869.

89. Schmucker, *Discourse in Commemoration of the Glorious Reformation,* 66, 96.

90. Bachman, *Sermon on the Doctrines and Disciplines,* 31.

91. Sandeen, "Distinctiveness of American Denominationalism," 226n14. For similar assessments, see Jordan, *Evangelical Alliance,* 34; and Wentz, *Pioneer in Christian Unity,* 285–92.

92. "The Union Meeting to Be Held in London in June Next," *Lutheran Observer,* January 30, 1846, 90.

93. Baird, *Religion in the United States,* 586, 588–89. On the significance of Baird's work, see Moore, *Religious Outsiders,* 5–7. On Baird and Schmucker, see Wentz, *Pioneer in Christian Unity,* 30.

94. Quotations and specific details in this paragraph are from Forster, *Zion on the Mississippi,* 91, 94, 110, 135, 567. Forster's work remains the most complete history of the Stephanite movement.

95. On the *Erweckung,* see Conser, *Church and Confession,* 27–96; Gäbler, *Geschichte des Pietismus,* 3:87–370; Ellis, *Politics and Piety;* and Kloes, *German Awakening.*

96. Forster, *Zion on the Mississippi,* 567.

97. For a similar comparison, see Todd, *Authority Vested,* 32.

98. Quotations and specific details in this paragraph are from Forster, *Zion on the Mississippi,* 288–89, 294, 353, 392, 422.

99. The most comprehensive biography of Walther is Suelflow, *Servant of the Word.* For works that situate Walther in his American context, see Dörfler-Dierken, *Luthertum und Demokratie,* 259–334; and Jordahl, "Schmucker and Walther."

100. C. F. W. W[alther] to Otto Herman Walther, May 4, 1840, in Meyer, *Letters of C. F. W. Walther,* 34, 38.

101. The theses are printed in Forster, *Zion on the Mississippi,* 523–25.

102. "Von dem Namen 'Lutheraner,'" *Lutheraner,* September 23, 1844, 5. For a translation of the first three volumes of this periodical, see Baseley, *C. F. W. Walther's Original "Der Lutheraner."*

103. "Von dem Namen 'Lutheraner,'" *Lutheraner,* October 5, 1844, 11.

104. Schieferdecker, "Abgedrungener Beweis, daß die Methodisten eine Secte sind," *Lutheraner,* May 3, 1845, 69–70.

105. "Antwort auf die neueste Vertheidigung der Union," *Lutheraner,* August 9, 1845, 100.

106. On primitivist movements in U.S. religion, see Hughes, *American Quest for the Primitive Church.* For a provocative comparison of Walther's movement to early Mormonism, see Brasich, "Mighty Fortress," 79–132.

107. "Von dem Namen 'Lutheraner,'" *Lutheraner,* September 23, 1844, 6.

108. For a similar observation, see Bratt, "Reorientation of American Protestantism," 76.

109. "Zur Beherzigung: Für die Leser des Lutheraners und des sogenannten Wahrheitsfreunds," *Lutheraner,* March 8, 1845, 55.

110. "Kirchliche Nachricht," *Lutheraner,* January 24, 1846, 43.

111. On Wyneken's life and early career, see Lindemann, *Fredrich Konrad Dietrich Wyneken;* and Bachmann, "The Rise of 'Missouri Lutheranism,'" 41–69.

112. The work originally appeared in Germany in 1843. The following year it was published in the United States by the Pittsburgh-based *Lutherischen Kirchenzeitung,* first as a series of articles and then as a tract. All quotations here are from Wyneken, *Distress of the German Lutherans in North America,* a translation of the 1843 edition.

113. Wyneken, *Distress of the German Lutherans,* 18, 25, 49–50.

114. On Neo-Lutheranism in Germany, see Conser, *Church and Confession,* 55–96. On Löhe, see Geiger, *Life, Work, and Influence of Wilhelm Loehe.*

115. Heintzen, "William Loehe and the Missouri Synod," 78.

116. *Lebenslauf von W. Sihler bis zu seiner Ankunft in New York,* 142. On Sihler, see Spitz, *Life in Two Worlds.*

117. Wyneken, *Distress of the German Lutherans,* 47.

118. Bachmann, "Rise of 'Missouri Lutheranism,'" 186–90.

119. Lindemann, *Fredrich Konrad Dietrich Wyneken,* 21.

120. Ein unsindirter Laie, "Die (Pseudo) Lutherische Hirtenstime," *Lutheraner,* November 17, 1846, 32.

121. F. Wyneken, "Wie unsere deutschen Lutheraner sich fangen lassen; oder die Füchse in Weinberge des Herrn," *Lutheraner,* May 30, 1846, 79.

122. "Vorwort des Herausgebers zum dritten Jahrgang des 'Lutheraner,'" *Lutheraner,* September 5, 1846, 1.

123. "The Reverend Mr. Stephan and His Congregation," *Lutheran Observer,* March 8, 1839, 2. For background, see Forster, *Zion on the Mississippi,* 84–88.

124. "Old Lutherans of the West," *Lutheran Observer,* November 28, 1845, 54.

125. See Bachmann, "Rise of 'Missouri Lutheranism,'" 149–74.

126. W. Sihler, "Gibt es Alt-und Neu-Lutheraner?," *Lutheraner,* May 16, 1846, 76.

127. W. Sihler, "Gibt es Alt-und Neu-Lutheraner?," *Lutheraner,* May 30, 1846, 77–78. See also F. Buenger, "Protestation gegen die Beneunung 'Altlutheraner,'" *Lutheraner,* July 12, 1845, 91.

128. For example, in a lengthy series of articles in the *Lutheraner* between October 17, 1846, and July 27, 1847, titled "Führt das alte Lutherthum nach Rom?," Walther never disputed the designation.

129. See Forster, *Zion on the Mississippi,* 240–44, 458–59; and Mundinger, *Government in the Missouri Synod,* 149, 207–8. On the Dreissiger, see Kamphoefner, "Dreissiger and Forty-Eighter."

130. Mundinger, *Government in the Missouri Synod,* 208n19.

131. Walther, "Bußtagspredigt über Jer. 18, 1–11," in *Casual-Predigten und-Reden,* 155. For a translation, see Walther, *Occasional Sermons and Addresses,* 78–82.

132. "Predigt gehalten am Reformationsfeßt, den 31. October 1847 in der Dreieinigkeitskirche der deutschen ev.-luth. Gemeinde Ungänderter Augsburgischer Confession zu St. Louis, Mo," *Lutheraner,* November 16, 1847, 42. For other examples, see "Aufruf zur Mission unter den heidnischen Indianern," *Lutheraner,* November 4, 1847, 36; and "Kirchliche Nachrichten auß Hannover und Preußen," *Lutheraner,* March 7, 1848, 133. See also Bachmann, "Rise of 'Missouri Lutheranism,'" 280–82.

133. Walther, "Bußtagspredigt über Jer. 18, 1–11," 160.

134. Wyneken, *Distress of the German Lutherans,* 46.

135. Walther, "Rede am 4. Juli gehalten vor einem christlichen Jünglingsverein," in *Lutherische Brosamen,* 365–67, 369. For a translation, see Walther, *From Our Master's Table,* 173–76.

136. See Mundinger, *Government in the Missouri Synod,* 163–98; and Bachmann, "Rise of 'Missouri Lutheranism,'" 199–224.

137. "Synodalverfassung," *Lutheraner,* September 5, 1846, 2.

138. "Vorwort des Herausgebers zum dritten Jahrgang des 'Lutheraner,'" 1–2.

139. "Ein Wort über Kirchenmelodien," *Lutheraner,* August 10, 1847, 140; "'Der deutsche Kirchenfreund,'" *Lutheraner,* December 28, 1847, 70; "Neue religiöse Zeitschrift," *Lutheraner,* March 23, 1847, 84.

140. Hermann, "A New German Synod—The German Evang. Lutheran Synod of Missouri, Ohio, and other States—Innovations—New Measures Unknown to Our Church, &c, &c," *Lutheran Observer,* September 3, 1847, 1.

141. "The Missouri (Old Lutheran) Synod," *Lutheran Standard,* November 8, 1848, 2.

142. See Bachmann, "Rise of 'Missouri Lutheranism,'" 206–14.

143. *Zweiter Synodal-Bericht der deutschen Ev.-Luth. Synode von Missouri,* 37–38. For a translation of Walther's address, see Harrison, *At Home in the House of My Fathers,* 1–9.

144. See, for example, Mundinger, *Government in the Missouri Synod;* and Rast, "Demagoguery or Democracy?"

145. In his first book, a defense the Missouri Synod's view of church polity, Walther wrote, "We willingly concede that the conditions in which we live here in America have had a decided influence." Walther, *Stimme unserer Kirche in der Frage von Kirche und Amt,* viii.

146. Bachmann makes a similar point in "Rise of 'Missouri Lutheranism,'" 234.

147. See Conkin, *American Originals;* and Moore, *Religious Outsiders.*

148. "Vorwort des Herausgebers zum dritten Jahrgang des 'Lutheraner,'" *Lutheraner,* September 5, 1846, 2.

149. Schaff, *Amerika,* 225–26.

150. On the Ohio Synod's early history, see Allbeck, *Century of Lutherans in Ohio,* esp. 61–67, 111–17.

151. The Pennsylvania Synod officially recommended the periodical in 1851. See Ferm, *Crisis in American Lutheran Theology,* 145.

152. Schaff, *Amerika,* 225.

153. On Greenwald, see Jensson, *American Lutheran Biographies,* 273–75.

154. "Introductory," *Lutheran Standard,* September 21, 1842, 2.

155. "'Lutheran Standard,'" *Lutheran Observer,* October 7, 1842, 3; "Unhandsome Innuendoes," *Lutheran Observer,* December 16, 1842, 2.

156. Nevin, *Anxious Bench,* 4–5, 55. For biographical information on Nevin, see Hart, *John Williamson Nevin.* For examples of examinations of Nevin's book that overlook its original context, see Bratt, "Religious Anti-Revivalism in Antebellum America," 96–99; and Holifield, *Theology in America,* 468.

157. "'The Anxious Bench. By the Rev. J. W. Nevin, D. D., Prof of Theology in the Seminary of the German Reformed Church. Published in Chambersburg, Pa.,'" *Lutheran Observer,* October 27, 1843, 3.

158. The first part appeared in the November 10, 1843, issue; the final on March 22, 1844. For another New Lutheran defense of the practice of revivals published in response to Nevin, see Weiser, *Mourner's Bench.*

159. "Correct Sentiments," *Lutheran Standard,* November 3, 1843, 2; Rev. Dr. Nevin, "The Anxious Bench," *Lutheran Standard,* November 10, 1843, 2.

160. Nevin, *Angstbank.*

161. Beta, "Mr. Editor," *Lutheran Standard,* January 12, 1844, 2. See also Alpha, "Mr. Editor," *Lutheran Standard,* December 22, 1843, 2–3; and Alpha, "Mr. Editor!," *Lutheran Standard,* February 16, 1844, 3.

162. See Wentz, "Relations Between the Lutheran and Reformed Churches."

163. See Donner, "'Neither Germans nor Englishmen, but Americans.'"

164. Henkel, *Carolinian Herald of Liberty.* For background on Henkel and the early Tennessee Synod, see Carpenter, "Augsburg Confession War."

165. Bachman, *Sermon on the Doctrines and Disciplines,* 12.

166. "'Evangelic Lutheran Tennessee Synod,'" *Lutheran Observer,* February 22, 1839, 2.

167. "Ev. Luth. Synod of Tennessee," *Lutheran Standard,* August 5, 1846, 2. On Spielmann, see Jensson, *American Lutheran Biographies,* 741–43.

168. "'The Tennessee Synod,'" *Lutheran Standard,* September 30, 1846, 2. For similar accusations, see Bachman, *Sermon on the Doctrines and Disciplines,* 13.

169. See especially the series "Friendly Letters to the Tennessee Synod," which began appearing in the *Lutheran Standard* on December 3, 1851, and continued until May 5, 1852.

170. "Tennessee Department," *Lutheran Standard,* August 11, 1852, 1.

171. *Minutes of the Evangelical Lutheran Tennessee Synod, 1861,* 6.

172. See, for example, "The 'General Synod,' and its Doctrines," *Lutheran Standard,* April 15, 1846, 3.

173. "Rev. M. Wallace's Address Before the Pseudo-General Synod of the Lutheran Church in the United States," *Lutheran Standard,* June 18, 1845, 2.

174. "Our Confessions," *Lutheran Standard,* February 14, 1849, 3.

175. "'Der Lutheraner,'" *Lutheran Standard,* January 17, 1849, 2.

176. "The General Synod," *Lutheran Standard,* October 11, 1848, 2.

177. Wentz, *History of the Gettysburg Theological Seminary,* 95, 172–74.

178. On these figures, see Jensson, *American Lutheran Biographies,* 648–54; and Breidenbaugh, *Pennsylvania College Book,* 161–62.

179. For examples of this claim, see Wentz, *Pioneer in Christian Unity,* 177; and Gustafson, *Lutherans in Crisis,* 117.

180. R[eynolds], "Introductory—The Objects and Position of the Evangelical Review," *Evangelical Review* 1, no. 1 (July 1849): 15, 17–18.

181. "'Evangelical Review,'" *Lutheran Observer,* July 7, 1848, 106; "The Evangelical Review," *Lutheran Observer,* September 15, 1848, 147.

182. L., "The Evangelical Review," *Lutheran Observer,* July 27, 1849, 118; J., "The Evangelical Review," *Lutheran Observer,* August 3, 1849, 121–22.

183. S. S. S[chmucker], "Evangelical Review: No. 2," *Lutheran Observer,* September 7, 1849, 142.

184. [Samuel Schmucker] to Beale [Schmucker], July 30, 1849, series 1, folder 5, Samuel Simon Schmucker and the Schmucker Family Papers, Musselman Library Special Collections, Gettysburg College, Pennsylvania (hereafter Schmucker Family Papers).

185. The debate between Reynolds and Schmucker appeared in the *Lutheran Observer* between September 21, 1849, and December 28, 1849.

186. Candor, "The Evangelical Review," *Lutheran Observer,* February 8, 1850, 230.

187. S. S. Schmucker, "Synod of Penn. and the General Synod," *Lutheran Observer,* March 4, 1853, 37.

188. "Union of the Synod of Pennsylvania with the General Synod," *Lutheran Standard,* April 20, 1853, 3.

189. "Meeting of the Joint Synod," *Lutheran Standard,* May 4, 1853, 2.
190. "Our General Synod," *Evangelical Review* 5, no. 2 (October 1853): 280.
191. Schaff, *Amerika,* 226–27, 236.

2. THE CRISES OF THE 1850S

1. Harkey, *Mission of the Lutheran Church,* 3, 6, 13–16, 18–19, 28. On Harkey, see Jensson, *American Lutheran Biographies,* 96–100.
2. This perspective originated in Ferm, *Crisis in American Lutheran Theology,* and has been carried forward by other standard accounts of mid-nineteenth-century Lutheranism, including Wentz, *Basic History,* and Gustafson, *Lutherans in Crisis.*
3. For statistics on antebellum immigration, see United States Bureau of the Census, *Historical Statistics,* 105–9.
4. For background, see Gienapp, *Origins of the Republican Party;* and Anbinder, *Nativism and Slavery.*
5. On the forty-eighters and the presumed "freedom-loving" nature of antebellum German Americans, see Efford, *German Immigrants, Race, and Citizenship,* 53–85; and Anderson, *Abolitionizing Missouri,* esp. 18–79. For the broader context, see Kamphoefner, *Germans in America.*
6. The most comprehensive study remains Schneider, *German Church on the American Frontier.*
7. Mann, *Lutheranism in America,* 93–94. On Mann, see Jensson, *American Lutheran Biographies,* 487–90. On the Wisconsin Synod, see Koehler, *History of the Wisconsin Synod.* On the Texas Synod, see Vardell, "Striving to Gather the Scattered," 1–28.
8. Harkey, *Mission of the Lutheran Church,* 6, 8.
9. For examples of pleas for outreach, see "The Germans Totally Uncared For," *Lutheran Observer,* November 8, 1850, 382; and "Help! Help!! Brethren," *Lutheran Observer,* July 11, 1851, 522. For examples of criticisms, see "Germans in this Country," *Lutheran Observer,* May 26, 1854, 86; and "German Population in the U. States," *Lutheran Observer,* August 19, 1853, 152.
10. Elias Schwartz Journal, November 6, 1857, A. R. Wentz Library, United Lutheran Seminary, Gettysburg, Pennsylvania; J. H. W. Stuckenberg to "Brother," February 26, 1859, box 1, folder 2, John Henry Wilbrand Stuckenberg Papers, Special Collections, Musselman Library, Gettysburg College, Pennsylvania.
11. S. S. Schmucker, "Vocation of the American Lutheran Church," *Evangelical Review* 2, no. 4 (April 1851): 491.
12. "Germans in America," *Lutheran Standard,* September 24, 1851, 2.
13. R., "What Shall We Do for Our German Population?," *Lutheran Standard,* April 19, 1854, 2.
14. See Schneider, *German Church on the American Frontier,* 372–74; Koehler, *History of the Wisconsin Synod,* 76–86; and Hattery, "Historical Development of the Doctrine of Unionism."
15. *Sechster Synodal-Bericht der deutschen evangel.-lutherischen Synode von Missouri,* 7. For a translation of Wyneken's address, see Harrison, *At Home in the House of My Fathers,* 359–67.
16. Wangelin, "Loehe's Lens," 37.
17. "Reisebericht des Redakteurs," *Lutheraner,* February 17, 1852, 97. For a translation of Walther's "Trip Report," see Harrison, *At Home in the House of My Fathers,* 19–106.
18. For the most complete translation, see Walther, *Church and the Office of the Ministry.*
19. On the early history of the Iowa Synod, see Ottersberg, "Evangelical Lutheran Synod of Iowa."

20. Bachmann, "Rise of 'Missouri Lutheranism,'" 319–20.

21. On antebellum Swedish and Norwegian immigrants, see Barton, *Folk Divided*, 3–70; and Blegen, *Norwegian Migration to America.*

22. The most comprehensive overview of Swedish American Lutheranism is Erling and Granquist, *Augustana Story.* On its early history, see Stephenson, *Founding of the Augustana Synod,* as well as biographies of key leaders: Ander, *T. N. Hasselquist;* and Rönnegård, *Prairie Shepherd.*

23. L. P. Esbjörn to [Eric Norelius], May 12, 1853, box 1, folder 1, Erik Norelius Papers, Evangelical Lutheran Church in America Archives, Elk Grove Village, Illinois (hereafter Norelius papers). On Norelius, see Johnson, *Eric Norelius.*

24. L. P. Esbjörn to [Eric Norelius], August 14, 1852, box 1, folder 1, Norelius Papers.

25. L. P. Esbjörn to [Eric Norelius], March 6, 1855, box 1, folder 2, Norelius Papers.

26. On the early history of Norwegian Lutheranism in the United States, see Rohne, *Norwegian American Lutheranism;* and Nelson and Fevold, *Lutheran Church Among Norwegian-Americans,* vol. 1.

27. On Johnson and his influence, see Nelson and Fevold, *Lutheran Church Among Norwegian-Americans,* 1:32–45.

28. "Indberetning fra Pastorerne Ottesen og Brandt om deres Reise til St. Louis, Missouri; Columbus, Ohio; og Buffalo, New York," *Kirkelig Maanedstidende* 2, no. 12 (October 1857): 476–89.

29. Schmucker, *American Lutheran Church,* 157–58, 244–45.

30. Quotations are from the 1847 constitution. Polack, "Our First Synodical Constitution," 3. Compare to the 1854 constitution in Meyer, *Moving Frontiers,* 149–50.

31. *Zweiter Synodal-Bericht der deutschen Ev.-Luth. Synode von Missouri,* 35–36.

32. Ferm, *Crisis in American Lutheran Theology,* 144–48.

33. "Union of the Synod of Pennsylvania with the General Synod," *Lutheran Standard,* April 20, 1853, 3.

34. "The Synod of Pennsylvania and the Symbolical Books," *Lutheran Standard,* June 1, 1853, 1.

35. *Definite Platform,* 2, 5.

36. The idea that the *Definite Platform* advanced new theological claims is implied in Ferm, *Crisis in American Lutheran Theology,* 192; and Nelson, *Lutherans in North America,* 233–34. It is stated explicitly in Holifield, *Theology in America,* 411.

37. *Definite Platform,* 5.

38. On the history and occasion of the document's composition, see Wentz, *Pioneer in Christian Unity,* 195–215. On Sprecher, see Bell, *Portraiture of the Life of Samuel Sprecher.*

39. *Definite Platform,* 6.

40. Mann, *Plea for the Augsburg Confession,* 6, 47. For a similar argument, see Hoffman, *Broken Platform.*

41. Ferm, *Crisis in American Lutheran Theology,* 243, 331–32.

42. "Pacific Overture," *Lutheran Observer,* February 15, 1856, 3.

43. Schmucker, *American Lutheranism Vindicated,* 4, 9. For the retraction of Schmucker and others, including Kurtz, see "Pacific Overture," *Lutheran Observer,* February 29, 1856, 3.

44. "A New Lutheran Synod," *Lutheran Observer,* December 11, 1857, 2.

45. See Stephenson, *Founding of the Augustana Synod,* 130–52.

46. Wentz, *Basic History,* 136. Essentially the same claim is made in Ferm, *Crisis in American Lutheran Theology,* 190; Nelson, *Lutherans in North America,* 226–27; and Kuenning, *Rise and Fall,* 174.

47. For example, see "Revivals," *Lutheran Observer,* March 6, 1857, 2–3; "Questions and Answers

Respecting Revivals," *Lutheran Observer,* October 2, 1857, 2–3; and "The Temperance Question," *Lutheran Observer,* January 22, 1858, 1. On the broader American evangelical context, see Smith, *Revivalism and Social Reform;* and Long, *Revival of 1857–58.*

48. Nearly six years after the publication of the *Definite Platform,* one writer claimed that the New Lutheran understanding of the Augsburg Confession was the view of "by far the largest number of Lutherans in America." "Intolerance," *Lutheran Observer,* July 5, 1861, 2.

49. "'American Recension of the Augsburg Confession,'" *Lutheran Standard,* October 19, 1855, 2–3.

50. Allbeck, *Century of Lutherans in Ohio,* 198.

51. "Die neue theologische Zeitschrift," *Lutheraner,* January 16, 1855, 86.

52. "Vorwort zu Jahrgang 1856," *Lehre und Wehre* 2, no. 1 (January 1856): 4–5. For a translation, see Suelflow, *Selected Writings of C. F. W. Walther: Editorials from "Lehre und Wehre,"* 11–14.

53. The most complete account of these meetings is Lueker, "Walther and the Free Lutheran Conferences."

54. "Vorwort zu Jahrgang 1857," *Lehre und Wehre* 3, no. 1 (January 1857): 1–2. For a translation, see Suelflow, *Selected Writings of C. F. W. Walther: Editorials from "Lehre und Wehre,"* 39–42.

55. "The General Conference," *Lutheran Standard,* October 16, 1856, 2.

56. "Historiches Zeitblatt und Literarischer Anzeiger," *Lutheran Standard,* December 10, 1858, 3.

57. "'The Lutheraner'—Our Respects," *Lutheran Standard,* November 11, 1859, 3.

58. C. F. W. Walther to "die deutsche ev.-luth. Gesamtgemeinde Ungeänderter Augsburgischer Konfession zu St. Louis," February 3, 1860, in Fürbringer, *Briefe von C. F. W. Walther,* 1:135. For a translation, see Harrison, *At Home in the House of My Fathers,* 142–45.

59. C. F. W. Walther, "Editorielle Correspondenz," *Lehre und Wehre* 6, no. 7 (July 1860): 194–95, 197. For background on the trip and a translation of this letter, see Meyer, "Walther's Letter from Zurich."

60. The most comprehensive biography of Passavant is Gerberding, *Life and Letters of W. A. Passavant.*

61. W. A. Passavant to "Dearest Sister" [Emma], June 16, 1840, William Alfred Passavant Letters, Zelienople Historical Society (hereafter Passavant Letters).

62. Passavant to "Dearest Sister," January 25, 1841, Passavant Letters.

63. "Proceedings of an Extra Session of the Pittsburg Synod of the Evang. Lutheran Church Held on the 14th of October, 1847, and Following Days," *Missionary,* January 1848, 2. For Kurtz's commendation, see "'The Missionary,'" *Lutheran Observer,* February 4, 1848, 18.

64. "The New Volume," *Missionary,* January 1852, 4. For the accusations by the *Lutheran Observer,* see "How We Are Misrepresented," *Lutheran Observer,* December 19, 1851, 615.

65. "To Our Readers," *Missionary,* January 3, 1856, 2.

66. "The Missionary," *Lutheran Observer,* January 18, 1856, 12.

67. Samuel, "What Does It Mean?," *Lutheran Observer,* March 7, 1856, 40.

68. For biographical information on Krauth, see Spaeth, *Charles Porterfield Krauth.*

69. Spaeth, *Charles Porterfield Krauth,* 1:18. Besides Spaeth's biography, the most extensive treatment of Charles Philip Krauth is Conser, *Church and Confession,* 263–73. For an expression of Krauth's moderate Lutheranism, see his inaugural editorial for the journal: C[harles] P[hilip] Krauth, "The Lutheran Church in the United States," *Evangelical Review* 2, no. 1 (July 1850): 1–16.

70. See especially the letters of February 14, 1843, March 26, 1843, and February 18, 1845, in Spaeth, *Charles Porterfield Krauth,* 1:89–92, 101–2.

71. Simon Schneeweiss, "The View of the Lutheran Church in Regard to the Sacramental Presence of Christ," *Lutheran Observer,* June 29, 1849, 102. On Krauth's authorship of this article, see Spaeth, *Charles Porterfield Krauth,* 1:161.

72. Charles P[orterfield] Krauth, "The Relation of Our Confessions to the Reformation, and the Importance of Their Study, with an Outline of the Early History of the Augsburg Confession," *Evangelical Review* 1, no. 2 (October 1849): 236.

73. Spaeth, *Charles Porterfield Krauth,* 1:160.

74. Gerberding, *Life and Letters of W. A. Passavant,* 166.

75. On Seiss, see Rast, "Joseph A. Seiss."

76. Diehl, *Biography of Rev. Ezra Keller,* 83.

77. A Virginian, "'The Church's Best State; or Constant Revivals of Religion: By Rev. S. W. Harkey, Frederick, Md.," *Lutheran Observer,* January 3, 1845, 1; January 10, 1845, 5; January 17, 1845, 9; January 24, 1845, 13.

78. J. A. Seiss, "The Necessity and Obligation of Confessions of Faith," *Evangelical Review* 4, no. 1 (July 1852): 1–34.

79. On Schmucker, see Jensson, *American Lutheran Biographies,* 685–90.

80. B. M. S[chmucker] to Chas. P. Krauth, December 22, 1849, in Spaeth, *Charles Porterfield Krauth,* 1:189–90.

81. [Samuel Schmucker] to Beale [Schmucker], March 5 and November 7, 1849, March 17, 1850, series 1, folder 5, Schmucker Family Papers.

82. Works that frame the confessional movement in the United States as an importation from Europe include Wentz, *Basic History,* 108–30; Tappert, *Lutheran Confessional Theology;* and Conser, *Church and Confession.*

83. See, for example, H. E. F. Guerike, "The Church, as Set Forth in the Confessions of Christendom," trans. C. Porterfield Krauth, *Evangelical Review* 5, no. 1 (July 1853): 17–34; Seiss, "Necessity and Obligation of Confessions of Faith," 1–34; and "Progress of Evangelical Religion in Germany," *Missionary,* December 1855, 92.

84. See, for example, Schmucker, *American Lutheranism Vindicated,* 57–63; "Anglo-Sax and J. H. A. B.' or German Theology in America," *Lutheran Observer,* February 8, 1856, 25; and "To the Evangelical Church Diet to be Held in Stuttgart, Germany, from the 21st to the 25th of September, 1857," *Lutheran Observer,* September 11, 1857, 1–2.

85. Schneeweiss, "View of the Lutheran Church in Regard to the Sacramental Presence of Christ," 102; Krauth, "Relation of Our Confessions to the Reformation," 240.

86. "Where Do We Stand?," *Lutheran and Missionary,* October 31, 1861, 2.

87. Krauth, *Christian Liberty,* 13–14, 28.

88. Seiss, "Necessity and Obligation of Confessions of Faith," 1–2.

89. "The 'Alte Lutheraner' (Old Lutherans) of the United States," *Missionary,* April 1855, 26.

90. "Where Do We Stand?," 2.

91. In his discussion of Moderate Lutherans, Philip Schaff did not mention Krauth, Passavant, Seiss, or any other young confessionalists. See Schaff, *Amerika,* 225–27.

92. Krauth, "Relation of Our Confessions to the Reformation," 242. See also Rast, "Joseph A. Seiss," 37–39; Gerberding, *Life and Letters of W. A. Passavant,* 59.

93. "'We Be Brethren,'" *Missionary,* February 7, 1856, 6.

94. C. P. K[rauth], "The General Synod," *Missionary,* April 30, 1857, 54.

95. "An Apology for Our Existence," *Lutheran and Home Journal,* July 6, 1860, 4.

96. "Where Do We Stand?," 2.

97. Krauth, *Poverty;* Seiss, *Claims of Sabbath Schools;* "Temperance and the Church," *Missionary,* February 10, 1859, 9; "Protracted Meetings," *Missionary,* February 17, 1859, 13–14.

98. See Fields, *Slavery and Freedom on the Middle Ground.*

99. "Slavery," *Lutheran Observer,* August 23, 1850, 339.

100. "The Authority of the Bible Misapplied: Polygamy—Slavery," *Lutheran Observer,* September 21, 1855, 158.

101. See, for example, "For Liberia," *Lutheran Observer,* August 8, 1851, 539; and "Religion in Liberia," *Lutheran Observer,* September 28, 1855, 160.

102. "Reply to a 'Member,'" *Lutheran Observer,* November 13, 1857, 3.

103. Morris Officer, "The African Slave Trade," *Evangelical Review* 9, no. 1 (July 1857): 42, 47. On Officer, see Imhoff, *Life of Rev. Morris Officer.*

104. Fortenbaugh, "American Lutheran Synods and Slavery," 86–87.

105. Schmucker, *Elements of Popular Theology* (1860), 330–36.

106. Stange, *Radicalism for Humanity,* 33–40.

107. Kuenning, *Rise and Fall,* 213.

108. Fortenbaugh, "American Lutheran Synods and Slavery," 74.

109. "Slavery in New Orleans," *Lutheran Standard,* April 21, 1852, 2; "End of the Slave Trade," *Lutheran Standard,* August 25, 1852, 3; "Modification of the Slave Law," *Lutheran Standard,* February 8, 1854, 3.

110. For example, in a lengthy sermon detailing the sins of the American nation, Krauth did not discuss slavery. Krauth, *Altar on the Threshing-Floor.*

111. Historian Paul Kuenning has contended that opposition to New Lutheranism stemmed in part from antagonism toward Schmucker's views on slavery. However, as Kuenning himself admits, "hard evidence or documented proof is lacking." Kuenning, *Rise and Fall,* 175.

112. Fortenbaugh, "American Lutheran Synods and Slavery," 86.

113. "Abstract of the Proceedings of the Middle Conference of the Pittsburg Synod," *Missionary,* October 1, 1857, 142.

114. "Free Speech," *Missionary,* December 10, 1857, 182.

115. For example, see "The Slave Trade," *Missionary,* March 3, 1859, 23; "Washington and Slavery," *Missionary,* March 29, 1860; and "The Slave Trade as It Is," *Missionary,* July 5, 1860, 96.

116. See Stephens, *Science, Race, and Religion in the American South.*

117. See, for example, Ford, *Deliver Us from Evil;* and Genovese and Fox-Genovese, *Fatal Self-Deception.*

118. John Bachman, "Strictures on Resolutions of the Middle Conference," *Missionary,* December 10, 1857, 181.

119. "Freedom Better than Bondage," *Missionary,* December 17, 1857, 186.

120. Noll, *Civil War as a Theological Crisis,* 36–37.

121. Brøndal, *Ethnic Leadership and Midwestern Politics,* 46–48.

122. Ander, "Swedish-American Newspapers"; Andersen, *Immigrant Takes His Stand,* 10–33; Rasmussen, *Civil War Settlers,* 61–98.

123. Andersen, *Immigrant Takes His Stand,* 65–67. On Solberg, see Solberg, "Reminiscences of a Pioneer Editor."

124. Ander, *T. N. Hasselquist*, 153. Andersen calls the opposition to slavery among Swedes "nearly unanimous." Andersen, *Immigrant Takes His Stand*, 69.

125. Widen, "Texas Swedish Pioneers and the Confederacy," 104; Hastvedt, "Recollections of a Norwegian Pioneer in Texas," 101–2.

126. An anonymous article containing two quotations from the sixteenth century may have been compiled by Walther. See "Melanchthon und Luther über Sclaverei," *Lehre und Wehre* 2, no. 11 (November 1856): 352.

127. A. B[iewend], "Die Sclaverei und die Bibel," *Lehre und Wehre* 2, no. 8 (August 1856): 225–33. Biewend briefly reiterated his views in A. B[iewend], "Welthändel," *Lutheraner*, January 27, 1857, 94. For similar defenses of slavery by both Protestants and Catholics, see Noll, *Civil War as a Theological Crisis*, 39–40, 51–52, 126–32.

128. Walther, "Bußtagspredigt über Jer. 18, 1–11," in *Casual-Predigten und-Reden*, 155.

129. "Freiheit oder Freckheit," *Lutheraner*, January 17, 1854, 86. On Boernstein and the *Anzeiger des Westens*, see Anderson, *Abolitionizing Missouri*.

130. "'Saint Louiser Volksblatt,'" *Lutheraner*, May 22, 1854, 158. For background, see Suelflow, *Servant of the Word*, 75–78.

131. "Das 'St. Louiser Volksblatt,'" *Lutheraner*, May 6, 1856, 147–50.

132. "'St. Louiser Volksblatt,'" *Lutheraner*, September 22, 1857, 22.

133. The most comprehensive study of this periodical is Peterson, *Popular Narratives and Ethnic Identity*.

134. "Etwas über Präsidentenwahlen," *Illustrirte Abend-Schule*, September 20, 1856, 134–35. On the *Volksblatt*'s endorsement, see Anderson, *Abolitionizing Missouri*, 77.

135. "Sklaverei," *Illustrirte Abend-Schule*, June 10, 1854, 1–2; "Der Sklavenmarkt in New-Orleans," *Illustrirte Abend-Schule*, April 19, 1856, 38–39.

136. "Prospectus der Illustrirten Abendschule," *Lutheraner*, February 14, 1854, 103.

137. Dietrich Gerstein to "Dear sister," September 10, 1856, in Kamphoefner and Helbich, *Germans in the Civil War*, 277.

138. Walther, "Rede am 4. Juli," 363.

139. See Kretzmann, "Francis Arnold Hoffmann."

140. Harkey, *Mission of the General Synod*, 8, 10, 12, 17, 28–29.

141. "The Review: The Church," *Evangelical Review* 10, no. 1 (July 1858): 12–13, 15.

142. "The Position of Our Church," *Lutheran and Home Journal*, September 7, 1860, 37.

143. Pacificator, "The Lutheran Church—No. 2," *Lutheran Observer*, June 8, 1860, 1, and "The Lutheran Church—No. 3," *Lutheran Observer*, June 15, 1860, 1.

144. "Lutheran Churches at York, Pa.—No. 1," *Lutheran Observer*, March 8, 1861, 1.

145. *Proceedings of the Nineteenth Convention of the General Synod*, 59.

3. LUTHERANS AND THE UNION, 1860–1863

1. "The Lutheran and Missionary," *Lutheran and Missionary*, October 31, 1861, 2.

2. "Don't Give Up the Ship," *Lutheran and Missionary*, October 31, 1861, 2.

3. Works that explore these developments include Byrd, *Holy Baptism of Fire and Blood;* Carwardine, *Righteous Strife;* Harlow, *Religion, Race, and the Making of Confederate Kentucky;* Holm,

Kingdom Divided; Miller et al., *Religion and the American Civil War;* Noll, *Civil War as a Theological Crisis;* Oshatz, *Slavery and Sin;* Rable, *God's Almost Chosen Peoples;* Scott, *Visitation of God;* Stout, *Upon the Altar of the Nation;* Volkman, *Houses Divided;* Wesley, *Politics of Faith;* and Wetzel, *American Crusade.* Another significant strain of scholarship examines how the Civil War shaped views of the millennium. See Aamodt, *Righteous Armies, Holy Cause;* Matsui, *Millenarian Dreams and Racial Nightmares;* and Wright and Dresser, *Apocalypse and Millennium.* Also important for the context of this study are works on other religious "outsiders," such as Curran, *American Catholics and the Quest for Equality;* Kurtz, *Excommunicated from the Union;* and Lehman and Nolt, *Mennonites, Amish, and the American Civil War.*

4. This is the case in histories of Lutheran confessional conflicts in the nineteenth-century United States. See Ferm, *Crisis in American Lutheran Theology;* Mauelshagen, *American Lutheranism Surrenders;* and Gustafson, *Lutherans in Crisis.* It also occurs in general histories of American Lutheranism, such as Wentz, *Basic History;* Nelson, *Lutherans in North America;* Lagerquist, *Lutherans;* and Granquist, *Lutherans in America.* An important exception is Kuenning, *Rise and Fall.* The only book on Lutherans and the war is more than one hundred years old. See Heathcote, *Lutheran Church and the Civil War.*

5. Kleppner, *Third Electoral System,* esp. 153–63; Swierenga, "Ethnoreligious Political Behavior." On the election of 1860 specifically, see Luebke, *Ethnic Voters and the Election of Lincoln;* Hokanson, *Swedish Immigrants in Lincoln's Time,* 52–67; and Andersen, *Immigrant Takes His Stand,* 77–82.

6. Bost, "Reverend John Bachman," 498.

7. McCandless, "Political Evolution of John Bachman," 28.

8. [Catherine Bachman], *John Bachman,* 362.

9. "The Secession Convention Prayer," John Bachman Papers, James R. Crumley Jr. Archives, Lutheran Theological Southern Seminary, Columbia, South Carolina. The original manuscript is found in the Charleston Museum.

10. According to the paper's editors, "Our circulation is larger than that of all other [Lutheran] papers combined." "The Lutheran Observer as an Advertising Medium," *Lutheran Observer,* March 15, 1861, 2.

11. "Peace," *Lutheran Observer,* February 15, 1861, 2.

12. "Civil War," *Lutheran Observer,* April 26, 1861, 2.

13. "Our Country," *Lutheran Observer,* May 17, 1861, 2.

14. "The Great Battle," *Lutheran Observer,* August 2, 1861, 2.

15. See, for example, "The Division of the Church," *Lutheran Observer,* October 11, 1861, 2; J. M. G., "Peace—No. 1," *Lutheran Observer,* December 6, 1861, 1, and "Peace—No. 2: How Best Promoted," *Lutheran Observer,* January 10, 1862, 1–2.

16. As late as the middle of May, the editors of the *Lutheran Observer* expressed uncertainty about whether their state would secede. See "Will Maryland Secede?," *Lutheran Observer,* May 17, 1861, 2. On views about secession in Maryland, see Robinson, *Union Indivisible.*

17. "The Interest of the Church in the Questions Which Agitate the Country," *Lutheran Observer,* December 28, 1860, 3.

18. "Will Our Church Be Divided?," *Lutheran Observer,* May 17, 1861, 2.

19. For the most complete overview of southern Lutheranism during the Civil War, see Anderson, *Lutheranism in the Southeastern States,* 26–85.

20. "The Observer—Its Foes and Its Friends," *Lutheran Observer*, June 7, 1861, 2.

21. "Southern Correspondence," *Lutheran Observer*, July 19, 1861, 2; July 26, 1861, 2.

22. A., "Conservatism," *Southern Lutheran*, September 28, 1861, 2.

23. See Anderson, *Lutheranism in the Southeastern States*, 34–36.

24. "Our National Troubles," *Missionary*, February 14, 1861, 14. For similar rhetoric from a Pennsylvania Synod minister, see Fry, *Trembling for the Ark of God*.

25. "War," *Missionary*, April 18, 1861, 50.

26. A Friend of His Country, "Is the 'Observer' in League with the Great Civil Rebellion?," *Missionary*, May 9, 1861, 62. See also the letter from "Stars and Stripes" in the same issue.

27. "A Singular Request," *Missionary*, June 27, 1861, 90.

28. On the contested politics in Philadelphia during the war, see Gallman, *Mastering Wartime*, esp. 170–93.

29. "Our Country," *Lutheran and Home Journal*, May 3, 1861, 68; "Character of the Present War," *Lutheran and Home Journal*, June 21, 1861, 92–93.

30. G. Krotel, "Resolutions of the Pennsylvania Synod," *Lutheran and Home Journal*, June 21, 1861, 90.

31. "A Sudden Conversion," *Missionary*, June 13, 1861, 82.

32. F. R. Anspach, "Past, Present and Future," *Lutheran Observer*, January 3, 1862, 2. See also "The Missionary's Misrepresentations," *Lutheran Observer*, June 21, 1861, 3.

33. *Proceedings of the Twentieth Convention of the General Synod*, 30–31.

34. "Our Country," *Lutheran Standard*, December 14, 1860. Worley assumed "entire control" of the paper in December 1859. "Prospectus," *Lutheran Standard*, December 9, 1859, 3. On Worley's life, see Mechling, *History of the Evangelical Lutheran District Synod of Ohio*, 206–7.

35. "Civil War," *Lutheran Standard*, April 26, 1861, 3.

36. See "The Way to Peace," *Lutheran Standard*, November 22, 1861, 1; and "The Church and the Present Politics of the Country," *Lutheran Standard*, April 1, 1863, 2.

37. On the Copperheads, or Peace Democrats, and their prominence in Ohio and other Midwestern states, see Klement, *Copperheads in the Middle West*; and Weber, *Copperheads*.

38. "Our Southern Friends and Brethren," *Lutheran Standard*, May 1, 1862, 2.

39. "Agents for the South," *Lutheran Standard*, July 15, 1862, 2.

40. *Proceedings of the Forty-Second Annual Convention of the Evangelical Lutheran Tennessee Synod*, 6.

41. J. C. Barb, "Lutheranism in Tennessee," *Lutheran Standard*, October 15, 1864, 8.

42. On the reaction of Scandinavian Americans to the war's outbreak, see Hokanson, *Swedish Immigrants in Lincoln's Time*, 68–80; Andersen, *Immigrant Takes His Stand*, 83–90; and Rasmussen, *Civil War Settlers*, 101–29.

43. C. F. W. Walther to J. M. Buehler, May 21, 1861, in Suelflow, *Selected Writings of C. F. W. Walther: Selected Letters*, 150.

44. "Vorwort der Redaction zum achtzehnenten Jahrgang des 'Lutheraner,'" *Lutheraner*, August 20, 1861, 1; C. F. W. W[alther], "Predigt, am allgemeinen Bußtag, den 26 Sept, dieses Jahres," *Lutheraner*, October 16, 1861, 35.

45. Suelflow, "History of Concordia Seminary, St. Louis," 111–12.

46. C. F. W. Walther to J. M. Buehler, May 21, 1861, in Suelflow, *Selected Writings of C. F. W. Walther: Selected Letters*, 150.

47. "'Sind die Untergebenen verbunden, der Obrigkeit Folge zu leisten, wenn dieselbe sie zu irgend einem Kriege ruft?'" *Lutheraner,* May 14, 1861, 156. For a translation, see Rein, "The Christian and Politics," 122.

48. Anderson, *Abolitionizing Missouri,* 171–72. See also Kolb, "C. F. W. Walther to A. F. Hoppe," 80.

49. C. F. W. Walther to Theo E. Buenger, May 7, 1861, in Suelflow, *Selected Writings of C. F. W. Walther: Selected Letters,* 148; Walther to Emilie [Walther], May 10, 1861, in Fürbringer, *Briefe von Walther,* 1:166.

50. Clausen, *Gjenmæle mod Kirkeraadet for den Norske Synode,* 19. For a translation, see Clausen, *Reply to the Church Council of the Norwegian Synod.*

51. Oath of Loyalty, February 12, 1862, Addendum, Civil War folder, box 4, Carl Ferdinand Wilhelm Walther Papers, Concordia Historical Institute, St. Louis, Missouri (hereafter Walther Papers). After the war, Walther was compelled to pledge his loyalty once again, this time to Missouri's new constitution. Walther viewed this order as contrary to both "the Word of God" and "the Constitution of the U.S." He eventually signed the oath, but only after being allowed to change the wording. See Meyer, *Moving Frontiers,* 237–38. On loyalty oaths in Missouri, see Volkman, *Houses Divided,* 135–60.

52. J. Biltz to "Dear sister," October 15, 1862, folder 8, Franz Julius Biltz Family Collection, Concordia Historical Institute, St. Louis, Missouri.

53. On these events, see Frizzell, "'Killed by Rebels.'"

54. A., "Rumors of Another Battle," *Southern Lutheran,* October 26, 1861, 2; "Another Victory," *Southern Lutheran,* December 20, 1862, 2.

55. J. B[achman], "A Reply to the Attack of the Rev. Benjamin Kurtz, D.D., Editor of the Lutheran Observer," *Southern Lutheran,* November 16, 1861, 2.

56. Dreher, *Sermon Delivered . . . June 13, 1861,* 5, 10, 12, 14.

57. "Bible Lessons for the Times: The Artful Question Met," *Lutheran and Missionary,* March 6, 1862, 74.

58. "Lessons of the Twelve-Month," *Lutheran and Missionary,* May 1, 1862, 106.

59. B. K[urtz], "'Let Us Alone,'" *Lutheran Observer,* August 15, 1862, 2.

60. R. W., "Can Our Present Terrible War Be Justified by Scripture?," *Lutheran Observer,* July 25, 1862, 1.

61. On the participation of German Americans, see Kamphoefner and Helbich, *Germans in the Civil War;* and Keller, *Chancellorsville and the Germans.* On Scandinavian Americans, see Rasmussen, *Civil War Settlers.* Valuable as these works are, they are more concerned with questions of ethnicity than of religious identity.

62. Twenty-two Lutheran chaplains were listed in *Lutheran Almanac for 1863,* 37. Not included was John H. W. Stuckenberg, possibly because he did not enlist until September 1862. On Sarner, see Armstrong, *For Courageous Fighting and Confident Dying,* 6.

63. Hedrick and Davis, *I'm Surrounded by Methodists,* 118.

64. Gerberding, *Life and Letters of W. A. Passavant,* 174–76.

65. Fritschel, *Story of One Hundred Years of Deaconess Service,* 27, 36; Herfarth, *Leben in zwei Welten,* 101.

66. See Faust, *This Republic of Suffering;* and Rable, *God's Almost Chosen Peoples,* 213–19.

67. For examples, see "The Meeting of the U.S. Christian Commission," *Lutheran Observer,* November 13, 1863, 3; "Christian Commission," *Lutheran Observer,* January 15, 1864, 3; "The Christian

Commission," *Lutheran and Missionary,* September 18, 1862, 187; and "The Meeting of the U.S. Christian Commission," *Lutheran and Missionary,* November 5, 1863, 7.

68. W., "Letter from New Orleans—The Christian Commission and the Lutheran," *Lutheran and Missionary,* September 1, 1864, 176.

69. Seiss, *Government and Christianity,* 9.

70. Williams, *Sermon Delivered in the Lutheran Churches of the Blain Charge,* 22; Ehrehart, *Discourse Delivered in St. Peter's Evan. Lutheran Church,* 5, 22.

71. Sadtler, *Rebellious Nation Reproved,* 4.

72. Focht, *Our Country,* 65; Anstaedt, *Loyalty to the Government,* 3.

73. Rasmussen, *Civil War Settlers,* 108, 128.

74. Andersen, *Immigrant Takes His Stand,* 85. See also Hokanson, *Swedish Immigrants in Lincoln's Time,* 68–80.

75. Rasmussen, *Civil War Settlers,* 171–213.

76. Delta, "Mr. Editor," *Lutheran Standard,* September 15, 1862, 2; E. H. S., "Political Preaching," *Lutheran Standard,* September 13, 1861, 2.

77. "Position of the Lutheran Church in the Present Crisis," *Lutheran Standard,* November 22, 1861, 2.

78. "Render unto Cesar the Things that are Cesar's; and unto God the Things that are God's," *Lutheran Standard,* November 8, 1861, 2–3.

79. "Neugläubige Predigtweise," *Lutheraner,* November 13, 1861, 54; "Vorwort der Redaction zum neunzehnenten Jahrgang des 'Lutheraner,'" *Lutheraner,* September 3, 1862, 3. See also "Vom Kriegsdienst der Christen," *Lutheraner,* September 3, 1862, 3–4.

80. "Pastor F. W. Richmann," *Lutheraner,* June 25, 1862, 182. On Richmann, see Kretzmann, "Lutheran Army Chaplain in the Civil War."

81. "Vorwort," *Abend Schule,* September 1, 1863, 2. See also "Ueber die beste Politik," *Illustrirte Abend Schule,* March 1, 1861, 97–98, and March 15, 1861, 105–6. The "Geschichte des Tages" section appeared in every issue. For examples of articles on Civil War–related news, see "General McClellan," *Illustrirte Abend Schule,* September 15, 1861, 13; and "Vorwort," *Illustrirte Abend Schule,* September 1, 1862, 1–2.

82. W[alther], "Predigt, am allgemeinen Bußtag," 35.

83. C. F. W. W[alther], "Bußtagspredigt, gehalten den 27. Nov. 1862 zu St. Louis, Mo.," *Lutheraner,* January 21, 1863, 82. For a translation, see Walther, *From Our Master's Table,* 130–34.

84. Byrd, *Holy Baptism of Fire and Blood,* 5. See also Rable, *God's Almost Chosen Peoples,* 80–83, 235–39; and Scott, *Visitation of God,* 97–138.

85. Wesley, *Politics of Faith,* 95. For a useful but incomplete overview of the various Lutheran approaches, see Brndjar, "'Political Preaching.'"

86. Anspach, "Past, Present and Future," 2.

87. "Partisan Politics," *Lutheran Observer,* April 17, 1863, 2.

88. "Religion and Politics," *Lutheran Observer,* May 2, 1862, 2.

89. J. H. B., "Politics in the Pulpit," *Lutheran Observer,* January 25, 1861, 1.

90. "Afraid of Politics," *Lutheran and Missionary,* November 6, 1862, 5. See also "The Religious Press and the Country," *Missionary,* May 16, 1861, 66.

91. "Bible Lessons for the Times: The Two Spheres," *Lutheran and Missionary,* April 3, 1862, 90.

92. "Bible Lessons for the Times: The Artful Question Met," 74.

93. See Ander, *T. N. Hasselquist,* 185–86; Ander, "Swedish-American Newspapers," 72–74; and Hokanson, *Swedish Immigrants in Lincoln's Time,* 61–64.

94. See Andersen, *Immigrant Takes His Stand,* 82–107.

95. P. A. P., "Position of the Lutheran Church in the Present Crisis," *Lutheran Standard,* November 22, 1861, 2; E. H. S., "Political Preaching," 2.

96. "The Church and the Present Politics of the Country," 2.

97. Wesley, *Politics of Faith,* 104–5.

98. *Verhandlungen der achten Jahresversammlung der Westlichen Districts,* 8. For a translation of this address, see Walther, *Essays for the Church,* 1:64–68. Though it is attributed to Walther in this collection of essays, the original proceedings indicate that the address was given by Gottlieb Schaller, the president of the Western District.

99. Th. Brohm, "Der Christ und die Politik," *Lutheraner,* May 14, 1861, 153–54. For a translation, see Rein, "The Christian and Politics," 119–21.

100. J. C. W. Lindemann, "Leset! Leset," *Lutheraner,* December 1, 1863, 49–51; "Der Präsident und die Satanspresse," *Illustrirte Abend Schule,* January 15, 1861, 1–2.

101. "Vorwort der Redaction zum neunzehnenten Jahrgang des 'Lutheraner,'" 1–2.

102. "Will Our Church Be Divided?," 2.

103. "Our National Crisis," *Evangelical Review* 13, no. 1 (July 1861): 143. For other examples, see C., "State of the Country," *Missionary,* May 9, 1861, 2; and Williams, *Sermon Delivered in the Lutheran Churches of the Blain Charge,* 14–15.

104. Gallagher, *Union War,* 34. For an important counterpoint to Gallagher's argument, see Oakes, *Freedom National.*

105. Anspach, "Past, Present and Future," 2.

106. B. K[urtz], "Politicians and Ministers," *Lutheran Observer,* February 14, 1862, 3.

107. "Lessons of the Twelve-Month," 106. See also "How to Make the Secessionists Laugh," *Lutheran and Missionary,* January 2, 1862, 38.

108. "Debate in General Synod on the Preamble and Resolutions on the State of the Country," *Lutheran Observer,* May 16, 1862, 2.

109. *Proceedings of the Twentieth Convention of the General Synod,* 30.

110. Conservator, "General Synod's Utterance on Slavery," *Lutheran Observer,* June 27, 1862, 2.

111. B. K[urtz], "The Late General Synod at Lancaster, PA.," *Lutheran Observer,* May 23, 1862, 2.

112. "A New Colonization Scheme," *Lutheran Observer,* December 27, 1861, 2.

113. B. K[urtz], "The President, the Constitution, and Slavery," *Lutheran Observer,* July 18, 1862, 2. See also B. K[urtz], "The Union Must Be Preserved at All Hazards, Though Slavery Should Perish," *Lutheran Observer,* September 19, 1862, 2.

114. "Our General Synod on the State of the Country," *Lutheran and Missionary,* May 15, 1862, 114.

115. "The General Synod and the Resolutions on the State of the Country," *Lutheran and Missionary,* July 3, 1862, 142.

116. "The General Synod," *Lutheran Standard,* June 2, 1862, 2.

117. Stange, *Radicalism for Humanity,* 41.

118. Van Alstine, *Thanksgiving Sermon,* 26, 28.

119. Stange, *Radicalism for Humanity,* 41. See also Kuenning, *Rise and Fall,* 214.

120. "Proclamation by the President of the United States," *Lutheran Observer,* September 26, 1862, 3; "The President's Proclamation," *Lutheran Observer,* January 16, 1863, 3.

121. "Emancipation," *Lutheran and Missionary,* September 25, 1862, 191; "Emancipation Proclamation," *Lutheran and Missionary,* January 8, 1863, 43.

122. "The Proclamation," *Lutheran and Missionary,* October 16, 1862, 201.

123. Gallagher, *Union War,* 76.

124. Schmucker authored only one published work during the Civil War, a sermon that made no mention of slavery. Schmucker, *Sermon on the Work of Grace.*

125. This view is found in Wentz, *Pioneer in Christian Unity;* and Kuenning, *Rise and Fall.*

126. Watchman, "The West Pennsylvania Synod," *Lutheran and Missionary,* September 24, 1863, 191.

127. In his only extant letter that discusses the war in detail, Schmucker described the conflict "as a *defensive* one on our land . . . in defence of *Republican* government . . . to perpetuate the principles of human liberty + popular rights." S. S. Schmucker to D. McConaughy, August 14, 1863, series 1, folder 7, Schmucker Family Papers.

128. M. Mielziner, "The Institution of Slavery Among the Ancient Hebrews, According to the Bible and the Talmud," trans. H. I. Schmidt, *Evangelical Review* 13, no. 3 (January 1862): 311–55; "The Universal Fatherhood of God and the Universal Brotherhood of Man, God's Argument Against Oppression," *Evangelical Quarterly Review* 14, no. 4 (July 1863): 578–99.

129. "The General Synod and the Resolutions on the State of the Country," 142.

130. B. K[urtz], "Judgments,—Their Origin, Secondary Cause, Use, and Remedy," *Lutheran Observer,* November 21, 1862, 2.

131. Or, as Mark Noll has memorably written, "It was left to those consummate theologians, the Reverend Doctors Ulysses S. Grant and William Tecumseh Sherman, to decide what in fact the Bible actually meant." Noll, *Civil War as a Theological Crisis,* 66.

132. Ander, "Swedish-American Newspapers," 73.

133. Rasmussen, *Civil War Settlers,* 121.

134. Rohne, *Norwegian American Lutheranism,* 206–7.

135. Clausen, *Gjenmæle mod Kirkeraadet for den Norske Synode,* 18, 20.

136. Rohne, *Norwegian American Lutheranism,* 214–15, 217.

137. On Craemer, see Heintzen, *Prairie School of the Prophets,* 42–110.

138. C[rämer], "Dr. Hengstenberg über die Sclavenfrage," *Lehre und Wehre* 8, no. 4 (April 1862): 106–10. On Hengstenberg, see Conser, *Church and Confession,* 35–36. On the curse of Canaan, see Haynes, *Noah's Curse;* and Whitford, *Curse of Ham.*

139. Knortz, *Gustav Seyffarth,* 11. For other details on his life, see Seyffarth, *Literary Life of Gustavus Seyffarth.*

140. See the letters found in folder 301, Walther Papers; Suelflow, *Correspondence of C. F. W. Walther,* 59; and Knortz, *Gustav Seyffarth,* 16.

141. G. Seyffarth to [Walther], June 11, 1862, folder 301, Walther Papers. In his reply, Walther wrote that he "never even suspected" Seyffarth of holding these views. C. F. W. W[alther] to Gustavus Seyffarth, June 17, 1862, in Suelflow, *Correspondence of C. F. W. Walther,* 60.

142. G. Seyffarth, "Ist die gegenwärtige Negersklaverei in Uebereinstimmung mit der Schrift oder nicht?," *Lutherische Herold,* October 15, 1862, 89–90. Seyffarth's appeal to the biblical prohibition against man-stealing was uncommon but not unique. See Noll, *Civil War as a Theological Crisis,* 44; and Oshatz, *Slavery and Sin,* 65–66.

143. G. Seyffarth, "Ist die gegenwärtige Negersklaverei in Uebereinstimmung mit der Schrift oder nicht?," *Lutherische Herold,* November 1, 1863, 97–98.

144. G. Seyffarth, "African Slavery; Is it Consistent or Inconsistent with the Scripture of the Old and New Testament?," *Lutheran and Missionary,* October 15, 1863, 1, October 22, 1863, 1–2; G. Seyffarth, "Ist die Erhaltung und Verbeitung der gegenwärtige Negersklaverei eine Sünde oder nicht?," *Lutherische Herold,* November 15, 1863, 105–6, December 1, 1863, 113–14.

145. "Vorwort," *Lehre und Wehre* 9, no. 2 (February 1863): 34, 43. For Walther's earlier comments on slavery, see W[alther], "Predigt, am allgemeinen Bußtag," 33; "Vorwort der Redaction zum neunzehnenten Jahrgang des 'Lutheraner,'" *Lutheraner,* September 3, 1862, 2; and "Abolitionismus," *Lutheraner,* November 26, 1862, 54. For the fullest treatment of Walther and slavery, see Manteufel, "Walther's View on Slavery."

146. "Die Sclaverei, im Lichte der heiligen Schrift betrachtet," *Lutheraner,* February 1, 1863, 90. The tract was published later that year as a book, under same title. For a summary of Sihler's argument, see Spitz, *Life in Two Worlds,* 111–15.

147. "Die Sclaverei, im Lichte der heiligen Schrift betrachtet," *Lutheraner,* February 15, 1863, 100.

148. "Die Sclaverei, im Lichte der heiligen Schrift betrachtet," *Lutheraner,* March 15, 1863, 115.

149. For an example of the similarities between the views of Missouri Synod theologians and other conservative American Protestants, see the positive review of *A Scriptural, Ecclesiastical, and Historical View of Slavery* by the Episcopalian bishop John Henry Hopkins, in *Lehre und Wehre* 11, no. 4 (April 1865): 102–13.

150. "Vorwort," *Lehre und Wehre* 9, no. 2 (February 1863): 43–44.

151. See Noll, *America's God;* and Noll, *Civil War as a Theological Crisis.* It should be noted that Old Lutherans did not use the term "common sense" or directly engage with the philosophical movement of the same name. Nevertheless, their frequent appeals to the "clear" and "plain" meaning of Scripture demonstrate the pervasiveness of this approach.

152. For an important exception, see McArver, "Better a 'Live Dog Than a Dead Lion.'"

153. See, for example, "A Precious Abolition Morsel," *Southern Lutheran,* December 21, 1861, 2; "Letters to Dr. Schmucker," *Southern Lutheran,* October 4, 1863, 2; and "Liberty," *Southern Lutheran,* February 7, 1863, 1.

154. *An Address to Christians Throughout the World,* 7, 9, 14. The address appeared on the first page of the *Southern Lutheran* in the May 23, May 30, and June 6, 1863, issues.

155. *Minutes of the First Convention of the General Synod of the Confederate States of America,* 3.

156. William Passavant praised "our foreign (German) brethren in Texas" for "remain[ing] true to their faith and to their adopted country." "The Lutheran Synod of Virginia," *Lutheran and Missionary,* May 1, 1862, 105. On the Union sentiment among Texas Germans, see Kamphoefner, "New Perspectives on Texas Germans and the Confederacy."

157. *Minutes of the First Convention of the General Synod of the Confederate States of America,* 4–5, 12.

158. *Lutheran Almanac for 1864,* 30.

159. "The Lutheran Church and Secession," *Lutheran and Missionary,* September 4, 1862, 178.

160. L. L. H., "The Great Battle at Gettysburg, July 1–3, 1863," *Lutheran and Missionary,* July 16, 1863, 150.

161. "Gettysburg," *Lutheran Observer,* July 31, 1863, 2; "God Giving Victory at Gettysburg," *Lutheran Observer,* August 14, 1863, 2.

162. *Address of the Hon. Edward Everett at the Consecration of the National Cemetery at Gettysburg,* 88. On Baugher, see Jensson, *American Lutheran Biographies,* 63–65.

1. "The Aimless Battle," *Lutheran and Missionary,* July 13, 1865, 150.

2. "Where Do We Stand?," *Lutheran and Missionary,* October 31, 1861, 2.

3. "The Lutheran and Missionary," *Lutheran and Missionary,* October 31, 1861, 2.

4. "The Two Foundations," *Lutheran and Missionary,* July 13, 1865, 150.

5. The two largest Civil War–era denominational schisms were the sectional splits among the Methodists in 1844 and the Baptists in 1845. The split between Old School and New School Presbyterians in 1837 involved roughly the same number of people as the General Synod schism. See Gaustad and Barlow, *New Historical Atlas,* 136–37; and *Lutheran Almanac for 1867,* 30. The only other American church division to occur during the first ten years after the Civil War was the breakoff of the tiny Reformed Episcopal Church from the Protestant Episcopal Church in 1873. See Guelzo, *For the Union of Evangelical Christendom.*

6. Virtually every Lutheran denominational history ignores or downplays the Civil War context of the General Synod schism. See, for example, Ferm, *Crisis in American Lutheran Theology;* Mauelshagen, *American Lutheranism Surrenders;* Wentz, *Basic History;* Nelson, *Lutherans in North America;* Gustafson, *Lutherans in Crisis;* Lagerquist, *Lutherans;* and Granquist, *Lutherans in America.* An exception to this trend is Kuenning, *Rise and Fall.*

7. "Aimless Battle," 150.

8. Impartiality, "Remarks on the Secession of the Synod of Pennsylvania from the General Synod," *Lutheran Observer,* September 28, 1866, 1.

9. See "Synod of Pennsylvania," *Lutheran and Home Journal,* July 6, 1860, 1; and "'Born Again of Baptism and the Holy Spirit,'" *Lutheran and Home Journal,* July 5, 1861, 100.

10. "The New Paper," *Lutheran Observer,* November 15, 1861, 2.

11. "Recommendation of 'The Lutheran and Missionary' by the Synod of Pennsylvania," *Lutheran and Missionary,* September 18, 1862, 185.

12. See, for example, "'American Lutheranism,'" *Lutheran and Missionary,* April 10, 1862, 94; and "Our General Synod: Theological Characteristics of the Era of Formation," *Lutheran and Missionary,* April 17, 1862, 98.

13. See, for example, "Where Do We Stand?," *Lutheran and Missionary,* October 31, 1861, 2; and B. K[urtz], "Where Do We Stand?," *Lutheran Observer,* January 17, 1862, 2.

14. See, for example, "Symbolic Analogy Between the Presbyterian and Lutheran Churches in the United States," *Lutheran Observer,* December 4, 1863, 2.

15. Samuel Schmucker had already used the terms in his 1856 book *American Lutheranism Vindicated.* For the use of these terms by the *Lutheran Observer,* see "The New Paper," 2; and An American Lutheran, "The General Synod: Her Present Basis the True One, and the Only One that Under Existing Circumstances Can Be Adopted," *Lutheran Observer,* May 2, 1862, 2. Krauth and others associated with the *Lutheran and Missionary* originally rejected the label. See "Old School and High Church," *Lutheran and Missionary,* October 31, 1861, 2. However, throughout his biography of Krauth, his son-in-law Adolph Spaeth used this terminology. See, for example, Spaeth, *Charles Porterfield Krauth,* 1:11, 316.

16. Spener, "The Peculiar and Distinctive Characteristics of the Lutheran Church," *Lutheran Observer,* March 21, 1862, 1–2.

17. K[urtz], "Where Do We Stand?," 2; Anti-Popery, "New Theology," *Lutheran Observer,* April 11, 1862, 1.

18. "A United Church," *Lutheran Observer*, March 1, 1861, 2–3.

19. K[urtz], "Where Do We Stand?," 2.

20. "Ignorance and Revivals," *Lutheran and Missionary*, August 7, 1862, 162. See also "Measures: New and Old," *Lutheran and Missionary*, June 26, 1862, 138.

21. "Revivals and Reports of Revivals," *Lutheran and Missionary*, December 18, 1862, 30. See also "Liturgies: A Little Common Sense About Them," *Lutheran and Missionary*, June 26, 1862, 138.

22. These include Tappert, *Lutheran Confessional Theology*; Conser, *Church and Confession*, 257–309; and Noll, *America's God*, 409–12. On the rare occasions when Krauth and other Old School Lutherans did refer to traditionalist movements like the Mercersburg Theology or the Oxford Movement, they expressed a mixture of appreciation and criticism. See, for example, "Dr. Nevin and the Lutheran Church," *Lutheran and Missionary*, April 16, 1863, 98; and "Puseyites in the Lutheran Church," *Lutheran and Missionary*, March 30, 1865, 90.

23. "The Doctrines of the Evangelical Lutheran Church," *Lutheran and Missionary*, February 13, 1862, 62.

24. For a lengthy expression of Krauth's biblicism, see his tract *The Bible a Perfect Book*, which went through two editions.

25. "A Sudden Conversion," *Missionary*, June 13, 1861, 82.

26. "'Born Again of Baptism and the Holy Spirit,'" 100.

27. "The Folly and Guilt of Intolerance," *Lutheran Observer*, March 8, 1861, 2.

28. B. K[urtz], "The General Synod and Other Cognate Subjects," *Lutheran Observer*, August 2, 1861, 2–3.

29. "Intolerance," *Lutheran Observer*, July 5, 1861, 2.

30. Cyril, "Revolutions and Secession in Church and State," *Lutheran Observer*, March 14, 1862, 1.

31. "Bud and Fruit: or Secessionism Before Secession," *Lutheran and Missionary*, May 1, 1862, 106.

32. "What Is Your Name?," *Lutheran and Missionary*, March 27, 1862, 86; "Something Greatly Needed," *Lutheran and Missionary*, May 1, 1862, 106. The editors of the *Lutheran Observer* also believed that the confessions' plain meaning could be apprehended by common sense; they simply disagreed with its teachings on the sacraments. See "The Interpretation of Confessions of Faith," *Lutheran Observer*, September 11, 1863, 3.

33. On Schaeffer, see Jensson, *American Lutheran Biographies*, 655–56.

34. B. K[urtz], "The Late General Synod at Lancaster, Pa.," *Lutheran Observer*, May 23, 1862, 2.

35. "The General Synod and the Resolutions on the State of the Country," *Lutheran and Missionary*, July 3, 1862, 142.

36. "The Late General Synod," *Lutheran and Missionary*, May 22, 1862, 118.

37. "Tendencies: Our Future," *Lutheran and Missionary*, May 22, 1862, 118.

38. "How Old Art Thou, and Is It Well with Thee?," *Lutheran Observer*, May 2, 1862, 2.

39. "'Born Again of Baptism and the Holy Spirit,'" 100.

40. "Sectarianism and Secessionism," *Lutheran and Missionary*, June 12, 1862, 130.

41. "Our Policy," *Lutheran Observer*, February 28, 1862, 2; "Sectarianism and Its Cure," *Lutheran and Missionary*, June 5, 1862, 126. These mottoes were repeated frequently by the papers' editors throughout the Civil War, and in the case of the *Lutheran and Missionary*, were printed on the paper's masthead.

42. T. Newton Kurtz, "Sale of the Lutheran Observer: A Few Parting Words by the Late Propri-

etor," *Lutheran Observer,* October 31, 1862, 2. On Conrad, see Jensson, *American Lutheran Biographies,* 144–46; and Wentz, *History of the Gettysburg Theological Seminary,* 378.

43. "Recommendation of 'The Lutheran and Missionary,'" 185.

44. See Conrad, *America's Blessings and Obligations* and *War for the Unity and Life of the American Union.*

45. "Another Spirit," *Lutheran and Missionary,* November 13, 1862, 10.

46. "Rev. Dr. Kurtz," *Lutheran and Missionary,* November 13, 1862, 10; "The New Staff," *Lutheran and Missionary,* November 13, 1862, 10.

47. "Our Neighbor: What the 'Lutheran' Says of Us and What We Say to the 'Lutheran,'" *Lutheran Observer,* November 21, 1862, 2.

48. "Some Friendly Words," *Lutheran and Missionary,* November 27, 1862, 18.

49. "Controversies of the Lutheran Church," *Lutheran and Missionary,* December 25, 1862, 34.

50. B., "Letter from Washington," *Lutheran Observer,* March 4, 1864, 2. For similar sentiments, see "Peace Versus War," *Lutheran Observer,* March 18, 1864, 2.

51. Kurtz, *Experimental (Not Ritual) Religion,* 8. Kurtz's sermon was never intended for publication, but due to the subsequent controversy surrounding its reception, it was published first in the *Lutheran Observer* in the October 23 and 30, 1863, issues, and shortly thereafter as a stand-alone publication. See "The Condemned Sermon," *Lutheran Observer,* November 13, 1863, 2.

52. Conservative, "The Spirit of the West Pennsylvania Synod," *Lutheran and Missionary,* October 1, 1863, 195.

53. B. K[urtz], "A Sermon, Privately and Publicly Condemned, and its Author Defamed in Public Print," *Lutheran Observer,* October 16, 1863, 2.

54. L. Sternberg, "The Lord's Supper," *Lutheran Observer,* October 9, 1863, 1. The first three installments of the essay appeared in the September 18, September 25, and October 2, 1863, issues. The article was originally published as L. Sternberg, "The Lord's Supper," *Evangelical Quarterly Review* 14, no. 4 (July 1863): 558–78. Later, it was printed as a tract with an introduction by Kurtz.

55. "The Lord's Supper," *Lutheran and Missionary,* October 15, 1863, 202; "Prof. Sternberg's Article," *Lutheran Observer,* September 18, 1863, 2.

56. "The Lutheran Unveiled," *Lutheran Observer,* October 23, 1863, 2. See also "The 'Lutheran and Missionary' Shows Its True Colors," *Lutheran Observer,* November 20, 1863, 2.

57. "Lutheran Unveiled," 2.

58. Kurtz, *Experimental (Not Ritual) Religion,* 7.

59. "Testing the Confessions by Scripture," *Lutheran and Missionary,* October 29, 1863, 2.

60. "Of Wit and Its Classification with a Digression of Logic," *Lutheran and Missionary,* October 29, 1863, 2.

61. "Lutheranism and Hyper-Lutheranism," *Lutheran Observer,* November 13, 1863, 2.

62. "What Has American Lutheranism Done?," *Lutheran Observer,* January 15, 1864, 2.

63. "The American Lutheran Church," *Lutheran and Missionary,* December 24, 1863, 34.

64. "The General Synod," *Lutheran Observer,* April 29, 1864, 2.

65. "The General Synod—Pia Desideria," *Lutheran and Missionary,* May 5, 1864, 110.

66. On the acceptance of the changes to the Augsburg Confession by Sprecher's church body, the English Ohio Synod, see Ferm, *Crisis in American Lutheran Theology,* 264.

67. Paul Kuenning, however, views slavery as key (*Rise and Fall,* 218–19).

68. Sprecher, *Providential Position of the Evangelical Church of This Country,* 11.

69. *Proceedings of the Twenty-First Convention of the General Synod,* 35–36.

70. *Proceedings of the Twenty-First Convention of the General Synod,* 17–19, 23–26.

71. *Proceedings of the Twenty-First Convention of the General Synod,* 39–40.

72. Jacobs, *History of the Evangelical Lutheran Church,* 459–61; Wentz, *Basic History,* 144.

73. *Proceedings of the Twenty-First Convention of the General Synod,* 41.

74. "Hopeful," *Lutheran Observer,* May 20, 1864, 2.

75. "The General Synod," *Lutheran and Missionary,* May 12, 1864, 114; "The Late General Synod," *Lutheran and Missionary,* May 19, 1864, 118; "The General Synod," *Lutheran and Missionary,* May 26, 1864, 123.

76. "The Synod of Pennsylvania," *Lutheran and Missionary,* June 2, 1864, 126; "The New Theological Seminary of the Ministerium of Pennsylvania and Adjacent States," *Lutheran and Missionary,* June 16, 1864, 134.

77. "The New Theolog'l Seminary," *Lutheran Observer,* June 10, 1864, 2.

78. "Why the Synod of Pennsylvania Wants to Establish a New Theological Seminary," *Lutheran and Missionary,* June 30, 1864, 142.

79. "The Theological Seminary of the Pennsylvania Synod," *Lutheran and Missionary,* July 21, 1864, 154.

80. Tappert, *History of the Lutheran Theological Seminary at Philadelphia,* 30–31.

81. "Is the New Theological Seminary Needed?," *Lutheran and Missionary,* August 11, 1864, 166.

82. "The Theological Seminary in Philadelphia: Is it on the Right Basis?," *Lutheran and Missionary,* September 1, 1864, 176.

83. "Is the New Theological Seminary Needed?," 166.

84. "Pure Doctrine in Our English Seminaries," *Lutheran Observer,* August 26, 1864, 2; "Keep it Before the Church," *Lutheran Observer,* September 16, 1864, 2.

85. "'Conservative and Liberal,'" *Lutheran Observer,* June 17, 1864, 2. See also "Who Are the Radicals?," *Lutheran Observer,* December 2, 1864, 2.

86. "New Theological Seminary," *Lutheran Observer,* September 2, 1864, 2.

87. "Secession—The New Seminary and the Cause," *Lutheran Observer,* January 20, 1865, 2.

88. Tappert, *History of the Lutheran Theological Seminary at Philadelphia,* 29.

89. For biographical information on Brown, see Jensson, *American Lutheran Biographies,* 115–19.

90. Brown's first article appeared as J. A. Brown, "The New Theology," *Evangelical Review* 9, no. 1 (July 1857): 91–109. Schmucker's reply appeared first as an article, S. S. Schmucker, "'The New Theology. By J. A. Brown' Again," *Evangelical Review* 9, no. 2 (October 1857): 256–67; and then again as a tract, Schmucker, *Rev. J. A. Brown's New Theology: Examined.* Brown then published his original article with a rejoinder to Schmucker's reply and other criticisms as Brown, *New Theology: Its Abettors and Defenders.*

91. Spaeth, *Charles Porterfield Krauth,* 1:410–11.

92. Wentz, *History of the Gettysburg Theological Seminary,* 169; Kuenning, *Rise and Fall,* 173. A more thorough treatment of the controversy is found in Gustafson, *Lutherans in Crisis,* 138–43.

93. Brown, *New Theology: Its Abettors and Defenders,* 38.

94. J. A. Brown to A. G. Medekind, August 19, 1864, James Allen Brown Papers, A. R. Wentz Library, United Lutheran Seminary, Gettysburg, Pennsylvania.

95. [Samuel Schmucker] to Beale [Schmucker], October 17, 1864, series 1, folder 5, Schmucker Family Papers.

96. "Our New Professor," *Lutheran Observer,* August 19, 1864, 2.

97. "The Theological Seminary of the General Synod: A History and Vindication," *Lutheran and Missionary,* December 1, 1864, 22.

98. "The Theological Seminaries at Gettysburg and Philadelphia: A Letter from Professor Brown and our Fraternal Reply to It," *Lutheran and Missionary,* December 22, 1864, 34. The two professors would continue a war of letters and articles over the next few months.

99. For examples of historians asserting that Brown's arrival at Gettysburg seminary signaled a move away from New School Lutheranism, see Wentz, *Basic History,* 145; and Kuenning, *Rise and Fall,* 173.

100. "The Coming Theological Conflict," *Lutheran Observer,* October 21, 1864, 2.

101. See Chesebrough, *No Sorrow Like Our Sorrow;* and Hodes, *Mourning Lincoln,* esp. 97–112.

102. "The Lesson of the Great Calamity," *Lutheran Observer,* May 5, 1865, 2; "Murder of the President," *Lutheran and Missionary,* April 20, 1865, 102.

103. Butler, *Martyr President;* Rhodes, *Sermon on the Occasion of the Assassination of Abraham Lincoln;* Krauth, *The Two Pageants;* Seiss, *Assassinated President;* Johnston, *Sermon Delivered on Thursday, June 1st, 1865.*

104. "Our Country: Peace," *Lutheran and Missionary,* February 9, 1865, 63; "Constitutional Amendment," *Lutheran Observer,* February 17, 1865, 2.

105. "The Lesson of the Great Calamity," 2.

106. "Duties of the Hour," *Lutheran and Missionary,* April 20, 1865, 102.

107. "Another Victory to Be Won," *Lutheran and Missionary,* May 11, 1865, 114.

108. "The Close of the War," *Lutheran Observer,* April 21, 1865, 2.

109. "Gettysburg and Philadelphia," *Lutheran and Missionary,* May 18, 1865, 118.

110. C[onrad], "Gettysburg and Philadelphia Contrasted," *Lutheran Observer,* June 16, 1865, 2. Conrad's articles appeared in every issue of the *Lutheran Observer* from June 9 to July 14, 1865.

111. "Aimless Battle," 150.

112. C[onrad], "The Unity of the Lutheran Church," *Lutheran Observer,* August 4, 1865, 2.

113. "Another Victory to Be Won," 114; "Duties of the Hour," 102.

114. "Reunion of the Church North and South," *Lutheran Observer,* June 30, 1865, 2.

115. "The Southern Lutheran Churches: What Shall Be Done with Them?," *Lutheran and Missionary,* July 27, 1865, 158. See also "What Shall We Do with Them?," *Lutheran and Missionary,* July 6, 1865, 146.

116. "Dissenting from Our Views," *Lutheran Observer,* July 21, 1865, 2; E. W. H., "The Southern Lutheran Churches: 'What Shall Be Done with Them?'," *Lutheran and Missionary,* July 27, 1865, 159.

117. "Southern Lutheran Churches—The Other Side of the Question," *Lutheran Observer,* August 4, 1865, 2; "The Southern Synods—A Reply to a Few Last Words," *Lutheran and Missionary,* August 10, 1865, 166.

118. "Dr. Bachman's Vindication," *Lutheran and Missionary,* October 26, 1865, 2.

119. "One Hundred and Eighteenth Convention of the Synod of Pennsylvania," *Lutheran and Missionary,* June 22, 1865, 138.

120. "The Lutheran and Missionary: Its Claims and Aims," *Lutheran and Missionary,* August 31, 1865, 170.

121. "Responses," *Lutheran Observer,* September 23, 1864, 2; "Ohio Letter," *Lutheran Observer,* October 21, 1864, 3.

122. Lutheranus, "Is the Lutheran Church Divided?," *Lutheran Observer,* January 27, 1865, 1.

123. Sprecher, *Apostolic Method of Realizing the True Ideal of the Church*, 12.

124. *Proceedings of the Twenty-Second Convention of the General Synod*, 3–5, 8–17, 25–28, 38–40.

125. "Proceedings of the 119th Annual Session of 'The Ministerium' of Pennsylvania and Adjacent States," *Lutheran and Missionary*, June 21, 1866, 133.

126. Anon, "Our Old Arm Chair," *Lutheran and Missionary*, August 16, 1866, 165. See also "What Shall They Do?," *Lutheran and Missionary*, August 30, 1866, 172; and "'What Shall They Do?' and the Lutheran Observer," *Lutheran and Missionary*, September 13, 1866, 180.

127. "Proceedings of the 119th Annual Session of 'The Ministerium' of Pennsylvania," 133. See also "Did the General Synod Violate Its Constitution by the Admission of the Franckean Synod at York," *Lutheran and Missionary*, August 16, 1866, 165.

128. Loyalty, "A Review of 'The Response of the Pennsylvania Delegation,'" *Lutheran Observer*, June 22, 1866, 1.

129. Loyalty, "Conspiracy to Destroy the General Synod," *Lutheran Observer*, July 6, 1866, 2.

130. F. W. C[onrad], "The Question at Issue between the Synod of Pennsylvania and the General Synod," *Lutheran Observer*, July 6, 1866, 1.

131. M., "The General Synod and the Synod of Pennsylvania," *Lutheran Observer*, July 13, 1866, 1.

132. "The Augustana (Scandinavian) Synod," *Lutheran and Missionary*, September 8, 1864, 181.

133. "Editorial Correspondence," *Lutheran and Missionary*, September 20, 1866, 184.

134. For background, see Braun, "Wisconsin's 'Turn to the Right'"; Grundmeier, "Pennsylvania's 'Youthful Daughter'"; and Koehler, *History of the Wisconsin Synod*, 37–133.

135. Koehler, *History of the Wisconsin Synod*, 98.

136. "Die lutherische Generalsynode, ihre Aufgabe und wir," *Evangelisch-Lutherisches Gemeinde-Blatt*, April 1, 1866, 2.

137. "Reise-Erinnerungen," *Evangelisch-Lutherisches Gemeinde-Blatt*, July 1, 1866, 4.

138. Fry, "Matthias Loy," 219.

139. See, for example, "The Missouri Synod," *Lutheran Standard*, May 15, 1864, 5; "Our Brethren in Missouri," *Lutheran Standard*, December 1, 1864, 5; "The Tendency of Unionism," *Lutheran Standard*, June 1, 1864, 5; and "Promiscuous Communion," *Lutheran Standard*, August 15, 1864, 2. See also his later testimony in Loy, *Story of My Life*, 193–99.

140. E. A. Brauer, "Vorwort," *Lehre und Wehre* 11, no. 1 (January 1865): 3. See also "Unfriendly Notices of the Ohio Synod," *Lutheran Standard*, February 15, 1865, 29.

141. "A While Away," *Lutheran Standard*, September 1, 1864, 4.

142. "The Proposed New General Synod," *Lutheran Standard*, July 1, 1866, 100.

143. Crämer, "Ueber das generalsynodistische Bekenntniß zur Augsb. Conf., 'insofern sie die Fundamentalallehren richtig darlegt,'" *Lehre und Wehre* 10, no. 11 (November 1864): 345.

144. "Synode von Pennsylvanien," *Lehre und Wehre* 10, no. 5 (May 1864): 152. A portion of this article was translated in the May 26, 1864, issue of the *Lutheran and Missionary*.

145. W[alther], "Die Synode von Pennsylvanien," *Lutheraner*, August 1, 1866, 183. A translation of Walther's article appeared in the August 16, 1866, issue of the *Lutheran and Missionary*.

146. "The Augustana Scandinavian Synod," *Lutheran and Missionary*, October 30, 1862, 1; "The Augustana Synod," *Lutheran and Missionary*, January 28, 1864, 53.

147. "Things in the Northwest," *Lutheran and Missionary*, December 8, 1864, 26; "Watertown, Wisconsin," *Lutheran and Missionary*, September 28, 1865; "Church Progress in Wisconsin," *Lutheran and Missionary*, January 11, 1866.

148. "The Lutheran Standard," *Lutheran and Missionary,* March 31, 1864; "Festival of the Reformation," *Lutheran and Missionary,* November 9, 1865, 186; "'The Proposed New General Synod,'" *Lutheran and Missionary,* July 12, 1866, 144.

149. "Our German Exchanges," *Lutheran and Missionary,* August 2, 1866, 156; "Our Church Intelligence," *Lutheran and Missionary,* August 16, 1866, 164.

150. "Where Do We Stand?," 2.

151. "The Symbolical Books and the Missouri Synod," *Lutheran and Missionary,* May 5, 1864, 111.

152. "'Old Lutherans,'" *Lutheran and Missionary,* October 5, 1865, 190.

153. "The Missouri Lutherans at Fort Wayne," *Lutheran and Missionary,* August 2, 1866, 156. See also Tappert, "Intercommunion in 1866."

154. "Politico-Radical Work," *Lutheran Standard,* December 1, 1864, 5; "Politics in the Pulpit," *Lutheran Standard,* May 15, 1865, 76.

155. Lehmann, "Proceedings of the 14th Convention of the German Evangelical Lutheran Synod of Wisconsin," 6. See also Lehmann, "Proceedings of the 15th Convention of the German Evangelical Lutheran Synod of Wisconsin," 9; and "Memorial Sermon Delivered April 19, 1865," John Bading Biographical File, Wisconsin Evangelical Lutheran Synod Archives, Waukesha.

156. Walther, "Am Nationalbußtage," in *Amerikanisch-Lutherische Epistel Postille,* 494, 496. For a translation, see Walther, *Standard Epistles,* 510–16.

157. See "Sclavenemancipation durch unsere Abolitionisten," *Lutheraner,* August 15, 1864, 189; and the book review by "W. St." in *Lehre und Wehre* 11, no. 4 (April 1865): 102–13.

158. *Proceedings of the Convention Held at Reading, 1866,* 3–5.

159. "What Shall They Do?," *Lutheran Observer,* September 14, 1866, 2. See also "Our Church Difficulties," *Lutheran Observer,* August 24, 1866, 2; and Impartiality, "Remarks on the Secession of the Synod of Pennsylvania," 1.

160. "'What Shall They Do?'" *Lutheran Observer,* September 7, 1866, 2.

161. "Our Ecclesiastical Situation," *Lutheran Observer,* August 3, 1866, 2.

5. CONSERVATIVE RECONSTRUCTION, 1866–1872

1. "Reconstruction," *Lutheran Observer,* May 7, 1869, 2.

2. "The New Era of the General Synod," *Lutheran Observer,* May 14, 1869, 2.

3. On the prioritization of reunion and reconciliation over racial equality among northern Christians, see Blum, *Reforging the White Republic;* and Brodrecht, *Our Country.* For other standard studies on reunion and reconciliation, see Silber, *Romance of Reunion;* Blight, *Race and Reunion;* and Janney, *Remembering the Civil War.*

4. "Lutheran Synods," *Lutheran and Missionary,* February 28, 1867, 74.

5. W[alther], "Vorwort zum neunundzwanzigsten Jahrgang des 'Lutheraner,'" *Lutheraner,* October 15, 1872, 10.

6. Summers, *Ordeal of Reunion,* 3. For other standard accounts of this period, see Foner, *Reconstruction;* and White, "Reconstructing the Nation," part 1 in *Republic for Which It Stands.*

7. "A Voice from the South," *Lutheran and Missionary,* January 4, 1866, 42–43; "Destitution at the South," *Lutheran and Missionary,* February 7, 1867, 62; "Letter from Virginia," *Lutheran and Missionary,* June 18, 1868, 139.

8. "The Late Convention of the Pittsburg Synod," *Lutheran and Missionary*, November 21, 1867, 18.

9. "Southern Sympathy," *Lutheran and Missionary*, March 15, 1866, 83.

10. The few articles in the paper that did mention the freedpeople simply reprinted the words of other Lutherans, with no editorial commentary. See "The Brooklyn Lectures: Pohlman, Stork and Conrad," *Lutheran and Missionary*, March 15, 1866, 83; and "The Freedmen," *Lutheran and Missionary*, October 25, 1866, 2.

11. When the "Our Country" section did appear, it usually dealt with cultural rather than political matters. See, for example, "Our Country: Dr. McCosh on the United States," *Lutheran and Missionary*, March 21, 1867, 87; and "Our Country: Americans Everywhere," *Lutheran and Missionary*, October 10, 1867, 204. On the few occasions when elections were mentioned, the articles scrupulously avoided taking sides. See, for example, Watchman, "The Election," *Lutheran and Missionary*, October 18, 1866, 200.

12. "Political Preaching," *Lutheran and Missionary*, December 14, 1865, 30.

13. On Seiss's leading role at the *Lutheran and Missionary*, see Rast, "Joseph A. Seiss," 59–60.

14. "Tidings," *Lutheran and Missionary*, May 4, 1871, 114.

15. John, "How Some Things Are to Be Done," *Lutheran and Missionary*, April 25, 1867, 106; Insulanus, "Letter from New York," *Lutheran and Missionary*, May 16, 1872, 122.

16. On Butler, see Ramshaw, "Rev. John G. Butler."

17. "The Church South, and Our Duty," *Lutheran and Missionary*, November 2, 1865, 6.

18. Butler, *God's Work—Our Ebenezer*, 13; Butler, *Courageous Thankfulness*, 9.

19. "The Healing of the Nation," *Lutheran and Missionary*, March 28, 1867, 91.

20. "Washington, D.C.," *Lutheran and Missionary*, August 5, 1869, 166.

21. "Living Issues," *Lutheran Observer*, November 17, 1865, 2.

22. "From the South," *Lutheran Observer*, January 5, 1866, 2; "The Relief of the South," *Lutheran Observer*, March 29, 1867, 2; "Appeal for and by the Lutherans of Wilmington, N.C.," *Lutheran Observer*, March 27, 1868, 2.

23. "The Presidential Election," *Lutheran Observer*, November 13, 1868, 2. On Conrad's role as the paper's principal editor, see F. W. C[onrad], "Our Editorial Work," *Lutheran Observer*, May 3, 1867, 2.

24. "Thanksgiving Day at Washington," *Lutheran Observer*, December 22, 1865, 3; Watchman, "The Duty of the Church Toward the Freedmen of the South," *Lutheran Observer*, January 19, 1866, 1; "The Freedmen," *Lutheran Observer*, January 18, 1867, 2.

25. Watchman, "Duty of the Church Toward the Freedmen of the South," 1.

26. Apart from the writings of Butler, the only endorsement of racial equality in the paper was Conrad's praise of the ratification of the Fifteenth Amendment. See "Universal Freedom," *Lutheran Observer*, April 8, 1870, 4. The paper, however, did continue to advocate for the freedpeople's education. See "A Plea for the Freedmen," *Lutheran Observer*, March 31, 1871, 5; and "Can the Negro Be Educated?," *Lutheran Observer*, October 6, 1871, 4.

27. "The Negroes of the South," *Lutheran Observer*, May 5, 1871, 2. For endorsements of colonization, see "Pennsylvania Colonization Society," *Lutheran Observer*, February 17, 1871, 3; "First Sunday in July," *Lutheran Observer*, June 23, 1871, 5; and "Notes and Comments," *Lutheran Observer*, March 8, 1872, 4. As late as 1867, Conrad had called colonization "uneconomical" and "not congenial to our free institutions." "The Freedmen," *Lutheran Observer*, January 18, 1867, 2.

28. See, for example, B[utler], "Letter from Washington," *Lutheran Observer*, October 25, 1872, 6.

29. The phrase comes from Gillette, *Retreat from Reconstruction*. For other studies on how northern conservatism led to the failures of Reconstruction, see Schwalm, *Emancipation's Diaspora;* Efford, *German Immigrants, Race, and Citizenship,* 199–216; Stanley, *Loyal West,* 98–174; and Lang, *Contest of Civilizations,* 359–98.

30. "Heavenly Citizenship," *Lutheran Observer,* May 19, 1871, 4. See also Conrad, *Ministers of the Gospel.*

31. For background, see Moore, *Founding Sins,* 120–35. On the paper's support for this amendment during the war, see B. K[urtz], "National Association for the Amendment of the Constitution of the United States," *Lutheran Observer,* December 9, 1864, 1; and "Rev. J. Swartz's Sermon on 'God and the Constitution,'" *Lutheran Observer,* March 17, 1865, 2.

32. "God and the Constitution," *Lutheran Observer,* March 1, 1867, 2. On the paper's continued support for this amendment, see "The Creed of the Nation," *Lutheran Observer,* December 10, 1869, 2; "God in the Constitution," *Lutheran Observer,* January 27, 1871, 4; and "The Religious Amendment," *Lutheran Observer,* February 16, 1872, 5.

33. "The Political Duties of Christians," *Lutheran Observer,* November 10, 1871, 4; "Notes and Comments," *Lutheran Observer,* November 8, 1872, 2. For similar remarks, see "Political Corruption," *Lutheran Observer,* January 19, 1872, 2; and "Notes and Comments," *Lutheran Observer,* October 25, 1872, 2.

34. Rasmussen, "'The States' Readmission Puts an End to All Civil and Political Questions,'" 204, 213. See also Andersen, *Immigrant Takes His Stand,* 136–52.

35. *Journal of the Twenty-Ninth Annual Session of the Franckean Evangelic Lutheran Synod,* 24–25.

36. In the proceedings of the Franckean Synod from 1866 to 1877, no mention is made of the subject of freedpeople's rights, but much space is devoted to the other three topics. For further background, see Scholz, *Press Toward the Mark,* 247–61.

37. "Our Wants," *Lutheran Visitor,* June 1866, 135. See also "Editorial," *Lutheran Visitor,* April 1866, 70–72.

38. Lutheranus, "A Lutheran Church in Washington City," *Lutheran Visitor,* October 6, 1869, 2–3. For other examples, see "Literary and Miscellaneous," *Lutheran Visitor,* May 1866, 152–54; and "Answer to the Observer," *Lutheran Visitor,* June 30, 1871, 2.

39. "G. or G.," *Lutheran Visitor,* July 26, 1872, 2. On the paper's (supposed) refusal to discuss politics, see "Political Meetings," *Lutheran Visitor,* June 9, 1870, 2.

40. See Johnson, *Black Christians,* 126–29, 138–48.

41. See Stowell, *Rebuilding Zion,* 130–45; Blum, *Reforging the White Republic,* 51–86; and Richardson, *Christian Reconstruction.*

42. W[alther], "Religiöse Politik," *Lutheraner,* April 15, 1867, 126. For other examples, see "Prediger und Politik," *Lehre und Wehre* 12, no. 11/12 (November/December 1866): 380; and W[alther], "Politik auf der Canzel," *Lutheraner,* November 15, 1872, 28–29.

43. C[rämer], "Warnung an alle Christen vor dem politischen Zeitblatt eines gewissen Marcus Thrane, betitelt 'Norske (Der norwegische) Amerikaner,'" *Lutheraner,* September 15, 1866, 114; W[alther], "Politische Blätter," *Lutheraner,* January 15, 1869, 77; C[rämer], "Selbst der in der Politik sonst ziemlich geschmeidige 'Observer,'" *Lehre und Wehre* 13, no. 11 (November 1871): 343.

44. "Editorial Notes," *Lutheran Standard,* September 15, 1872, 141; "Thanksgiving Day," *Lutheran Standard,* December 1, 1870, 180. For similar sentiments, see "Politics in the Pulpit," *Lutheran Standard,* May 15, 1865, 76; and "Editorial Notes," *Lutheran Standard,* January 1, 1872, 5.

45. W[alther], "Religiöse Politik," 126.

46. W[alther], "Politik in der Kirche," *Lutheraner,* November 1, 1865, 36; W[alther], "Negerstimmrecht und die Kirche," *Lehre und Wehre* 11, no. 12 (December 1865): 375–76.

47. Clausen, *Gjenmæle mod Kirkeraadet for den Norske Synode,* 75.

48. Preus's account is found in *Historisk Fremstilling,* 35. Clausen's account is found in *Gjenmæle mod Kirkeraadet for den Norske Synode,* 76–80. While abroad, Preus also argued his case in a lecture before the Norwegian Mission Society. See Preus, *Vivacious Daughter,* 161–73.

49. The theses were printed in *Historisk Fremstilling,* 48; a translation can be found in Rohne, *Norwegian American Lutheranism,* 219.

50. Clausen, *Gjenmæle mod Kirkeraadet for den Norske Synode,* 83.

51. C. F. W. Walther to [A. C. Preus], January 8, 1869, in Helmke, "Was American Slavery a Sinful Institution?," 247–48.

52. Even in the early twentieth century, a prominent Norwegian Synod theologian still defended his church body's stand on the slavery question. See U. V. Koren, "Hvorfor er der ingen kirkelig Enighed mellem norske Lutheranere i Amerika? Svar til Hr. M. Ulvestad og til mange andre," in Koren, *Samlede Skrifter,* 3:463–65. For a translation, see DeGarmeaux, *U. V. Koren's Works,* 490–539.

53. For representative examples, see "Thanksgiving Day," *Lutheran and Missionary,* December 3, 1868, 26; J. H. Werfelmann, "Predigt, gehalten am allgemeinen Lands-Dank-und Bettage, dem 26. November 1868," *Lutheraner,* July 15, 1869, 169–72; and "Thanksgiving Discourse," *Lutheran Observer,* December 9, 1870, 2. For an exception to this general trend, see Holloway, *Sermon Preached in the English Evangelical Lutheran Church.*

54. "Our Annual Thanksgiving," *Lutheran Observer,* November 29, 1872, 2. See also "The Nation's Thanksgiving," *Lutheran Observer,* November 19, 1869, 2.

55. C. F. W., "Evangelical Lutheran Church: Her Mission and Her Present Task," *Lutheran and Missionary,* January 31, 1867, 58; "Thanksgiving Day," *Lutheran Standard,* December 1, 1870, 180; W[alther], "Religionsfreiheit in Amerika," *Lutheraner,* February 1, 1867, 85.

56. "Tidings," *Lutheran and Missionary,* May 4, 1871, 114.

57. "The Pittsburg Synod," *Lutheran and Missionary,* November 8, 1866, 10.

58. Anon, "Our Old Arm Chair," *Lutheran and Missionary,* August 16, 1866, 165.

59. "The Pittsburg Synod," 10.

60. W[alther], "Die Synode von Pennsylvanien," *Lutheraner,* August 1, 1866, 183.

61. "Norwegian Lutheran Synod," *Lutheran and Missionary,* October 11, 1866, 197.

62. *Lutheran Almanac for 1866,* 31.

63. *Proceedings of the Convention Held at Reading, 1866,* 6–16.

64. "The Convention of Lutheran Synods at Reading," *Lutheran and Missionary,* December 20, 1866, 34.

65. "Schism," *Lutheran Observer,* March 15, 1867, 2; Anti-Schismatic, "An Emphatic Rebuke," *Lutheran Observer,* April 5, 1867, 3.

66. "The Recent Convention at Reading, Pa.," *Lutheran Watchman,* January 1, 1867, 3–4.

67. "Die Convention zu Reading zum Zweck der Bildung einer neuen Generalsynode," *Lutheraner,* January 1, 1867, 71.

68. "The General Convention," *Lutheran Standard,* January 1, 1867, 4; "Proceedings of the Sixteenth (Special) Meeting of the Ev. Lutheran Joint Synod of Ohio and Adjoining States, Convened at Hamilton, Butler Co., O., June 13–19, 1867," *Lutheran Standard,* September 1, 1867, 138–39.

69. "Extreme Symbolism," *Lutheran Observer,* April 5, 1867, 2.

70. "The Joint Synod of Ohio and the General Council," *Lutheran and Missionary,* July 18, 1867, 154.

71. Pacificator, "The Pennsylvania Synod and the General Synod," *Lutheran and Missionary,* January 10, 1867, 47. For a similar argument, see "Don't Touch That Flag," *Lutheran and Missionary,* October 17, 1867, 205.

72. "Extracts from Correspondents," *Lutheran and Missionary,* February 14, 1867, 66.

73. "A Word from Fort Wayne," *Lutheran and Missionary,* December 5, 1867, 27.

74. C. P. Krauth, "The General Council: Its Difficulties and Encouragements," *Lutheran and Missionary,* December 12, 1867, 29.

75. *General Council of the Evangelical Lutheran Church in America: First Convention,* 20.

76. "The General Council at Fort Wayne," *Lutheran and Missionary,* December 5, 1867, 26.

77. "Convention ev.-lutherischer Synoden zu Reading, Pa, vom 11. bis 13. December 1866," *Lehre und Wehre* 13, no. 1 (January 1867): 20.

78. *General Council of the Evangelical Lutheran Church in America: First Convention,* 12, 16–19.

79. "The 'Lutheran Standard' and the General Council," *Lutheran and Missionary,* January 2, 1868, 42.

80. "The 'Lutheran' on Ohio and Missouri," *Lutheran Standard,* August 1, 1868, 116–17. See also C[rämer], "Conferenz zwischen den Präsidenten unsrer und der Ohio-Synode," *Lutheraner,* August 15, 1868, 188–89.

81. "Missouri and Ohio," *Lutheran and Missionary,* July 23, 1868, 158.

82. "What Prevents a Union of Lutherans?," *Lutheran and Missionary,* September 3, 1868, 182.

83. "The 'Four Points' in the General Council," *Lutheran Observer,* October 23, 1868, 2.

84. For a full transcription, see "The General Council of the Evangelical Lutheran Church in America," *Lutheran and Missionary,* November 26, 1868, 22–23. For background, see Huber, "Controversy over Pulpit and Alter Fellowship," 133–48.

85. *General Council of the Evangelical Lutheran Church in America: Second Convention,* 22–25.

86. "The General Council," *Lutheran and Missionary,* December 3, 1868, 26.

87. "1868," *Lutheran and Missionary,* December 17, 1868, 34.

88. "The General Council," *Lutheran Standard,* December 1, 1868, 182.

89. See Ottersberg, "Evangelical Lutheran Synod of Iowa," 663–81.

90. "Urkunde über die friedliche Einigung zwischen der Ehrw. ev.-luth. Synode von Missouri und der ev.-luth. Synode von Wisconsin," *Evangelisch-Lutherisches Gemeinde-Blatt,* November 15, 1868, 1.

91. *General Council of the Evangelical Lutheran Church in America: Second Convention,* 25.

92. For background, see Koehler, *History of the Wisconsin Synod,* 128–33; and Braun, "Wisconsin's 'Turn to the Right,'" 88–90.

93. "Equivocal Character of the Decision of the Four Points," *Lutheran Observer,* January 15, 1869, 2; "The Wisconsin Synod Leaves the General Council," *Lutheran Observer,* July 16, 1869, 2.

94. "The Union of the Lutheran Church," *Lutheran Observer,* January 22, 1869, 2.

95. J. A. Brown, "Sermon," *Lutheran Observer,* May 15, 1868, 1–2. See also J. A. Brown, "The Evangelical Lutheran Church in the United States," *Bibliotheca Sacra* 25, no. 3 (July 1868): 435–500.

96. J. A. B[rown], "The General Synod, and the General Council," *Lutheran Observer,* July 3, 1868, 1.

97. "Close Communion and Exchange of Pulpits—Our Position," *Lutheran and Missionary,* August 13, 1868, 170; "What Prevents a Union of Lutherans?," *Lutheran and Missionary,* September 3, 1868, 182.

98. "Our Missouri Accusers," *Lutheran and Missionary,* February 25, 1869, 74; "Letter from New York," *Lutheran and Missionary,* March 18, 1869, 86.

99. "The Missouri Synod," *Lutheran and Missionary,* September 30, 1869, 198; "The Joint Synod of Ohio and Missouri," *Lutheran and Missionary,* October 14, 1869, 206.

100. "The Wisconsin Synod," *Lutheran and Missionary,* July 22, 1869, 158.

101. "What's in a Name?," *Lutheran Observer,* September 14, 1866, 2.

102. *Minutes of the Third Convention of the General Synod of the Confederate States of America,* 28, 34. On Bernheim and the *Evangelical Lutheran,* see Jensson, *American Lutheran Biographies,* 88; and Anderson, *Lutheranism in the Southeastern States,* 224–26.

103. "The Evangelical Lutheran," *Lutheran and Missionary,* September 20, 1866, 184.

104. "Southern General Synod," *Lutheran Observer,* May 10, 1867, 2.

105. "Our Ecclesiastical Situation," *Lutheran Observer,* August 3, 1866, 2.

106. "Southern General Synod," 2; "'The Evangelical Lutheran,'" *Lutheran Observer,* September 14, 1866, 2.

107. X. C. R., "The Lutheran Church in the Shenandoah Valley, Virginia," *Lutheran Observer,* May 31, 1867, 2. See also "Our Church in the South," *Lutheran Observer,* May 31, 1867, 2; and B., "Trip South—General Synod in North America—What I Saw and Heard—Impressions!," *Lutheran Observer,* June 17, 1867.

108. *Proceedings of the Twenty-Fourth Convention of the General Synod,* 64.

109. "The Power of the Truth," *Lutheran and Missionary,* August 1, 1867, 162.

110. "Our Church in the South," *Lutheran and Missionary,* November 24, 1870, 22.

111. "How Are We to Understand It?," *Lutheran and Missionary,* June 17, 1869, 138.

112. "A Question Answered," *Lutheran Observer,* June 25, 1869, 2.

113. For other examples of this reconciliatory rhetoric, see "The Southern Churches," *Lutheran Observer,* June 4, 1869, 2; and "The Proposed Convention," *Lutheran and Missionary,* February 23, 1871, 74.

114. On Rude and the *Lutheran Visitor,* see Jensson, *American Lutheran Biographies,* 637–38; and Anderson, *Lutheranism in the Southeastern States,* 226–31.

115. "The Lutheran Observer *Again,*" *Lutheran Visitor,* January 26, 1870, 2.

116. "What Should We Do?," *Lutheran and Visitor,* February 24, 1869, 1.

117. "The Lutheran Church," *Lutheran Visitor,* June 22, 1870, 2.

118. "North Carolina Synod," *Lutheran Visitor,* September 28, 1870, 2; "Our North Carolina Brethren," *Lutheran Visitor,* November 23, 1870, 2. For background, see Anderson, *Lutheranism in the Southeastern States,* 230–32.

119. G. Diehl, "The Southern General Synod," *Lutheran Observer,* June 24, 1870, 1.

120. Sic Semper, "Free Conference," *Lutheran Visitor,* March 3, 1871, 2.

121. J. Hawkins, "The Free Conference," *Lutheran Visitor,* March 10, 1871, 2.

122. See, for example, Vigilans, "That Free Conference," *Lutheran Visitor,* February 24, 1871, 2; and One of the People, "Very Strange," *Lutheran Visitor,* March 24, 1871, 2.

123. "The Proposed Southern Conference," *Lutheran and Missionary,* March 16, 1871, 86.

124. "Dr. Seiss' Conference," *Lutheran Visitor,* May 19, 1871, 2; "Dr. Rude on the Union of the Lutheran Church," *Lutheran Observer,* June 2, 1871, 5.

125. "Painful and Mortifying," *Lutheran Visitor,* March 31, 1871, 2.

126. Seiss reported on the meeting in "Our Visit South," *Lutheran and Missionary,* July 6, 1871, 150.

127. "A Flash in the Pan," *Lutheran Visitor*, August 25, 1871, 2.

128. "A Theological Funeral," *Lutheran Visitor*, October 20, 1871, 2.

129. "Both Sides of the Question," *Lutheran Visitor*, September 8, 1871, 2.

130. "North Carolina Synod," *Lutheran Visitor*, September 22, 1871, 2.

131. Anderson, *Lutheranism in the Southeastern States*, 233–38.

132. Corrected, "Shall We Go?," *Lutheran Visitor*, March 8, 1872, 2.

133. See, for example, "Dr. Rude's Manifesto," *Lutheran Observer*, September 29, 1871, 5; G. Diehl, "The Growth of Our Church," *Lutheran Observer*, December 22, 1871, 1; and "Ecclesiastical Signs," *Lutheran Observer*, March 8, 1872, 4.

134. Watchman, "Shall We Go?," *Lutheran Visitor*, March 29, 1872, 2.

135. Lutheranus, "'X. J. R.,'" *Lutheran Visitor*, April 12, 1872, 3.

136. "Emphatic Declaration," *Lutheran Visitor*, May 24, 1872, 2; "Editorial Brevities," *Lutheran Observer*, May 24, 1872, 2. On the rejection of the northern delegate, see Anderson, *Lutheranism in the Southeastern States*, 239–40.

137. Lutheranus, "Our General Synod," *Lutheran Visitor*, June 7, 1872, 2.

138. Walther, *Die evangelisch-lutherische Kirche*, 50–51, 146, 152. The most complete English translation is Walther, *True Visible Church*.

139. See, for example, [Walther], *Antwort auf die Frage;* and Meyer, "Walther's Letter from Zurich."

140. "The Evang Lutheran Church the True Visible Church of God on Earth," *Lutheran Standard*, March 1, 1867, 38.

141. Walther's book was translated and published in the *Lutheran Standard* from June 1 to August 15, 1869. For examples of the paper echoing the Missouri Synod, see "Luther's Proof that the Evangelical Lutheran Is the True Old Church, Whilst the Papal Is a New and False Church, Fallen Away from the Old True Church," *Lutheran Standard*, August 15, 1869, 122–23; and "How to Find the True Church," *Lutheran Standard*, March 15, 1871, 166.

142. Braun, "Wisconsin's 'Turn to the Right,'" 88–90.

143. W[alther], "Wieder eine Friedensbotschaft!," *Lutheraner*, November 1, 1868, 37.

144. "Rechtgläubig aber auch recht gläubig," *Evangelisch-Lutherisches Gemeinde-Blatt*, June 15, 1870, 1. For other examples, see "Etwas gegen das Wandern von einer rechtgläubigen Gemeinde zu einer anderen," *Evangelisch-Lutherisches Gemeinde-Blatt*, May 15, 1871, 69–70; and "Gottes Wort und Luther's Lehr' / Vergehet nun und nimmermehr!," *Evangelisch-Lutherisches Gemeinde-Blatt*, November 1, 1871, 2.

145. See, for example, "Among the Missourians," *Lutheran and Missionary*, July 2, 1868, 145; "The 'Lutheraner' on the Pennsylvania Synod," *Lutheran and Missionary*, August 20, 1868, 174; and "Unfortunate," *Lutheran and Missionary*, February 11, 1869, 66.

146. "Is the Lutheran Church the Only Church?," *Lutheran and Missionary*, February 17, 1870, 70.

147. Krauth, *Conservative Reformation*, xiv, 122, 146, 169, 186. For background on the book's composition, see Spaeth, *Charles Porterfield Krauth*, 2:299–314.

148. Krauth, *Conservative Reformation*, 181–83; Walther, *Die evangelisch-lutherische Kirche*, 114–27.

149. For a useful overview, see Arand, *Testing the Boundaries*, 53–118.

150. Walther, *Die evangelisch-lutherische Kirche*, 138, 142.

151. *General Council of the Evangelical Lutheran Church in America: First Convention*, 21. For a fuller discussion, see Krauth, *Conservative Reformation*, 201–328.

152. N. W., "'The Lutheran' as the Champion of the Council," *Lutheran Standard,* November 15, 1870, 172.

153. "Die falschen Stützen der modernen Theorie von den offenen Fragen," *Lehre und Wehre* 14, no. 4 (April 1868): 202.

154. "The Last Ditch," *Lutheran and Missionary,* December 1, 1870, 26.

155. Simeon, "The Strength and Glory of the Lutheran Church—No. 3," *Lutheran Observer,* December 25, 1868, 1. For a similar evaluation, see J. A. Brown, "The Distinctive Peculiarities of the Lutheran Church," *Lutheran Observer,* September 24, 1869, 1.

156. S. Sprecher, "The Folly of Exclusiveness—and the Practicability of Christian Union," *Lutheran Observer,* March 4, 1870, 1; "The Union of the Lutheran Church," *Lutheran Observer,* May 13, 1870, 4.

157. S. Sprecher, "The Two Methods," *Lutheran Observer,* January 4, 1867, 1; S. Sprecher, "The Meaning of the Struggle Between the Two Methods—The Effort to Realize the Protestant Ideal of the Church," *Lutheran Observer,* December 13, 1867, 1.

158. "The Lutheran Not the Only True Church," *Lutheran Observer,* May 10, 1872, 2; Simeon, "Strength and Glory of the Lutheran Church," 1; "The Right to the Name Lutheran," *Quarterly Review of the Evangelical Lutheran Church* 2, no. 1 (January 1872): 139–40.

159. See, for example, Peter Bergstresser, "Symbolism Not Protestantism," *Lutheran Observer,* March 1, 1867, 1; M. Valentine, "True Lutheran Christianity—II," *Lutheran Observer,* April 17, 1868, 3; and "The Standard of Lutheranism," *Lutheran Observer,* December 9, 1870, 4.

160. "The Union of the Lutheran Church," *Lutheran Observer,* January 22, 1869, 2. One especially provocative article described the General Council as the Missouri Synod's slave. See "The General Council Under the Lash of Missouri," *Lutheran Observer,* February 28, 1868, 2.

161. S. Sprecher, "The Character and Spirit of the Evangelical Lutheran Church, as Represented by the General Synod," *Lutheran Observer,* February 7, 1868, 1.

162. [Stuckenberg], *Ninety-Five Theses,* 8, 38. On the authorship of this tract, see Evjen, *Life of J. H. W. Stuckenberg,* 173.

163. "Protestant Infallibility," *Quarterly Review of the Evangelical Lutheran Church* 2, no. 2 (April 1872): 165–66.

164. *Proceedings of the Twenty-Second Convention of the General Synod,* 44–45.

165. "Editorial Catechization," *Lutheran Observer,* August 2, 1867, 2. For a similar evaluation, see "'No Creed but the Bible,'" *Lutheran Observer,* November 12, 1869, 2.

166. See, for example, "Conservatism," *Lutheran Observer,* June 28, 1867, 2; "Spirit of Extreme Symbolism," *Lutheran Observer,* April 17, 1868, 2; and "Theological Tendencies," *Lutheran Observer,* March 4, 1870, 1.

167. "Union in the Lutheran Church," *Quarterly Review of the Evangelical Lutheran Church* 1, no. 2 (April 1871): 243, 249, 259. On Brown's authorship of this article, see "Union in the Lutheran Church," *Lutheran Observer,* May 12, 1871, 4.

168. "The American Element in the General Council," *Lutheran Observer,* December 27, 1867, 2; "Private Judgment," *Lutheran Observer,* November 5, 1869, 2.

169. S. Sprecher, "True Lutheranism: The Meaning of the Struggle," *Lutheran Observer,* January 31, 1868, 1.

170. "The Lutheran's Description of Extreme Symbolism," *Lutheran Observer,* October 30, 1868, 2.

171. "The American Element in the General Council," *Lutheran Observer,* December 27, 1867, 2.

172. "Luther and Rome," *Lutheran Observer,* November 20, 1868, 2. For a similar evaluation, see "Luther and Liberty," *Lutheran Observer,* December 6, 1867, 2.

173. "Evangelical Lutheran Church in America and the 'American Lutheran Church,'" *Lutheran and Missionary,* January 10, 1867, 46.

174. "The General Synod, &c.," *Lutheran and Missionary,* July 13, 1871, 154.

175. Krauth, *Conservative Reformation,* 159–60.

176. "Has Genuine Lutheranism Any Prospect of Maintaining Itself in America?," *Lutheran Watchman,* November 15, 1866, 171–73. This article was reprinted in the December 15, 1866, issue of the *Lutheran Standard.* On Schmidt, see Jensson, *American Lutheran Biographies,* 671–74.

177. *Sechszehnter Synodal-Bericht der Allgemeinen Deutschen Evang.-Luth. Synode von Missouri,* 13–15. For a translation of this address, see Walther, *From Our Master's Table,* 255–59. For similar sentiments, see W[alther], "Vorwort zum neunundzwanzigsten Jahrgang des 'Lutheraner,'" 10.

178. "Memorial, Containing a Comprehensive Statement of the Reasons Why the Synods Forming 'The Evangelical Synodical Conference' Could Not Join Any of the Existing Unions of Synods Bearing the Lutheran Name," *Lutheran Standard,* May 15, 1872, 98.

179. Krauth, *Conservative Reformation,* viii.

180. "Union in the Lutheran Church," *Quarterly Review of the Evangelical Lutheran Church* 1, no. 2 (April 1871): 243, 249.

181. "The Chicago Conference," *Lutheran Standard,* February 1, 1871, 20.

182. For the decisions of the November 1871 meeting, see "The Synodical Conference," *Lutheran Standard,* December 1, 1871, 180; and W[alther], "'Synodalconferenz,'" *Lutheraner,* December 1, 1871, 36–37. For background, see Schuetze, *Synodical Conference,* 51–58.

183. "The Free Conference at Chicago," *Lutheran Observer,* February 10, 1871, 1. For similar evaluations, see "Editorial Brevities," *Lutheran Observer,* December 8, 1871, 4; and "Synodical Conference," *Lutheran Observer,* December 22, 1871, 1.

184. "The Contemplated Synodical Conference," *Lutheran and Missionary,* January 18, 1872, 54.

185. "Tidings," *Lutheran and Missionary,* February 16, 1871, 70; "Missourism Applied to History," *Lutheran and Missionary,* March 16, 1871, 86; Insulanus, "Letter from New York," *Lutheran and Missionary,* March 9, 1871, 82.

186. *Denkschrift,* 32–33. The chief author of this document was Friedrich Schmidt, but the other delegates at the meeting reviewed the text and helped to make revisions. An English translation was published in the *Lutheran Standard* from May 15 to July 1, 1872.

187. *Verhandlungen der ersten Versammlung der Evangelisch-Lutherischen Synodal-Conferenz,* 4, 10, 12–13. For a translation of Walther's sermon, see Harrison, *At Home in the House of My Fathers,* 193–201.

188. For these statistics, see *Lutheran Almanac for 1878,* 22–23; and Kopenhaver et al., *Lutheran Church Year Book for 1919,* 84–85. In 1918, the National Lutheran Council was formed. Since this organization was more of a loose confederation, the Synodical Conference could be considered the largest Lutheran union until 1962, when the Lutheran Church in America was founded. See Wiederaenders, *Historical Guide,* 141–42; and Nelson, *Lutheranism in North America,* 18–21, 135.

6. THE TRIUMPH OF CONFESSIONAL CONSERVATISM, 1872–1900

1. H. K. Carroll, "American Lutherans and Their Divisions," *Methodist Quarterly Review* 64, no. 3 (July 1882): 427–28. For further background, see Grundmeier, "American Lutherans and Their Divisions," 83–87.

2. For standard overviews of the Gilded Age, see Trachtenberg, *Incorporation of America;* Edwards, *New Spirits;* and White, *Republic for Which It Stands.*

3. For accounts of postbellum immigration, see Archdeacon, *Becoming American,* esp. 27–172; and Daniels, *Coming to America,* esp. 121–284.

4. These phrases come from Marty, *Protestantism in the United States.* Of course, as several historians have shown, some religious groups did not fit neatly into either "party." See, for example, Jacobson and Trollinger, *Re-Forming the Center.*

5. Juster, *Disorderly Women,* ix.

6. For statistics from 1820 to 1900, see United States Bureau of the Census, *Historical Statistics,* 105–6, 116–17; for estimates of immigration before 1820, see Daniels, *Coming to America,* 6.

7. For state-by-state statistics on German and Nordic immigrants, see Merriam, *Twelfth Census of the United States,* 732–35, 810–11, 818–19.

8. In 1900, Lutherans in Texas belonged to seven different synods, none of which belonged to the United Synod of the South. See Vardell, "Striving to Gather the Scattered," x.

9. For context, see Scheidt. "Linguistic Transition in the Muhlenberg Tradition"; and Blanck, *Creation of an Ethnic Identity.*

10. Carroll, "American Lutherans and Their Divisions," 442.

11. Numerous examples could be cited. Three of the most significant are Ferm, *Crisis in American Lutheran Theology;* Tappert, *Lutheran Confessional Theology;* and Gustafson, *Lutherans in Crisis.*

12. For background, see Zachhuber, *Theology as Science;* and Purvis, *Theology and the University.*

13. Carroll, "American Lutherans and Their Divisions," 436–37.

14. *Walther's Works: All Glory to God,* 1, 4, 19, 22. The lectures originally appeared in the proceedings of the Missouri Synod's Western District conventions from 1873 to 1886.

15. On usury and life insurance, see Albers, "History of Attitudes Within the Missouri Synod Toward Life Insurance"; on the marriage of in-laws, see Schuetze, *Synodical Conference,* 65–66.

16. "Political Parties and Principles and Religious Parties and Principles," *Lutheran Witness,* March 21, 1890, 156.

17. For one of the most extensive attacks, see Brockmann, *Christian und Ernst.* For a sampling of the frequent condemnation of "secret societies" in the periodicals of the Missouri Synod, see R. L. "Geheime Gesellschaften," *Lutheraner,* August 1, 1887, 119–20; and C. Dreyer, "The Anti-Christian Character of Secret Societies," *Lutheran Witness,* July 21, 1891, 26.

18. A. G[raebner], "Von geheimen Farmerverbindungen," *Lutheraner,* January 28, 1890, 18. See also J. Müller, "Kann ein lutherischer Christ Mitglied des Nordamerikanischen Turnerbundes sein?," *Lutheraner,* April 22, 1890, 70–73; and "Why Christians Should Not Join the Secret Order of the Grand Army of the Republic," *Lutheran Witness,* December 21, 1890, 109.

19. Gruber, *Erinnerungen an Professor C. F. W. Walther,* 71.

20. Stellhorn, *Schools of The Lutheran Church—Missouri Synod,* 182.

21. See Koehler, *History of the Wisconsin Synod,* 162, 187.

22. "Thesen über das rechte Verhältniß zu dem hiesigen Freischulwesen, besprochen auf der Versam-

mlung des westlichen Districts der Synode von Missouri, Ohio u. a. St.," *Lutheraner,* August 15, 1870, 188; *Fünfzehnter Synodal Bericht der Allgemeinen Deutschen Evang.-Luth. Synode von Missouri,* 88.

23. G., "Gemeindeschulen," *Lutheraner,* September 1, 1876, 134; W[alther], "Gemeindeschulen," *Lutheraner,* February 15, 1873, 76.

24. The most exhaustive account of these disputes is Haug, "Predestination Controversy"; the most succinct treatment is Thuesen, *Predestination,* 148–68.

25. Thuesen, *Predestination,* 157–58.

26. U. V. Koren, "Hvad den norske Synode har villet og fremdeles vil," in *Samlede Skrifter,* 3:445. For a translation, see DeGarmeaux, *U. V. Koren's Works,* 3:403–89. For background, see Gjerde, "Conflict and Community."

27. For biographical details on Pieper, see Graebner, *Dr. Francis Pieper.*

28. For examples, see Greenwald, *True Church;* J. A. Seiss, "Our Confessions in English," *Lutheran Church Review* 1, no. 3 (July 1882): 218–20; and Spaeth, *General Council,* 12.

29. H. E. Jacobs, "The Confessional Principle and the Confessions: A Memorial of the Jubilee of 1880," *Lutheran Quarterly* 11, no. 1 (January 1881): 14, 18. See also Jacobs, *Book of Concord.*

30. H. E. J[acobs], "Preface," in Hutter, *Compend of Lutheran Theology,* vi. See also Schmid, *Doctrinal Theology of the Evangelical Lutheran Church.*

31. For a full account, see Huber, "Controversy over Pulpit and Alter Fellowship," 133–227.

32. *General Council of the Evangelical Lutheran Church in America: Second Convention,* 23–25.

33. *Minutes of the Ninth Convention of the General Council,* 17. The declaration was sometimes referred to as the Galesburg Rule.

34. Krauth, *Theses on the Galesburg Declaration,* 1, 4, 30. For a comprehensive statement of his church fellowship principles, see Charles P. Krauth, "The Relations of the Lutheran Church to the Denominations Around Us," in Jacobs, *First Free Lutheran Diet,* 27–69.

35. Spaeth, *Charles Porterfield Krauth,* 2:208.

36. "A Few Explanations," *Lutheran and Missionary,* September 27, 1877, 408. For Seiss's theses, see "Twenty-Four Propositions on the Galesburg Declaration," *Lutheran and Missionary,* September 20, 1877, 404. For further evidence of the widespread agreement on the principles of the Galesburg Declaration, see the numerous letters of support written to Krauth by General Council pastors, in "Correspondence Regarding the Galesburg Rule," Charles Porterfield Krauth Papers, Lutheran Archives Center, Philadelphia, Pennsylvania.

37. R. L., "General Council," *Lehre und Wehre* 25, no. 11 (November 1879): 341; F. P[ieper], "General-Council," *Lutheraner,* December 15, 1879, 189.

38. Beck, *Lutheran Elementary Schools,* 281–85.

39. "Concerning the Dogma of Predestination: Opinion Given by the Faculty of the Theological Seminary at Philadelphia in Answer to a Request Made by the New York Ministerium," *Lutheran Church Review* 3, no. 3 (July 1884): 235. For background on the General Council's response, see Haug, "Predestination Controversy," 837–57.

40. C. P. K[rauth] to C. Spielmann, April 7, 1876, in Spaeth, *Charles Porterfield Krauth,* 2:236.

41. On Spaeth, Jacobs, and the confessionalism of the Philadelphia seminary's faculty in the late nineteenth and early twentieth centuries, see Tappert, *History of the Lutheran Theological Seminary at Philadelphia,* 69–75.

42. J. A. Brown, "The Four General Bodies of the Lutheran Church in the United States, Wherein

They Agree, and Wherein They Might Harmoniously Co-Operate," in Jacobs, *First Free Lutheran Diet,* 85–86.

43. H. Ziegler, "The Value to the Lutheran Church of Her Confessions," in Baum and Kunkelman, *Second Free Lutheran Diet,* 59, 70–71.

44. *Proceedings of the Thirty-First Convention of the General Synod,* 44.

45. On Valentine and Richard, see Wentz, *History of the Gettysburg Theological Seminary,* 317–20, 325–28.

46. M. Valentine, "The Effort to Reconstruct History in the Interest of the General Council," *Lutheran Quarterly* 16, no. 4 (October 1886): 593; J. W. Richard, "Melanchthon and the Augsburg Confession," *Lutheran Quarterly* 28, no. 3 (July 1898): 379; Richard, "The Confessional History of the General Synod," *Lutheran Quarterly* 25, no. 4 (October 1895): 473. See also Valentine, "General Synod," 39–46.

47. L. A. Gotwald, "Lutheran Confessionalism in the General Synod: A Reply to the Charges of My Assailants," in [Gotwald], *Trial of Luther A. Gotwald,* 51, 60, 76.

48. "Copy of Charges as Preferred Against Dr. Gotwald by A. Gebhart, Joseph R. Gebhart, and E. E. Baker," in [Gotwald], *Trial of Luther A. Gotwald,* 4. For background, see Gotwald Jr., "Trial of Luther A. Gotwald."

49. *Proceedings of the Thirty-Seventh Convention of the General Synod,* 63.

50. *Proceedings of the Fortieth Convention of the General Synod,* 83–84.

51. *Proceedings of the Forty-Sixth Convention of the General Synod,* 126.

52. Jordan, *Evangelical Alliance,* 73–74, 83–84; Schmucker, *True Unity of Christ's Church.*

53. "Use and Abuse of Denominationalism," *Lutheran Quarterly* 1, no. 1 (January 1878): 104, 110.

54. *Proceedings of the Thirty-Third Convention of the General Synod,* 56.

55. See, for example, *Proceedings of the Thirty-First Convention of the General Synod,* 43; and "Revivals," *Lutheran Observer,* February 2, 1872, 5.

56. *Proceedings of the Thirty-Second Convention of the General Synod,* 193.

57. "Revivals," *Lutheran Observer,* December 23, 1887, 4.

58. The debates and discussions over worship in the General Synod (and among other American Lutherans) during this era were complex and contested. For a helpful summary, see Wentz, *Basic History,* 221–29.

59. "The General Synod: Fortieth Biennial Convention: Des Moines, Ia, May 29th, 1901," *Lutheran Observer,* June 7, 1901, 3.

60. See Hutchison, *Modernist Impulse;* and Dorrien, *Making of American Liberal Theology.*

61. "Darwin und der Urmensch," *Lehre und Wehre* 17, no. 7 (July 1871): 212. See also W[alther], "Ueber Darwin's neueste Schrift," *Lehre und Wehre* 19, no. 2 (February 1873): 64; and "Darwinismus," *Lehre und Wehre* 28, no. 10 (October 1882): 476–77.

62. G. St., "Schulbibel in Deutschland," *Lehre und Wehre* 36, no. 5 (May 1890): 167. See also "Zur Thorheit der modernen Bibelkritik," *Lehre und Wehre* 17, no. 12 (December 1872): 376; G. St., "Antikritisches," *Lehre und Wehre* 35, no. 11 (November 1889): 344–49; and Theo Engelder, "Higher Criticism," *Lutheran Witness,* March 21, 1893, 154.

63. Loy, *Fallacy of Liberalism,* 19.

64. Lindemann, *Astronomische Unterredung.*

65. For a concise summary of the Missouri Synod's theological position near the end of the nine-

teenth century, see Pieper, *Unsere Stellung in Lehre und Praxis*. For further context, see Suelflow, "History of the Missouri Synod During the Second Twenty-Five Years," 68–244.

66. On the views in both the General Council and the General Synod, see Deitz, "Eastern Lutheranism in American Society."

67. H. V. Hilprecht, "The Essential Task of Old Testament Science at the Present Time," *Lutheran Church Review* 10, no. 4 (October 1891): 287, 279.

68. Schmauk, *Negative Criticism,* 29, 129. On Schmauk, see Sandt, *Theodore Emanuel Schmauk.*

69. Seiss, *Moses and the Higher Criticism,* 20, 24.

70. M. Valentine, "Inaugural Discourse," *Lutheran Quarterly* 14, no. 4 (October 1884): 602–5. For other negative assessments of higher criticism and Darwinian evolution, see George U. Wenner, "The Line of Cleavage: Essential Dogmatic Differences Between the Liberal and Positive Schools of Theology," *Lutheran Quarterly* 27, no. 1 (January 1897): 50–62; and Junius B. Fox, "Oriental Archæology and the Old Testament," *Lutheran Quarterly* 27, no. 4 (October 1897): 559–75.

71. For example, one article advanced a form of the "day-age theory" but argued that "the theory of evolution fails" to explain human "intellect" and "self-consciousness," which were the result of a special "act of divine creation." A. E. Deitz, "Evolution as Taught in Scripture," *Lutheran Quarterly* 27, no. 2 (April 1897): 215. In another, James Richard explicated a "believing criticism" but insisted that theologians must assert "not that the Bible *contains* the word of God, but that it *is* the word of God." Loenhard Staehlin, "Christianity and Holy Scripture," trans. J. W. Richard, *Lutheran Quarterly* 23, no. 1 (January 1893): 10. On the wide range of views presented in the *Fundamentals,* see Marsden, *Fundamentalism and American Culture,* 118–23.

72. See Andersen, *Rough Road to Glory;* and Brøndal, *Ethnic Leadership and Midwestern Politics.*

73. A. G[raebner], "Kirche und Staat," *Lutheraner,* March 26, 1889, 51. See also "Staat und Kirche," *Lehre und Wehre* 35, no. 4 (April 1889): 130; and "Church and State," *Lutheran Witness,* December 7, 1898, 99–100.

74. The first three quotations are from the proceedings of the Missouri Synod's Central District, in Suelflow, "History of the Missouri Synod during the Second Twenty-Five Years," 245–46; the final two quotations are from A. G[raebner], "Kirche und Staat," *Lutheraner,* April 9, 1889, 58.

75. Walther, *Communism and Socialism,* 7–8. That Walther's tract was translated into English demonstrates its popularity. For the original German edition, which went through a second edition eight years after its original printing, see Walther, *Communismus und Socialismus.*

76. "Politik in der Kirche," *Lehre und Wehre* 23, no. 5 (May 1877): 154; "Church and State," *Lutheran Witness,* October 21, 1899, 76.

77. C. P. Krauth, "Church Polity," *Lutheran Church Review* 4, no. 1 (January 1885): 59.

78. Hiram Peters, "The Lord's Day and the State," *Lutheran Church Review* 12, no. 2 (April 1893): 167–69.

79. Charles P. Krauth, "The Sermon: Its Material and Text," *Lutheran Church Review* 1, no. 2 (April 1882): 81.

80. Krauth, *Caesar and God,* 15; "Congratulatory Address, by Rev. C. P. Krauth, D.D., LL.D., at the Inauguration of Prof. Julius D. Dreher, as President of Roanoke College, Salem, Virginia, October 17th, 1879," *Lutheran and Missionary,* December 4, 1879, 863.

81. W. J. Mann, "A Sign of the Times," *Lutheran Church Review* 2, no. 3 (July 1883): 180–81. See also "Christianity and the Nation," *Lutheran and Missionary,* July 22, 1880, 2; "Notes," *Lutheran and*

Missionary, July 28, 1881, 2; and C. W. Schaeffer, "The Church and the Times," *Lutheran Church Review* 10, no. 2 (April 1891): 83–97.

82. S. A. Holman, "Human Ordinances in the Church," *Lutheran Quarterly* 10, no. 3 (July 1880): 345–46.

83. D. M. Gilbert, "The Relation of the Church to Questions of Governmental Policy," *Lutheran Quarterly* 19, no. 4 (October 1889): 590. A similar argument was made by Samuel S. Schmucker's youngest son, a federal judge in Maryland. See Samuel D. Schmucker, "The Relation of the Church to the State," *Lutheran Quarterly* 35, no. 4 (October 1905): 501–21.

84. J. Wagner, "The Pulpit and the Problems of Modern Life," *Lutheran Quarterly* 21, no. 3 (July 1891): 413–15, 421–23. For a similar argument, see E. D. Weigle, "The Ministry and Current Social Problems," *Lutheran Quarterly* 24, no. 4 (October 1894): 467–80.

85. See Jensen, *Winning of the Midwest;* Kleppner, *Third Electoral System;* and Swierenga, "Ethnoreligious Political Behavior."

86. On Gilded Age moral reform movements more generally, see Foster, *Moral Reconstruction;* on the temperance movement specifically, see Pegram, *Battling Demon Rum.*

87. On the social gospel, see Susan Curtis, *Consuming Faith;* and Evans, *Social Gospel in American Religion.*

88. Trauger, *True Temperance,* 4, 27, 31. The tract went through five editions, including a publication by the Ohio Synod's publishing house. See also Sihler, *Wider das Gewohnheits-Trinken.*

89. C. W. Schaeffer, "What Should Be the Attitude of the Lutheran Church to the So-Called Reforms of the Day?," in Baum and Kunkelman, *Second Free Lutheran Diet,* 202, 204.

90. "Alcohol and the State," *Lutheran Quarterly* 8, no. 1 (January 1878): 137. Throughout the tenure of Frederick Conrad as editor, the *Lutheran Observer* continued to promote temperance. See Deitz, "Eastern Lutheranism in American Society," 196.

91. H. C. Haithcox, "Prohibition," *Lutheran Quarterly* 17, no. 3 (July 1887): 359–60.

92. "Warning," *Lutheran Observer,* September 13, 1901, 10; David H. Bauslin, "The Socialization of the Church," *Lutheran Quarterly* 44, no. 2 (April 1914): 178.

93. For the fullest treatment, see Rudnik, "Missouri Synod's Stand on the Labor Question."

94. Walther, *Communism and Socialism,* 6.

95. G., "Zur Arbeiterfrage: Ein Gespräch," *Lutheraner,* April 15, 1886.

96. Walther, *Communism and Socialism,* 29, 74.

97. Deitz, "Eastern Lutheranism in American Society," 194–201. See also Granquist, "American Lutheran Reactions to the Labor Movement."

98. See, for example, Charles S. Albert, "The Church and the Labor Problem," *Lutheran Quarterly* 17, no. 2 (April 1887): 248–59; Adam Stump, "Christ and the Labor Movement," *Lutheran Quarterly* 20, no. 3 (July 1890): 435–45; and Samuel Wagenhals, "The Industrial Situation," *Lutheran Church Review* 14, no. 2/3 (April/July 1895): 148–64.

99. M. Valentine, "The Ethical Aim of Christianity," *Lutheran Quarterly* 22, no. 4 (October 1892): 532–33.

100. For the most comprehensive study, see Schaefer, "Avoiding the Hornet's Nest."

101. F. P[ieper], "Frauenstimmrecht im Staat Missouri," *Lehre und Wehre* 41, no. 2 (February 1895): 59; F. P[ieper], "Frauenstimmrecht vor dem Senat der Vereinigten Staaten," *Lehre und Wehre* 33, no. 2 (February 1887): 56.

102. A. G[raebner], "Frauenrechte," *Lutheraner,* April 2, 1894, 71–72. For a similar evaluation, see "Scripture on the Woman Question," *Lutheran Witness,* February 7, 1898, 132. On Graebner, see Lagerquist, *Lutherans,* 183–84.

103. E. W. H., "Should Women Be Made Voters?," *Lutheran Observer,* May 20, 1870, 3; E. Greenwald and J. Fry, "The Work of Believing Women," *Lutheran and Missionary,* July 11, 1872, 153.

104. Theodore E. Schmauk, "Holy Scripture and Questions of the Day," *Lutheran Church Review* 18, no. 3 (July 1899): 497.

105. Theodore E. Schmauk, "A History of Authority, and of the Right to Rule, in Christian Society, in Its Bearings on the Woman Question," *Lutheran Church Review* 18, no. 3 (July 1899): 544, 551.

106. For a similar observation, see Lohrmann, "Lutherans and the Nineteenth Amendment," 54.

107. T. W. Dosh, "The Religious Condition of the Colored People, and What Ought to Be Done in Their Behalf by the Lutheran Church," in Baum and Kunkelman, *Second Free Lutheran Diet,* 237–38; George E. Titzell, "The Lutheran Church and Negro Evangelization," *Lutheran Church Review* 9, no. 2 (April 1890): 131, 139.

108. Wentz, *History of the Evangelical Lutheran Synod of Maryland,* 125–26.

109. On Wiseman and Redeemer Lutheran Church, see Teigen, "Rev. Daniel E. Wiseman"; and Wentz, *History of the Evangelical Lutheran Synod of Maryland,* 312–14. There were also a few Black Lutheran churches in late nineteenth-century New York. See Scholz, *Press Toward the Mark,* 214–18.

110. Quotes in Lueking, *Mission in the Making,* 112, 141. For statistics, see Dickinson, *Roses and Thorns,* 57.

111. See Nelson, *Lutheranism in North America,* 135; and Johnson, *Black Christians,* 177.

112. Duncan, *Dear Church.*

113. This argument is made in Deitz, "Eastern Lutheranism in American Society," 239–78, and echoed in Nelson, *Lutherans in North America,* 348–56. Regarding Lutherans' conservatism during the Gilded Age, Mark Granquist contends, "Although they were aware of many of these modern developments and recognized their challenges, American Lutherans during this period were simply too busy gathering in the masses of immigrants." Granquist, *Lutherans in America,* 205.

114. For examples, see Hope, *German and Scandinavian Protestantism,* 217–568; and Nelson, *Lutheranism and the Nordic Spirit of Social Democracy.*

115. On these Catholic divisions in the late nineteenth-century United States, see Dolan, *In Search of an American Catholicism,* 71–126.

116. Sihler, *Gedanken eines Lutheraners,* 7. For similar sentiments, see Walther's synodical address in *Sechszehnter Synodal-Bericht der Allgemeinen Deutschen Evang.-Luth. Synode von Missouri,* 9–17.

117. A. G[raebner], "Kirche und Staat," *Lutheraner,* March 26, 1889, 50–51. For a similar argument, see Adolphus Biewend, "Luther's Reformation and Its Influence on America," *Lutheran Witness,* October 21, 1882, 82–83, 86–87.

118. Seiss, "Our Country: A Sermon Preached July 4, 1886," in *The Christ and His Church,* 369, 375. For similar claims from General Council Lutherans, see "The Thirty-First of October: An Address Delivered by Rev. Prof. W. J. Mann, D.D., in the Theological Seminary of the Evan. Luth. Ch., at Phila., on the Anniversary of the Reformation, Oct. 31, 1872," *Lutheran and Missionary,* December 12, 1872, 33; and H. Peters, "A Thanksgiving Sermon," *Lutheran Church Review* 18, no. 4 (October 1899): 734–46.

119. J. G. Butler, "An Hour with the Fathers: Is Our Nation Christian?—A Centennial Thought,"

Quarterly Review of the Evangelical Lutheran Church 6, no. 4 (October 1876): 522–23; David H. Bauslin, "The Reformation and Civil Liberty," *Lutheran Quarterly* 22, no. 4 (October 1892): 561. See also David A. Buehler, "The Influence of the Reformation upon Civil Liberty," *Lutheran Quarterly* 14, no. 1 (January 1884): 113–27; and Abraham L. Guss, "Luther and Religious Liberty," *Lutheran Quarterly* 16, no. 2 (April 1886): 222–32.

120. A. Graebner, "Epochs of Lutheranism in America," in *Reden, gehalten einer Versammlung der mit der Missouri-Synode verbundenen lutherischen Gemeinden Chicagos,* 23, 25. For similar ideas about the Synodical Conference as a whole, see Sieker, *Gesegnete Wirksamkeit.*

121. Spaeth, *General Council,* 28. See also H. E. Jacobs, "The Mission of the Lutheran Confession in America," *Lutheran Church Review* 15, no. 2 (April 1896): 132–33.

122. Sprecher, *Groundwork of a System of Evangelical Lutheran Theology,* 35, 38. For a similar evaluation, see E. J. Wolf, "Lutheranism in the General Synod," *Lutheran Quarterly* 21, no. 2 (April 1891): 285–303.

123. Seiss, "Our Fathers in America: A Jubilee Discourse," in *The Christ and His Church,* 364.

124. For a particularly virulent example, see J. G. Butler, "Facing the Twentieth Century," *Lutheran Quarterly* 30, no. 1 (January 1900): 61–68.

125. S. E. Ochsenford, "Lutheran History," *Lutheran Church Review* 7, no. 2 (April 1888): 120, 123. See also S. E. Ochsenford, "The Lutheran Church in America," *Lutheran Church Review* 4, no. 1 (January 1885): 12–28.

126. Lee M. Heilman, "Lutheranism in American Liberty Vindicated," *Lutheran Quarterly* 24, no. 1 (January 1894): 82, 86, 92, 96–98.

127. J. Schte, "The Repeal of the Bennett Law and One of Those Campaign Speeches Which Set Forth the Inconsistency and Tyranny of Such Law," *Lutheran Witness,* February 21, 1891, 137–38; "The Fight for Parochial Schools in Wisconsin," *Lutheran Witness,* October 7, 1890, 69–70. For context, see Johnston, "American Ideals in German Print."

128. A. G[rabner], "Kirche und Staat," *Lutheraner,* April 23, 1889, 65–66.

129. F. B[ente], "Lutherthum und Americanerthum," *Lehre und Wehre* 48, no. 11 (November 1902): 322–25. This article was translated into English and published in the January 1904 issue of the *Theological Quarterly.* On Bente, see Josephine Bente, *Biography of Dr. Friedrich Bente.*

130. For the statistics about Lutheran educational, charitable, and literary institutions, see Sheeleigh, *Lutheran Almanac and Year Book for 1901,* 26–30.

131. Carroll, "American Lutherans and Their Divisions," 427.

132. For biographical information on Stuckenberg, see Evjen, *Life of J. H. W. Stuckenberg.*

133. In one of the rare instances of a female writer being given a voice in a nineteenth-century Lutheran theological publication, Mary Stuckenberg made the case for expanding educational access so that "women be matured and trained to true womanliness." Stuckenberg, "Thoughts on Woman's Education," *Lutheran Quarterly* 17, no. 4 (October 1887): 579.

134. Stuckenberg to A. H. F. Fischer, September 2, 1902, in Evjen, *Life of J. H. W. Stuckenberg,* 456.

135. Stuckenberg, *Orthodox Lutheranism in Germany,* 13–14, 25. See also Stuckenberg, *Greetings from the Fatherland,* esp. 3–5.

136. The influence of European thought on postbellum "American Lutherans" can be seen in the work of Stuckenberg's mentor, Samuel Sprecher. For example, Sprecher translated, but never published, portions of the *History of Protestant Theology* by the German mediating theologian Isaak A.

Dorner. See folder CB 4.1, Samuel Sprecher Papers, Archives and Special Collections, Thomas Library, Wittenberg University, Springfield, Ohio. The influence of Dorner and other German theologians on Sprecher is also evident in the copious references to them in his theological textbook. See Sprecher, *Groundwork of a System of Evangelical Lutheran Theology.*

137. As R. Laurence Moore has shown, a similar phenomenon was found among Roman Catholics in the late nineteenth century. Moore, *Religious Outsiders,* 48–71.

138. *Sechszehnter Synodal-Bericht der Allgemeinen Deutschen Evang.-Luth. Synode von Missouri,* 14.

139. *Denkmal der dritten Jubelfeier der Concordienformel,* 233. For a translation, see Harrison, *At Home in the House of My Fathers,* 213–23.

EPILOGUE

1. Lewis, *Compilation of the Messages and Speeches of Theodore Roosevelt,* 549. For examples of Lutheran reactions to Roosevelt's address, see "President Roosevelt on the Lutheran Church," *Lutheran Observer,* February 3, 1905, 5; and "President Roosevelt on the Lutheran Church," *Augustana Journal,* February 15, 1905, 3–4.

2. On German Americans and World War I, see Luebke, *Bonds of Loyalty.* For a useful account of the Missouri Synod during the war, see Wetzel, *American Crusade,* 125–48.

3. See, for example, Graebner, "Acculturation of an Immigrant Lutheran Church."

4. See Rudnick, *Fundamentalism and the Missouri Synod;* and Echols, "Charles Michael Jacobs."

5. Vergilius Ferm, foreword to *What Is Lutheranism?,* viii.

6. See, for example, Granquist, "Lutherans and the New Deal."

7. *Minutes of the Third Biennial Convention of the United Lutheran Church in America,* 72, 75, 79.

8. United States Bureau of the Census, *Historical Statistics,* 105.

9. For Lutheran statistics, see Kopenhaver, *Lutheran Church Year Book for 1922,* 45; and Nelson, *Lutheranism in North America,* 135. Between 1920 and 1960, membership in Congregationalist, Methodist, and Presbyterian congregations did not even double, while the number of Baptists, Episcopalians, and Roman Catholics increased at a slightly lower rate than did the number of Lutherans. See Gaustad and Barlow, *New Historical Atlas,* 80, 98, 100, 137, 157, 180.

10. "The New Lutheran," *Time Magazine,* April 7, 1958, EBSCO-host.

11. See Braun, *Tale of Two Synods;* and Burkee, *Power, Politics, and the Missouri Synod.*

12. See Trexler, *High Expectations;* and Granquist, *Lutherans in America,* 323–51.

13. On the present-day divisions within the Lutheran Church—Missouri Synod, see Sauer, "Field Guide to the Missouri Synod."

14. See Nelson, *Lutheranism in North America,* 135; Gaustad and Barlow, *New Historical Atlas,* 80, 157; and Grammich et al., *2020 U.S. Religion Census,* 88–94.

15. Noll, "Lutheran Difference," 34–36.

16. Noll, "American Lutherans Yesterday and Today," 14–16.

17. Noll, "Lutheran Difference," 31.

18. See, for example, Berger, "On Lutheran Identity in America"; and Braaten, *Because of Christ,* 165–71.

APPENDIX

1. "Statistics of the Lutheran Church for 1830," *Lutheran Observer,* September 1, 1831, 44; *Lutheran Almanac for the Year of Our Lord and Saviour Jesus Christ 1851,* 45; *Lutheran Almanac for 1861,* 32–33; *Lutheran Almanac for 1873,* 30; Sheeleigh, *Lutheran Almanac and Year Book for 1901,* 84–85.

BIBLIOGRAPHY

PRIMARY SOURCES

Manuscript Collections

Concordia Historical Institute, St. Louis, Missouri
  Franz Julius Biltz Family Collection
  Carl Ferdinand Wilhelm Walther Papers
Evangelical Lutheran Church in America Archives, Elk Grove Village, Illinois
  Erik Norelius Papers
Gettysburg College, Special Collections, Musselman Library, Pennsylvania
  Samuel Simon Schmucker and the Schmucker Family Papers
  John Henry Wilbrand Stuckenberg Papers
Lutheran Archives Center, Philadelphia, Pennsylvania
  Charles Porterfield Krauth Papers
Lutheran Theological Southern Seminary, James R. Crumley Jr. Archives, Columbia,
    South Carolina
  John Bachman Papers
Roanoke College Archives, Virginia
  David F. Bittle Papers
United Lutheran Seminary, A. R. Wentz Library, Gettysburg, Pennsylvania
  James Allen Brown Papers
  Samuel Simon Schmucker Papers
  Elias Schwartz Journal
Wisconsin Evangelical Lutheran Synod Archives, Waukesha
  John Bading Biographical File
Wittenberg University, Archives and Special Collections, Thomas Library, Springfield, Ohio
  Samuel Sprecher Papers
Zelienople Historical Society, Pennsylvania
  William A. Passavant Letters

Bibliography

Periodicals

Abend Schule
American Biblical Repository
Augustana Journal
Bibliotheca Sacra
Evangelical Quarterly Review
Evangelical Review
Evangelisch-Lutherisches Gemeinde-Blatt
Kirkelig Maanedstidende
Illustrirte Abend-Schule
Lehre und Wehre
Liberator
Lutheran and Home Journal
Lutheran and Missionary
Lutheran Church Quarterly
Lutheran Church Review

Lutheran Observer
Lutheran Quarterly
Lutheran Standard
Lutheran Visitor
Lutheran Watchman
Lutheran Witness
Lutheraner
Lutherische Herold
Methodist Quarterly Review
Missionary
Quarterly Review of the Evangelical
    Lutheran Church
Southern Lutheran
Theological Quarterly
Time

Church Proceedings and Almanacs

Baum, W. M., and J. A. Kunkelman, eds. *Second Free Lutheran Diet in America: Philadelphia, November 5–7, 1878: The Essays, Debates, and Proceedings.* Philadelphia, 1879.

Denkschrift enthaltend eine eingehende Darlegung der Gründe weshalb die zur Synodal-Conferenz der evangel.-luther. Kirche von Nord-Amerika zusammentretenden Synoden sich nicht an eine der hierzulande schon bestehenden lutherisch benannten Verbindungen von Synoden haben anschließen können. Columbus, 1871.

Extracts from the Minutes of the Twelfth Meeting of the Evangelical Lutheran Synod and Ministerium, of South Carolina and Adjacent States, convened at St. Nicholas Church, Barnwell District, SO. CA. on Saturday the Fourteenth November, 1835 [...]. Columbia, SC, 1836.

Fünfzehnter Synodal-Bericht der Allgemeinen Deutschen Evang.-Luth. Synode von Missouri, Ohio u. a. Staaten vom Jahre 1872. St. Louis, 1872.

General Council of the Evangelical Lutheran Church in America: First Convention, Fort Wayne, Indiana, November 20 to 26, A.D. 1867. Pittsburgh, 1867.

General Council of the Evangelical Lutheran Church in America: Second Convention, Pittsburgh, Penn'a: November 12 to 18, A.D. 1868. Pittsburgh, 1868.

Jacobs, H[enry] E[yster], ed. *First Free Lutheran Diet in America: Philadelphia, December 27–28, 1877: The Essays, Debates and Proceedings.* Philadelphia, 1878.

Journal of the Twenty-Ninth Annual Session of the Franckean Evangelic Lutheran Synod, Convened at Frey's Bush, Montgomery Co., N.Y., June 7th to June 11th, 1866. Albany, 1866.

Kopenhaver, W. M., ed. *Lutheran Church Year Book for 1922.* United Lutheran Publication House, 1922.

Bibliography

Kopenhaver, W. M., Grace M. Sheeleigh, and Carl Ackermann, eds. *The Lutheran Church Year Book for 1919*. Lutheran Publication Society, 1919.

Lehmann, Arnold O., trans. "Proceedings of the 14th Convention of the German Evangelical Lutheran Synod of Wisconsin and Other States Held in the First German Evangelical Lutheran Congregation in Manitowoc, Wisc." *WELS Historical Institute Journal* 18, no. 1 (April 2000): 3–20

———, trans. "Proceedings of the 15th Convention of the German Evangelical Lutheran Synod of Wisconsin and Other States held in the German Evangelical Lutheran Church of Watertown, Wis. June 22 to 28, 1865." *WELS Historical Institute Journal* 14, no. 2 (October 1996): 3–26.

———, trans. "Wisconsin Synod Synodical Proceedings, 1849–1860: Proceedings of 1849, 1850, 1851," *WELS Historical Institute Journal* 9, no. 1/2 (1991): 3–7.

The Lutheran Almanac for 1861. Baltimore, 1861.

The Lutheran Almanac for 1863. Baltimore, 1863.

The Lutheran Almanac for 1864. Baltimore, 1864.

The Lutheran Almanac for 1866. Baltimore, 1866.

The Lutheran Almanac for 1867. Baltimore, 1867.

The Lutheran Almanac for 1873. Baltimore, 1873.

The Lutheran Almanac for 1878. Baltimore, 1878.

The Lutheran Almanac for the Year of Our Lord and Saviour Jesus Christ 1851. Baltimore, 1851.

Minutes of the Evangelical Lutheran Tennessee Synod, Held in St. John's Church, Lexington District, S.C., November 9–14, A.D. 1861. Greensborough, NC, 1861.

Minutes of the First Convention of the General Synod of the Evangelical Lutheran Church of the Confederate States of America Held at Concord, N.C., May 20–26, 1863. Columbia, SC, 1864.

Minutes of the Ninth Convention of the General Council of the Evangelical Lutheran Church in America, Held in the Evan. Lutheran Church, Galesburg, Ill., Oct. 7th to 12th, A.D. 1875. Pittsburgh, 1875.

Minutes of the Third Biennial Convention of the United Lutheran Church in America: Buffalo, N.Y., October 17–25, 1922. United Lutheran Publication House, 1922.

Minutes of the Third Convention of the General Synod of the Evangelical Lutheran Church in the Confederate States of America, [. . .] Held at St. John's Church, and at Mount Pleasant, N.C., June 14–18, 1866. Savannah, 1866.

Proceedings of the Convention Held by Representatives from Various Evangelical Lutheran Synods in the United States and Canada Accepting the Unaltered Augsburg Confession, at Reading, Pa., Dec. 12, 13, and 14, A.D. 1866 [. . .]. Pittsburgh, 1867.

Proceedings of the Fortieth Convention of the General Synod of the Evangelical Lutheran Church in the United States of America: In Session at Des Moines, Iowa, May 29 to June 6, 1901. Lutheran Publication Society, 1901.

Proceedings of the Forty-Second Annual Convention of the Evangelical Lutheran Tennessee Synod, Held in Grace Church, Catawba County, North Carolina, From 4th to 7th October, 1862. Greensborough, NC, 1863.

Bibliography

Proceedings of the Forty-Sixth Convention of the General Synod of the Evangelical Lutheran Church in the United States of America in Session at Atchison, Kan. May 14–21, 1913. Lutheran Publication Society, 1913.

Proceedings of the Nineteenth Convention of the General Synod of the Evangelical Lutheran Church in the United States: Assembled in Pittsburg, Pa., From the 19th to the 26th of May, 1859. Gettysburg, 1859.

Proceedings of the One Hundred and Third Annual Session of the German Evangelical Lutheran Ministerium of Pennsylvania and the Adjacent States, Convened in Pottsville, Schuylkill County, Pa., May 26–29, 1850. Philadelphia, 1850.

Proceedings of the Sixth General Synod of the Evan. Luth. Church in the United States: Convened at Frederick, Md., Oct. & Nov. 1831. Schoharie, NY, 1831.

Proceedings of the Thirty-First Convention of the General Synod of the Evangelical Lutheran Church in the United States: Convened in Springfield, O., May 16–22, 1883. Philadelphia, 1883.

Proceedings of the Thirty-Second Convention of the General Synod of the Evangelical Lutheran Church in the United States: Convened in Harrisburg, Pa., May 27–June 2, 1885. Philadelphia, 1885.

Proceedings of the Thirty-Seventh Convention of the General Synod of the Evangelical Lutheran Church in the United States of America: In Session at Hagerstown, Md., June 5–13, 1895. Philadelphia, 1895.

Proceedings of the Thirty-Third Convention of the General Synod of the Evangelical Lutheran Church in the United States of America: In Session at Omaha, Neb., June 1st–13th, 1887. Philadelphia, 1887.

Proceedings of the Twentieth Convention of the General Synod of the Evangelical Lutheran Church in the United States: Assembled in Lancaster, Pa., May, 1862. Gettysburg, 1862.

Proceedings of the Twenty-First Convention of the General Synod of the Evangelical Lutheran Church in the United States: Assembled in York, Pa., May, 1864. Gettysburg, 1864.

Proceedings of the Twenty-Fourth Convention of the General Synod of the Evangelical Lutheran Church in the United States: Assembled in Washington, D.C., May, 1869. Lancaster, PA, 1869.

Proceedings of the Twenty-Second Convention of the General Synod of the Evangelical Lutheran Church in the United States: Assembled in Fort Wayne, Ind., May, 1866. Philadelphia, 1866.

Report of the Transactions of the Evangelical Lutheran Tennessee Synod, During Their Twelfth Session, Held in Buehler's Church, Sullivan County, Tenn. from Monday 12th, to Friday the 16th September, 1831. New Market, VA, 1832.

Sechster Synodal-Bericht der deutschen evangel.-lutherischen Synode von Missouri, Ohio und andern Staaten vom Jahre 1850. St. Louis, [1852].

Sechszehnter Synodal-Bericht der Allgemeinen Deutschen Evang.-Luth. Synode von Missouri, Ohio u. a. Staaten, versammelt als Erster Delegaten-Synode zu Fort Wayne, Ind., im Jahre 1874. St. Louis, 1874.

Sheeleigh, Grace E., ed. *The Lutheran Almanac and Year Book for 1901.* Lutheran Publication Society, 1901.

Bibliography

Verhandlungen der achten Jahresversammlung der Westlichen Districts der deutschen evang.-lutherischen Synode von Missouri, Ohio u. a. Staaten im Jahre 1862. St. Louis, 1862.

Vierter Synodal-Bericht der deutschen evangel.-lutherischen Synode von Missouri, Ohio und andern Staaten vom Jahre 1850. St. Louis, 1851.

Zweiter Synodal-Bericht der deutschen Ev.-Luth. Synode von Missouri, Ohio u. a. Staaten vom Jahre 1848. 2nd ed. St. Louis, 1876.

Other Published Primary Sources

Address of the Hon. Edward Everett at the Consecration of the National Cemetery at Gettysburg, 19th November 1863, with the Dedicatory Speech of President Lincoln, and the Other Exercises of the Occasion [...]. Boston, 1864.

An Address to Christians Throughout the World: By a Convention of Ministers Assembled at Richmond, Va., April, 1863. Philadelphia, 1863.

Anspach, F. R. *A Discourse Pronounced on Sabbath Evening, July 4, 1852, in the Lutheran Church of Hagerstown, on the Death of Henry Clay.* Hagerstown, MD, 1852.

Anstaedt, P. *Loyalty to the Government: A Thanksgiving Sermon Delivered in Selinsgrove, Pa., on the 6th of August 1863.* Selinsgrove, PA, 1863.

[Bachman, Catherine L.]. *John Bachman, D.D., LL.D., Ph.D.: Pastor of St. John's Lutheran Church, Charleston.* Charleston, 1888.

Bachman, John. *An Address Delivered Before the Washington Total Abstinence Society of Charleston, S.C., on Wednesday Evening, July 27th, 1842.* Charleston, 1842.

———. *A Sermon on the Doctrines and Disciplines of the Evangelical Lutheran Church, Preached at Charleston, S.C., November 12th, 1837.* Charleston, 1837.

Baird, Robert. *Religion in the United States of America: Or an Account of the Origin, Progress, Relations to the State, and Present Condition of the Evangelical Churches in the United States* [...]. Glasgow, 1844.

Baseley, Joel R., ed. and trans. *C. F. W. Walther's Original Der Lutheraner Volumes One Through Three (1844–47).* Mark V, 2012.

Baugher, H. L. *The Christian Patriot: A Discourse Address to the Graduating Class of Pennsylvania College, September 15, 1861.* Gettysburg, 1861.

Bell, P. G. *A Portraiture of the Life of Samuel Sprecher D.D., LL.D.* Lutheran Publication Society, 1907.

Bente, Josephine. *Biography of Dr. Friedrich Bente.* Concordia, 1936.

Bittle, David F. *A Plea for Female Education.* Hagerstown, MD, 1852.

———. *Remarks on New Measures.* Staunton, VA, 1839.

Braaten, Carl E. *Because of Christ: Memoirs of a Lutheran Theologian.* William B. Eerdmans, 2010.

Breidenbaugh, E. S., ed. *The Pennsylvania College Book, 1832–1882.* Philadelphia, 1882.

Brockmann, J. H. *Christian und Ernst: Eine Besprechung über die Lehre der Odd-Fellows oder Sonderbaren Brüder auf Grundlage heiliger Schrift* [...]. St. Louis, 1872.

Brown, J. A. *The New Theology: Its Abettors and Defenders.* Philadelphia, 1857.

Buck, Charles. *A Theological Dictionary, Containing Definitions of All Religious Terms; a Comprehensive View of Every Article in the System of Divinity; an Impartial Account of All the Principal Denominations* [. . .]. Philadelphia, 1830.

Bureau of the Census. *Religious Bodies: 1906, Part 1: Summary and General Tables.* Government Printing Office, 1910.

Butler, J[ohn] Geo. *Courageous Thankfulness: Twentieth Pastoral Anniversary, July 4, 1869, St. Paul's Lutheran Church, Washington, D.C.* Washington, DC, 1869.

———. *God's Work—Our Ebenezer: Eighteenth Anniversary of the Pastorate of J. George Butler, of St. Paul's Lutheran Church, Washington, D.C., July 7, 1867.* Washington, DC, 1867.

———. *The Martyr President: Our Grief and Duty.* Washington, DC, 1865.

Carroll, H[enry] K. *The Religious Forces of the United States: Enumerated, Classified, and Described on the Basis of the Government Census of 1890.* New York, 1893.

Clausen, C. L. *Gjenmæle mod Kirkeraadet for den Norske Synode: i Anledning af dets Skrift, kaldet: "Historisk fremstilling af den Strid som i Aarene 1861 til 1868 inden for den Norske Synode i Amerika har været ført i Anledning af Skriftens Lære om Slaveri."* Chicago, 1869.

———. *Reply to the Church Council of the Norwegian Synod.* Translated by John R. Nielsen. Concordia Seminary, 1952.

Conrad, F[rederick] W. *America's Blessings and Obligations: A Discourse Delivered in Trinity Lutheran Church, Lancaster, Pa., on the Day of National Thanksgiving, November 26, 1863.* Lancaster, 1863.

———. *Ministers of the Gospel, the Moral Watchmen of the Nation: A Discourse Delivered in the English Lutheran Church, Chambersburg, Pa.* Gettysburg, 1865.

———. *The War for the Unity and Life of the American Union: A Thanksgiving Discourse, May 15, 1864.* Chambersburg, PA, 1864.

Definite Platform, Doctrinal and Disciplinarian, for Evangelical Lutheran District Synods: Construed in Accordance with the Principles of the General Synod. Philadelphia, 1855.

DeGarmeaux, Mark, ed. and trans. *U. V. Koren's Works.* 4 vols. Lutheran Synod Book Company, 2013–2017.

Diehl, M. *Biography of Rev. Ezra Keller, D.D., Founder and First President of Wittenberg College.* Springfield, OH, 1859.

Dreher, Daniel I. *A Sermon Delivered* [. . .] *June 13, 1861: Day of Humiliation and Prayer as per Appointment of the President of the Confederate States of America.* Salisbury, NC, 1861.

Ehrehart, Charles J. *A Discourse Delivered in St. Peter's Evan. Lutheran Church, Middletown, Pa.: On Thanksgiving Day, November 27, 1862.* Lancaster, PA, 1862.

Ferm, Vergilius, ed. *What is Lutheranism? A Symposium in Interpretation.* Macmillan, 1930.

Focht, D. H. *Our Country: Two Sermons, etc.* Gettysburg, 1862.

Fry, Jacob. *Trembling for the Ark of God: or, the Danger and Duty of the Church in the Present Crisis: A Sermon Preached in the First Lutheran Church, Carlisle, Pa. on Sunday Evening, Dec. 30, 1860.* Carlisle, PA, 1861.

Fürbringer, L., ed. *Briefe von C. F. W. Walther an seine Freunde, Synodalgenossen und Familienglieder.* 2 vols. Concordia, 1915–1916.

Bibliography

Gerberding, G. H. *The Life and Letters of W. A. Passavant, D.D.* Young Lutheran, 1906.

Giustiniani, L. *Papal Rome, As It Is, by a Roman.* Baltimore, 1843.

[Gotwald, Luther A.] *Trial of Luther A. Gotwald., D.D., Professor of Practical Theology in Wittenberg Theological Seminary, Springfield, Ohio, April 4th and 5th, 1893, upon Charges of Disloyalty to the Doctrinal Basis of Said Theological Seminary.* Philadelphia, 1893.

Graebner, Theodore. *Dr. Francis Pieper: A Biographical Sketch.* Concordia, 1931.

Greenwald, E[mmanuel]. *The True Church: Its Way of Justification; and Its Holy Communion: In Three Discourses.* Philadelphia, 1876.

Gruber, J. L. *Erinnerungen an Professor C. F .W. Walther und seine Zeit: Zum Druck befördert durch seine Kinder.* Lutheran Literary Board, 1930.

Grundmeier, Timothy D., ed. "American Lutherans and Their Divisions, by H. K. Carroll." *Journal of the Lutheran Historical Conference* 7 (2019): 83–109.

Hanser, Carl Johann Otto. *Irrfahrten und Heimfahrten: Erinnerungen aus meinem Leben.* Lutheran Publishing Company, 1910.

Harkey, Simeon W. *The Church's Best State; or Constant Revivals of Religion.* Baltimore, 1842.

———. *The Mission of the General Synod: A Sermon Delivered in the English Evangelical Lutheran Church, Pittsburg, Pa., May 19, 1859, at the Opening of the Nineteenth Convention of the General Synod of the Evangelical Lutheran Church in the United States.* Philadelphia, 1859.

———. *The Mission of the Lutheran Church in America: Being an Address Delivered in the First Presbyterian Church of Springfield, Illinois, on Sabbath Evening, November 14th, 1852, upon the Occasion of the Inauguration of the Author as Professor of Theology in "Illinois State University."* Springfield, 1853.

Harrison, Matthew C., ed. *At Home in the House of My Fathers: Presidential Sermons, Essays, Letters, and Addresses from the Missouri Synod's Great Era of Unity and Growth.* Concordia, 2011.

Hastvedt, Knudt Olson. "Recollections of a Norwegian Pioneer in Texas." Edited and translated by C. A. Clausen. *Norwegian-American Studies and Records* 12 (1941): 91–104.

Hedrick, David T., and Gordon Barry Davis Jr., eds. *I'm Surrounded by Methodists: Diary of John H. W. Stuckenberg, Chaplain of the 145th Pennsylvania Volunteer Infantry.* Thomas, 1995.

Helmke, John E., ed. and trans. "Was American Slavery a Sinful Institution?" *Concordia Historical Institute Quarterly* 72, no. 4 (Winter 1999): 231–50.

Henkel, David. *Carolinian Herald of Liberty, Religious and Political.* Salisbury, NC, 1821.

Historisk Fremstilling af den Strid, som i Aarene 1861 til 1868 indenfor den norske Synode i Amerika har været ført i Anledning af Skriftens Läre om Slaveri [. . .]. Madison, 1868.

Hoffman, John N. *The Broken Platform: or, A Brief Defence of Our Symbolical Books Against Recent Charges of Alleged Errors.* Philadelphia, 1856.

Hutter, Leonard. *Compend of Lutheran Theology: A Summary of Christian Doctrine, Derived from the Work of God and the Symbolical Books of the Evangelical Lutheran Church.* Translated by H. E. Jacobs and G. F. Spieker. Philadelphia, 1868.

Imhoff, Alex J. *The Life of Rev. Morris Officer, A.M.* Dayton, OH, 1876.

Jacobs, Henry E[yster]. *The Book of Concord; or, the Symbolical Books of the Evangelical Lutheran Church* [. . .]. 2 vols. Philadelphia, 1882, 1888.

———. *A History of the Evangelical Lutheran Church in the United States.* New York, 1893.

Jensson, J. C., ed. *American Lutheran Biographies, or Historical Notices of Over Three Hundred and Fifty Leading Men of the American Lutheran Church, from its Establishment to the Year 1890.* Milwaukee, 1890.

Johnston, E. S. *Sermon Delivered on Thursday, June 1st, 1865, the Day of Special Humiliation and Prayer in Consequence of the Assassination of Abraham Lincoln.* Harrisburg, PA, 1865.

Kamphoefner, Walter D., and Wolfgang Helbich, eds. *Germans in the Civil War: The Letters They Wrote Home.* Translated by Susan Carter Vogel. University of North Carolina Press, 2006.

Knortz, Karl. *Gustav Seyffarth: Eine Biographische Skizze.* New York, 1886.

Kolb, Robert, ed. and trans. "C. F. W. Walther to A. F. Hoppe: A Letter." *Concordia Historical Institute Quarterly* 42, no. 3 (May 1969): 79–84.

Koren, Paul, ed. *Samlede Skrifter af Dr. Theol. V. Koren.* 4 vols. Lutheran Publishing House Bogtrykkeri, 1911–1912.

Krauth, C[harles] P[hilip]. *Address Delivered on the Anniversary of Washington's Birth-day, at the Request of the Union Abstinence Society of Gettysburg.* Gettysburg, 1846.

Krauth, Charles Porterfield. *The Altar on the Threshing-Floor: A Discourse Delivered in the First Eng. Evan. Lutheran Church, Pittsburgh, Pa. on Thanksgiving Day, Nov. 26, 1857.* Pittsburgh, 1857.

———. *The Bible a Perfect Book: An Address Delivered Before the Bible Society of Pennsylvania College and of the Theological Seminary, April 13, 1852.* 2nd ed. Gettysburg, 1857.

———. *Caesar and God; or, Politics and Religion. A Sermon.* Philadelphia, 1874.

———. *Christian Liberty in its Relation to the Usages of the Evangelical Lutheran Church: The Substance of Two Sermons Delivered in St. Mark's Evangelical Lutheran Church, Philadelphia, Sunday, March 25th, 1860.* Philadelphia, 1860.

———. *The Conservative Reformation and Its Theology: As Represented in the Augsburg Confession, and in the History and Literature of the Evangelical Lutheran Church.* Philadelphia, 1871.

———. *Theses on the Galesburg Declaration on Pulpit and Altar Fellowship, Prepared by Order of the General Council.* Philadelphia, 1877.

———. *The Two Pageants: A Discourse Delivered in the First Eng. Evan. Lutheran Church, Pittsburgh, Pa. Thursday, June 1st, 1865.* Pittsburgh, 1865.

Kurtz, B[enjamin]. *Experimental (Not Ritual) Religion, the One Thing Needful: A Sermon Delivered in Newville, Pa., Before the West Pennsylvania Synod, September 18th, 1863.* Baltimore, 1863.

———. *Why Are You a Lutheran? or a Series of Dissertations, Explanatory of the Doctrines, Government, Discipline, Liturgical Economy, Distinctive Traits, &c., of the Evangelical Lutheran Church in the United States.* Baltimore, 1843.

Bibliography

Lewis, Alfred Henry, ed. *A Compilation of the Messages and Speeches of Theodore Roosevelt, 1901–1905*. Bureau of National Literature and Art, 1906.

Lindemann, J. C. W. *Astronomische Unterredung zwischen einem Liebhaber der Astronomie und mehreren berühmten Astronomen der Neuzeit, worin deutliche Auskunst gegeben wird über die Untrüglichkeit des Kopernikanischen Sonnen-Systems*. St. Louis, 1873.

———. *Fredrich Konrad Dietrich Wyneken: An Evangelist Among the Lutherans of North America*. Edited by Adriane Dorn, Marvin Huggins, and Robert E. Smith. Translated by Sieghart Reim. Concordia Theological Seminary Press, 2010.

Loy, M[atthias]. *The Fallacy of Liberalism*. Columbus, 1883.

———. *The Story of My Life*. Lutheran Book Concern, 1905.

Mann, W. J. *Lutheranism in America: An Essay on the Present Condition of the Lutheran Church in the United States*. Philadelphia, 1857.

———. *A Plea for the Augsburg Confession, in Answer to the Objections of the Definite Platform: An Address to All Ministers and Laymen of the Evangelical Church of the United States*. Philadelphia, 1856.

Mechling, George Washington. *History of the Evangelical Lutheran District Synod of Ohio: Covering Fifty-Three Years, 1857–1910*. Dayton, OH, 1911.

Merriam, William R., ed. *Twelfth Census of the United States, Taken in the Year 1900*. United States Census Office, 1901.

Meyer, Carl S., ed. and trans. *Letters of C. F. W. Walther: A Selection*. Fortress Press, 1969.

———, ed. *Moving Frontiers: Readings in the History of the Lutheran Church—Missouri Synod*. Concordia, 1964.

———, ed. and trans. "Walther's Letter from Zurich: A Defense of Missouri's Unity and Confessionalism." *Concordia Theological Monthly* 32, no. 10 (October 1961): 642–55.

Morris, John G. *Bibliotheca Lutherana: A Complete List of the Publications of all the Lutheran Ministers in the United States*. Philadelphia, 1876.

Nevin, J[ohn] W[illiamson]. *The Anxious Bench*. Chambersburg, PA, 1843.

———. *Die Angstbank*. Translated by A. B. Bierdemann. Canton, OH, 1844.

Niebuhr, H. Richard. *The Social Sources of Denominationalism*. Henry Holt, 1929.

Oehlschlaeger, C. J., *The Evangelical Lutheran Church: The True Visible Church of God on Earth*. Columbus, 1880.

Pieper, F[rancis]. *Unsere Stellung in Lehre und Praxis: Vortrag geholten von der Delegatensynode 1893 der Synode von Missouri, Ohio und anderen Staaten*. St. Louis, 1896.

Polack, W. G., trans. "Our First Synodical Constitution." *Concordia Historical Institute Quarterly* 16, no. 1 (April 1943): 1–18.

Preus, Herman Amberg. *Vivacious Daughter: Seven Lectures on the Religious Situation Among Norwegians in America*. Edited and translated by Todd W. Nichol. Norwegian-American Historical Association, 1990.

Reden, gehalten einer Versammlung der mit der Missouri-Synode verbundenen lutherischen Gemeinden Chicagos im Art Institute am 3. September 1893. St. Louis, 1893.

Rein, Sieghart, trans. "The Christian and Politics." *Concordia Historical Institute Quarterly* 84, no. 2 (Summer 2011): 119–22.

Bibliography

Rhodes, M. *A Sermon on the Occasion of the Assassination of Abraham Lincoln, Late President of the United States, Delivered on Wednesday, April 19, 1865* [...]. *in the Evangelical Lutheran Church, Sunbury, Penn'a.* Sunbury, 1865.

Sadtler, B. *A Rebellious Nation Reproved: A Sermon* [...] *on the Day of Humiliation, Fasting and Prayer, September 26, 1861.* Easton, PA, 1861.

Sandt, George W. *Theodore Emanuel Schmauk, D.D., L.L.D.: A Biographical Sketch with Liberal Quotations from his Letters and other Writings.* United Lutheran Publication House, 1921.

Schaff, Philip. *America: A Sketch of the Political, Social, and Religious Character of the United States of North America* [...]. New York, 1855.

———. *Amerika: Die politischen, socialen und kirchlich-religiösen Zustände der Vereinigten Staaten von Nordamerika* [...]. Berlin, 1854.

Schmauk, Theodore E. *The Negative Criticism and the Old Testament: An All Around Survey of the Negative Criticism from the Orthodox Point of View* [...]. Lebanon, PA, 1894.

Schmid, Heinrich. *The Doctrinal Theology of the Evangelical Lutheran Church, Exhibited, and Verified from the Original Sources.* Translated by Charles A. Hay and Henry E[yster] Jacobs. Philadelphia, 1876.

Schmucker, S[amuel] S[imon]. *The American Lutheran Church, Historically, Doctrinally, and Practically Delineated, in Several Occasional Discourses.* Springfield, OH, 1851.

———. *American Lutheranism Vindicated; or, Examination of the Lutheran Symbols, on Certain Disputed Topics.* Baltimore, 1856.

———. *Appeal in Behalf of the Christian Sabbath.* New York, [1845].

———. *Appeal to the Churches, with a Plan for Catholic Union.* New York, 1838.

———. *The Christian Pulpit, the Rightful Guardian of Morals, in Political No Less than in Private Life: A Discourse Delivered at Gettysburg, Oct. 26, the Day Appointed by the Governor, for Public Humiliation, Thanksgiving and Prayer.* Gettysburg, 1846.

———. *A Discourse in Commemoration of the Glorious Reformation of the Sixteenth Century, with a Reference to the Relation Between the Principles of Popery and our Republican Institutions: Delivered Before the Evangelical Lutheran Synod of West Pennsylvania.* New York, 1838.

———. *Elements of Popular Theology, with Special Reference to the Doctrines of the Reformation, as Avowed Before the Diet at Augsburg, in MDXXX.* Andover, MA, 1834.

———. *Elements of Popular Theology, with Special Reference to the Doctrines of the Reformation, as Avowed Before the Diet at Augsburg, in MDXXX.* 5th ed. Philadelphia, 1846.

———. *Elements of Popular Theology, with Special Reference to the Doctrines of the Reformation, as Avowed Before the Diet at Augsburg, in MDXXX.* 9th ed. Philadelphia, 1860.

———. *Fraternal Appeal to the American Churches, with a Plan for Catholic Union, on Apostolic Principles.* New York, 1839.

———. *Fraternal Appeal to the American Churches: With a Plan for Catholic Union on Apostolic Principles.* 1839. Edited by Frederick K. Wentz. Reprint, Fortress Press, 1965.

———. *The Happy Adaptation of the Sabbath-School System to the Peculiar Wants of Our Age and Country: A Sermon, Preached at the Request of the Board of Managers of the American Sunday School Union, Philadelphia, May 20th, 1839.* Philadelphia, 1839.

———. *The Intellectual and Moral Glories of the Christian Temple: Illustrated from the History of the Evangelical Lutheran Church: A Synodical Discourse.* Baltimore, 1824.

———. *Rev. J. A. Brown's New Theology: Examined.* Gettysburg, 1857.

———. *Sermon on the Work of Grace, or Revival of Religion at Antioch, Preached in the Evangelical Lutheran Church, in Hanover, Pa., January 6th, 1862.* York, PA, 1862.

———. *The True Unity of Christ's Church: Being a Renewed Appeal to the Friends of the Redeemer, on Primitive Christian Union, and the History of its Corruption.* New York, 1870.

Seiss, Joseph A. *The Assassinated President, on the Day of National Mourning for Abraham Lincoln, at St. John's (Lutheran) Church, Philadelphia, June 1st, 1865.* Philadelphia, 1865.

———. *The Christ and His Church: Some Occasional, Special, and Other Sermons.* Board of Publication of the General Council, 1902.

———. *The Claims of Sabbath Schools: An Address Delivered in the M.E. Church to the Sunday School Union Society of Cumberland, on the Evening of January 21st, 1850.* Cumberland, MD, 1850.

———. *Ecclesia Lutherana: A Brief Survey of the Evangelical Lutheran Church.* 4th ed. Philadelphia, 1871.

———. *Government and Christianity: A Sermon for the Times.* Philadelphia, 1861.

———. *Moses and the Higher Criticism: A Sermon, Preached at the Meeting of the Ministerium of Pennsylvania in St. John's Church, Allenstown, May 31, 1896.* Philadelphia, 1896.

———. *The Ravages of Intemperance: An Address Delivered at the Grand Temperance Rally in Shepherdstown, Va., February 22, 1845.* Baltimore, 1845.

Seyffarth, Gustavus. *Literary Life of Gustavus Seyffarth: An Auto-Biographical Sketch.* New York, 1886.

Sieker, J. H. *Die Gesegnete Wirksamkeit der treulutherischen Kirche unseres Landes.* New York, 1883.

Sihler, W[ilhelm]. *Die Sklaverei im Lichte der Heiligen Schrift betrachtet.* Baltimore, 1863.

———. *Gedanken eines Lutheraners bei dem Herannahen der 100jährigen Gedächtnissfeier des Bestehens des Nordamerikanischen Staatenbundes.* St. Louis, 1876.

———. *Lebenslauf von W. Sihler bis zu seiner Ankunft in New York.* St. Louis, 1879.

———. *Wider das Gewohnheits-Trinken: Epheser 5,18: Eine lutherische Lehr-, Straf- und Lockpredigt.* St. Louis, 1882.

Smith, Chas. Adam. *The Ground of National Consolation and Hope: A Sermon Occasioned by the Death of Zachary Taylor, [...] Delivered in the Third Lutheran Church of Rhinebeck, Sabbath Morning, July 21, 1850.* Albany, 1850.

Solberg, Carl Fredrik. "Reminiscences of a Pioneer Editor." Edited by Albert O. Barton. *Norwegian-American Studies and Records* 1 (1926): 110–25.

Spaeth, Adolph. *Charles Porterfield Krauth.* Vol. 1, *1823–1859.* New York, 1898.

———. *Charles Porterfield Krauth.* Vol. 2, *1859–1883.* General Council Publication House, 1909.

———. *The General Council of the Evangelical Lutheran Church in North America.* Philadelphia, 1885.

Sprecher, Samuel. *The Apostolic Method of Realizing the True Ideal of the Church: A Sermon*

Delivered at the Opening of the General Synod of the Evangelical Lutheran Church in the United States, at Fort Wayne, Indiana, May 17th, 1866. Baltimore, 1866.

———. *The Groundwork of a System of Evangelical Lutheran Theology.* Philadelphia, 1879.

———. *The Providential Position of the Evangelical Church of This Country, at This Time: A Sermon Delivered at the Opening of the General Synod, at York, Pennsylvania, May Fifth, 1864.* Selinsgrove, PA, 1864.

Stange, Douglas C., ed. "Document: Bishop Daniel Alexander Payne's Protestation of American Slavery." *Journal of Negro History* 52, no. 1 (January 1967): 59–64.

———, ed. "Dr. Samuel Simon Schmucker and the Inculcation of Moderate Abolitionism." *Concordia Historical Institute Quarterly* 40, no. 2 (July 1967): 78–83.

———, ed. "The One Hundred and Twenty-Fifth Anniversary of a Fraternal Appeal." *Concordia Historical Institute Quarterly* 40, no. 1 (April 1967): 43–48.

Sternberg, L[evi]. *The Lord's Supper.* Baltimore, 1864.

Strong, Josiah. *Our Country: Its Possible Future and Its Present Crisis.* New York, 1885.

Stuckenberg, J[ohn] H. W. *Greetings from the Fatherland.* Dayton, OH, 1892.

———. *Ninety-Five Theses, for the Seventh Semi-Centennial Jubilee of the Reformation: With Notes and Appendix.* Baltimore, 1868.

———. *Orthodox Lutheranism in Germany and the Confessional Position of the General Synod of the Evangelical Lutheran Church in the United States [...].* Dayton, OH, 1892.

Suelflow, August R., ed. and trans. "Nietzsche and Schaff on American Lutheranism." *Concordia Historical Institute Quarterly* 23, no. 4 (January 1951): 145-58.

———, ed. *Selected Writings of C. F. W. Walther: Editorials from "Lehre und Wehre."* Translated by Herbert J. A. Bouman. Concordia, 1981.

———, ed. *Selected Writings of C. F. W. Walther: Selected Letters.* Translated by Roy A. Suelflow. Concordia, 1981.

Suelflow, Roy A., ed. and trans. *Correspondence of C. F. W. Walther.* Concordia Seminary, 1980.

Tappert, Theodore G., ed. "Intercommunion in 1866." *Concordia Historical Institute Quarterly* 40, no. 1 (April 1967): 42.

———, ed. *Lutheran Confessional Theology in America, 1840–1880.* Oxford University Press, 1972.

Trauger, J. L. *True Temperance in the Light of God's Word.* St. Louis, 1880.

Valentine, M[ilton]. "The General Synod." In *The Distinctive Doctrines and Usages of the General Bodies of the Evangelical Lutheran Church in the United States,* 34–61. Philadelphia, 1895.

Van Alstine, N[icholas]. *Thanksgiving Sermon: A Specific Remedy for National Calamities; Preached in the Evangelic Lutheran Church of Minden, Montgomery Country, N.Y., November 28, 1861.* Albany, 1862.

Walther, C. F. W. *Amerikanisch-Lutherische Epistel Postille: Predigten über die meisten epistolischen Perikopen des Kirchenjahrs u. freie Texte.* St. Louis, 1882.

———. *Antwort auf die Frage: Warum sind die symbolischen Bücher unserer Kirche von denen, welcher Diener derselben werden wollen, unbedingt zu unterscheiben?* St. Louis, 1858.

———. *Casual-Predigten und -Reden.* St. Louis, 1889.

———. *The Church and the Office of the Ministry.* Edited by Matthew C. Harrison. Translated by John Theodore Mueller. Concordia, 2012.

———. *Communism and Socialism: Minutes of the First German Evangelical Lutheran Congregation U. A. C. at St. Louis, Mo.* Translated by D. Simon. St. Louis, 1879.

———. *Communismus und Socialismus: Verhandlungen der ersten deutschen evang.-luth. gemeinde U. A. C. zu St. Louis, Mo.* St. Louis, 1878.

———. *Die evangelisch-lutherische Kirche, die wahre sichtbare Kirche Gottes auf Erden: Ein Referat für die Verhandlungen der Allgemeinen Evangelisch-Lutherischen Synode von Missouri, Ohio u. a. Staaten bei Gelegenheit der Sitzungen derselben zu St. Louis, Mo., den 31. October 1866 und folgende Tage.* St. Louis, 1867.

———. *Die Stimme unserer Kirche in der Frage von Kirche und Amt.* Erlangen, 1852.

———. *Essays for the Church.* 2 vols. Edited by Aug[ust] R. Suelflow. Concordia, 1992.

———. *From Our Master's Table.* Translated by Joel R. Baseley. Mark V, 2008.

———. *Lutherische Brosamen: Predigten und Reden, seit 1847 theils Pamphletform, theils in Zeitschriften bereits erschienen, in Sammelband aufs Neue dargeboten.* St. Louis, 1876.

———. *Occasional Sermons and Addresses.* Translated by Joel R. Baseley. Mark V, 2008.

———. *Standard Epistles.* Translated by Donald E. Heck. Concordia Theological Seminary Press, 1986.

———. *The True Visible Church: An Essay for the Convention of the General Evangelical Lutheran Synod of Missouri, Ohio, and Other States, for its Sessions at St. Louis, Mo., October 31, 1866.* Translated by John Theodore Mueller. Concordia, 1963.

———. *Walther's Works: All Glory to God.* Edited by John C. Wohlrabe Jr. Concordia, 2016.

Weiser, R. *The Mourner's Bench: or, an Humble Attempt to Vindicate New Measures.* 1844.

Williams, J. T. *Sermon Delivered in the Lutheran Churches of the Blain Charge, on the National Fast-Day, September 26th, 1861.* Gettysburg, 1861.

Wyneken, Fr[iedrich]. *Die Noth der deutschen Lutheraner in Nordamerika: Ihren Glaubensgenossen in der Heimat ans Herz gelegt.* Erlangen, 1843.

———. *The Distress of the German Lutherans in North America: Laid upon the Hearts of the Brethren in the Faith in the Home Country.* Edited by R. F. Rehmer. Translated by S. Edgar Schmidt. Concordia Theological Seminary Press, 1986.

SECONDARY SOURCES

Books

Aamodt, Terrie Dopp. *Righteous Armies, Holy Cause: Apocalyptic Imagery and the Civil War.* Mercer University Press, 2002.

Ahlstrom, Sydney E. *A Religious History of the American People.* Yale University Press, 1972.

Allbeck, Willard D. *A Century of Lutherans in Ohio.* Antioch Press, 1966.

Anbinder, Tyler. *Nativism and Slavery: The Northern Know Nothings and the Politics of the 1850s.* Oxford University Press, 1992.

Ander, O. Fritiof. *T. N. Hasselquist: The Career and Influence of a Swedish-American Clergyman, Journalist and Educator.* Augustana Book Concern, 1931.

Bibliography

Andersen, Arlow W. *The Immigrant Takes His Stand: The Norwegian-American Press and Public Affairs, 1847–1872*. Norwegian-American Historical Association, 1953.

———. *Rough Road to Glory: The Norwegian-American Press Speaks Out on Public Affairs, 1875 to 1925*. Balch Institute Press, 1990.

Anderson, H. George. *Lutheranism in the Southeastern States, 1860–1886: A Social History*. Mouton, 1969.

Anderson, Kristen Layne. *Abolitionizing Missouri: German Immigrants and Racial Ideology in Nineteenth-Century America*. Louisiana State University Press, 2016.

Arand, Charles P. *Testing the Boundaries: Windows to Lutheran Identity*. Concordia, 1995.

Archdeacon, Thomas J. *Becoming American: An Ethnic History*. Free Press, 1983.

Armstrong, Warren B. *For Courageous Fighting and Confident Dying: Union Chaplains in the Civil War*. University Press of Kansas, 1998.

Ayers, Edward L. *The Thin Light of Freedom: The Civil War and Emancipation in the Heart of America*. W. W. Norton, 2017.

Baer, Friederike. *The Trial of Frederick Eberle: Language, Patriotism, and Citizenship in Philadelphia's German Community, 1790 to 1830*. New York University Press, 2008.

Barton, H. Arnold. *A Folk Divided: Homeland Swedes and Swedish Americans, 1840–1940*. Southern Illinois University Press, 1994.

Beck, Walter H. *Lutheran Elementary Schools in the United States: A History of the Development of Parochial Schools and Synodical Educational Policies and Programs*. Concordia, 1939.

Blanck, Dag. *The Creation of an Ethnic Identity: Being Swedish American in the Augustana Synod, 1860–1917*. Southern Illinois University Press, 2006.

Blegen, Theodore C. *Norwegian Migration to America*. 2 vols. Norwegian-American Historical Association, 1931–1940.

Blight, David W. *Race and Reunion: The Civil War in American Memory*. Belknap Press of Harvard University Press, 2001.

Blum, Edward J. *Reforging the White Republic: Race, Religion, and American Nationalism, 1865–1898*. Louisiana State University Press, 2005.

Braun, Mark E. *A Tale of Two Synods: Events That Led to the Split Between Wisconsin and Missouri*. Northwestern Publishing House, 2003.

Brekus, Catherine A. *Strangers & Pilgrims: Female Preaching in America, 1740–1845*. University of North Carolina Press, 1998.

Brodrecht, Grant R. *Our Country: Northern Evangelicals and the Union During the Civil War Era*. Fordham University Press, 2018.

Brøndal, Jorn. *Ethnic Leadership and Midwestern Politics: Scandinavian Americans and the Progressive Movement in Wisconsin, 1890–1914*. Norwegian-American Historical Association, 2004.

Brown, Candy Gunther. *The Word in the World: Evangelical Publishing, Writing, and Reading in America, 1789–1880*. University of North Carolina Press, 2004.

Burkee, James C. *Power Politics and the Missouri Synod: A Conflict that Changed American Christianity*. Fortress Press, 2011.

Burton, Orville Vernon. *The Age of Lincoln*. Hill and Wang, 2007.

Bibliography

Butler, Jon. *Awash in a Sea of Faith: Christianizing the American People.* Harvard University Press, 1990.

Byrd, James P. *A Holy Baptism of Fire and Blood: The Bible and the American Civil War.* Oxford University Press, 2021.

Carwardine, Richard. *Evangelicals and Politics in Antebellum America.* Yale University Press, 1993.

———. *Righteous Strife: How Warring Religious Nationalists Forged Lincoln's Union.* Alfred A. Knopf, 2025.

Chesebrough, David B. *No Sorrow Like Our Sorrow: Northern Protestant Ministers and the Assassination of Abraham Lincoln.* Kent State University Press, 1994.

Cirillo, Frank J. *The Abolitionist Civil War: Immediatists and the Struggle to Transform the Union.* Louisiana State University Press, 2023.

Coburn, Carol K. *Life at Four Corners: Religion, Gender, and Education in a German-Lutheran Community, 1868–1945.* University of Kansas Press, 1992.

Coffman, Elesha J. *Turning Points in American Church History: How Pivotal Events Shaped a Nation and a Faith.* Baker Academic, 2024.

Conkin, Paul K. *American Originals: Homemade Varieties of Christianity.* University of North Carolina Press, 1997.

Conser, Walter H. *Church and Confession: Conservative Theologians in Germany, England, and America, 1815–1866.* Mercer University Press, 1984.

Conzen, Kathleen Neils. *Making Their Own America: Assimilation Theory and the German Peasant Pioneer.* Berg, 1990.

Cross, Whitney R. *The Burned-over District: The Social and Intellectual History of Enthusiastic Religion in Western New York, 1800–1850.* Cornell University Press, 1982.

Curran, Robert Emmett. *American Catholics and the Quest for Equality in the Civil War Era.* Louisiana State University Press, 2023.

Curtis, Susan. *A Consuming Faith: The Social Gospel and Modern American Culture.* Johns Hopkins University Press, 1991.

Daly, John Patrick. *When Slavery Was Called Freedom: Evangelicalism, Proslavery, and the Causes of the Civil War.* University Press of Kentucky, 2002.

Daniels, Roger. *Coming to America: A History of Immigration and Ethnicity in American Life.* 2nd ed. HarperPerennial, 2002.

Dickinson, Richard C. *Roses and Thorns: The Centennial Edition of Black Lutheran Mission and Ministry in the Lutheran Church—Missouri Synod.* Concordia, 1977.

Dolan, Jay P. *In Search of an American Catholicism: A History of Religion and Culture in Tension.* Oxford University Press, 2002.

Dörfler-Dierken, Angelika. *Luthertum und Demokratie: Deutsche und amerikanische Theologen des 19. Jahrhunderts zu Staat, Gesellschaft, und Kirche.* Vandenhoeck & Ruprecht, 2001.

Dorrien, Gary J. *The Making of American Liberal Theology: Imagining Progressive Religion, 1805–1900.* Westminster John Knox Press, 2001.

Dorsey, Bruce. *Reforming Men and Women: Gender in the Antebellum City.* Cornell University Press, 2002.

Bibliography

Dubbs, Joseph Henry. *History of Franklin and Marshall College*. Franklin and Marshall College Alumni Association, 1903.

Edwards, Rebecca. *New Spirits: Americans in the Gilded Age, 1865–1905*. 3rd ed. Oxford University Press, 2015.

Efford, Alison Clark. *German Immigrants, Race, and Citizenship in the Civil War Era*. Cambridge University Press, 2013.

Ellis, David L. *Politics and Piety: The Protestant Awakening in Prussia, 1816–1856*. Brill, 2017.

Erling, Maria, and Mark Granquist. *The Augustana Story: Shaping Lutheran Identity in North America*. Augsburg Fortress, 2008.

Escott, Paul D. *The Worst Passions of Human Nature: White Supremacy in the Civil War North*. University of Virginia Press, 2020.

Evans, Christopher H. *Histories of American Christianity: An Introduction*. Baylor University Press, 2013.

———. *The Social Gospel in American Religion*. New York University Press, 2017.

Evjen, John O. *The Life of J. H. W. Stuckenberg: Theologian, Philosopher, Sociologist, Friend of Humanity*. Lutheran Free Church, 1938.

Farrelly, Maura Jane. *Anti-Catholicism in America, 1620–1860*. Cambridge University Press, 2018.

Faust, Drew Gilpin. *This Republic of Suffering: Death and the American Civil War*. Alfred A. Knopf, 2008.

Ferm, Vergilius. *The Crisis in American Lutheran Theology: A Study of the Issue Between American Lutheranism and Old Lutheranism*. Century, 1927.

Fields, Barbara Jeanne. *Slavery and Freedom on the Middle Ground: Maryland During the Nineteenth Century*. Yale University Press, 1985.

Finke, Roger, and Rodney Stark. *The Churching of America: Winners and Losers in Our Religious Economy, 1776–2005*. Rutgers University Press, 2005.

Foner, Eric. *Reconstruction: America's Unfinished Revolution, 1863–1877*. Harper and Row, 1988.

Ford, Bridget. *Bonds of Union: Religion, Race, and Politics in a Civil War Borderland*. University of North Carolina Press, 2016.

Ford, Lacy K. *Deliver Us from Evil: The Slavery Question in the Old South*. Oxford University Press, 2009.

Forster, Walter O., *Zion on the Mississippi: The Settlement of the Saxon Lutherans in Missouri, 1839–1841*. Concordia, 1953.

Foster, Gaines M. *Moral Reconstruction: Christian Lobbyists and the Federal Legislation of Morality, 1865–1920*. University of North Carolina Press, 2002.

Fritschel, Herman L. *A Story of One Hundred Years of Deaconess Service by the Institution of Protestant Deaconesses Pennsylvania, and the Lutheran Deaconess Motherhouse at Milwaukee, Wisconsin, 1849 to 1949*. Lutheran Deaconess Motherhouse, 1949.

Furniss, Jack. *Between Extremes: Seeking the Political Center in the Civil War North*. Louisiana State University Press, 2024.

Bibliography

Gäbler, Ulrich, ed. *Geschichte des Pietismus.* Vol. 3, *Der Pietismus in neunzehnten und zwanzigsten Jahrhundert.* Vandenhoeck & Ruprecht, 2000.

Gallagher, Gary W. *The Union War.* Harvard University Press, 2011.

Gallman, J. Matthew. *Mastering Wartime: A Social History of Philadelphia During the Civil War.* Cambridge University Press, 1990.

Gaustad, Edwin Scott, and Philip L. Barlow. *New Historical Atlas of Religion in America.* Oxford University Press, 2001.

Geiger, Erika. *The Life, Work, and Influence of Wilhelm Loehe 1808–1872.* Translated by Wolf Knappe. Concordia, 2010.

Genovese, Eugene, and Elizabeth Fox-Genovese. *Fatal Self-Deception: Slaveholding Paternalism in the Old South.* Cambridge University Press, 2011.

Gienapp, William E. *The Origins of the Republican Party, 1852–1856.* Oxford University Press, 1987.

Gillette, William. *Retreat from Reconstruction, 1869–1879.* Louisiana State University Press, 1982.

Gin Lum, Kathryn. *Heathen: Religion and Race in American History.* Harvard University Press, 2022.

Gjerde, Jon. *Catholicism and the Shaping of Nineteenth-Century America.* Edited by S. Deborah Kang. Cambridge University Press, 2012.

Glaser, Elisabeth, and Hermann Wellenreuther, eds. *Bridging the Atlantic: The Question of American Exceptionalism in Perspective.* Cambridge University Press, 2002.

Goen, C. C. *Broken Churches, Broken Nation: Denominational Schisms and the Coming of the American Civil War.* Mercer University Press, 1985.

Grabbe, Hans-Jürgen, ed. *Halle Pietism, Colonial North America, and the Young United States.* Franz Steiner Verlag, 2008.

Graham, Stephen Ray. *Cosmos in the Chaos: Philip Schaff's Interpretation of Nineteenth-Century American Religion.* William B. Eerdmans, 1995.

Grammich, Clifford, Erica J. Dollhopf, Mary L. Gautier, et al. *2020 U.S. Religion Census: Religious Congregations and Adherents Study.* Association of Statisticians of American Religious Bodies, 2023.

Granquist, Mark. *Lutherans in America: A New History.* Fortress Press, 2015.

Grasso, Christopher. *Skepticism and Faith: From the Revolution to the Civil War.* Oxford University Press, 2018.

Grubb, Farley Ward. *German Immigration and Servitude in America, 1709–1920.* Routledge, 2011.

Guelzo, Allen C. *For the Union of Evangelical Christendom: The Irony of Reformed Episcopalians.* Pennsylvania State University Press, 1994.

Gustafson, David A. *Lutherans in Crisis: The Question of Identity in the American Republic.* Fortress Press, 1993.

Gutacker, Paul J. *The Old Faith in a New Nation: American Protestants and the Christian Past.* Oxford University Press, 2023.

Bibliography

Hahn, Steven. *A Nation Without Borders: The United States Its World in an Age of Civil Wars, 1830–1910.* Viking, 2017.

Hall, David W., ed. *The Practice of Confessional Subscription.* University Press of America, 1995.

Harlow, Luke E. *Religion, Race, and the Making of Confederate Kentucky, 1830–1880.* Cambridge University Press, 2014.

Harper, Keith, ed. *American Denominational History: Perspectives on the Past, Prospects for the Future.* University of Alabama Press, 2008.

Harrold, Stanley. *Border War: Fighting over Slavery Before the Civil War.* University of North Carolina Press, 2010.

Hart, D. G. *John Williamson Nevin: High Church Calvinist.* P&R, 2005.

———. *The Lost Soul of American Protestantism.* Rowman and Littlefield, 2002.

Haselby, Sam. *The Origins of American Religious Nationalism.* Oxford University Press, 2015.

Hatch, Nathan O. *The Democratization of American Christianity.* Yale University Press, 1989.

Haynes, Stephen R. *Noah's Curse: The Biblical Justification of American Slavery.* Oxford University Press, 2002.

Heathcote, Charles William. *The Lutheran Church and the Civil War.* Fleming A. Revell, 1919.

Heintzen, Erich H. *Prairie School of the Prophets: The Anatomy of a Seminary, 1846–1976.* Concordia, 1989.

Herfarth, Margit. *Leben in zwei Welten: Die amerikanische Diakonissenbewegung und ihre deutschen Wurzeln.* Evangelische Verlagsanstalt, 2014.

Hodes, Martha. *Mourning Lincoln.* Yale University Press, 2015.

Hokanson, Nels. *Swedish Immigrants in Lincoln's Time.* Arno Press, 1979.

Holifield, E. Brooks. *Theology in America: Christian Thought from the Age of the Puritans to the Civil War.* Yale University Press. 2003.

Holm, April E. *A Kingdom Divided: Evangelicals, Loyalty, and Sectionalism in the Civil War Era.* Louisiana State University Press, 2017.

Hope, Nicholas. *German and Scandinavian Protestantism, 1700–1918.* Clarendon Press, 1995.

Howard, Thomas Albert. *God and the Atlantic: America, Europe, and the Religious Divide.* Oxford University Press, 2011.

Hughes, Richard T., ed. *The American Quest for the Primitive Church.* University of Illinois Press, 1988.

Hutchison, William R. *The Modernist Impulse in American Protestantism.* Harvard University Press, 1976.

Jackson, Erika K. *Scandinavians in Chicago: The Origins of White Privilege in Modern America.* University of Illinois Press, 2019.

Jacobsen, Douglas G., and William Vance Trollinger Jr., eds. *Re-Forming the Center: American Protestantism, 1900 to the Present.* William B. Eerdmans, 1998.

Jacobson, Matthew Frye. *Whiteness of a Different Color: European Immigrants and the Alchemy of Race.* Harvard University Press, 1998.

Janney, Caroline E. *Remembering the Civil War: Reunion and the Limits of Reconciliation.* University of North Carolina Press, 2013.

Jensen, Richard. *The Winning of the Midwest: Social and Political Conflict, 1888–1896.* University of Chicago Press, 1971.

Johnson, Emeroy. *Eric Norelius: Pioneer Midwest Pastor and Churchman.* Augustana Historical Society, 1954.

Johnson, Jeff G. *Black Christians: The Untold Lutheran Story.* Concordia, 1991.

Jordan, Philip D. *The Evangelical Alliance for the United States of America, 1847–1900: Ecumenism, Identity, and the Religion of the Republic.* Edwin Mellen Press, 1982.

Juster, Susan. *Disorderly Women: Sexual Politics and Evangelicalism in Revolutionary New England.* Cornell University Press, 1994.

Kamphoefner, Walter D. *Germans in America: A Concise History.* Rowman and Littlefield, 2021.

Kazal, Russell A. *Becoming Old Stock: The Paradox of German-American Identity.* Princeton University Press, 2004.

Keller, Christian B. *Chancellorsville and the Germans: Nativism, Ethnicity, and Civil War Memory.* Fordham University Press, 2007.

Kidd, Thomas S., and Barry Hankins. *Baptists in America: A History.* Oxford University Press, 2015.

Klement, Frank L. *The Copperheads in the Middle West.* University of Chicago Press, 1960.

Kleppner, Paul. *The Third Electoral System, 1853–1892: Parties, Voters, and Political Cultures.* University of North Carolina Press, 1979.

Kloes, Andrew. *The German Awakening: Protestant Renewal after the Enlightenment, 1815–1848.* Oxford University Press, 2019.

Koehler, John Philipp. *The History of the Wisconsin Synod.* Edited and translated by Karl Koehler and Leigh Jordahl. Sentinel, 1970.

Kuenning, Paul P. *The Rise and Fall of American Lutheran Pietism: The Rejection of an Activist Heritage.* Mercer University Press, 1988.

Kurtz, William B. *Excommunicated from the Union: How the Civil War Created a Separate Catholic America.* Fordham University Press, 2016.

Lagerquist, L. DeAne. *From Our Mothers' Arms: A History of Women in the American Lutheran Church.* Augsburg Publishing House, 1987.

———. *The Lutherans.* Greenwood Press, 1999.

Landry, Stan M. *Ecumenism, Memory, and German Nationalism, 1817–1917.* Syracuse University Press, 2014.

Lang, Andrew F. *A Contest of Civilizations: Exposing the Crisis of American Exceptionalism in the Civil War Era.* University of North Carolina Press, 2021.

Lee, James Ambrose, II. *Confessional Lutheranism and German Theological Wissenschaft.* Walter de Gruyter, 2022.

Lehman, James O., and Steven M. Nolt. *Mennonites, Amish, and the American Civil War.* Johns Hopkins University Press, 2007.

Long, Kathryn. *The Revival of 1857–58: Interpreting an American Religious Awakening.* Oxford University Press, 1998.

Longenecker, Stephen L. *Gettysburg Religion: Refinement, Diversity, and Race in the Antebellum and Civil War Border North.* Fordham University Press, 2014.

Luebke, Frederick C. *Bonds of Loyalty: German-Americans and World War I.* Northern Illinois
University Press, 1974.

———, ed. *Ethnic Voters and the Election of Lincoln.* University of Nebraska Press, 1971.

Lueking, F. Dean. *Mission in the Making: The Missionary Enterprise Among Missouri Synod
Lutherans, 1846–1963.* Concordia, 1964.

Marsden, George. *Fundamentalism and American Culture: The Shaping of Twentieth-Century
Evangelicalism, 1870–1925.* Oxford University Press, 1980.

Marty, Martin E. *Protestantism in the United States: Righteous Empire.* Charles Scribner's Sons,
1986.

Matsui, John H. *Millenarian Dreams and Racial Nightmares: The American Civil War as an
Apocalyptic Conflict.* Louisiana State University Press, 2021.

Mauelshagen, Carl. *American Lutheranism Surrenders to Forces of Conservatism.* University of
Georgia Division of Publications, 1936.

McKivigan, John R. *The War Against Proslavery Religion: Abolitionism and the Northern
Churches, 1830–1865.* Cornell University Press, 2009.

Miller, Randall M., Harry S. Stout, and Charles Reagan Wilson, eds. *Religion and the American
Civil War.* Oxford University Press, 1998.

Moore, Joseph S. *Founding Sins: How a Group of Antislavery Radicals Fought to Put Christ in
the Constitution.* Oxford University Press, 2015.

Moore, R. Laurence. *Religious Outsiders and the Making of Americans.* Oxford University Press,
1986.

Mullen, Lincoln. *The Chance of Salvation: A History of Conversion in America.* Harvard
University Press, 2017.

Mullin, Robert Bruce, and Russell E. Richey, eds. *Reimagining Denominationalism:
Interpretive Essays.* Oxford University Press, 2010.

Mundinger, Carl S. *Government in the Missouri Synod.* Concordia, 1947.

Nelson, E. Clifford. *Lutheranism in North America, 1914–1970.* Augsburg Publishing House,
1972.

———, ed. *The Lutherans in North America.* Fortress Press, 1980.

Nelson, E. Clifford, and Eugene L. Fevold. *The Lutheran Church Among Norwegian-
Americans: A History of the Evangelical Lutheran Church.* Vol. 1, *1825–1890.* Augsburg
Publishing House, 1960.

Nelson, Robert H. *Lutheranism and the Nordic Spirit of Social Democracy.* Aarhus University
Press, 2017.

Noll, Mark A. *America's Book: The Rise and Decline of a Bible Civilization, 1794–1911.* Oxford
University Press, 2022.

———. *America's God: From Jonathan Edwards to Abraham Lincoln.* Oxford University Press,
2002.

———. *The Civil War as a Theological Crisis.* University of North Carolina Press, 2006.

———. *A History of Christianity in the United States and Canada.* 2nd ed. William B.
Eerdmans, 2019.

Nolt, Steven M. *Foreigners in Their Own Land: Pennsylvania Germans and the Early Republic.* Pennsylvania State University Press, 2002.

Nord, David Paul. *Faith in Reading: Religious Publishing and the Birth of Mass Media in America.* Oxford University Press, 2004.

Oakes, James. *Freedom National: The Destruction of Slavery in the United States, 1861–1865.* W. W. Norton, 2013.

Oshatz, Molly. *Slavery and Sin: The Fight Against Slavery and the Rise of Liberal Protestantism.* Oxford University Press, 2012.

Pegram, Thomas E. *Battling Demon Rum: The Struggle for a Dry America.* Ivan R. Dee, 1998.

Perry, Seth. *Bible Culture and Authority in the Early United States.* Princeton University Press, 2018.

Peterson, Brent O. *Popular Narratives and Ethnic Identity: Literature and Community in Die Abendschule.* Cornell University Press, 1993.

Phillips, Christopher. *The Rivers Ran Backward: The Civil War and the Remaking of the American Middle Border.* Oxford University Press, 2016.

Porterfield, Amanda. *Conceived in Doubt: Religion and Politics in the New American Nation.* University of Chicago Press, 2012.

Purvis, Zachary. *Theology and the University in Nineteenth-Century Germany.* Oxford University Press, 2016.

Rable, George C. *God's Almost Chosen Peoples: A Religious History of the American Civil War.* University of North Carolina Press, 2010.

Rasmussen, Anders Bo. *Civil War Settlers: Scandinavians, Citizenship, and American Empire, 1848–1870.* Cambridge University Press, 2022.

Richardson, Joe Martin. *Christian Reconstruction: The American Missionary Association and Southern Blacks, 1861–1890.* University of Alabama Press, 2008.

Riforgiato, Leonard R. *Missionary of Moderation: Henry Melchior Muhlenberg and the Lutheran Church in English America.* Bucknell University Press, 1980.

Robinson, Michael D. *A Union Indivisible: Secession and the Politics of Slavery in the Border South.* University of North Carolina Press, 2017.

Roeber, A. G. *Palatines, Liberty, and Property: German Lutherans in Colonial British America.* Johns Hopkins University Press, 1998.

Rohne, John Magnus. *Norwegian American Lutheranism up to 1872.* Macmillan, 1926.

Rönnegård, Sam. *Prairie Shepherd: Lars Paul Esbjorn and the Beginnings of the Augustana Lutheran Church.* Translated by G. Everett Arden. Augustana Book Concern, 1952.

Rudnick, Milton L. *Fundamentalism and the Missouri Synod: A Historical Study of Their Interaction and Mutual Influence.* Concordia, 1966.

Sarna, Jonathan D., ed. *Minority Faiths and the American Protestant Mainstream.* University of Illinois Press, 1998.

Schneider, Carl E. *The German Church on the American Frontier: A Study in the Rise of Religion Among the Germans of the West.* Eden, 1939.

Scholz, Robert F. *Press Toward the Mark: History of the United Lutheran Synod of New York and New England, 1830–1930.* Scarecrow Press, 1995.

Schuetze, Armin W. *The Synodical Conference: Ecumenical Endeavor.* Northwestern Publishing House, 2000.

Schwalm, Leslie. *Emancipation's Diaspora: Race and Reconstruction in the Upper Midwest.* University of North Carolina Press, 2009.

Scott, Sean A. *A Visitation of God: Northern Civilians Interpret the Civil War.* Oxford University Press, 2011.

Sernett, Milton C. *North Star Country: Upstate New York and the Crusade for African American Freedom.* Syracuse University Press, 2002.

Silber, Nina. *The Romance of Reunion: Northerners and the South, 1865–1900.* University of North Carolina Press, 1994.

Sinha, Manisha. *The Slave's Cause: A History of Abolition.* Yale University Press, 2016.

Smith, Adam I. P. *The Stormy Present: Conservatism and the Problem of Slavery in Northern Politics, 1846–1865.* University of North Carolina Press, 2017.

Smith, Timothy L. *Revivalism and Social Reform: American Protestantism on the Eve of the Civil War.* Johns Hopkins University Press, 1980.

Snay, Mitchell. *Gospel of Disunion: Religion and Separatism in the Antebellum South.* University of North Carolina Press, 1997.

Spitz, Lewis W. *Life in Two Worlds: Biography of William Sihler.* Concordia, 1968.

Stange, Douglas C. *Radicalism for Humanity: A Study in Lutheran Abolitionism.* Oliver Slave, 1970.

Stanley, Matthew E. *The Loyal West: Civil War and Reunion in Middle America.* University of Illinois Press, 2016.

Stellhorn, August C. *Schools of The Lutheran Church—Missouri Synod.* Concordia, 1963.

Stephens, Lester D. *Science, Race, and Religion in the American South: John Bachman and the Charleston Circle of Naturalists, 1815–1895.* University of North Carolina Press, 2000.

Stephenson, George M. *The Founding of the Augustana Synod, 1850–1860.* Augustana Book Concern, 1927.

Stout, Harry S. *Upon the Altar of the Nation: A Moral History of the Civil War.* Viking, 2006.

Stowell, Daniel W. *Rebuilding Zion: The Religious Reconstruction of the South, 1863–1877.* Oxford University Press, 1998.

Strobert, Nelson T. *Daniel Alexander Payne: The Venerable Preceptor of the African Methodist Episcopal Church.* University Press of America, 2012.

Strom, Jonathan, Hartmut Lehmann, and James Van Horn Melton, eds. *Pietism in Germany and North America 1680–1820.* Ashgate Publishing, 2009.

Suelflow, August R. *Servant of the Word: The Life and Ministry of C. F. W. Walther.* Concordia, 2000.

Summers, Mark W. *The Ordeal of Reunion: A New History of Reconstruction.* University of North Carolina Press, 2014.

Sweeney, Douglas A., and Charles E. Hambrick-Stowe, eds. *Holding on to the Faith: Confessional Traditions in American Christianity.* University Press of America, 2008.

Tappert, Theodore G. *History of the Lutheran Theological Seminary at Philadelphia, 1864–1964.* Lutheran Theological Seminary, 1964.

Thomas, James R. *A Rumor of Black Lutherans: The Formation of Black Leadership in Early American Lutheranism.* Fortress Press, 2024.

Thuesen, Peter J. *Predestination: The American Career of a Contentious Doctrine.* Oxford University Press, 2009.

Todd, Mary. *Authority Vested: A Story of Identity and Change in the Lutheran Church—Missouri Synod.* William B. Eerdmans, 2000.

Tomek, Beverly C. *Colonization and Its Discontents: Emancipation, Emigration, and Antislavery in Antebellum Pennsylvania.* New York University Press, 2011.

Trachtenberg, Alan. *The Incorporation of America: Culture and Society in the Gilded Age.* 25th anniversary ed. Hill and Wang, 2007.

Trexler, Edgar R. *High Expectations: Understanding the ELCA's Early Years, 1988–2002.* Augsburg Fortress, 2003.

Turpin, Andrea L. *A New Moral Vision: Gender, Religion, and the Changing Purposes of American Higher Education, 1837–1917.* Cornell University Press, 2016.

Tyrrell, Ian R. *American Exceptionalism: A New History of an Old Idea.* University of Chicago Press, 2021.

———. *Sobering Up: From Temperance to Prohibition in Antebellum America, 1800–1860.* Greenwood Press, 1978.

United States Bureau of the Census. *Historical Statistics of the United States, Colonial Times to 1970.* U.S. Government Printing Office, 1975.

Volk, Kyle G. *Moral Minorities and the Making of American Democracy.* Oxford University Press, 2014.

Volkman, Lucas P. *Houses Divided: Evangelical Schisms and the Crisis of the Union in Missouri.* Oxford University Press, 2018.

Voorhees, Amy B. *A New Christian Identity: Christian Science Origins and Experience in American Culture.* University of North Carolina Press, 2021.

Walters, Ronald G. *American Reformers, 1815–1860.* Rev. ed. Hill and Wang, 1997.

Watkins, Jordan T. *Slavery and Sacred Texts: The Bible, the Constitution, and Historical Consciousness in Antebellum America.* Cambridge University Press, 2021.

Weber, Jennifer L. *Copperheads: The Rise and Fall of Lincoln's Opponents in the North.* Oxford University Press, 2006.

Wellenreuther, Hermann. *Citizens in a Strange Land: A Study of German-American Broadsides and Their Meaning for Germans in North America, 1730–1830.* Pennsylvania State University Press, 2013.

Wentz, Abdel Ross. *A Basic History of Lutheranism in America.* Muhlenberg Press, 1964.

———. *History of the Evangelical Lutheran Synod of Maryland of the United Lutheran Church in America, 1820–1920.* Evangelical Press, 1920.

———. *History of the Gettysburg Theological Seminary of the General Synod of the Evangelical Lutheran Church in the United States and of the United Lutheran Church in America, Gettysburg, Pennsylvania, 1826–1926.* United Lutheran Publication House, 1926.

Bibliography

———. *Pioneer in Christian Unity: Samuel Simon Schmucker.* Fortress Press, 1967.

Wesley, Timothy L. *The Politics of Faith during the Civil War.* Louisiana State University Press, 2013.

Wetzel, Benjamin J. *American Crusade: Christianity, Warfare, and National Identity, 1860–1920.* Cornell University Press, 2022.

White, Richard. *The Republic for Which It Stands: The United States During Reconstruction and the Gilded Age, 1865–1896.* Oxford University Press, 2017.

Whitford, David M. *The Curse of Ham in the Early Modern Era: The Bible and the Justifications for Slavery.* Ashgate Publishing, 2012.

Wiederaenders, Robert C. *Historical Guide to Lutheran Church Bodies of North America.* Lutheran Historical Conference, 1998.

Wokeck, Marianne S. *Trade in Strangers: The Beginnings of Mass Migration to North America.* Pennsylvania State University Press, 1999.

Wood, Gordon S. *The Radicalism of American Revolution.* Alfred A. Knopf, 1992.

Wright, Ben. *Bonds of Salvation: How Christianity and Limited American Abolitionism.* Louisiana State University Press, 2020.

Wright, Ben, and Zachary W. Dresser, eds. *Apocalypse and Millennium in the American Civil War Era.* Louisiana State University Press, 2013.

Yacovazzi, Cassandra L. *Escaped Nuns: True Womanhood and the Campaign Against Convents in Antebellum America.* Oxford University Press, 2018.

Zachhuber, Johannes. *Theology as Science in Nineteenth Century Germany: From F. C. Baur to Ernst Troeltsch.* Oxford University Press, 2013.

Articles and Book Chapters

Ahlstrom, Sydney E. "The Lutheran Church and American Culture: A Tercentenary Retrospect." *Lutheran Quarterly* 9, no. 4 (November 1957): 321–42.

Albers, James W. "Perspectives on the History of Women in the Lutheran Church—Missouri Synod During the Nineteenth Century." *Lutheran Historical Conference: Essays and Reports* 9 (1982): 137–83.

Ander, O. Fritiof. "Swedish-American Newspapers and the Republican Party, 1855–1875." In *Augustana Historical Society Publications Number 2*, 64–78. Augustana Book Concern, 1933.

Benne, Robert. "David Bittle (1811–1876): The Americanist Founder of Roanoke College." *Lutheran Quarterly* 27, no. 3 (Autumn 2013): 321–43.

Berger, Peter L. "On Lutheran Identity in America." *Lutheran Quarterly* 20, no. 3 (Autumn 2006): 337–47.

Blum, Edward J., Tracy Fessenden, Prema Kurien, and Judith Weisenfeld. "Forum: American Religion and 'Whiteness.'" *Religion and American Culture* 19, no. 1 (Winter 2009): 1–35.

Bonomi, Patricia U. "'Watchful Against the Sects': Religious Renewal in Pennsylvania's German Congregations, 1720–1750." *Pennsylvania History* 50, no. 4 (October 1983): 273–83.

Bowman, Matthew, and Samuel Brown. "Reverend Buck's Theological Dictionary and the Struggle to Define American Evangelicalism, 1802–1851." *Journal of the Early Republic* 29, no. 3 (Fall 2009): 441–73.

Bratt, James D. "Religious Anti-Revivalism in Antebellum America." *Journal of the Early Republic* 24, no. 1 (Spring 2004): 65–106.

———. "The Reorientation of American Protestantism, 1835–1845." *Church History* 67, no. 1 (March 1998): 52–82.

Braun, Mark E. "Wisconsin's 'Turn to the Right.'" *Concordia Historical Institute Quarterly* 75, no. 1 (Spring 2002): 31–48, and no. 2 (Summer 2002): 80–100.

Brndjar, John M. "'Political Preaching' During the Civil War." *Lutheran Quarterly* 14, no. 4 (November 1962): 320–27.

Carpenter, Robert C. "Augsburg Confession War: Lutheran Confessional Beliefs, Rev. David Henkel, and Creation of the Tennessee Synod." *Lutheran Historical Conference: Essays and Reports* 22 (2006): 110–45.

Donner, William W. "'Neither Germans nor Englishmen, but Americans': Education, Assimilation, and Ethnicity Among Nineteenth-Century Pennsylvania Germans." *Pennsylvania History* 75, no. 2 (Spring 2008): 197–226.

Edmonds, Albert Sydney. "The Henkels, Early Printers in New Market, Virginia, with a Bibliography." *William and Mary Quarterly,* 2nd ser., 18, no. 2 (April 1938): 174–95.

Erling, Maria. "American Lutherans and Slavery." *Seminary Ridge Review* 16, no. 1 (Autumn 2013): 22–37.

Fogleman, Aaron. "Migration to the Thirteen British North American Colonies, 1700–1775: New Estimates." *Journal of Interdisciplinary History* 22, no. 4 (Spring 1992): 691–709.

Fortenbaugh, Robert. "American Lutheran Synods and Slavery, 1830–60." *Journal of Religion* 13, no. 1 (January 1933): 72–92.

———. "The Representative Lutheran Periodical Press and Slavery, 1831–1860." *Lutheran Church Quarterly* 8, no. 2 (April 1935): 151–72.

Frizzell, Robert W. "'Killed by Rebels': A Civil War Massacre and Its Aftermath." *Missouri Historical Review* 71, no. 4 (July 1977): 369–95.

Gjerde, Jon. "Conflict and Community: A Case Study of the Immigrant Church in the United States." *Journal of Social History* 19, no. 4 (Summer 1986): 681–97.

Gjerde, Jon, and Peter Franson. "'Still the Inwardly Beautiful Bride of Christ': The Development of Lutheranism in the United States." In *Luther zwischen den Kulturen: Zeitgenossenschaft—Weltwirkung,* edited by Hans Medick and Peer Schmidt, 190–211. Vandenhoeck & Ruprecht, 2004.

Gotwald, Luther A., Jr. "The Trial of Luther A. Gotwald." *Currents in Theology and Missions* 36, no. 2 (April 2009): 118–27.

Granquist, Mark A. "American Lutheran Reactions to the Labor Movement in the 1890s." *Journal of the Lutheran Historical Conference* 10 (2020): 73–89.

———. "Lutherans and the New Deal." *Journal of the Lutheran Historical Conference* 5 (2015): 127–41.

Bibliography

Groh, John E. "Revivalism Among Lutherans in America in the 1840s." *Concordia Historical Institute Quarterly* 43, no. 1 (February 1970): 29–43, and no. 2 (February 1970): 59–78.

Grundmeier, Timothy D. "Pennsylvania's 'Youthful Daughter': Reexamining the Early History of the Wisconsin Synod." *Wisconsin Lutheran Quarterly* 122, no. 2 (Spring 2025): 89–140.

Johnston, Wade R. "American Ideals in German Print: The Opposition of the Evangelical Lutheran Synodical Conference to the 1889 Bennett Law in Wisconsin." *Journal of the Lutheran Historical Conference* 4 (2014): 211–20.

Jordahl, Leigh D. "Schmucker and Walther: A Study of Christian Response to American Culture." In *The Future of the American Church*, edited by Philip J. Hefner, 71–90. Fortress Press, 1968.

Kamphoefner, Walter D. "Dreissiger and Forty-Eighter: The Political Influence of Two Generations of German Political Exiles." In *Germany and America: Essays on Problems of International Relations and Immigration*, edited by Hans L. Trefousse, 89–102. Brooklyn College Press, 1980.

———. "New Perspectives on Texas Germans and the Confederacy." In *The Fate of Texas: The Civil War and the Lone Star State*, edited by Charles D. Grear, 105–19. University of Arkansas Press, 2008.

Köllman, Wolfgang, and Peter Marschalck. "German Emigration to the United States." *Perspectives in American History* 7 (1973): 499–544.

Kretzmann, Karl. "Francis Arnold Hoffmann: Cofounder of the Missouri Synod, Financier, Cofounder of the Republican Party, Acting Governor of Illinois During the Civil War, Agricultural Expert, Journalist." *Concordia Historical Institute Quarterly* 18, no. 2 (July 1945): 37–54.

———. "A Lutheran Army Chaplain in the Civil War." *Concordia Historical Institute Quarterly* 17, no. 4 (January 1945): 97–102.

Lohrmann, Martin J. "Lutherans and the Nineteenth Amendment: American Lutheran Views of Women's Suffrage." *Journal of the Lutheran Historical Conference* 5 (2015): 51–61.

Lueker, Erwin L. "Walther and the Free Lutheran Conferences of 1856–1859." *Concordia Theological Monthly* 15, no. 8 (August 1944): 529–63.

Maffly-Kipp, Laurie F. "The Burdens of Church History." *Church History* 82, no. 2 (June 2013): 353–67.

Manteufel, Thomas. "Walther's View on Slavery." *Concordia Historical Institute Quarterly* 86, no. 4 (Winter 2013): 12–23.

McArver, Susan Wilds. "Better a 'Live Dog Than a Dead Lion': The Remarkable and Unlikely Life of Manuel Simeon Corley, South Carolina Abolitionist, Unionist, Teetotaler, and Scalawag." *Journal of the Lutheran Historical Conference* 7 (2017): 19–55.

McCandless, Peter. "The Political Evolution of John Bachman: From New York Yankee to South Carolina Secessionist." *South Carolina Historical Magazine* 108, no. 1 (January 2007): 6–31.

Noll, Mark A. "American Lutherans Yesterday and Today." In *Lutherans Today: American*

Bibliography

Lutheran Identity in the 21st Century, edited by Richard Cimino, 3–25. William B. Eerdmans, 2003.

———. "A Good Time for Looking Back." *Lutheran Quarterly* 29, no. 3 (Fall 2015): 315–23.

———. "The Lutheran Difference." *First Things,* February 1992, 31–40.

Ramshaw, Paul D. "The Rev. John G. Butler of Washington, DC." *Journal of the Lutheran Historical Conference* 11 (2021): 122–57.

Rasmussen, Anders Bo. "'The States' Readmission Puts an End to All Civil and Political Questions': Scandinavian Immigrants and Debates over Racial Equality During the Impeachment of President Andrew Johnson." *Swedish-American Historical Quarterly* 66, no. 4 (October 2017): 202–17.

Rast, Lawrence R., Jr. "Demagoguery or Democracy? The Saxon Emigration and American Culture." *Concordia Theological Quarterly* 63, no. 4 (October 1999): 247–68.

Roeber, A. G. "Henry Melchior Muhlenberg: Orthodox Pietist." In *Henry Melchior Muhlenberg—The Roots of 250 Years of Organized Lutheranism in North America: Essays in Memory of Helmut T. Lehmann,* edited by John W. Kleiner, 1–20. Edwin Mellen Press, 1998.

———. "J. H. C. Helmuth: An Interpreter of Lutheranism in the Early Republic." *Lutheran Historical Conference: Essays and Reports* 17 (1996): 1–19.

Rudnik, Milton. "The Missouri Synod's Stand on the Labor Question, 1879–1901." *Concordia Historical Institute Quarterly* 45, no. 2 (May 1972): 89–105.

Sandeen, Ernest R. "The Distinctiveness of American Denominationalism: A Case Study of the 1846 Evangelical Alliance." *Church History* 45, no. 2 (June 1976): 222–34.

Sauer, Paul Robert. "A Field Guide to the Missouri Synod." *Lutheran Forum* 42, no. 2 (Summer 2008): 6–8.

Schaefer, Benjamin P. "Avoiding the Hornet's Nest: Woman Suffrage and Synodical Conference Lutherans." *Concordia Historical Institute Quarterly* 96, no. 3 (Fall 2023): 9–58.

Smith, Timothy L. "Religion and Ethnicity in America." *American Historical Review* 83, no. 5 (December 1978): 1155–85.

Stange, Douglas C. "Editor Benjamin Kurtz of the *Lutheran Observer* and the Slavery Crisis." *Maryland Historical Magazine* 62, no. 3 (September 1967): 285–99.

———. "Lutheran Involvement in the American Colonization Society." *Mid-America* 49, no. 2 (April 1967): 140–51.

Suelflow, Roy A. "The History of Concordia Seminary, St. Louis, 1847–1865." *Concordia Historical Institute Quarterly* 24, no. 2 (July 1951): 49–68, and no. 3 (October 1951): 97–124.

Swierenga, Robert P. "Ethnoreligious Political Behavior in the Mid-Nineteenth Century: Voting, Values, Cultures." In *Religion and American Politics: From the Colonial Period to the Present,* edited by Mark A. Noll and Luke E. Harlow, 145–68. Oxford University Press, 2007.

Teigen, Philip M. "Rev. Daniel E. Wiseman (1858–1942): African-American Pastor to District of Columbia Lutherans," *Journal of the Lutheran Historical Conference* 5 (2015): 7–30.

Bibliography

Wangelin, William R. "Loehe's Lens: Wilhelm Loehe's Critique of Democratic Principles in the Missouri Synod During the Revolutions of 1848/49." *Concordia Historical Institute Quarterly* 86, no. 2 (Summer 2013): 30–47.

Wentz, Abdel Ross. "Relations Between the Lutheran and Reformed Churches in the Eighteenth and Nineteenth Centuries," *Lutheran Church Quarterly* 6, no. 3 (July 1933): 300–27.

Widen, Carl T. "Texas Swedish Pioneers and the Confederacy." *Swedish-American Pioneer Quarterly* 12, no. 3 (July 1961): 100–107.

Dissertations and Theses

Albers, James W. "The History of Attitudes Within the Missouri Synod Toward Life Insurance." ThD diss. Concordia Seminary, St. Louis, 1972.

Bachmann, E. Theodore. "The Rise of 'Missouri Lutheranism.'" PhD diss., University of Chicago Divinity School, 1946.

Baglyos, Paul A. "In This Land of Liberty: American Lutherans and the Young Republic, 1787–1837." PhD diss., University of Chicago Divinity School, 1997.

Bost, Raymond. "The Reverend John Bachman and the Development of Southern Lutheranism." PhD diss., Yale University, 1963.

Brasich, Adam S. "A Mighty Fortress: American Religion and the Construction of Confessional Lutheranism." PhD diss., Florida State University, 2017.

Deitz, Reginald W. "Eastern Lutheranism in American Society and American Christianity, 1870–1914: Darwinism, Biblical Criticism, the Social Gospel." PhD diss., University of Pennsylvania, 1958.

Echols, James Kenneth. "Charles Michael Jacobs, the Scriptures, and the Word of God: One Man's Struggle against Biblical Fundamentalism among American Lutherans." PhD diss., Yale University, 1989.

Fry, Charles George. "Matthias Loy, Patriarch of Ohio Lutheranism, 1828–1915." PhD diss., Ohio State University, 1965.

Gollner, Philipp. "Good White Christians: How Religion Created Race and Ethnic Privilege for Immigrants in America." PhD diss., University of Notre Dame, 2016.

Graebner, Alan. N. "The Acculturation of an Immigrant Lutheran Church: The Lutheran Church—Missouri Synod, 1917–1929." PhD diss., Columbia University, 1965.

Hattery, John W. "The Historical Development of the Doctrine of Unionism of the Lutheran Church—Missouri Synod." STM thesis, Lutheran Theological Seminary, Gettysburg, 1970.

Haug, Hans R. "The Predestination Controversy in the Lutheran Church in North America." PhD diss., Temple University, 1968.

Heintzen, Erich H. "William Loehe and the Missouri Synod, 1841–1853." PhD diss., University of Illinois, 1964.

Huber, Donald L. "The Controversy over Pulpit and Alter Fellowship in the General Council of the Evangelical Lutheran Church, 1866–1889." PhD diss., Duke University, 1971.

Koenning, Alton R. "Henkel Press: A Force for Conservative Lutheran Theology in Pre-Civil War Southeastern America." PhD diss., Duke University, 1972.

Ottersberg, Gerhard Sigmund. "The Evangelical Lutheran Synod of Iowa and Other States, 1854–1904." PhD diss., University of Nebraska, Lincoln, 1949.

Rast, Lawrence R. "Joseph A. Seiss and the Lutheran Church in America." PhD diss., Vanderbilt University, 2003.

Scheidt, David Lee. "Linguistic Transition in the Muhlenberg Tradition of American Lutheranism." STD diss., Temple University, 1963.

Suelflow, Roy A. "The History of the Missouri Synod During the Second Twenty-Five Years of Its Existence, 1872–1897." ThD diss., Concordia Theological Seminary, 1946.

Vardell, Russell Alan. "Striving to Gather the Scattered: The Texas-Louisiana Synod and its Predecessor Bodies, 1851–1987." PhD diss., University of Houston, 1992.

INDEX

Augustana Synod: formation of, 56–57; growth in postbellum era, 167; joins the General Council, 144; as Moderate Lutherans, 81, 141; and Norwegian Synod, 139, 141; and Old School Lutherans, 125, 127; pro-Union views in, 81, 128

Bachman, John: defends slavery, 67–69, 100; as New Lutheran leader, 26–29, 59, 67; as president of Confederate General Synod, 101; rejects sectional reconciliation, 122; studies in Germany, 63; supports ecclesiastical reunion, 150, supports secession, 76, 83; and Tennessee Synod, 41
Bacon, Leonard, 25
Bading, Johannes, 126, 146
Baird, Robert, 29
Bakke, Nils, 184
Bancroft, George, 187
baptismal regeneration, 27, 34, 41, 55, 106, 173, 197
Baptists, 6, 10, 19, 20, 21, 24, 32, 68–69, 72, 104, 132, 164, 165, 176, 195, 234n5, 256n9
Bassler, Gottlieb, 142
Baugher, H. L., 102
Beecher, Henry Ward, 88, 163
Beecher, Lyman, 28
benevolent empire, 22
Bennett Law, 187
Bente, Friedrich, 188
Bernheim, Gotthardt, 148
biblical criticism, 168, 176–77, 194, 252n71
biblicism, 2, 24, 37, 99, 168. *See also* common sense reasoning; *sola scriptura*
Biewend, August, 70
Bittle, David, 23, 27, 100
Black Americans. *See* African Americans
Boernstein, Heinrich, 70–71
Bonhoeffer, Dietrich, 1
Book of Concord, 2, 53–54, 58, 117, 155, 171, 193, **197**. *See also* Augsburg Confession; confessionalism; Formula of Concord; symbol
Booth, John Wilkes, 120
Brown, J. A., 118–19, 123, 146–47, 157, 173, 175
Brown, John, 76
Buck, Charles, 27

Buffalo Synod, 34, 52
Bull Run, Battle of, 77
burned-over district, 26
Burton, Orville Vernon, 8
bushwhackers, 82
Butler, John, 134–37, 183

Calvin, John, 187
Campbell, Alexander, 32
Carroll, Henry, 163, 167, 168, 189
Carwardine, Richard, 24
Catholics. *See* Roman Catholics
chaplains in the Civil War, 84–85
Chicago World's Fair, 186
chiliasm. *See* millennialism
Christian Amendment, 136
Christian Commission, 85
Christiania (Oslo), University of, 52, 97, 139
church fellowship, 3, 50, 54, 65, 126, 144–46, 155, 163, 169, 171–72, 174–75, 191, 194. *See also* Four Points; Galesburg Declaration; unionism
Church Society of the West. *See* Evangelical Synod of the West
church-state separation. *See* religious liberty
civil religion. *See* American exceptionalism; religious nationalism
Civil War era, defined, 8
Clausen, C. L., 69, 97, 139
colonization, 25, 66, 93, 136
Columbus Theological Seminary, 38, 43, 50, 52
common sense reasoning, 18, 100, 233n151, 235n32
communism, 99, 178, 181
Compromise of 1850, 66
Concordia Seminary (St. Louis): during Civil War, 81–82; faculty members of, 70, 97–98, 170, 188; founding of, 37; and Norwegian Synod, 52
confessional movement (in the General Synod): and American ideals, 63–64; on General Synod, 64–65, 72, 74, 103; on German Lutheranism, 63; leaders of, 59–63; and Moderate Lutherans, 64; and Old Lutherans, 64; and Old School Lutheranism, 105, 200; and patriotism, 84; and politics, 75–76, 88–89; on preserving the Union, 74, 79; on slavery, 67–69, 92–94

Index

Index

Index

Lutheran Church Review, 177, 187

Lutheran Congregations in Mission for Christ, 194

Lutheran Observer, **198–99**; anti-Catholicism of, 28; confessional movement leaders and, 59–61; on confessionalism, 106, 112, 121, 156–57; editorship of, 23, 66, 76, 84, 110; on Evangelical Alliance, 28–29; on *Evangelical Review*, 43; on General Council, 142–43, 145–46, 156; on German immigrants, 49; on German Lutheranism, 63; on Lutherans' relationship with mainstream Protestants, 73; and Moderate Lutherans, 41–43; as New Lutheran paper, 23, 57, 65, 77, 84; and New School–Old School disputes, 104–14, 116–19, 121, 123–25, 130; and Old Lutherans, 34, 36; on Philadelphia seminary's founding, 116–17; and politics, 24, 88, 136; as principal Lutheran publication, 23, 57, 76; and Reconstruction, 131, 135–36; and religious nationalism, 84–85, 101–2, 110, 140; on revivalism, 23, 106, 175; on secession crisis, 77–79, 107–8; on slavery and emancipation, 24–25, 65–66, 91–95; and southern Lutherans, 77–78, 122, 148–51; Swedish Lutherans and, 52; on Synodical Conference, 160; on temperance, 23–24, 106, 253n90; on women, 27, 182

Lutheran Quarterly, 187

Lutheran Standard, **199**; on Anxious Bench, 40; editorship of, 38, 41–42, 80, 126, 228n34; founding of, 38; on General Synod, 41–42, 55, 57; and German immigrants, 50; on Missouri Synod, 36, 42, 58, 94, 153–54; as Moderate Lutheran "organ," 38; and New Lutherans, 38–39; on political preaching, 89–90, 94, 128, 138; on religious nationalism, 86–87; and secession crisis, 80; on slavery, 67; Swedish Lutherans and, 52; and Tennessee Synod, 41, 80–81

Lutheran Theological Seminary in Philadelphia, 116–21, 123, 127, 171, 173, 187

Lutheran Visitor, 137, 149–52

Lutheraner, **199**; and American exceptionalism, 35; and Civil War, 81–82, 87; founding of, 31; and Missouri Synod's founding, 36; on New

Lutherans, 34–35; and Old Lutheranism, 33–35; and politics, 70–71, 90, 138, 181; and "true Lutheranism," 31–32; and unionism, 50

Lutherische Herold, 98

Machen, J. Gresham, 176

Maffly-Kipp, Laurie, 9

Mann, W. J., 48, 56, 105, 117

Marsden, George, 7–9

Maryland Synod, 56, 60, 183

Mayflower, 30

McClellan, George, 119

Melanchthon, Philip, 197

Melanchthon Synod, 56

Mennonites, 4

Mercersburg Theology, 39, 235n22

Methodist Quarterly Review, 163

Methodists, 6, 10, 15, 19–21, 24, 32, 34, 37, 61, 72, 104, 132, 148, 165, 176, 180, 234n5, 256n9. *See also* African Methodist Episcopal Church

Mid-Atlantic states, political culture of, 11, 137. *See also specific synods*

Middle Border in Civil War era, 11

Midwest: becomes center of American Lutheranism, 165–66; political culture of, 11, 137. *See also* Northwest Territory; *and specific synods*

millennialism, 144, 155, 227n3

Minnesota Synod, 160

Missionary, 60–61, 64, 67–69, 78–79, 84, 198

Missouri Synod: and Alpha Synod, 184; and American liberty, 37, 54, 71, 87, 140, 158–59, 185, 188, 190; antebellum size of, 37–38, 50, 59; and church fellowship, 169; and congregationalism, 37, 51; constitution of, 36, 54; founding of, 36–38; and General Council, 141–44, 154–56, 171–72; and General Synod, 42, 127; and German immigrants, 50, 167; and Lutherans in Germany, 50–51; and modernism, 176–77; as national church body, 36, 70, 201; and Norwegian Synod, 52, 81, 96–97, 139, 180; and Ohio Synod, 58, 126, 145, 153–54; and Old School Lutherans, 127–28; and parochial schools, 169–70; and politics, 70–71, 90, 128–29, 138–39, 178–79, 187;

Index

Missouri Synod (*continued*)
postbellum growth of, 130, 132, 161, 167, 186;
and Predestination Controversy, 170; and
slavery, 70, 96–100, 129, 139–40; as Synodical
Conference leader, 159–61, 167, 192, 201; and
the Union, 81–83, 87; and Wisconsin Synod,
50, 146, 154; and women's rights, 182. *See also*
Concordia Seminary; Lutheran Church—
Missouri Synod; *Lutheraner*
Moderate Lutherans, **199**; and *Anxious Bench,* 40;
and confessionalism, 54–55; and *Definite
Platform,* 56–57; described by Philip Schaff,
16, 38, 44; and *Evangelical Review,* 43, 72; and
General Synod, 41–44, 72; and German
culture, 40, 64; and German immigrants,
48–50; and Old Lutherans, 42; and Old
School Lutherans, 105, 125; and politics, 76;
and Scandinavian immigrants, 51–52; and
slavery, 67, 81; and Tennessee Synod, 40–41
modernism. *See* biblical criticism; evolutionary
theory; new theology; social gospel
Moe, Olaf Edvard, 1–2
Moore, R. Laurence, 10, 256n137
Moravians, 17, 61
Mormons, 10, 66, 217n106
Morse, Sidney, 28
Muhlenberg, Frederick, 17
Muhlenberg, Heinrich Melchior, 17–18, 150
Murphy, Francis, 181

National Council of Churches, 193
National Lutheran Council, 248n188
nationalism. *See* American exceptionalism;
religious nationalism
Neo-Lutheranism in Germany. *See Erweckung*
Nevin, John Williamson, 39–40, 62
Newberry College, 118
New Lutherans, **200**; and confessional movement,
59–65, 200; and confessionalism, 53–54; and
Definite Platform, 55–57; described by Philip
Schaff, 15–16; and *Evangelical Review,* 43; and
evangelicalism, 22–24, 28–29; and General
Synod, 21–22, 72, 198; and German
immigrants, 49; and German Reformed, 40;
and German theology, 63; and Moderate

Lutherans, 38–42, 199; and New School
Lutheranism, 106, 200; and Old Lutherans,
34–36, 200; and political parties, 24, 75–76;
and Roman Catholicism, 27–28; and
Scandinavian immigrants, 51–52; and the
secession crisis, 77–79; and slavery, 24–27,
65–67, 91–95; in the South, 23, 26, 41, 67; and
women's roles, 27
new measures. *See* revivalism
New School Lutherans, **200**; and American ideals,
113, 140, 157–58; and conflicts with Old School
during Civil War, 104, 107–12, 117–19, 121–22,
124–25, 130; on the General Council, 142,
145–47; and the General Synod, 108, 113–16,
123; and German Lutheranism, 190; origins of,
105–6; on Reconstruction, 131, 135–37; and
southern Lutherans, 122, 148–50; on
temperance, 181; theology of, 106, 112–13, 121,
156–57, 159, 173–75, 189, 197
new theology, 164, 168, 176. *See also* biblical
criticism; evolutionary theory
New York Synod (or Ministerium), 141, 144, 166
Newberry College, 118
Niebuhr, H. Richard, 1–2
Noll, Mark, 7–8, 18–19, 68, 195, 232n131
Nolt, Steven, 19, 21
Nordic Americans. *See specific ethnic groups*
Norelius, Eric, 52, 125
North American Lutheran Church, 195
North Carolina Synod, 40, 100, 138, 150–52
Northern Illinois Synod, 52, 56, 125
Northwest Territory, 16
Norwegian Americans: immigration of, 51–52,
165–66; and politics, 69–70, 89, 137, 180;
pro-Union views of, 86. *See also* Augustana
Synod; Norwegian Synod
Norwegian Synod: founding of, 52; and General
Council, 141–42, 144; and Missouri Synod, 52,
81, 96–97; and slavery, 81, 96–97, 139; and
Synodical Conference, 159, 167, 170

Odd Fellows. *See* secret societies
Officer, Morris, 66
Ohio Synod: and confessional adherence, 54, 57;
founding of, 38; and General Council, 141–

Walther, C. F. W. (*continued*)
127; on the labor movement, 180–81; as leading voice of postbellum Lutheranism, 130; legacy of, 170, 195; and *Lehre und Wehre* founding, 57–58; and *Lutheraner* founding, 31–32; and Missouri Synod founding, 36; and Ohio Synod, 42, 58, 145; as Old Lutheranism's leader, 33–34, 37–38; on parochial schools, 170; political views of, 35, 70–71, 91, 138–39, 178–79; and Predestination Controversy, 170; primitivist ideas of, 32; signs loyalty oath, 82; on slavery, 70, 96–99, 139–40; and Synodical Conference founding, 132, 160–61; travels to Germany, 50, 58–59; on "true visible church," 153–55, 161
Washington, George, 150
Wayland, Francis, 25, 68–69
Wellenreuther, Hermann, 18
Wentz, Abdel Ross, 21
Wesley, John, 23
Wesley, Timothy, 88
West Pennsylvania Synod, 43, 56, 111
Western Virginia Synod, 100
Whig Party, 24, 48
Whitefield, George, 23
whiteness, 10
Wilson, Woodrow, 192
Wisconsin Evangelical Lutheran Synod (WELS), 194–95, 201. *See also* Wisconsin Synod

Wisconsin Synod: and General Council, 144, 146; growth in postbellum era, 167, 169; increasing conservatism in 1860s, 125–27; joins Synodical Conference, 159–60; and Missouri Synod, 50, 146, 154; as Moderate Lutherans, 48–49, 125; and politics, 128. *See also* Wisconsin Evangelical Lutheran Synod
Wiseman, Daniel, 183
Wittenberg College, 62, 114, 156, 189
Wittenberg Seminary, 174
Wittenberg Synod, 66
women: in Lutheran churches, 6–7; rights of, 182–83, 189; roles of, 27; and temperance, 188–189. *See also* deaconesses
Women's Christian Temperance Union, 189
Wood, Gordon, 20
World Council of Churches, 193
World Evangelical Alliance. *See* Evangelical Alliance
World War I, 192
Worley, Daniel, 80–81, 86–87, 89–90, 94, 228n34
Worms, Diet of, 158, 186
Wyneken, Friedrich, 32–37, 50

York, Pennsylvania. *See* General Synod: 1864 convention of
Young Men's Christian Association, 169, 175

Zwingli, Ulrich, 113

www.ingramcontent.com/pod-product-compliance
Lightning Source LLC
Chambersburg PA
CBHW030257100426
42812CB00002B/473

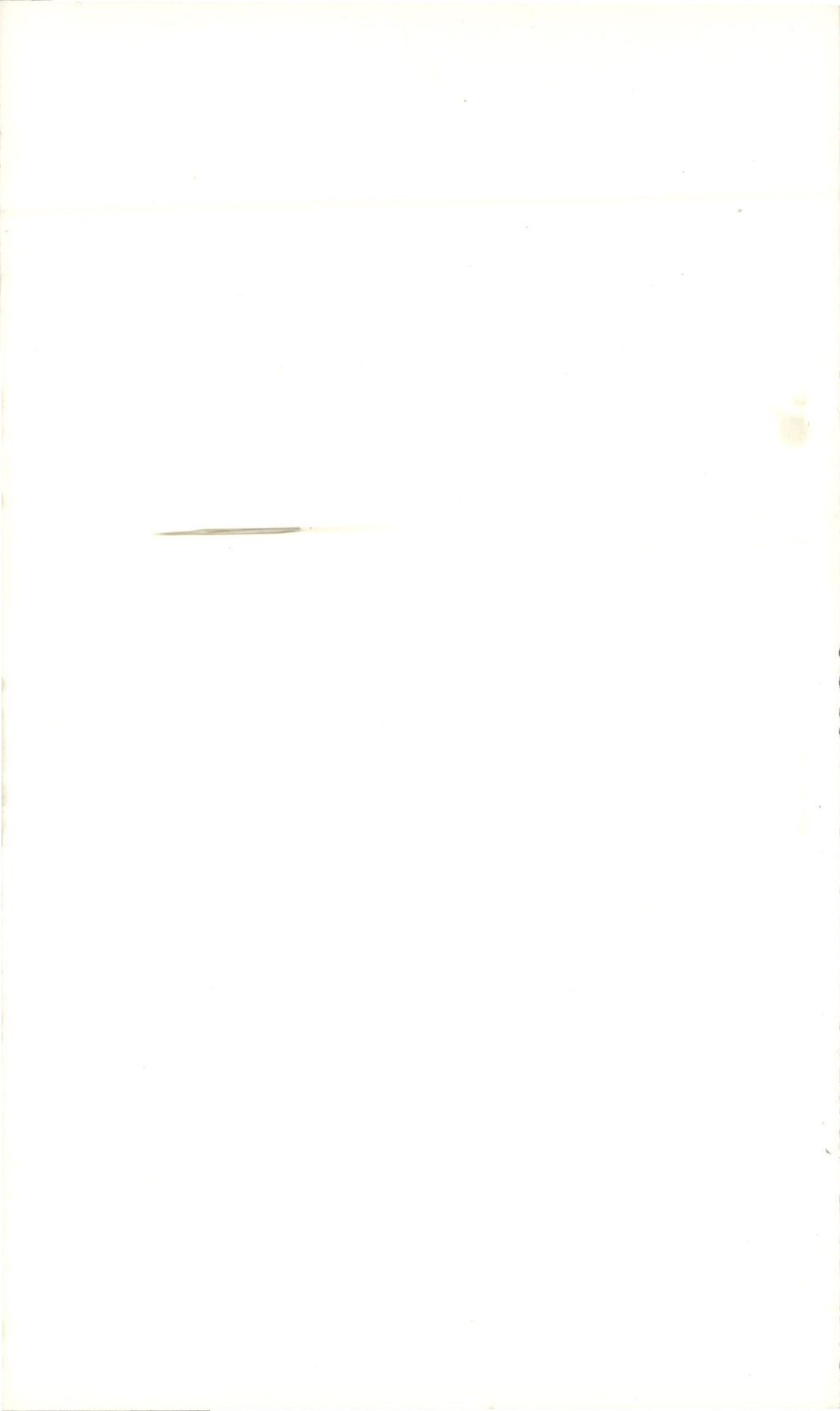